SOCIAL WORK ADMINISTRATION

Other books by HARLEIGH B. TRECKER

Citizen Boards at Work
Goals for Social Welfare 1973-1993
Social Group Work: Principles and Practices

SOCIAL WORK ADMINISTRATION

Principles and Practices
Revised Edition

HARLEIGH B. TRECKER

University Professor Emeritus of Social Work
School of Social Work
University of Connecticut

ASSOCIATION PRESS • NEW YORK

SOCIAL WORK ADMINISTRATION

Copyright © 1977, 1971 by Association Press
291 Broadway, New York, N.Y. 10007

Library of Congress Catalog Card Number: 77–21622

Library of Congress Cataloging in Publication Data
Trecker, Harleigh Bradley, 1911–
  Social work administration.

  Bibliography: p. 319
  Includes index.
  1. Public welfare administration. I. Title.
HV40.T74 1977   658'.91'361   77–21622
ISBN 0–8096–1925–3

PRINTED IN THE UNITED STATES OF AMERICA

to my granddaughters Molly
and Sophia Trecker with love

Contents

The Administrator and Work Productivity
The Staff Member as a Part of the Agency
What the Professional Social Worker Wants from
   Administration
The Staff Member's Responsibility to Administration
Code of Ethics of the Social Worker
Authority and Administration
A Survey of Staff Attitudes
Delegation of Responsibility to Staff Members
Differential Use of Staff
Job Satisfaction and Staff Retention

Administrative Philosophy and the Board
Functions of the Administrative Board
The Administrator at Work with the Board
Administrators Describe Their Role with Their Boards
The Administrator and the Chairman of the Board
The Administrator, the Board, and Policy-making
Many Persons Involved in Policy-making
Problems of Administrators and Boards

The Importance of Participation
Obtaining Significant Participation
The Poor as a Constituent Group
Client Complaints and Pressures
The Need to Work Together
In Summary

Definition of Communication
The Administrator and the Communication System
Agency Structure and Communication
Criteria of Effective Communication

What Is Organization?
Models of Organization
Hierarchy, Bureaucracy, and Power

Creating the Effective Organization
Criteria of Adequacy for Structure and Organization
Some Emerging Trends
The Responsibility of the Administrator for Planning
Steps in Planning
The Responsibility of the Administrator for Coordination

**PART II: The Practice of Administration
Cases, Papers and Documents for Study**

Figures

Introduction

In its first edition, SOCIAL WORK ADMINISTRATION: PRINCIPLES AND PRACTICES won wide recognition as a book for administrators of the nation's social welfare enterprises and for those social workers who aspire to take on administrative jobs. Students of social work found it of value in their graduate education. In addition, it has been helpful to professional workers in related and allied fields where the goals of human service are reasonably congruent. It was read by many professionals and volunteers in social work who, while not necessarily carrying primary administrative responsibilities themselves, sought a deeper understanding of the work of the administrator and the complexities of the administrative task.

There is a continuing need for a book of this kind. Social welfare is a large field and is growing each year. New programs under governmental and voluntary auspices call for an ever-increasing number of administrators, and many social workers assume administrative positions each year. Although the literature is expanding, there is no other volume that puts together social work administration principles and practices. There is general agreement that the way social work services are administered is of great importance to the persons served, to the community, and ultimately to the nation. There is also agreement that the work of the administrator becomes more and more demanding during times of unprecedented change. Leadership tasks and responsibilities must be accepted as crucial to the well-being of the agency the administrator represents and the people served.

It remains true, however, that no area of human understanding is untouched by change for very long, and social work is no exception. In preparing this revised edition, the author took into account the changes that have taken place in the community and in the practice of social work administration since the first edition was published. Efforts have been made to update the content in the light of new studies, new writings, and new experiences. At some points, material from the first edition has been elaborated. In many cases, material has been eliminated or replaced with more current information.

Social work administration is viewed as an adaptive process, and a comparison is made between the assumptions of the classical management school and the humanistic school. Attention is given to a diagnostic approach to problem solving. Because more and more administrators are taking the lead in advocating social change, advocacy is considered. Likewise, the emerging concept of community participation and control in agency affairs is elaborated. The importance of worker satisfaction and job retention is reviewed, and further attention is given to agency structure and its impact on communication. The various models of agency organization are discussed, and the criteria of adequacy for structure and organization are included.

In Part II, all the illustrative items are new and are published here for the first time in book form. All of them have been tested out in the classroom.

The Bibliography of Selected Readings is completely updated and undoubtedly represents the most comprehensive listing of its kind to be found today.

As in the earlier edition, this book is divided into two parts: Part I is essentially a presentation of theory. Part II includes a selection of cases and documents as illustrative materials to be used for classroom teaching or for agency in-service training programs. This material is presented separately so that instructors and readers can be free to choose material as the need arises and to adapt it to their own approaches.

This is a book to be read and studied. Hopefully, the reader will read Part I in sequence because there is a logic to the way in which the chapters are offered. Social work administration is discussed and defined in Chapter 1. The role of social work administrators is detailed in Chapter 2. The setting of the social agency is discussed in Chapter 3, and the community is examined in Chapter 4. Chapter 5 concentrates on the role of the administrator with the staff. In Chapter 6, the administrator at work with the board is reviewed. Chapter 7 looks at the administrator and the constituency. Communication is discussed in Chapter 8. Organization, planning, and coordination are considered in Chapter 9. Chapter 10 is devoted to administrators and decision-making. Policy determination is the focus of Chapter 11. Administration and resource utilization is outlined in Chapter 12. Evaluation, growth, and change are considered in Chapter 13. In the final chapter, the principles of social work administration are summarized.

In many ways, this book is a culmination of many years of both administration and the teaching of administration on the part of the author. Readers familiar with his earlier works, GROUP PROCESS IN ADMINISTRATION, NEW UNDERSTANDINGS OF ADMINISTRATION, and CITIZEN BOARDS AT WORK, will recognize that this volume is an extension and a refinement of the major ideas offered in these books. Yet it must be admitted that over the years there have been striking and significant changes in the field, and there has been a corresponding change in the author's comprehension and grasp of all that is involved in administration. While his basic philosophy has not changed, the details of how one proceeds in the administrative situation have changed as a result of the experiences he has had. In this book, the point of view expressed and the methods proposed represent a maturing and farsighted projection as to what will be required in the future.

While the author takes full responsibility for both the contributions and shortcomings of this book, it must be said that many people have participated directly and indirectly. It is impossible to name them as individuals because so many have been involved. Faculty members, staff members, and students at the University of Connecticut School of Social Work, where the author has worked as dean and professor for over twenty-five years, have given much in the way of ideas, suggestions, and illustrations. Furthermore, and hopefully not to their disadvantage, they have been a testing ground for the author's ideas and usually a source of challenge to the theories and methods he pursues. Sharp questioning by students over many years in the classroom has done much to make the author constantly clarify his views and state them clearly. The students, too, have put their ideas into this work and much credit is due them.

When it was first established in 1963, the author had the privilege of serving as chairman of the Council of Social Work Administration of the National Association of Social Workers. The stimulating experience did much to help him think through the many facets of the administrative role and also deepened his conviction that social work administration is a method in social work practice and that it should be so regarded.

Thus, scores of people have had a part in this work, and if they see their ideas and expressions recorded herein, it is hoped that they will be gratified. No way can be thought of to assign to each person his rightful credit because by now even the writer himself is a product of all that has influenced him over these many years.

Special thanks go to Miss Thelma Caruso, who did more than type the manuscript. She handled the sometimes "messy" copy with good spirit and did an outstanding job in helping to meet deadlines.

In the Introduction to the first edition of this book, a wonderful group of people were mentioned who deserve great appreciation and high commendation. They are my wife, Audrey; sons, Jerrold and James; and daughters-in-law, Janice and Barbara. Their encouragement, support, and confidence has continued to be a source of great strength. Anyone who has this kind of family is indeed fortunate, and probably he is a better administrator and a better writer because of what he gets from his loved ones.

HARLEIGH B. TRECKER
University Professor of Social Work
School of Social Work
University of Connecticut

West Hartford, Connecticut

PART I

METHODS AND PRINCIPLES

1 The Meaning of Administration in Social Work

Administrators of the social services are responsible for helping millions of people meet some of their basic needs. These administrators, along with their co-workers, are called upon daily to make decisions of profound importance to the lives of the people they serve. While their tasks are often huge, complex, and arduous, the personal rewards are great. Because of the efforts of social work administrators who staff the nation's social agencies, many individuals are given the professional help they need at the time they need it.

Social Work Administration as an Adaptive Process

In all administration, there are generic aspects or processes. These processes include such items as purposing or setting objectives, planning, organizing, policy-setting, staffing, budgeting, decision-making, evaluating, and providing continuous leadership. But these basic processes must be adapted to the substantive field, whether it be social work, education, health, business, or government. Each of these fields has specific knowledge, understandings, and values that are pertinent to the given field or program. Consequently, the generic processes listed earlier must be adapted to the substantive field, and the administrator must know the field and identify strongly with it. This is especially true in social work. In addition to adapting the generic processes to the substantive field, the administrator must adapt them to the type of organization involved. In social work, they may be governmental or voluntary agencies. They have different geographic service areas and may render different kinds of help. Likewise, there are differences in the organization format of education, health, business, and so on, and these differences must be understood. Not only must the generic processes be adapted to the substantive area and organizational type but they also must be adapted to the general environment, which includes the community, state, or nation; cooperating or competing groups; regulatory bodies or support sources. In summary, the generic processes of all administration must be adapted to the substantive field, organizational type, and the general environment.

Some Assumptions About Social Work Administration

As was stated in the Introduction, this book is based upon the propositions that social work administration is a *method* in social work practice and that social work agencies should be administered by social work administrators. Thus, certain important assumptions have been made. *First,* social work administrators must have an understanding and acceptance of and a deep commitment to basic social work values. *Second,* social work administrators must have substantial knowledge of social work as a professional service to people. *Third,* social work administrators must have a strong identification with the profession of social work and its fundamental purposes. *Fourth,* social work administrators must know and integrate social work practice and administrative theory. *Fifth,* social work administrators are primarily engaged in establishing effective working relationships with and between people. Providing services in line with agency purposes is basically a matter of organizing, coordinating, and motivating the staff to their highest levels of achievement. *Sixth,* social work administrators are responsible for the quality of services rendered. As Fanshel clearly says, "The manner in which social welfare programs are administered—the efficiency of operation, the clarity of administrative goals, and the degree of rationalization of procedure—has an immediate impact upon the lives of many human beings. Poorly administered services can have as telling an effect as poor diagnosis in casework treatment or inept professional leadership of social groups." [1]

Social work administration is seen, therefore, as a method practiced by social work administrators to enable all people involved in the agency's work to fulfill their responsibilities in accordance with their functions and to make maximum use of resources to the end that the agency provide the best possible social services to the people of the community.

Social work administration is a process of working with people in ways that release and relate their energies so that they use all available resources to accomplish the purpose of providing needed community services and programs. People, resources, and purposes are thus brought together by administration in a continuous, dynamic process. Social work administration is a process of working *with people* to establish and maintain a system of cooperative effort. This way of looking at administration implies a wide distribution of responsibility throughout the whole agency. Many people have administrative responsibilities. Some people, such as agency executives and certain others, have primary responsibility for overall administrative leadership. They must understand that administration as a process has at least three interrelated dimensions. (See Figure 1.) A central dimension is the task or work assignment within the agency structure. Another dimension is the community within which the agency works. A third dimension is the psychosocial one within which people release their feelings and energies. It is this release of energy and feeling, properly channeled and directed by administrators, that enables people to accomplish their tasks in relation to the goals of agency service.

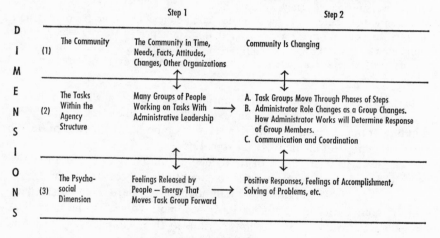

Figure 1
The Administrative Process

Substantive Content of Social Work Administration

It is further assumed that social work administration has a substantive content and method that makes it different from the administration of other enterprises. The difference arises out of the nature and purpose of social work as well as social work's values and methods. It is assumed that for a person to administer social work he must know both the content of social work and the skills of administration. As Millett points out:

I happen to agree that management or organization, in many different settings and for many different ends, does in fact encounter common problems and make use of common techniques. But, I would agree that these common problems and common techniques are necessarily subordinate to the peculiar substantive problems of any particular enterprise. Professionalism in American society means special competence in special fields of learning and skill. These professional specializations have to do with law, medicine, theology, the scholarly disciplines, public school administration, accounting, business management, national defense, engineering, and many other fields. Every professional field of competence may involve organizational and management problems; indeed, I would insist that every field in some degree sooner or later does. But what remains preeminent in professional experience is the professional competence of the individual. When the professional man or woman becomes involved in management and organization, he or she brings to the background of these particular problems the points of view and understandings of the profession. These points of view and these understandings are important, I believe, in the solution or in the handling of organizational and management problems in any particular enterprise. I do not wish to pursue further the question of professional competence versus management competence. . . . I will record simply my own conclusion that there is a management competence different from or supplementary to professional competence, that in any particular organization both competencies are essential to administrative leadership, and that in order of priority professional competence must take precedence over management competence.[2]

It is assumed that social work administration is work with people. It is a dynamic process based on an ever-increasing knowledge and understanding of human behavior, human relations, and human organization. The basic concepts and elements from social casework, social group work, and community organization are of fundamental importance in administration, as well. Social work administration is a continuous process in which many persons share. (See Figure 2.) Staff members, board members, clients, and the community must engage in or become involved in the overall administrative process at points appropriate to their contribution and function. It is assumed that the role of the social work administrator is essentially a dynamic leadership role designed to energize people toward the fulfillment of the objectives of the social work program. It is assumed that the social welfare agency is the structural framework within which administrative tasks are carried on. This agency structure inevitably conditions and controls the specifics of the administrative process in a given situation. It is assumed that social work purposes, policies, and procedures are always interrelated in a dynamic way and tend to become the focus of administrative action and decision. Inasmuch as social agencies are wholes and their parts are interrelated, administration likewise must be thought of as a total process rather than a series of segmented acts.

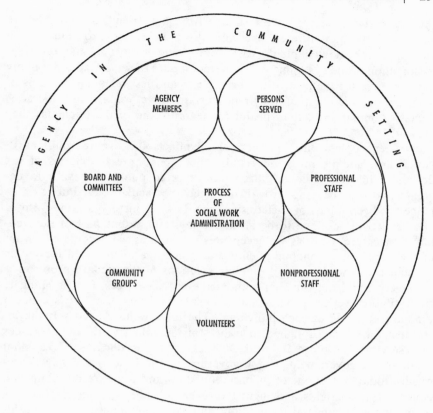

Figure 2
Administration as a Continuous Process

The Importance of Social Work Administration

It is assumed that the quality of services rendered by the social work agency is definitely influenced by the kind of administration the agency has. Because of the inseparable nature of administration and service, the quality of agency program is dependent in a large measure upon the quality of agency administration. The increasing magnitude of the social work task places more and more emphasis upon the necessity of good administration. No matter how one views it, from the standpoint of costs or the standpoint of needs met, social services are large and important in society and must have competence in the administrative realm.

As Vinter puts it, "The American social welfare system has attained a scope and complexity which would strain the credulity of bygone humanitarians. New services constantly emerge, and existing agencies continue to expand. Aid and succor once available from kin, friend, or neighbor are now routinely 'administered' according to 'policies and procedures' as a part of a 'coordinated plan' (with appropriate 'recording and review'). Recognition of today's immensely different modes of service does not imply any nostalgia for the past, with its simpler—and less adequate patterns of help. But acceleration of the trend toward large welfare bureaucracies impels examination of their distinctive features and of the dilemmas they present." [3]

As Clegg points out, "Public welfare affects the lives of millions of Americans, and its programs require the expenditure of billions of tax dollars. While the average citizen has expected public assistance to decrease and disappear, its growth has been spectacular. . . . Public assistance has been a part of society since the dawn of history. In one form or another it will continue to be an increasingly important part of our economic structure. Only as we accept this fact and as we become cognizant of the social and economic phenomena which spawn the need for public assistance will we begin to formulate solutions to the welfare problem." [4]

Society could not function without the social services, for, as Hungate says, "Public welfare programs are tangible evidence of society's concern for the well-being of each individual. The local welfare agency is the instrument of society designed to transform individual work and resources into services for those in need. Public welfare is one of the essential processes of government. Every governmental jurisdiction of any consequence today has as one of its basic functions and prime responsibilities a concern for the rights and digntiy of every member of society. There is increasing governmental recognition that every individual must be considered as a person whose basic needs must be provided in times of stress and also as a potentially effective member of his group and of society as a whole. The individual is the most important resource of modern society, and any enduring governmental system must be concerned with the welfare of every person within its jurisdiction." [5]

The social work ethic fosters responsibility for keeping agency programs and the values of the profession reasonably consonant with the values and needs of the community. Social work knowledge enhances the administrator's ability to integrate program goals, immediate resources, immediate client needs, and community resources. By virtue of the scope, magnitude, and impact of the administrator's job, he needs a systematic approach to organizing the various disciplines and knowledge inherent in good administrative practice.

Fink makes this clear when he says, "Since the administration of a social welfare program is the keystone for maximum efficiency and effectiveness in achievement of agency goals, social work's concern with administrative principles and practices, as with research, has emerged in terms particular to social work. It is social work in an administrative setting and not administration in a social work setting which distinguishes the direction of the social welfare agency from the administration of other kinds of enterprises. The social work administrator is committed to the values and objectives of social work. He is responsible for nurturing the use of social work knowledge and methods for the achievement of acceptable services. Theoretical and technical knowledge applicable to administrative tasks respecting such matters as organizational processes, fiscal operations and control, operational analysis and personnel administration are, of course, essential prerequisites to successful social work administration. The most effective social work administrator, however, is one who uses social work's own rich understanding and experience in human relationships in carrying out the administrative duties necessary to ensure acceptable services for professionally acceptable purposes." [6]

Many Social Workers Engaged in Administration

When the National Association of Social Workers made a study of its membership, it was interesting to note that a large percentage of social workers were engaged in administration as a primary function. The study reported: "General administration is the primary function most frequently checked by the male respondents, and the percentage is exactly twice as high as that for females—40.0 as compared with 20.1 per cent." The study also reported: "An almost equally large number of women are in general administration as are in supervision, 20.1 and 20.8 per cent respectively." Supervision was cited as their primary function by 15.9 percent of the male respondents. When asked to check their primary, secondary, and tertiary job functions, the respondents reported that 28.7 percent of them were engaged in general administration as a primary function; 7.5 percent as a secondary function, and 9.0 percent as a tertiary function. It is clear that a large number of professional social workers are fulfilling administrative roles in either a primary or secondary sense.[7]

Changing Definitions of Social Work Administration

Kidneigh was one of the first authorities to look upon social work administration as an area of social work practice. He said, "Social work administration can be defined as the process of transforming social policy into social services. This definition also includes the process of utilizing the experience gained in transforming social policy into social services to make recommendations that will modify the social policy. It is thus a two-way process: (1) a process of transforming policy into concrete social services, and (2) the use of experience in recommending modification of policy." [8]

Spencer has presented many scholarly discussions of the administration method in social work. She defines administration as follows: "Administration of social agencies is the process of securing and transforming community resources (human and financial) into a program of community service. This process of securing and transforming resources involves the active participation of board (or legislative body), executive, staff and volunteers or constituency in varying degrees. Administration in social work is concerned in a major way with enterprise determination which includes goal formation. It is *not* limited to the management and utilization of resources according to plans provided by an external body." [9]

Stein, a recognized authority, says, "Definitions of administration abound, but central to those most accepted currently is the concept of administration as a process of defining and attaining the objectives of an organization through a system of coordinated and cooperative effort. This concept stresses the administrative process, not just the responsibilities of management; defining objectives, which connote the need to modify and reshape them, to be conscious of goals, and not to take them for granted; reaching these objectives, described as the central responsibility of management and the underlying *raison d'être* of administrative process, the latter not then being an end in itself; involvement of people and their contributions in a planned pattern of cooperation, rather than administration being the activities of the executive group only." [10]

Johns says, "Administration is the process of setting objectives and establishing policies, creating and maintaining an organization, making plans and carrying them out, evaluating the results. It is an inclusive process, shared by everyone in an organization . . . it is a cooperative function, a pervasive function. Everyone participates in it; everyone is affected by it." [11]

Newman defines administration as "the guidance, leadership and control of the efforts of a group of individuals toward some common goal. . . . The work of any administration can be divided into the following basic processes; planning, organizing, assembling, directing and controlling." [12]

Administration may be defined as "the determination and clarification of function; the formulation of policies and procedures; the delegation of authority; the selection, supervision and training of staff; and the mobilization and organization of all available and appropriate resources to the end that the purposes of the agency can be fulfilled." [13] The above definition by Mayo is condensed and summarized by Schwartz when he says, "Administration is the process and the organization of people working toward objectives which entail the production of goods or the provision of services." [14]

Rodney states, "In essence, administration is the process that mobilizes an organization's resources, human and material, to attain predetermined goals." [15]

Hungate calls attention to the fact that "Administration is the total functional activity and behavioral influence involved in attaining program goals." [16]

In another definition, environment is stressed: "Administration is the creation of an environment—of an appropriate physical setting, of a favorable psychological climate, and of an established pattern for the interpersonal relationships required for the efficient discharge of an organization's function." [17]

From the public health field, it is observed that "Administration is a process by which the potentials of men and of materials are synthesized and activated for the achievement of defined goals." [18]

In a classic definition, Tead says, "Administration is the process and agency which lays down the broad object for which an organization and its management are to strive, which establishes the broad policies under which they are to operate, and which gives general oversight to the continuing effectiveness of the total organization in reaching the objective sought." [19]

In a discussion of the administrative function, it is suggested: "The function of administration is to 'carry out' or 'execute' or 'implement' policy decisions, or to coordinate activity in order to accomplish some common purpose, or simply to achieve cooperation in the pursuit of a shared goal." [20]

Blum and Leonard say, "The word 'administration' encompasses the efforts required to initiate and guide the entire series of agency procedures. Included are the determination of the ends or objectives of the agency, procurement and organization of the means or resources necessary to achieve those ends, the conception and effective carrying through of plans that best utilize available resources to achieve the desired objectives, and finally, evaluation of the effectiveness and efficiency of the effort and its impact on the shaping of new or modified objectives." [21]

McGill observes that "The art of administration, whether university administration or the operation of a business, is to take a whole configuration of problems that one faces and attempt to untangle the threads—identify the major difficulties and go after them systematically." [22]

Sarri says, "Administration is defined as a method of social work practice rather than as an area of knowledge and research. It is that method which is concerned primarily with the following activities: 1. translation of societal mandates into operational policies and goals to guide organizational behavior; 2. design of organizational structures and processes through which goals can be achieved; 3. securing resources in the form of materials, staff, clients, and societal legitimation necessary for goal attainment and organizational survival; 4. selection and engineering of the necessary technologies; 5. optimizing organization behavior directed toward increased effectiveness and efficiency; 6. evaluation of organization performance to facilitate systematic continuous problem solving." [23]

The common elements that appear in all of these definitions can be summarized as follows:

1. Administration is a continuous, dynamic process.
2. The process is set into motion in order to accomplish a common purpose or goal.
3. The resources of people and material are harnessed so that the common purpose or goal may be achieved.
4. Coordination and cooperation are the means by which the resources of people and material are harnessed.
5. Implicit in the definition are the elements of planning, organization, leadership, and artistry.

Major Areas of Administrative Responsibility

If it is agreed that administration has a major leadership role to fulfill in the work of the agency, what are some of the major areas within which administration should take leadership?

First, administration is responsible for giving leadership to the continuing process of identifying social welfare needs in the community where the agency serves. Naturally, attention will be devoted to those areas of need that are in the general realm of the agency's service mandate. However, administration must be concerned about needs broadly defined even though programs for meeting those needs may ultimately be assigned to some other agency. In the need identification process, administrators are seen as working with the board, the staff, clientele, other agencies, and the community as expert analysts of problems, trends, and possible programs.

Second, administration is responsible for giving leadership to the matter of defining, redefining, interpreting, and utilizing agency purposes as guides for programs and services. Perhaps no task is more demanding or more difficult. However, without clear objectives, it is impossible for an agency to operate efficiently or evaluate its work.

Third, administration is responsible for giving leadership to provisioning the agency in terms of financial resources, facilities, staff, and other forms of support. Administration always has the responsibility to inform the community what is needed in the way of resources to do the job. Furthermore, administration has to work diligently through every available channel to see to it that these resources are obtained.

Fourth, administration is responsible for giving leadership to the development of the agency's program of services. To be sure, this task is widely shared with the professional staff and with others, but it ultimately is the job of administration to see to it that the program meets the needs of the community.

Fifth, administration is responsible for giving leadership to the development of a form of organization and structure that will provide for the coordination of the efforts of all persons engaged in the work of the agency and that will support the program of services.

Sixth, administration has a major responsibility for giving leadership to the process of policy formation, procedure development, and general operating principles. Without clearly stated policies and procedures, it is impossible for any agency to operate soundly and efficiently.

Seventh, administration is responsible for giving leadership to the continuous assessment and evaluation of how well the agency is doing its job. Here it is assumed that objectives are clear, standards have been set, and criteria of evaluation are understood and followed.

Eighth, administration is responsible for giving leadership to the change process. In a dynamic and changing age with new needs emerging all of the time, most agencies are in a process of change during their entire history. When administration is change-oriented and takes responsibility for helping to bring about needed changes, it can be assumed that the agency will remain viable.

While the eight points given above are by no means all that could be written, it does seem that they are the major ones, and if they are done, one can expect a generally healthy and effective administration. (See Figure 3.)

Functions of Administration

Hammond and others list three functions of administration. They are: "1. *Structuring of the organization as an administrative function.* If such organizations must exhibit sustained rather than *ad hoc* activity it follows that the actions of their component parts must be patterned and controlled, rather than random. While custom, convention and habit provide a basis for common action, administered organizations must channel and modify such activity in order to meet their specific needs. 2. *Definition of purpose as an administrative function.* If administered organizations have delimited, specialized purposes, it follows that these purposes must be selected and articulated. Organizational goals do not spring automatically out of the performance of non-administrative tasks. In a dynamic context, goals do not remain obvious but mechanisms for their evaluation, reflection, implementation, and periodic revision must be institutionalized. As such activities as bolt-turning, temperature-taking, or rifle-firing do not in themselves define and prescribe collective goals, the definition of purposes is a function of administration. 3. *Management of the organization-environment exchange system as a function of administration.* Some of the necessary exchanges between the organization and the environment occur in the performance of non-administrative activity; but the very essence of organization is task specialization, which calls for coordination. Hence, the management of the system of exchange between an organization and its environment becomes primarily a function of administration. At a minimum this applies to the acquisition and dispersement, from and to the larger system (a) of legitimation or authority; (b) of personnel; (c) of tools, equipment or other facilities; and (d) of a medium of exchange."[24]

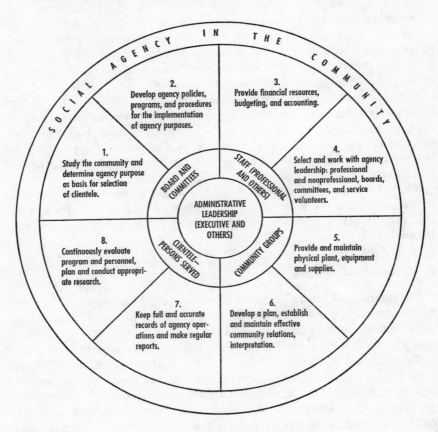

Figure 3
The Unitary Nature of the Administrative Process—
Functions Performed—Groups Involved

Administration as a Social Work Method

The practice of administration as a social work method must encourage wide participation in the decision-making process, rather than centralized decision-making. Within the organization, mutual confidence and consensus rather than imposed authority, and coercion, must be the major integrative forces. Moreover, responsibility for program decision-making is placed in the hands of the professionally competent and knowledgeable and is exercised on the basis of rationality.

By the nature of its value commitment, social work administration is practiced within a humanistic frame of reference. It views the organizational setting as a dynamic and complex set of relationships among people to achieve both organizational and individual goals. In order to carry out a relating and releasing function, the consultative or democratic form of administration encourages relevant participation by the principals of the agency (board, staff, and client groups) at all levels. It seeks to give its philosophical framework practical meaning by encouraging full and free communication and by providing an atmosphere that encourages emotional expression and self-realization of human needs within the work situation.

Thus, social work administration implements on an organizational level many of the values that characterize the social worker's relationship to people. It extends the belief in the dignity and worth of the individual and his right to self-determination to the level of the agency's system as a whole. It believes that encouragement of full participation at all levels is not only ethically correct but that it is the only type of system that will permit human and organizational growth under conditions of change. Thus, it accepts a human rather than a mechanistic view of administration.

The purposes of any agency mirror the underlying value and philosophy of service that the agency represents. Administrative efforts to instill both staff and community with this sense of purpose may be cited as an enabling function. Wise and continuous use of purpose by the administrator may be seen as one of the ways in which individuals and groups are enabled to function more effectively in the production of services and in interpersonal relationships affecting the provision of services. Interpretation of purpose in the community also enables the service population and the sources of political, financial, and community support to have a clearer understanding of agency function. Purpose, therefore, becomes the primary point of reference for the administrator, and it should guide all his actions.

The knowledge of the social work administrator differs from that utilized by other social work practitioners on several counts. He must have a deeper understanding of the agency as a whole, of the agency in the community, and of the position of the agency within the network of social welfare institutions. The social work administrator must also be able to perceive systematically the implications of policy formulations and must be able to give rational priority to agency objectives.

Poe gives us a helpful schema when he compares the assumptions of the classical scientific management school of thought with administrations guided by the humanistic approach.[25]

A COMPARATIVE LOOK AT ASSUMPTIONS ABOUT ADMINISTRATION

Assumptions	Classical Scientific Management	Humanistic Approach
1. Philosophical assumptions about man	Man prefers to be directed. Man is not creative. Man desires little responsibility. Man finds work distasteful.	When appropriately motivated, man strives for creativity, responsibility, self-direction, and self-actualization.
2. Goal	Organizational goal, productivity and efficiency	Respect and growth of persons within the fulfillment of service delivery
3. Structure	Concept of mechanics, separation of parts and functions	Interrelationships and interdependence of all components into a whole
4. Orientation	Focus strictly on tasks	An emphasis on human relationships while fulfilling tasks
5. Size	Largeness implies productiveness and efficiency	Small enough for effective communications and relationships
6. View of administration	The technological control and business part of the organization	A human service; coordination of the human aspects of the organization
7. Functional expectations	Compliance to orders	Building personal commitment, trust, and responsibility
8. Positions	Confined to definitions and delineation by area of specialty for which one is hired	Flexible application of people's interests and skills to jointly resolve organizational problems and tasks
9. Decision-making (Power level)	Authority and control from the few at the top of the hierarchy	Shared leadership participation and input
10. Sense of responsibility	A feeling of responsibility *for* others	Being responsible *for* one's self and *to* others
11. Programming	Consumer adjusts to program	Programs adapt to the consumer
12. Clinical Orientation	Focus on problems and weaknesses	Focus on skills, strengths, and areas of growth needs

Administration Faces Emerging Issues

The rapid growth of the social services and the increasing responsibilities of administrators have brought into focus a number of issues. The dictionary definition of the word *issue* is: "a point in debate or controversy on which the parties take affirmative and negative positions; a presentation of alternatives between which to choose or decide."

Among the several issues undergoing resolution are first how the administrator is seen and how his responsibilities are defined. Here the range may be wide with some feeling that the administrator's job in social work is primarily that of inside "management" of agency operations. Others feel that the administrator occupies and must exercise a leadership role with his efforts directed not only toward inside operations but increasingly toward the wider community. If one sees the administrator as being primarily concerned with maintaining the institution in terms of the status quo, then there will be little expectation that he will carry a leadership role with major responsibility for innovating. If, on the other hand, it is assumed that the administrator has responsibility for leading the organization in new directions, he must then have a real desire to seek changes, not only in his agency but also in society, that provide adequate standards of community welfare services for all.

The sheer size of the social welfare enterprise gives rise to other issues. With social welfare operations becoming increasingly complex, there are problems inherent in bureaucracy and centralization. The agency may seem to be impersonal, and administrative decisions may seem to be made far from the point of impact of the services. A point of issue, therefore, is how to decentralize operations so that the staff providing the professional services and the persons in need of the services will be involved in basic decision-making that is compatible with their experience and authority.

An issue of increasing magnitude today is the confusion between the policy-making function and the administrative function. Considerable conflict results when there is a lack of clarity between the policy-making task on the one hand and the tasks associated with carrying out policy.

The issue of accountability for results is also important. Measures of the effectiveness of social work programs are not adequate. Performance criteria for professional staff are also limited. This would seem to indicate that administrators will be giving an increasing amount of time and attention to the whole matter of how they guarantee to the public the efficacy of the programs they direct.

The conflicts between the values of social work and those of the community often come to a sharp focus in the office of the administrator. Here it is clear that administrators have a crucial role in reconciling the values of the profession with those of the community, always in relating them to the needs and to the best interests of the client. Because different communities hold different values at different times and because needs are always changing, the administrator and his board and staff must constantly seek to communicate with and interpret to groups that represent divergent but readily known points of view.

Today, there are many diverse staffing patterns, including the use of undergraduate social work majors to provide services and the emergence of paraprofessionals to function as aides. Administrators have a real responsibility to work out staffing patterns that result in the best possible services to people.

Services are being increasingly decentralized and taken out to the neighborhoods. This trend is not fully understood or recognized by some agencies, but it must be reckoned with.

It is the rare agency that has a single funding source. At present, most agencies are multiple-funded, securing monetary resources from a variety of governmental units, federated financing campaigns, voluntary gifts, and fees. Financing thus becomes a varied pattern with different agencies and must be understood by administrators.

Multiservice programs have come into being in recent years, and many agencies that formerly provided a single service are now engaged in a much wider range of service activities calling for highly developed skills in coordination.

Agency coalitions have appeared in many places, and agency administrators have to decide about which agencies they will ally themselves with in terms of their fundamental mission.

More sophisticated management technology is appearing daily, and computers play a larger part in information gathering, storing, and retrieval. Sometimes administrators have to weigh the added expense involved in using these new technologies against the real benefits to be gained.

There is much more client and community involvement in policy- and decision-making than was true even a decade ago. Consequently, the administrator must decide how this growing movement will be harnessed to the good of all.

In essence, administrative effectiveness is dependent on a wide number of variables that must be adapted to the time, the place, and the particular circumstances. The task is to identify and assess those factors indigenous to a specific environment that militate against or argue for a specific approach.

NOTES

1. David Fanshel, "Administrative Research in Social Welfare: A Review of Current Trends," in *Research in Social Welfare Administration* (New York: National Association of Social Workers, 1962), p. 11.
2. John D. Millett, *Organization for the Public Service* (New York: Van Nostrand Reinhold Co., a Division of Litton Educational Publishing Inc., 1956), pp. 5–6.
3. Robert D. Vinter, "The Social Structure of Service," in Alfred J. Kahn, ed., *Issues in American Social Work* (New York: Columbia University Press, 1959), p. 243.
4. Reed K. Clegg, *The Welfare World* (Springfield, Ill.: Charles C. Thomas Publisher, 1968), pp. vii–viii.
5. Joseph I. Hungate, Jr., *A Guide for Training Local Public Welfare Administrators* (Washington, D.C.: U.S. Department of Health, Education and Welfare—Welfare Administration, Bureau of Family Services, Division of Technical Training, 1964), p. 15.
6. Arthur E. Fink, C. Wilson Anderson, and Merrill B. Conover, *The Field of*

Social Work, 5th ed. (New York: Holt, Rinehart, and Winston, Inc., 1968), pp. 8–9.

7. Alfred M. Stamm, "NASW Membership: Characteristics, Deployment, and Salaries," in *Personnel Information* (New York: National Association of Social Workers, May 1969), pp. 39–40.

8. John Kidneigh, "Social Work Administration—An Area of Social Work Practice?" *Social Work Journal* (April 1950), p. 58.

9. Sue Spencer, *The Administration Method in Social Work Education* (New York: Council on Social Work Education, 1959), p. 26.

10. Herman Stein, "Administration," in *Encyclopedia of Social Work* (New York: National Association of Social Workers, 1965), p. 58.

11. Ray Johns, *Executive Responsibility* (New York: Association Press, 1954), p. 30.

12. William H. Newman, *Administrative Action,* 2nd edition (New York: Prentice-Hall, Inc., 1963), pp. 4–5.

13. Leonard Mayo, "Administration of Social Agencies," in *Social Work Yearbook, 1945* (New York: Russell Sage Foundation, 1945), p. 15.

14. Edward E. Schwartz, "Some Views on the Study of Social Welfare Administration," in David Fanshel, ed., *Research in Social Welfare Administration— Its Contributions and Problems* (New York: National Association of Social Workers, 1962), p. 42.

15. Lynn S. Rodney, *Administration of Public Recreation* (New York: The Ronald Press, 1964), p. 26.

16. Joseph I. Hungate, Jr., *A Guide for Training Local Public Welfare Administrators* (Washington, D.C.: U.S. Department of Health, Education and Welfare, 1964), p. 5.

17. Group for the Advancement of Psychiatry, *Administration of the Public Psychiatric Hospital* (New York: Group for the Advancement of Psychiatry, 1960), p. 123.

18. Ruth B. Freeman and Edward M. Holmes, Jr., *Administration of Public Health Services* (Philadelphia: W. B. Saunders Company, 1960), p. 21.

19. Ordway Tead, *Democratic Administration* (New York: Association Press, 1954), p. 67.

20. Herbert Kaufman, "The Administrative Function," in David L. Sills, ed., *International Encyclopedia of the Social Sciences* (New York: The Macmillan Company and The Free Press, 1968), Vol. I., p. 61.

21. Henrick L. Blum and Alvin R. Leonard, *Public Administration—A Public Health Viewpoint* (New York: The Macmillan Company, 1963), p. 396.

22. From President William J. McGill, *Columbia Report* (Winter 1974), p. 2.

23. Rosemary C. Sarri, "Administration in Social Welfare," in *Encyclopedia of Social Work* (Washington, D.C.: National Association of Social Workers, 1971), Vol. I, pp. 42–43.

24. Peter B. Hammond et al., "On the Study of Administration," in James D. Thompson, ed., *Comparative Studies in Administration* (Pittsburgh: University of Pittsburgh Press, 1959), pp. 6–7.

25. William Poe, *The Hidden Agenda—The Administration of Mental Health and the Mental Health of Administration,* Ph.D. dissertation, April 1975, School of Education, University of Massachusetts, Amherst, Mass.

2 Social Work Administrators

It is the point of view of this book that, in order to administer the social services, key administrators must have social work education and experience. The special nature of social work administration results from the complex social welfare system in America and the nature of the social needs with which this system is designed to deal. In other words, social work administration has social purposes that it is pledged to fulfill. Furthermore, the social work administrator works with a number of different individuals and groups. Some of the groups are the staff, the board, and the clientele. In addition, the social work administrator has the dual responsibilities of professional leadership and agency operations. Social work itself provides a substantive body of knowledge, understandings, principles, skills, and *values* that is the foundation of the work to be done. There is a social work culture that must be understood.

Social Work Agencies and the World of Business Administration

To be sure, there are administrative subpositions in social agencies that do not necessarily require social work education, for example, business management, physical plant and equipment maintenance, and perhaps public relations. However, even persons working in these areas must have a deep understanding of social work purposes and a deep commitment to social work goals and values. Such subadministrators should be limited in their work to their areas of competence and should be responsible to the leadership of the social work executive.

It should be pointed out that the social work agency is a nonprofit concern, and it has different measures of efficiency than does the profit-making business. In the case of business, one measure of evaluation is the extent to which profits are made. In the case of the social agency, the measure is the extent to which human needs are met. In addition, business organizations are essentially competitive, and social agencies are essentially cooperative. They are cooperative in that they seek wide sharing of their knowledge and discoveries and endeavor to unite their efforts in the services they perform for their clientele.

Another differentiating factor is that in the world of business the customer can "shop around" and make his own choice as to which concern he will patronize. Frequently in the field of social work, the client does not have much of a choice, particularly in terms of governmental programs because they are authorized to meet the needs of categorical groups. When the network of social services is carefully organized, there should be a minimum of duplication of effort and a concentration upon coverage of particular groups and services to meet particular problems. While the administration of business and industry shares common problems with social work administration and other forms of administration, it seems increasingly clear that to administer the social work enterprise it is necessary that the administrator have both training and experience in social work.

As Ryan points out, "the executive who is a specialist is traditionally an expert in his field, for example, in social work or perhaps in one of its categories such as child welfare or group work. He has been educated quite thoroughly in this field and has been a practitioner for a good part of his professional life. Through the subsequent processes of supervision, consultation, or teaching, and largely on the basis of expert performance in these roles concerning the specialty, he has now arrived at an executive position. His technical knowledge of social work, or a particular portion of the field, and his performance in the specialty has been recognized as excellent by both professionals and lay persons alike. In this executive position, he is able to shape his learning into a professional program of high ideals based on the body of knowledge of social work. This expertise is a legitimate basis for authority in the agency and usually disposes workers to obey. The social work staff respond with loyalty to this fellow professional who also is committed to the goals of the agency and the profession. With the combined bases of expertise, legitimate role, and loyalty of professional staff, any specialist executive has a solid foundation upon which to function as an administrator." [1]

The Professional Social Work Administrator

What do we mean by professional social work administration?

First, the administrator is behaving professionally when he strives for objectivity and seeks and uses factual material in administration. This is another way of saying that the professional person seeks to make use of knowledge and understanding as a basis for skill and that knowledge and understanding replace unconsidered judgment and unfounded opinion.

Second, the professional administrator is behaving professionally when he works purposefully and planfully and knows what the administrative role is and what it is designed to accomplish. In other words, purpose becomes so much a part of the administrator that every action is governed by the consideration of whether or not the step taken will lead toward professional goals.

Third, the administrator is behaving professionally when he exercises conscious self-discipline or control over self at all times. The administrator's own needs are kept out of the situation insofar as possible. Sensitivity to others is basic. Obviously, this kind of administrator works in the public interest and wants to contribute to man's well-being. In short, professional integrity is based on the concept that the public interest is always above self-interest.

Fourth, the administrator is behaving professionally when he seeks constantly to make decisions on the basis of the values of the profession. Administrators seek diligently to formulate for themselves the convictions by which they live and which become the basis for choices or decisions, especially where matters of principle are involved.

Understandings Needed by the Social Work Administrator

In an earlier publication, the author defined "administration as a process through which staff, board, constituency, and community, individually and collectively in the developing agency setting, are enabled by administrators to fulfill their responsibilities as individuals and groups in accordance with their function, skill, and ability in terms of the whole agency to the end that their agency provides the best possible service to the people of the community." [2] Thus, the administrator's job is seen as that of working with people to establish and maintain a system of cooperative effort. This implies a functional distribution of responsibility widely throughout the whole agency.

The administrative job seems to have two important dimensions. *First,* there is the dimension of the problem, project, or task on which people are working. *Second,* there is the psychosocial dimension of feelings released by people as they work on these tasks. It is the release of energy with feelings properly channeled and directed that enables people to accomplish their tasks. An element in this dimension is movement, which means that as people work on problems they grow and change. Thus, the administrative process is dynamic and has the possibility of being analyzed in terms of various steps that occur. In the administrative process, it is further assumed that the securing of agreement among people, the making of decisions, and the carrying out of decisions are interwoven and inter-related. Of great significance is the assumption that the administrator's job is primarily a matter of establishing effective working relationships with and between people. It is basically a matter of understanding and influencing human motivation.

Although all social work practitioners are expected to have an understanding of community processes and cultural determinants, the social work administrator, as chief planner and coordinator, must have a more sophisticated understanding of these areas. However, this does not mean that the social work administrator is responsible for gathering all of this information, but rather that under a system of consultative relationship, two-way communication between staff members will be encouraged so that other members may be motivated to share in this responsibility.

The social work administrator must also have a knowledge of the agency and its structure and policies, and how these factors relate to the provision of services. Knowledge of the agency includes an awareness of the role responsibilities and tasks attached to each position and the reciprocal interaction between positions.

The knowledge of how to work through the agency and the community may be considered method knowledge. This level of understanding incorporates the notion that the social work administrator, like other social work practitioners, will know how to work effectively with individuals and with groups in order to achieve value modifications. This approach recognizes that all of us have needs for status, growth, and self-fulfillment that affect our interaction in our work environment. This means that the administrator must be person-centered as well as task-oriented. The administrator's recognition of motivational factors makes possible the provision of an organized work environment in which a system of cooperative effort will release these human feelings and will relate them in a meaningful and coordinated way.

The social work administrator's understanding of people will help him to focus upon the informal group structure that arises within every formal organization. These informal groupings are important to the individual, for a person's reactions and views provide the basis for the person's self-image. The informal structures may either compete with or facilitate the formal organizational structure, and the social work administrator must have knowledge of their value as "safety valves" as well as their dysfunctional consequence. By interacting with individuals on a group basis, the social work administrator encourages a more democratic process of decision-making. This is another way of saying that if the administrator is to function as an enabler, he must have knowledge of the agents of both change and stability within the organization.

If social work administrators are to work effectively in creating a planned and coordinated system of relationships, they must have a knowledge of self, of the quality of their interactions with others, and of the relationship of their own needs and actions to the purposes of the agency. In working through and with others, the social work administrator must make a responsible and conscious use of self. This means that the social work administrator must work purposefully and planfully. Administrators must communicate their inner sense of purpose to relevant others and must consciously judge all of their actions by their relation to purpose. When the social work administrator judges actions in terms of the needs of the people being served, work is then planfully carried out. When he strives to implement the values of social work, the work is responsible and professional. The administrator who practices the social work method must assume responsibility for decisions while creating an atmosphere that will enable others to share in this decision-making process. The social work

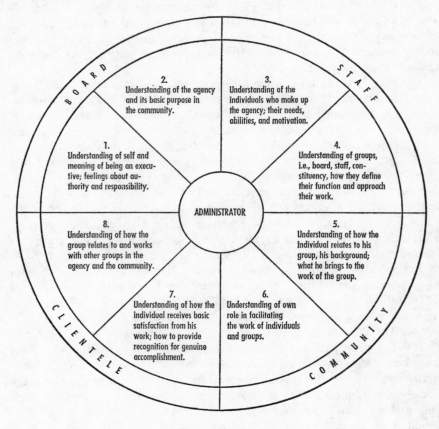

Figure 4
Basic Understandings Needed by the Administrator

administrator must base decisions upon sound professional principles and knowledge and must place the public interest, the interest of the person served, above any self-interest.

As pictured in Figure 4, the administrator must understand self, the agency, individuals, and groups that make up the agency and how they work together.

The Multiple Roles of the Administrator

As Mayo pointed out, "The modern social work administrator finds himself playing a number of different roles within his own organization; i.e., to a certain extent he must identify with the clients and also with the staff because these have to do with his professional responsibilities; by virtue of the fact that he is an administrator, he must identify with the board and to some extent he must see things through the eyes of the most conservative elements of the community, and outside of his organization he must identify not only with the agency he administers, be it public or private, but with the community as a whole and its needs. In other words, he must be an expert administrator looking to the interest of his own organization and pushing its program forward; at the same time he must be coordinator and champion of the community as a whole, and above all, as a professional person he feels certain political interests and concerns to which he is expected to be responsive. I regard these various responsibilities, obligations, and pressures to be extremely difficult when it comes to keeping them in balance and when it comes to maintaining one's own professional integrity." [3] Figure 5 illustrates the multidimensional role of the administrator.

A study of institutional change has commented: "The administrator has to live in a multi-dimensional world with a responsibility for taking action in dealing with concrete problems. He must constantly seek multi-functional solutions. This forces him into many paradoxical situations. The administrator must constantly strive to maintain a consistency in his own behavior while accepting the fact that his behavior will always appear inconsistent from any simple, one-dimensional frame of reference. He must constantly seek for solutions that resolve conflicts between the interests of several dimensions, but accept the fact that such conflicts are inevitable and never-ending. He must constantly seek to change behavior in the social system as a viable entity. He must seek a perfection of balanced development but accept the inevitability of imperfection. He must place heavy emphasis upon achieving organization purposes and must maintain the perspective of an outside observer, but not lose his impassioned involvement with the results of the system." [4]

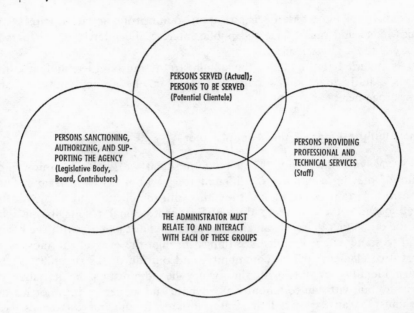

Figure 5
The Multidimensional Role of the Administrator

Scope and Importance of the Administrative Task

In recent years, it has become increasingly evident that the social work administrator has the ultimate and total responsibility for the work of the agency. The impact of the agency's services flows out from the central administration. Much of what the client, the staff, and the board feels or senses about the agency is set by the skill of the administrator. The decisions made by the administrator are far-reaching and seldom can be undone. Decisions made today tend to affect the agency for many years hence. Consequently, the administrator who must make choices among a number of alternatives is always exercising considerable influence. It can also be said that the growth of the agency and to a major extent the growth of the profession of social work is related to the kind of administration it enjoys. Therefore, the leadership role of the administrator cannot be overestimated.

Tead brings this out when he says, "By an administrator, I shall mean an individual who has the top directive responsibility (or who is an assistant to such an individual) to whom is assigned the initiative in the conduct of an organization for its overall planning, staffing, organizing, or structuring, directing, delegating, overseeing, and evaluating including the use of such objective measures as may be available in the premises. The administrator is the chief facilitator, expediter, and integrator of diversified but necessary functions and labors on the part of a variety of associated individuals and groups." [5]

Characteristics of the Administrator's Job

In discussing the characteristics of the executive's job, an institute group noted: "(1) He is responsible for seeing that work is performed by others; (2) he has to make decisions; (3) he works *through* others; he delegates responsibility; (4) he must use authority; (5) he is the channel between a higher authority and the staff; (6) he is a facilitator; (7) he is a trouble-shooter; (8) he is responsible for keeping the enterprise 'running'; (9) he is responsible for being a 'leader.' " [6]

The executive must have a well-formulated and progressive philosophy of social work. He must project a sound sense of direction for the agency. Administrators must have real capacity to form good working relationships with the staff, the clientele, and the community. They have to be able to keep their poise in the midst of often-conflicting opinions and values.

A community agency describes its administration in the following terms: "C.P.I.'s administration headed by an executive director bears over-all responsibility for coordinating and supervising the agency's six divisions and for dealing with the numerous outside agencies with which C.P.I. is allied or on which it is dependent. The executive staff, for example, makes certain that board policies are implemented; conducts negotiations with state, federal and private funding agencies; handles legal affairs through the office of the general counsel and implements directives and special instructions issued by funding agencies. Working closely with C.P.I.'s executive and deputy director is the personnel division, whose functions also include property management and purchasing. This division maintains personnel records and administers employee benefits, interviews potential employees, and is in charge of supplies, equipment, and training materials for C.P.I. programs and projects. It is responsible for leaseholds on such properties as the Skill Center, the young men's and young women's residential centers, and numerous neighborhood employment centers and Community Services offices. Maintenance of financial records; disbursement of grant-in-aid funds; conduct of delegate-agency field audits; preparation of periodic financial statements for federal, state and private funding sources; processing of invoices and billings, and handling of delegate-agency requisitions are among the functions of the accounting division. Headed by the comptroller, the division also maintains detailed accounts of all funds which support programs." [7]

The Council on Social Work Administration of the National Association of Social Workers has spelled out a detailed list of the administrator's functions. In their words: "The administrator, directing and co-ordinating all operations with the assistance of appropriate staff, is responsible for the quality and effectiveness of the total agency program and for seeing that things get done well and on time. He sets the tone of the agency. In carrying out his duties the administrator has a shared responsibility with the official body to whom he is accountable. He is specifically responsible for the following:

1. Giving leadership to policy-making bodies and staff.
2. Identifying, in a continuing process, social needs that can be met by his agency.
3. Taking leadership in defining and redefining agency purposes.
4. Formulating, recommending, and evaluating policy in relation to the agency's mission.
5. Developing and planning short-term and long-range programs with readiness for adaptation to changing conditions and new needs.
6. Maintaining a leadership role in meeting community needs.
7. Developing leadership in appropriate policy-making bodies.
8. Maintaining positive relationships with community leaders and forces, especially in the constellation of social agencies, both voluntary and governmental.
9. Interpreting the agency to the community and developing a proper public image and financial support.
10. Establishing and maintaining positive relationships with current and potential users of the agency's services.
11. Projecting the budget and obtaining financial resources.
12. Recruiting, employing, and developing the staff.
13. Organizing and directing the staff and resources.
14. Providing conditions, resources, and climate conducive to optimum staff utilization and development for productive effectiveness.
15. Administering the financial assets and resources.
16. Maintaining records and reports as a basis for accountability and evaluation.
17. Evaluating program achievements and personnel effectiveness in accordance with goals and standards.
18. Accounting to the appropriate policy-making bodies and to the community for the total agency program and operation." [8]

Friedlander sums it up in these words: "The main administrative functions of a private or public social agency may be divided into nine activities: 1) fact-finding; 2) analysis of social conditions and of services to meet human needs; 3) decision on the way of reaching this objective; 4) planning and allocating resources; 5) setting up organizational structure and work assignments; 6) staffing the agency; 7) supervising and controlling personnel and finances; 8) recording and accounting; and 9) supplying financial resources." [9]

Pathways to Administration

There is no accurate information on the educational background of today's social work administrators. There are several pathways to administrative responsibility. For example, many administrators begin their professional social work practice in the area of direct service. They then assume supervisory responsibility, then subadministrative responsibility, and then assume the executive role or the overall leadership of the agency. McDonald says, "The Family Service movement has been a solid supporter of the view that the chances for success of an administrator are enhanced if he has come up 'through the chairs'—caseworker, supervisor, executive. In small agencies—and a great number of voluntary social agencies of all kinds are not large—this seems especially true. The executive is not purely an administrator—he also functions as practitioner and supervisor. This matter of agency size, then, may be one pertinent spot where there is an administrative issue." [10]

Another route to social administrative responsibility is the route of transfer from other fields of endeavor. It is not known how many administrators have come into social work from other fields such as education, government service, or the like. It would seem to be true, however, that a certain number of administrators now in practice have come from fields other than social work.

With reference to the field of education, the U.S. Office of Education states, "It would be much easier to recruit people if we knew more about what sort of stuff the successful administrator is made of. Although attributes such as sensitivity, courage, style, and even charisma are as essential to the good administrator as mental ability and scholarship, they are less easily measured, and therefore not often enough considered in recruitment and preparation programs. A true appreciation of the importance of these personal qualities might result in the broadening of the range of people we consider for top jobs in education. In some cases, personal leadership qualities should perhaps even take precedent over particular functional skills, when those skills could be just as easily delegated to another person. Leadership qualities, after all, are relatively rare, while functional skills are not." [11]

In recent years, a number of schools of social work have developed specializations or concentrations in social work administration, and other schools are now embarking on such ventures. In future years, it can be expected that more and more administrative positions will be filled by persons who have specialized in administration in graduate schools of social work.

Increasing Importance of Basic Qualifications for Social Work Administrators

The social work administrator must have a broad background of social work experience and practice. He must have a professional degree in social work and hopefully a specialization in administration, and must have a deep commitment to the values of social work. He must have good health and vitality to cope with the many pressures related to the administrative job. The administrator should be a person who has the capacity to organize time and set priorities among the many things that have to be done. Well-developed communication skills are essential so that he will be able to present their views to the various groups with whom they work. He must have a highly developed sensitivity to the needs of persons and a high sensitivity to the social problems of the community. The administrator must be able to do long-range thinking and planning and must have ability to set goals for the agency. He must have the ability to listen and hear and learn from many people. The administrator must be a growing person, capable of responding to the challenges for change in the agency and in the profession.

In a penetrating discussion of administration, Tead suggests that to be successful in administrative work people must have "1) superior intellectual capacity, 2) ability for achievement, that is, able to get things done, 3) willingness to assume responsibility, 4) ability to participate as a wise counselor and guide, 5) a solid sense of security of one's own status in the hurly-burly organized relationships and events." He goes on to suggest that the professional worker needs sheer physical and nervous vitality and drive. The ability to think logically, rationally, with problem-solving skills that get the point more quickly than the average person are listed. He suggests that he must be willing to take on the burdens of repsonsibility for decisions and action. He stresses ability to get along with people in a sincerely and friendly yet firm way. He underlines the importance of being able to communicate by voice and pen in effective ways. He says, "We are talking about intellectual capacity which is in some considerable measure innate and unlearned, about high level purposes, about a contagious enthusiasm for goals and methods needed to achieve them, about a total personal drive that catches others up into group loyalty, persistent striving, and gratification simultaneously obtained for personal desires and to those satisfactions realized through one's creative institutional contribution." [12]

The following qualities seem to be necessary if one is to undertake administrative responsibility in social work. Anyone who wants to do administrative work must be willing to assume responsibility. They must be willing to take risks because inevitably administrators make "chancy" decisions. They must be happy in getting work done through other people and must be willing to forego the satisfactions that come from rendering direct service to clients. They have to be the kind of person who can live with conflicting interests and can live with the uncertainties of the job. Because the administrative job is never routine and never is it possible to plan too far ahead, the administrator must know how to cope with the unknown, the unpredictable, and the inevitable emergency problems. The potential administrator must have a high level of energy and must be able to work long hours. In addition, he should be able to take and handle criticism and must forego too much need to be liked. They must be receptive to the communications of other people and must develop a thoughtful style in hearing and listening. They must be able to handle the authority component in their role without becoming authoritarian. They must be able to say "no" without becoming negative. They must have patience and persistence as they give leadership to the progress of the agency. They must be willing to accept certain inroads into their personal life because the administrative job does not necessarily end at the close of the work day. They must be able and willing to set priorities and make decisions about the use of their own time.

Skills of the Social Work Administrator

The Council on Social Work Administration of the National Association of Social Workers describes the skills needed by administrators in these words: "The skill of the social work administrator refers to his ability to perform well the specified tasks related to his various functions. It is made up of administrative knowledge and experience combined with certain innate characteristics. Administrative skills include the ability to do the following: 1. Think and plan ahead realistically. 2. Assess the feasibility of a particular plan. 3. Consider alternative ways of doing things. 4. Foresee and appraise the likely impact of decisions. 5. Set priorities. 6. Make decisions. 7. Handle multiple roles and tasks simultaneously. 8. Maintain personal equilibrium. 9. Understand the functioning of the bureaucratic system and of organizational theory and utilize this understanding to achieve agency goals. 10. Get others to work productively utilizing specific talents of individuals and groups and offsetting their limitations. 11. Use and delegate authority constructively. 12. Communicate effectively with others. 13. Act decisively. Possession of these skills may be of varying degrees and combinations so that a wide range of performance style may be observed among notably successful social work administrators." [13]

Another important skill of the administrator is that of communicating feelings and values. The administrator carries a heavy responsibility for the communication of feelings and values between groups and individuals to help them find common ground. In addition, the administrator is responsible for the communication of ideas, orally and in writing, to individuals, committees, groups, and organizations. Moreover, administrators must be skillful in finding and preparing facts in usable form and must know how to help individuals and groups do their own fact-finding and properly use relevant facts. Perhaps the most important skill of all is that of helping individuals make responsible decisions. This means help with problem identification, sorting and ranking of problems, seeing interrelationships among problems, problem-solving, and evaluating the consequences of proposed solutions. These are all related to the process of responsible decision-making. Also, the administrator must have skill in policy and program analysis coupled with skill in policy formulation. These twin skills of analysis and formulation are fundamental to the administrator's ability to help individuals and groups analyze problems and make decisions.

In discussing the skills of the effective administrator, Katz describes technical, human, and conceptual skills, which he defines as follows: *"Technical skill* . . . and understanding of, and proficiency in, a specific kind of activity, particularly one involving methods, processes, procedures or techniques. Technical skill involves specialized knowledge, analytical ability within that specialty, and facility in the use of the tools and techniques of the specific discipline. *Human skill* . . . the executive's ability to work effectively as a group member and to build cooperative effort within the team he leads. *Conceptual skill* . . . the ability to see the enterprise as a whole; it includes recognizing how the various functions of the organization depend on one another, and how changes in any one part affect all the others. Recognizing those relationships and perceiving the significant elements in any situation, the administrator should then be able to act in a way which advances the over-all welfare of the total organization." [14]

Program Directors and Social Service Administrators in Host Settings

In community centers, it is customary for program staff members to carry a considerable amount of administrative responsibility. As Schatz says, "Program staff members are deeply involved in daily administration. Just as the executive director administers the total agency, the program director administers the total Center program and the program department heads administer their respective departments. Although the scope of responsibility of the program director and of the program department directors may be more limited, administrative functions are the same. They have responsibility within their respective jurisdictions for: 1. Defining departmental objectives. 2. Translating objectives into specific programs based on members' needs and interests. 3. Determining what personnel, facilities, materials and budget are required to put the program into operation. 4. Obtaining and coordinating all the necessary factors. 5. Recruiting, training, scheduling and supervising program personnel. 6. Processing intake of members into the program. 7. Maintaining records of programs and participation. 8. Reviewing and evaluating the program in terms of enrollment and participation, quality of leadership, use of facilities, budget. 9. Program planning for the next season based on the evaluation of the current season's experience." [15]

Directors of social service in hospitals, schools, courts, and other host settings are responsible for the administration of the social work program. Referring to medical social work, Moss says, "The director of the social service department should be responsible to the administrator of the medical agency for planning, organizing, assembling resources, directing and controlling the social work activities throughout the agency. This is the proper organizational relationship, regardless of the source of funds which maintain these activities, or the particular part of the medical agency to which the social service department may be related. The methods used and results achieved are also the responsibility of the director. He should be given the authority commensurate with these responsibilities." [16]

In discussing the directorship of a social service department in a hospital setting, Phillips goes into the matter of skills and knowledge required. It is her belief "that social work training and practice experience are essential prerequisites for the job. There are those who believe that 'the generalist,' well-trained in administration, can function successfully as a social service director. Perhaps those who hold this belief conceive of the role in a different way. If the premise that the social work director must set and maintain professional standards for his discipline is valid, then only a professionally trained person can function adequately in this role. However, professional training and practice experience are not the only requisites. Even assuming the presence of these elusive qualities—'leadership ability' and 'organizational ability'—the skilled social worker is not adequately prepared through casework and supervisory roles to become a department director. Administrative knowledge must be acquired. By and large, this is done through accumulated experience 'on the job.' . . . Chief among the things the director must learn as he assumes his role is how to adapt social work knowledge and skill to the administrative task. Knowledge of human behavior, the meaning of interpersonal and group dynamics, skill in working with people or groups, ability to set goals and limits, capacity to observe what is happening, are all necessary and useful to the administrative role. In using them, however, the director must focus on the broad goal of patient care and the concept of muliti-discipline responsibilities required to fulfill the goal. He must learn to center on the administrative mechanism through which patient needs are met rather than solely meeting patient needs. He must learn to see his associates as individuals with professional roles rather than as isolated personalities. He must develop an ability to generalize and an acute sense of timing that will permit him to intervene appropriately in behalf of the patient. Usually, the director should not become concerned about an individual patient situation—that is the caseworker's function. Rather, the director must concern himself with the meaning of specific patient problems to the total social service program and its place in medical care. When it is necessary to intervene in behalf of the patient or a group of patients, the director must know when, how, and with whom. If he does not, he stands to jeopardize casework process and/or interdepartmental functional relationships." [17]

A Diagnostic Approach to Administrative Problem-Solving

The social work administrator must give leadership to the problem-solving process. There is never a week when some problem does not come to the desk of the administrator. Some of the "minor" ones can be "solved" or at least "dealt with" on the spot. Other problems are more complicated and require a diagnostic approach on the part of the administrator. Such an approach is outlined below in a series of steps that have proven to be helpful.

Step One: Define the problem. Discuss it with the people involved, and agree as to what the major problem is and what the subproblems are.

Step Two: Look for causative factors. There must be some reason why this problem has come up at this time. Search for agreement on possible reasons for the problem.

Step Three: Gather necessary facts and information available about the problem, and list other items to be sought and make assignments as to who is to do the fact-gathering and pulling together of information.

Step Four: Determine who must be involved in developing a solution to the problem. Here one should consider the competence of various persons in the agency, community, and client population and the contributions they might make.

Step Five: List the *central issues* that seem to be raised by the problem as defined and related to the facts uncovered.

Step Six: Decide on some possible or tentative ways of approaching the problem. During this step, the administrator must create a climate in which different approaches are considered. The idea-getting process should be separated from the idea-evaluation process lest the latter inhibit the former. The administrator must avoid approving or disapproving tentative ideas during this exploratory period.

Step Seven: After checking out all alternate approaches to problem solution, go to work on the course that seems to have the most agreement and potential.

Step Eight: While the work goes on, develop a procedure for frequent checking back and conferring with the problem-solving group or individuals.

Step Nine: When a solution is agreed upon, put the procedure and plan into operation.

Step Ten: Evaluate the entire process, and if it is not working, retrace your steps and try another way.

Growing Leadership Responsibility of the Administrator

One of the dilemmas faced by many administrators is whether they should be primarily concerned with inspiration or administration. The fact seems to be that they must take responsibility for both. They must spend their time identifying emerging problems so that they may deal with them before they become too severe, they must understand the basis for the problems that are emerging, and they must deal with these problems with a clear sense of the purpose of their agency.

Likert says, "Of all the tasks of management, managing the human component is the central and most important task, because all else depends upon how well it is done." [18]

Leadership can be defined as the ability one has to inspire people to work together in the achievement of a common objective. Zalesnik says, "The crux of leadership is the acceptance of responsibility." [19]

As Gardner observes: "Very few of our most prominent people take a really large view of the leadership assignment. Most of them are simply tending the machinery of that part of society to which they belong. The machinery may be a great corporation or a great government agency or a great law practice or a great university. These people tend it very well indeed, but they are not pursuing a vision of what the total society needs. They have not developed a strategy as to how it can be achieved, and they are not moving to accomplish it. One does not blame them, of course. They do not see themselves as leaders of the society at large, and they have plenty to do handling their own specialized role. Yet it is doubtful that we can any longer afford such widespread inattention to the largest questions facing us. We achieved greatness in an era when changes came more slowly than now. The problems facing society took shape at a stately pace. We could afford to be slow in recognizing them, slow in coping with them. Today, problems of enormous import hit us swiftly. Great social changes emerge with frightening speed. We can no longer afford to respond in a leisurely fashion." [20]

The social work administrator gives, shows, and takes leadership at various times. In what ways does the administrator show, give, or take leadership? It would seem that the social work administrator gives, takes, and shows leadership in two broad but interrelated categories. First is the category of giving leadership to the internal operating affairs of the agency. Here would be included such matters as policy formulation, program development, personnel development, evaluation, and long-range planning. Thus, within the agency, the administrator should be persistently and consistently giving leadership to these various functions. The second broad category would be external. Here the agency within the community setting must be considered. This means that the administrator would be taking initiative to help people know, understand, and hopefully be in support of the important work of the agency because they feel the essential need for it in the lives of the people of the community. The administrator in giving leadership in this area would work with other organizations that share kindred goals and that have a reasonable congruency of values and convictions about the kind of community it should be.

It has been stated that social work must have a broad base of community sanction. This would seem to imply that the administrator would work with the community to create and maintain this sanction. In giving this leadership, the administrator must be guided by a professional philosophy and values. This has been described as social statesmanship and the ability to give guidance to the change process.

As Dimock says, "All large-scale organizations need strong, constructive, imaginative leadership to pull together all the elements of the program which otherwise tend to fly apart, and to focus the organization's attention on the consumer instead of on bureaucracy's inner tensions, moods, and petty concerns. The larger the body, the greater the centrifugal force it develops and the greater is the likelihood that the parts will be separated from the whole; that segmentation will drain the program's energies and halt enterprise. It is integrative leadership that keeps the parts together, and hence leadership is more necessary in large bureaucratic institutions than it is in smaller, more informal, competitive ones. But irrespective of size, organization alone never solves the administrative problem. There must be some one person at the top to watch over the program so as to keep it together, to keep it responsible, to combat self-centeredness, to promote innovation and vitality. And there must be extension of leadership on subordinate levels so as to form a kind of network through which the influences of the top man is carried throughout the organization." [21]

Green points out that "in large formal organizations, the very size usually means an increase in the need for leadership, co-ordination, and control. Professional social workers, however, take pride in their technical skills and prefer to be able to use initiative and self-direction in employing these skills. The bureaucracy limits the practitioner through its regulations, procedures, and systems of hierarchical supervision." [22]

In a penetrating discussion of the problems of leadership, Barber makes the following observations: "If this rhetorical distrust of leadership corresponded to a genuine emergence of equality in our society, some might welcome it as a sign of coming of age of American democracy. But the absence of leaders is more often a symptom of decay in representative democracy than a harbinger of maturity. Leadership is precisely what distinguishes a representative democracy and permits a collection of self-interested private citizens and special interests to act as a civic entity on behalf of public purposes. Leadership is not a surrogate for participation in a representative democracy, it is a necessary condition. Without leaders, a citizenry is unlikely to remain active; without active citizens, responsive leaders are not likely to emerge, and leaders who do emerge are unlikely to remain responsive.

"It is, in fact, the distinctive feature of democratic leadership that it defies the traditional Carlylean choice: it is produced neither by great men (although it can create great men), nor by great challenge (although it can be catalyzed by great challenges). It arises, however, out of great purposes—a delicate consensus tenable only when the polity is able to define common goals. To put it another way, democratic leaders are authoritative but not authoritarian figures: they lead a people by following it. Potentially they may be as corruptible as authoritarians, but they are accountable. Accountability—the specter of electoral defeat or even recall —compels them to be followers.

"Walter Lippmann wrote many years ago; 'Leaders are the custodians of the nation's ideals, of the beliefs it cherishes, of its permanent hopes, of the faith which makes a nation out of a mere aggregation of individuals.' " [23]

Knowledge of Self and the Administrative Job

The administrative job places many opportunities and challenges before anyone who would undertake it. Social work administrators, prior to undertaking administrative assignments, have to ask whether or not they have the personality and the temperament to perform satisfactorily in this work. Administrators have *total* responsibility for the work of their agencies. The risks they take are great and the emotional drain upon them is likely to be heavy. The social work administrator is exposed to many forces, and most of the work has to be done before the public. The job is fraught with stresses and pressures. The social work administrator thus must reconcile various conflicting points of view and must balance off the many pressures that are always present.

The administrator must maintain many relationships simultaneously. (See Figure 6.) He must make decisions—complicated decisions. In addition, the social work administrator must decide how to use time, what priorities to adopt, what choices to make, and what decisions to make first. The social work administrator receives far less supervision than does the direct service worker. The administrative role changes from that of serving clients directly to the multiple role of helping other people to help clients. Also, the administrator must frequently say no, and in doing so, he may not seem to be the "giving" person that others would like. Nevertheless, setting limits and helping people to work within limits is a very important part of the administrator's responsibility. Along with this is the ever-present necessity to compromise because there are never enough resources to meet all of the needs that should be met. In light of the above, it seems clear that the administrator must have an increasing amount of self-knowledge, self-awareness, and self-insight prior to entry into administrative work and throughout all of the time that such responsibilities are carried.

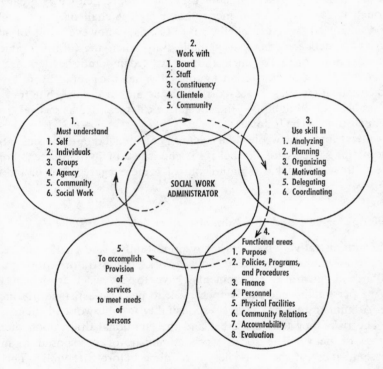

Figure 6
Social Work Administrators
Interrelationship of Understandings, Skills, Functions, Goals

The Administrator at Work

When one studies the social work administrator at work, seven primary task areas stand out.

1. *Purpose and goal determination*—Skillful administrators make wise and continuous use of purpose. It is their primary point of reference. It influences and guides their every move. Why is it so important that administrators place emphasis upon purpose? As David puts it, "objectives are not merely goals; they are motivating forces for action, and we move toward them or retreat by concerted action. As a practical matter, objec-

tives which have been developed and defined by one group lose some and at times all of their motivating force for action when they are passed on to another group. The success of objectives in stimulating action is proportionate to the spirit of participation in determining the objective. . . . Among people who are to take action, the process of thinking about objectives is more important than the final words in which they are put on paper. The words of others may be near platitudes, those you forge yourself have life. . . . Objectives, in order to motivate a group into action, must be far enough away and general enough to motivate people with different characteristics to work toward the same goals, perhaps by different means. Action-stimulating objectives, therefore, must be close enough to excite individuals to action far enough away to allow diverse people to work together and not so far away as to induce despair." [24]

2. *Providing an organized work environment*—Administrators are necessarily concerned in a major way with providing an organized work environment. Every social work agency is a community of people, dynamic, evolving, and changing. All of the needs of people including their needs for status, recognition, and growth are brought into the agency. It is necessary for the administrator to organize these various people into a system of cooperative work groups so that they will be seen and felt as working together. Administrators are spending more and more time trying to create healthy humanly organized work environments. It is known that when there is a contagious enthusiasm and a positive outlook on the part of the administrative leader there is a marked association between this and the success of the staff group. Studies have shown that the pride people take in their work is associated with the pride that is shown by the administrator. It is well known that the climate or atmosphere of the work environment makes a great deal of difference in the way the job is done. When professional administrators strive to create an atmosphere that is essentially free, relaxed, and comfortable, people get together in a cooperative way. As Argyris says, "The task of a leader is to create a warm congenial atmosphere in which individuals feel free to bring out any attitudes and feelings they may have, no matter how unconventional, absurd or contradictory they may be. Wherever possible people should feel as free to withhold expression as they should feel free to give expression." [25]

3. *Facilitating communication within the organization*—Administrators must know and understand how to facilitate communication within their organization. Some would argue that skill in creating and maintaining channels for effective communication is perhaps the most important skill to be had by the administrator.

4. *Establishing relationships*—Administrators must be concerned in a major way with establishing effective relationships with and between many people who carry forward the tasks of the agency. How the administrator behaves, works with, and relates to people clearly affects the kinds of

behavior responses he gets back from people. The way the administrator behaves in his perception, understanding, and sensitivity toward the behavior of the people in the situation are interrelated. What the administrator sees in the situation, his judgment, his inferences about it tend to control administrative behavior. Inasmuch as individuals and groups change with experience, the administrator must redefine his role as such changes occur. His primary moves and subsequent directions are determined not in a prearranged sequence but in terms of where the people are and what they need from him and how well he is related to them. The effective administrator is one who knows how to release the energy of people and how to help relate their separate energies together so that they may be thought of as a united team.

As Glover and Hower say:

The qualities which, to our way of thinking, distinguish the administrator are his ability to think and act responsively, to perceive and respond to environmental realities, to work cooperatively with others, and to work effectively and with satisfaction within the group and generally to provide leadership in getting the required work done. . . . Our reason for emphasizing attitude, judgment, and understanding is something like this: We conceive of the administrator as being confronted with, and as being part of, constantly changing situations—situations which are always unique, always related to the past and to the future. What he may usefully do about one particular situation today is unlikely to be exactly appropriate in the situation as it will have evolved tomorrow, or in still another situation (also unique) which has a different past and a still different future. Moreover, we do not think that a human situation, by an action on the part of the administrator, can be channeled into a simple predeterminable course of evolution in which it will remain—through a sort of kinetic inertia—and in which it will inevitably unfold just as planned. The administrator may start action as planned. But what follows thereafter depends upon the successive reactions that the administrator encounters, the "feedback" that he obtains, and what he himself does in relation to the developing events. He can start a series of interactions, but no one can see very far into the future what the course of events may be. Accordingly, we think that the very idea of an administrative "solution" or "answer" to a situation—especially a "solution" or "answer" which can be applied to other situations—is essentially misleading. The job of the administrator as we see it is to live with his organization from day to day and from year to year, contributing what he can to the development of the organization as the circumstances permit and his own qualifications allow. Judgment, attitude, point of view, way of approaching problems, and such—not "solutions" or "answers"—will help the administrator understand the evolving situation of which he is a part and will help him to decide what, if anything, he should and can do at this moment and at the next.[26]

5. *Planning and coordination*—Administrators are naturally concerned in a major way with the processes of planning and coordination. Effective

work with the staff, the board, and the constituency must be based upon a carefully conceived plan or design that has been thoughtfully worked out. Planning is a matter of using considered and thoughtful judgment in place of haphazard cluttered thinking or careless judgment. Planning is more and more appropriate and more needed than it was during simpler times. Effective planning carries with it the notion that administrators are clear on what purposes are to be achieved and are clear about what is being planned for. It makes good sense to know what we are trying to have happen to people as a result of our work. Planning also implies that what is to be done will be done *together* and that people will be involved in deciding what is to be done. The administrator has the responsibility to bring a sense of wholeness and a sense of totality to the planning process. When people are engaged in planning together and in coordinating their efforts under the leadership of a competent professional administrator, there is reason to believe that these individuals will experience a sharp sense of discovery and a new awareness of the many dimensions of the total program.

6. *Dynamics of change*—Administrators are concerned in a major way with understanding and facilitating change within their organization. Everyone would agree that programs are changing very rapidly today and that the community is also undergoing considerable change. Thus, administrators have to be skillful in facilitating the change process.

Dimock says, "The administrator who can rise above his daily tasks and see his institution with a fresh eye is the one capable of providing energy and drive and of preventing the onset of decline. Unfortunately many administrators are limited to trouble-shooting, to the settling of immediate and often petty crises, and to keeping their noses to the grindstone; as a result, they have no time or energy left over to devote to questions of morale, inspiration, and vitality." [27]

7. *Dynamic Leadership Role*—Administrators are concerned in a major way with defining their own dynamic leadership role. As Selznick sees it: "Group leadership is far more than the capacity to mobilize personal support. It is more than the maintenance of equilibrium through the routine solutions of everyday problems; it is the function of the leader statesman to define the ends of group existence, to design an enterprise instinctively adapted to these ends, and to see to it that the design becomes a living reality." [28]

The Administrator's Responsibility as an Advocate

It is the special responsibility of the social agency, the administrative staff particularly, to serve as advocates (an advocate is one who pleads the cause of another) for people whose needs are not being met. Advocacy means working internally within the agency and externally within the community.

Frequently, legislative matters are involved if new and more adequate programs are to be provided. Almost always it is necessary to strive for more substantial appropriation of funds to meet the ever-increasing unmet needs.

Advocacy does not mean "politicizing" either the agency or the administrator but speaking out strongly in behalf of those many persons who have little or no voice or power. It is essentially a matter of continuous interpretation of unrecognized or ignored problems so that better services will be provided.

A growing pattern is that of agency coalitions with civic and community groups that are committed to similar human service goals. In such cases, advocacy becomes a central task of the agency administrator, board, and staff with full commitment to the goals jointly agreed upon and with understanding as to the methods to be used.

It is reasonable to expect that the role of advocate will become increasingly important for all administrators in the years ahead.

Primary and Basic Administrative Duties

One of the essential tasks of any administrator is to define the agency's emerging problems and help structure the ongoing debate over those problems among staff, board, clients, and community. The administrator should give leadership in securing wide in-put and various alternatives and should assist the decision-making groups in reaching a consensus as to which of several paths to follow.

Another primary task of administrators is to develop and release the energies of all persons worked with and help them to acquire the strength, security, and confidence that enable them to cope with and solve the inevitable problems that arise in day-to-day work.

The administrative person must always seek to achieve a diagnostic understanding of the total situation. In addition, all administrators must appreciate and utilize the ever-changing forces that operate in all phases of the problem-solving process. Furthermore, administrators must make use of relationships as the force that makes change possible, always respecting the integrity of the people involved and always with a disciplined and professional use of self.

NOTES

1. John J. Ryan, "Social Work Executive: Generalist or Specialist?" *Social Work,* April 1963, pp. 26–27.
2. Harleigh B. Trecker, *Group Process in Administration* (New York: Association Press, 1950), p. 4.

3. Leonard Mayo, *Excerpts from Letters Received.* Council on Social Work Administration (New York: National Association of Social Workers, February 1965), pp. 2–3.

4. Paul R. Lawrence, *The Changing of Organizational Behavior Patterns* (Cambridge: Harvard University Graduate School of Business Administration, 1958), pp. 225–226.

5. Ordway Tead, "Reflections on the Art of Administration," *Hospital Administration,* Winter 1959, p. 8.

6. *Proceedings of Workshop on Social Agency Administration—Leadership and the Social Welfare Executive,* Richmond Professional Institute, School of Social Work, Richmond, Va., April 12–14, 1967, p. 7.

7. *C.P.I.—The Human Story,* Annual Report of Community Progress, Inc., New Haven, Conn., 1968, p. 25.

8. *Social Work Administration* (New York: National Association of Social Workers, March 1968), pp. 6–7.

9. Walter A. Friedlander, *Introduction to Social Welfare,* 3rd ed. (Englewood Cliffs, N.J.: Prentice-Hall, Inc., 1968), p. 202.

10. Joseph McDonald, "The Administrator—Hub of the Social Agency" (New York: Family Service Association of America, June 1965, mimeographed), p. 2.

11. Harold Howe II, *The People Who Serve Education* (Washington, D.C.: U.S. Department of Health, Education and Welfare, 1969), pp. 7–8.

12. Ordway Tead, *Administration: Its Purpose and Performance* (New York: Harper & Row, 1959).

13. *Social Work Administration* (New York: National Association of Social Workers, March 1968), p. 9.

14. Robert L. Katz, "Skills of an Effective Administrator," *Harvard Business Review,* January–February 1955, pp. 34–42.

15. Harry Schatz, "Administrative Role and Function of Center Program Staff," *Jewish Community Center Program Aids,* Winter 1962–63, pp. 1–2.

16. Celia R. Moss, *Administering a Hospital Social Service Department* (Washington, D.C.: American Association of Medical Social Workers, 1955), p. 21.

17. Beatrice Phillips, "A Director Examines the Director's Role," *Social Work,* October 1964, pp. 98–99.

18. Rensis Likert, *The Human Organization—Its Management and Values* (New York: McGraw-Hill Book Company, 1967), p. 1.

19. Abraham Zaleznik, *Human Dilemmas of Leadership* (New York: Harper & Row, 1966), p. 1.

20. John W. Gardner, "The Antileadership Vaccine." Reprinted from the 1965 Annual Report, Carnegie Corporation of New York, p. 7.

21. Marshall E. Dimock, *Administrative Vitality—The Conflict with Bureaucracy* (New York: Harper & Row, 1959), p. 175.

22. A. D. Green, "The Professional Worker in the Bureaucracy," *Social Service Review,* March 1966, pp. 72–73.

23. Benjamin Barber, "Command Performance," *Harpers,* April 1975, pp. 52–53.

24. Donald K. David, "The Objectives of Professional Education," in *Education for Professional Responsibility* (Pittsburgh: Carnegie Institute of Technology, 1948), pp. 11–12.

25. Chris Argyris, *Executive Leadership—An Appraisal of a Manager in Action* (New York: Harper and Brothers, 1953), p. 112.

26. John Glover and Ralph Hower, *The Administrator—Cases on Human Relations in Business* (Homewood, Ill.: Richard D. Irwin, 1963), pp. xvii–xix.

27. Dimock, *Administrative Vitality,* p. 50.

28. Philip Selznick, *Leadership in Administration* (Evanston, Ill.: Row, Peterson, 1957), p. 37.

3 The Social Work Agency

Administrators must have a deep and growing understanding of their agency as a human enterprise. In addition, they must help the people who work for or are served by it to understand it as a dynamic, changing entity with a history, purposes, and ways of getting work done.

The modern social agency is a complex social system involving many people. These may include the board, administrative staff, other staff, volunteers, members, clients, or persons served, and the supporting community. To bind all of these people together into a functioning whole is a major responsibility of administration. When the administrator understands the agency as a social system, he sees it as a whole because each part bears a relation to every other part and all are interdependent.

In fact, the social agency might be thought of as a watch made up of many interdependent parts that interact with one another. These parts must be kept in balance and must have a source of energy or power to keep them moving together. This energy or power in the social agency is provided by the people who make up the agency and work together under the leadership of the administration.

Social System

Many authorities have made use of the concept of social system in their study of administration.

Kast says, "Under the systems concept, the business organization is viewed as a series of sub-systems which include the individual, the informal work groups, the formal organization, and finally the environmental system which has a direct impact upon the business organization. Furthermore, under the systems concept, consideration must be given to the means for interrelating and coordinating these various sub-systems.

These parts are integrated through various processes, such as the information and communication network, the decision system, and built-in equilibrium mechanisms which exist in every organization." [1]

Albers says, "A system is commonly defined as consisting of parts that are connected or combined to form a whole. Such a definition is so universal as to include almost any variety of phenomena. Indeed, it would be difficult to find something that cannot be so categorized. The universe, the solar system, a society, an economy, an industry, an automobile, a house, a football game, a coffee pot, a book, a human being, a wolf, a worm, and a dictionary are examples of systems. Some of these systems are aspects of other systems and are themselves composed of subsystems. Scientists are still not sure they have found the basic building block of the universe or whether there is a more comprehensive system than the universe." [2]

In writing about the mental health field, Brown says, "The systems analysis approach involves looking at any person, institution, or service in the context of all related persons, institutions, and services. A service implies a network of integrated elements. In mental health programs, these elements are the services and facilities that provide prevention, diagnosis, treatment, and rehabilitation. Many separate institutions and many kinds of services are involved in providing these types of care. Accordingly, we are faced with a dual problem. On the one hand we must plan for the individual units or agencies and services themselves, and on the other hand we must plan for their integration into a composite whole of mental health activities." [3]

Frey views the hospital as a social system and illustrates how helpful it is to see it in this manner. She says, "A social system is an entity or whole made up of interacting parts. It contains within it small subsystems that interact with each other and in relationship to the whole. An analogy can be made between the social system and a mobile in which all the parts are interconnected so that even a slight breeze will cause all the parts to shift and move through a series of new positions and relationship patterns before coming to rest at a new and different balance. Viewing the hospital as such an entity of interacting parts and subsystems that operate in relationship to each other is exceedingly helpful to an understanding of particular needs of the patient population. For example, in one hospital poor salaries, a shortage of nurses, geriatrics patients restricted to bed instead of being up and about, a depressive, hopeless institutional atmosphere and a social work case load with only a few elderly patients in it were all interacting and interdependent aspects of several subsystems within the system. A change in any one of these situations would be expected to bring about shifts at the other points in the system. In this example there is clearly a need for an active rehabilitation program with the elderly patients. How to meet this need depends upon a consideration not just of the case load but of the totality of the system. (This includes the characteristics of the particular system and the essential elements of the social work profession: value, purpose, knowledge, sanction, and methods which determine the social work functions in the setting.)" [4]

As Johnson points out:

The school as a social system has a network of patterned relationships of people, each category of whom has distinctive role-sets or a group of associated roles. The form these relationships have taken in the public school are the outgrowth of its purpose, i.e., the giving and receiving of instruction or the teaching-learning objectives. The classroom teacher is, therefore, at the heart of the social system but is surrounded by those above and below him in status. These statuses carry authority inherent in the responsibilities attached to them. They also result in a system of prescribed relations such as social distance, formality in communication, thus giving stability and predictability to behavior and mutual expectations. The structure of the school tends to be hierarchical with power vested in the superintendent and, in turn, in the principal. The larger the school, the more likelihood of autocratic administration; the better the rapport between the members of the system, the less likelihood of autocratic administration.

A number of forces affect the equilibrium of the social system: (1) The internal organization of the school, (2) The external environment of the school, and (3) The social worker as specialist in the school social system. . . . The school as a social system is a complex phenomenon. The social worker in the school must be cognizant of its general outlines, able to accept his place in the system, and well enough oriented to discern what aspects of his experience are characteristic of the social system and what aspects are peculiar and perhaps modifiable. Such knowledge lends consistency and purposiveness to the service he is in the school to render. Of importance also is more definitive agreement among social workers on what comprises the role-set of the school social worker.[5]

Kast points out how useful it is to administrators to understand their organization as a social system. He says, "The systems concept is a useful way of thinking about the function of management. It provides a framework for visualizing internal and external environmental factors as an integrated whole. It allows recognition of the proper place and function of sub-systems. The systems within which management operates are necessarily complex. It is important to recognize the integrated nature of specific systems, including the fact that each system has both inputs and outputs and can be viewed as a self-contained unit. But it is also important to recognize that business and industry are a part of larger systems, such as an industry and the total society. General systems theory is concerned with developing a systematic, theoretical, framework for describing general relationships of the empirical world." [6]

Hartley does an excellent job in describing the characteristics and properties of social systems in his publication dealing with educational planning.[7]

Dolgoff sees organizations as sociotechnical systems with such inputs from the environment as manpower, money, materials, information, and energy, which go through subsystems that are managerial, technological, and psychosocial. Outputs such as products, services, product information, and social and personal satisfaction then flow into the environment, and feedback from the environment keeps the system constantly up-to-date.[8]

Social Work Agencies—Instruments of Society

Social work agencies are instruments of society. They have been established by governmental or voluntary effort to meet the social needs of people. In America, there is a dual system of meeting social welfare needs. When the needs of people are properly expressed, legislative bodies grant authorization to governmental or private bodies to provide services. Many of these authorized agencies are large.

As Coughlin observes, "Modern society is a society of large social institutions. As we have forsaken a laissez-faire social philosophy, so we have moved away from a society that places a premium on individualism to a society that values the social institutions to which individuals belong. These institutions, both public and private, have increased in size and importance. Social role is an important concept; but more and more important for understanding modern society are the institutions that comprise the social system. The main actors in society today are organizations. This means that whereas previously men looked to individuals for certain social verifications, now they seek those verifications in organizations; qualities which formerly were attributes of individuals have taken on an institutionalized character. . . . Therefore, we live in a society that is increasingly based on the principles of the welfare state, and a society in which power largely resides in large institutions." [9]

Descriptions of Governmental and Voluntary Agencies

The case examples of agencies that follow illustrate the role of voluntary and governmental agencies in the fields of child and family services, youth guidance, community centers, residential treatment, and work with the aged. These agencies as social systems with purposes and organization are representative of what many communities offer. The way people receive services is outlined, and some of the structural characteristics of the agencies are given.

Child and Family Agency of Belltown—
A District Office of a Voluntary Agency

The Hamilton District Office of the Child and Family Agency of Belltown provides four programs of service to the Greater Belltown area. They are: Family Service, Services to Unmarried Parents, Foster Home Care, and Homemaker Service.

Most of the agency's clients come because of breakdown or threatened breakdown in some area of family life. There might be a marital problem, a financial concern, behavior problems with children at home or at school, or a myriad of other reasons why, at a certain point or in a crisis situation, a family is no longer able to handle the stress and strain; therefore it seeks help. Although the voluntary family agency is designed to meet the needs of the people in Belltown, it is important to remember that it is one of several available agencies. At Child and Family Service, persons receive counseling with emphasis on their own self-determination.

Most persons approach the agency first by way of the telephone. At the time of the first telephone call, the person is asked to state generally why he is seeking help, and then an appointment is set up for an intake interview. In this interview, the social worker explores with the client his problem as he sees it. The person is asked to tell about the ways he has previously coped with his problem and how he thinks the agency will be able to help him. An effort is made to help the client state what his expectations are. During this intake interview, it is explained to him that he may be assigned a different worker later on if the agency and he wish to continue the relationship. Assignments are made on the basis of the presenting problem. Three workers handle the general counseling program, one person heads up services to unmarried parents, another person is in charge of foster home care.

Because one person heads up services to unmarried parents, all such cases are referred to her. An important part of this service is the concrete help given with living arrangements during pregnancy, prenatal care, hospitalization, financial assistance when needed, and legal aid. Counseling is given to help the mothers plan responsibly for their own future and the future of their babies.

One person is in charge of foster home care. This offers the babies of unmarried mothers responsible care while permanent plans are being made for them. It also serves children who need a substitute home. After careful placement, the social worker consults regularly with the foster parents and the child.

Homemaker service is designed to provide help for a limited period of time in emergency situations. The agency attempts to match the homemaker and the client as compatibly as possible. Specific duties are explained to the homemaker and close touch is kept to ascertain that things are running smoothly. The homemaker's primary job is to keep the family together rather than simply to provide domestic aid.

If someone calls the agency about adoption, an appointment is set up with the representative from Belltown who visits the different districts regularly in order to discuss the needs, desires, and eligibility of those applying for both their own and the future adoptive child's best interests.

No matter in which division of services the client falls, the social worker in a family agency should be continually aware of the priority of the needs of the individual. There are many who come to a family agency representing problems that can best be met through other resources in the community. A knowledge of these resources and the ability to make a good referral are perhaps the most important services a family agency can render.

Everyone who resides in the district is eligible for services. This is decided during the intake interview, when the agency's fee schedule is discussed. The fee schedule is based on a sliding scale, and no one is turned away because of inability to pay. Services are made known by auxiliaries in their publicity related to fund-raising, in folders distributed by auxiliaries, and by staff participation in community organizations.

Becoming a Client at the Johnson Family Service Agency

The process of becoming a client at the Johnson Family Service Agency begins with a visit or, more commonly, with a telephone call. The prospective client gets in touch with the agency and inquires about help. In the case of the person walking in, he is met in the hall by the receptionist. At this point, the receptionist asks the client to state the purpose for his visit. He is then asked to wait in an attractive and comfortable waiting room until a social worker can see him. The agency has a rotating system of intake, with each worker taking his turn for one half-day. The scheduled intake worker attempts to see the prospective client as soon as possible. If this is not feasible, then an intake interview is offered for the earliest possible date.

If the prospective client telephones, he is referred to the intake worker, and an initial interview is set for the earliest possible time that scheduling and convenience for the client allow. The system of intake at the agency is set up so that in each half-day there are two scheduled appointments. This means that the intake worker who sets up an interview by telephone, arranges the appointment for the client to see another social worker. As each period on intake lasts four hours for the individual worker, and only two interviews are permitted in this period, the appointment time is set up for the client's convenience.

The next step is for the prospective client to come for his appointment. Usually, the client is early, and he is asked to wait in the waiting room.

The intake worker sees him at the appointed time and begins the interview. The purpose of this interview is to determine whether or not the still-prospective client has a problem with which the agency can deal. If this is not the case, then an appropriate referral is made. If the difficulty is one that the agency can handle, then the worker inquires into the nature of the problem. The initial phases of study and diagnosis are begun at this time. The decision as to whether or not the client is to be accepted for continuing service is made by the intake worker. If the client is accepted, the fee is established and thereby becomes part of the initial contract. There is no charge for the intake interview; for subsequent interviews, the client has the choice of being billed by mail or paying the receptionist at each visit. At the conclusion of the interview, the client is told that the agency will get in touch with him within ten days. Some intake workers keep the cases that they interview initially. Caseload size may prohibit this, and if so, the client is told who his permanent worker will be. The client then leaves and awaits a telephone call so a mutually convenient time can be set up for subsequent interviews.

The intake worker records the interview and includes a tentative diagnosis and treatment plan. This material, along with the fee rate and factual information on the client, is sent to the Business Office for entry into the records of the agency. If another agency department such as Homemaker Service is necessary, then the intake worker refers this information to this department.

The complete intake process takes from one to three weeks. For a family service agency, intake is very important. The goal is for the client to see as few people as possible during the intake procedure. The client may talk on the phone with one social worker, and then he never sees more than two others. Another goal is to provide competent service to the client from the initial contact forward.

The Smith Youth Guidance Center

It is the general policy of the Smith Youth Guidance Center that the parents of the child in question call the agency to schedule an appointment. If another agency should call regarding this family, a request is made that the parents place the initial call. When the initial call is made by a parent, it is received by an application secretary, who makes note of the name, address, and telephone number. The call is then returned by a professional staff person who is drawn from a pool of available staff members scheduled to handle initial calls at a designated time during any particular week.

After the call is returned by the staff member, the application reflecting a request for service (if it is deemed an appropriate request to the clinic) is referred to a pool that is administered by the chief of the Psychiatry

Department. As staff personnel have time available to see new applications, they secure such applications from the pool.

All cases are seen in short-term contact unless there is an administrative designation otherwise. Short-term contact includes up to fifteen interviews with a family. If the person seeing the mother or father in a case desires a diagnostic evaluation of the child, such an evaluation is conducted by the parents' worker or by personnel primarily from the Departments of Psychiatry or Psychology, who maintain a diagnostic pool of personnel available to do such evaluations. All diagnostic evaluations are done within an orientation that attempts to answer questions that are answerable. The decision about the case is not the responsibility of the person in the diagnostic role. Rather, the decisions about the case are made by the worker who has primary contact with the case. Such a worker may call upon his supervisor for consultation regarding the direction a particular case may take, but it is not the responsibility of the person doing the diagnostic evaluation on a child to tell the worker in the case how the case should be managed.

After a case is seen, if it is felt that it will require extended therapy and that this is something that will be useful and profitable to the family, the worker involved in the case brings it to an Extended Therapy Planning Conference, which is led by the director of the clinic. The decision to bring it to conference can be made after one interview or up to fifteen. At the time of the conference, the case is considered for extended therapy and, if accepted, assignment of the case is made via referral to the staff person maintaining time schedules of available professional hours. At the time of this conference, the worker presenting the case justifies why it should be seen in long-term treatment and spells out what the goals of such treatment would be. All extended treatment cases are evaluated every six months in formal Evaluation Conferences, which are headed by designated professional staff members. This conference is primarily directed toward establishing whether treatment is achieving the goals as set down at the time of the Extended Therapy Planning Conference.

Anderson Community House

The goal of the Anderson Community House is to work with disadvantaged or underachieving individuals in all of the neighborhoods of the city. The primary focus is on in-school and out-of-school youth. Through group work services, the agency hopes that these young people will be able to develop their potential abilities. Agency organization follows agency philosophy. In most instances, youth do not come to the agency but are more likely to be approached in a variety of situations by a group work supervisor, an outreach worker, a volunteer, or a part-time worker out in the community. Particular attention is paid to reaching out to young people who live in a housing project, attend an elementary school, and are clients of a multiservice antipoverty agency. In addition to working with youth, the agency is responsible for making its services available to grass roots organizations seeking to bring services into their neighborhoods. The agency also works with the community school team in developing special services for teenagers. The agency functions as a community organization in many respects. The detached or outreach workers are constantly seeking out areas of need that would not otherwise be discovered.

Abbott Community Center

When a potential new member comes to the Abbott Community Center, his first contact is with the receptionist-secretarial office staff. This initial contact with non-social work staff has important implications for the kind of information that the individual obtains about the agency. Because the office staff members are so important in the initial reception of the new member, the social work administrator and the division supervisors work with the office staff to help them be sensitive and accurate.

This initial step gains even further significance when one realizes that the members of the center are not for the most part referrals from other agencies who have already interpreted the role of the center to them, but instead are people drawn to the center by word of mouth, mailings or other circulars, or through some other contact in the community. For these people, then, it is important that the office staff present a pleasant reception and an accurate interpretation of what kinds of services are available to them.

The decision as to particular services offered and which divisions are involved is primarily determined by the age of the person applying and whether or not the individual is applying for single or family membership. The professional staff of the agency is set up on the basis of services to particular age divisions. These are, the Nursery Division, the Junior Division, the 'Tween Division, the Young Adult Division, and the Senior Division. If the individual is applying for a single membership, the office staff worker will refer him to the professional staff member in charge of the particular division under which his age is encompassed. If the person is applying for a family membership, the office staff worker will refer him to all staff members pertinent to the age groupings of his family. The process of referral to the appropriate staff member is a very informal one. As most new members come in "off the street," they are usually referred to an available staff member as soon as possible and without a formal appointment. An appointment is made only when none of the staff is available for an intake interview and tour of the facilities. The informal nature of this process reflects the goals and purposes of the community center. People who come to the center come because they are interested in the group services available to them. It is the task of the social work staff member to further clarify and interpret the goals and purposes of the agency, to explain the structure of the agency, to be sensitive to the needs of the individual, and in this way to establish a contract between the agency and the person that involves both agency services and the payment of fees.

It is the informal nature of the center's intake procedure that provides a major source of problems and administrative concern. Although it is important for the intake process of such a center to be flexible and informal, it is equally important that this process be under constant administrative supervision and total staff discussion in order that the informal process not succumb to its inherent tendency to become more casual and less sensitive and accurate. A continuing staff discussion and in-service training course on this matter of intake is being developed by the administrator.

A State Child Welfare Agency

The type of service given to a client at Child Welfare Services depends on the nature of the referral and the unit that provides the service. The agency has two intake units: one that handles referrals from the court and other agencies and one that is exclusively responsible for protective cases. Until fairly recently, the only source of referral to Child Welfare Services was the court. The agency now accepts voluntary placements and receives referrals from other agencies and interested citizens. Nevertheless, referrals from the court still make up the greatest number of cases served by the agency.

When a child is referred by the court, the judge requires a social history that includes a psychiatric evaluation, an assessment of the parents' capacity to help the child, and a treatment plan. The Intake Unit is responsible for compiling this information and returning to court with a recommendation. The judge usually accepts the agency's recommendation, which may be for either commitment, legal supervision, or detention. With any of the recommendations, the case is then referred to the area worker who is responsible for providing service to the child and the family. If the child is removed from his home, he is referred to the Direct Care Unit. Because the majority of these children come from highly disorganized families, the goal of direct care is long-term foster care or adoption. If adoption appears to be an appropriate plan, the case is then referred to the Adoption Unit. When a child does return home from a court appearance, detention, or placement in a foster home, legal supervision is usually assigned to the agency to give the family support and help it improve conditions for the child. A referral is sometimes made to the Home Services

Unit if the family appears motivated to accept intensive casework services. The referrals to Home Services, however, are quite selective because of strengths expected from these families. Usually, when legal supervision is assigned, the case is referred to an area worker who is responsible for following through on the treatment plan. The main problem with legal supervision is that many of the workers have such high caseloads that their only opportunity to see a family is following a crisis. Obviously, this type of casework is ineffective for achieving long-range goals. Unfortunately, the majority of cases at Child Welfare Services have been assigned legal supervision, and if a crisis does not occur within a year after the referral, the case is closed.

The second intake department is within the Protective Unit. Cases are referred to this unit by the police or interested citizens. The bulk of referrals concern children who have been neglected, abused, or abandoned. These cases remain in this unit following the intake study, and service is provided to the parents and children. After removal from the home, the children are either detained at the center or prepared for placement in foster homes. The purpose of this service is to help parents with difficulties that have led them to neglect or abuse their children. Court studies are often recommended to provide a concurrent evaluation of the family situation. The long-range goal is to return the child to his own home and help him adjust to his family and the community.

Because many of the children referred to Child Welfare Services through either intake unit come from multiproblem families, the long-range goal of returning the child to his family is often impossible to achieve. For this reason, it is the responsibility of Child Welfare Services and the social work profession to recruit more effectively for foster homes. This would enable the agency to at least partially achieve its long-range goal.

A Residential Treatment Center for Emotionally Disturbed Children

The Mountain Road Residential Treatment Center for emotionally disturbed children is an agency of state government. It receives requests for intake from several sources: public schools, juvenile courts, child guidance clinics, and the public welfare agency. In addition, many referrals are made by the parents. No matter what the origin of the referral, intake requests are given to the supervisor of intake, who outlines the general criteria of intake to the referring person. For the most part, initial inquiries are handled by the intake supervisor's telephone screening. Occasionally, the intake supervisor does see the referring person to screen applications in more detail. Following this period of initial screening, the case is assigned to a social worker, psychiatrist, or other trained clinic personnel on the basis of the problem presented and the technical and professional skill deemed necessary by the intake supervisor and clinic director to proceed with the intake study. This intake study determines the type of program most useful to the clients, if in fact any program at Mountain Road can be of service.

Following the assignment of the case to a social worker, the first task is a review of the case material by the social worker and the intake or casework supervisor. If an agency has referred the case, an early step is the notification of the referring agency that the intake phase of the program has begun. The notification of the referring agency also allows the social worker to introduce himself to that agency. Another major step in providing service is the initial contact with the parents. The social worker writes them a letter of introduction. Included in this letter are questions about the parents' idea of the problem, when it began, what they have done about it, and also a convenient appointment time is requested of them so they might come to see the worker.

Following receipt of the parents' letter, a first appointment is made. During the initial interview, the parents' letter is discussed, the agency's program is interpreted, and, following determination of the parents' interest at continuing beyond the first interview, the fee schedule is discussed. In conjunction with the fee schedule explanation, an appointment is made with the director of the agency so that he may discuss with the parents their ability to contribute financially to the diagnostic cost and the cost of treatment if the child is accepted for a treatment program. After the meeting with the director, the parents and the child are given an appointment with the psychiatrist (if this is considered necessary), the school principal, and the assistant director who is in charge of all treatment programs. Finally, the family is seen by the director of Group Life who describes the various types of residential plans of care, such as Day Care, Residence, and Group Homes. If there are noted medical problems with the child, the parents and the child are also seen by the nurse. In conjunction with these interviews arranged by the social worker, he also sees the family to ascertain background information to assess the parents' and the child's ability to utilize the intensive, structured treatment facilities found at Mountain Road.

Following the period of intake evaluation, those individuals who have met with the parents and child, meet together at an Intake Conference to determine what program at Mountain Road can be most beneficial to the family. In the event the case is not accepted, a recommendation is made to refer the child elsewhere. This decision is given to the parents as well as assistance in making a new referral. If the child is accepted, the social worker, as "case control," continues to coordinate treatment programs within and without the institution. In this contact with the family, the social worker encourages and facilitates their participation in the Mountain Road program either as a participant observer or, more basically, to keep the parents in contact with the treatment areas of the institution. By such activity, the parents are kept aware of their child's progress. In addition, the parents, by participating with staff in the treatment program, are able to use this participation as a model of child care or "corrective experience" in interaction with their child. Periodic staff conferences of all treatment staff update and evaluate the parents' and the child's programs and ascertain new ways for them to utilize treatment.

A City Center for the Aged

When a prospective member arrives at the Senior Center, he is usually greeted and helped by a volunteer worker. The volunteer, who is an elderly member, talks to the interested person about the various services rendered by the center. If there are any unusual questions or circumstances, the potential member is referred to a staff person. Generally, the volunteer, after describing the agency services, helps the new member fill out a simple application form, collects the one dollar membership fee, and provides the new member with a membership card.

The staff workers at the center become involved with new members by attempting to meet the various requests for services. Part of the membership application consists of a checklist, where agency services and opportunities are listed. The new member chooses his own services by checking his interests. The staff persons then follow up each request by arranging for the new member to be invited into groups in which he is interested. If the member had indicated no interests, the staff person talks with him, either personally or over the telephone, to encourage him and to stimulate his interest in some activity.

The above process is generally true; the major exceptions are referrals. If an older person is referred to the center by another agency or person, the staff discusses with the referring agent the goals for that member's participation, and they select appropriate group activities or arrange for personal counseling with the referred member.

The giving of service to a new member involves not only the volunteers and the program staff but also the various group leaders. The instructors of classes or interest groups are informed by the staff that a new member would like to join their group and are asked to help the member become a part of the group.

The process of receiving and providing service to new members is flexible and informal. For example, a new member may initially have no desire to join a group, preferring rather to sit in the lounge or to play cards. The staff members are aware of this and always give the new member time to feel comfortable with the agency and its clientele before encouraging him to pursue more involving interests. Often a new member will be recruited by an active center member and will have already been oriented to the agency's functions. These persons usually know what services they want and may make their own arrangements accordingly. The process of rendering services to new Senior Center members, then, involves the volunteers, the program staff, and the group leaders and instructors.

Understanding the Agency Structure

The way the individual or family is received by the social work agency is representative of the care and attention the administrator has given to the matter of structure. Certainly, structure is a vital factor in the extent to which the person gets the services needed.

Taylor stresses the fact that the social work administrator must "understand the nature of organizational structure as a factor in service" and must have "awareness of the consequences of such structuring for staff and clients . . . and a willingness to examine his own role in relation to others within the organization." She goes on to stress the fact that the administrator must understand the agency as an organized service in terms of both its formal structure and its informal structure. Under the former, she suggests knowledge of personnel allocated by function, formalization of relationships in a constellation of roles—that is, worker-supervisor, worker-client, and supervisor-director. Insofar as informal structure goes, she indicates that it refers to the spontaneous patterns of relationship growing out of shared personal interests that focus on the work situation. She suggests that the informal structure has cohesion and unrecognized but real identity and persists over a period of time. She recognizes that there is a potential conflict between efficiency and economy as organizational goals and professional values. She suggests that service is sometimes limited by function or budgetary restrictions rather than by client needs. She sees a potential conflict between the agency as a means of social control and professional belief in human worth and dignity.[10]

Social work administrators are necessarily concerned in a major way with providing an organized work environment. Every social work agency is a company of people, dynamic, evolving, and changing. All of the needs of people, including their needs for status, recognition, and growth, are brought into the agency. It is necessary to organize these various people into a system of cooperative work groups so that they will be seen and felt as working together. Organization is a process of so relating people to one another that they function at their maximum capacity. Organization charts are visual aids for showing this proposed organization, but charts by themselves do not develop an organization. Only when people feel that their needs and goals are being met can it be said that there is an effective human organization.

As Tyler has observed about educational administration, "a college or a university may be viewed as a complex social structure which involves not only individual statuses within the institution, but also relationships without. . . . It is this complex structure involving ambiguous responsibilities and conflicting expectations that breeds misunderstanding and dissension. Studies of effective social institutions indicate certain essential characteristics. Each of the members has a clear perception of his role and of his status in the organization. The perceptions of their several roles by various members of the organization are reasonably congruent when the institution is composed of individuals with different abilities and functions and when their effectiveness depends largely upon their own exercise of initiative, originality, and judgment, the leadership of the institution depends less on rules and directives for achieving some unity and much more on the development among the members of shared values and purposes." [11] While written in relation to educational institutions, Tyler's observations seem to have considerable relevance for social agencies as well.

The Council on Social Work Administration of the National Association of Social Workers says, "The effective application of knowledge and the exercise of administrative skills are in large measure affected by the conditions under which the administrator and his agency function. The administrator has major responsibility for creating favorable conditions for optimum productivity of services. At the same time, his own effectiveness is influenced by enabling or limiting conditions. Among the conditions conducive to effective administration are these: (1) Knowledge and skill of the executive equal to the demands of the job. (2) The delineation of the authority of the administrator and of other staff commensurate with their responsibilities. (3) The appropriate definition of the functions of the policy-making body and its relationship to the administrator. (4) The commitment of the policy-making body to the purposes of the agency and a readiness for change including expansion or retrenchment. (5) The relatedness of the agency's purpose and program to the needs of the people and community it strives to serve. (6) Adequate understanding and support of the agency's purposes and program by the various communities and groups it serves or to which it is related. (7) The availability of resources—physical, financial, and personnel—essential to carry out the program. (8) Salary and other benefits sufficient to attract and hold personnel." [12]

Organizational Lifestyle

In every social agency, an organizational lifestyle is apparent. This style or way of doing things sets a pattern for the agency and quite frequently attracts people to join it. In addition, agency style influences the future and creates a distinctive set of possibilities for it. The effective social agency develops an organizational lifestyle that is characterized by real emphasis on cooperation and collaboration. The communication channels are kept open and are well used. There is a mutual understanding on the part of the administration, the staff, the board, and the clientele. All groups understand how decisions are made and at what levels it is appropriate for them to take part. The effective agency encourages broad participation by staff, clients, board members, and the community. The effective agency attempts to make maximum use of informal communication. The agency recognizes and utilizes the specific resources that it has at hand in the way of staff members and working funds. The effective agency utilizes thoughtful procedures for working through matters of conflict and change.

In recognition of this impact of organizational lifestyle on the nature of the institution, Hamlin called for a lifestyle at George Williams College that

Emphasizes collaboration with
  (1) communication channels which are well known, kept open and well used;
  (2) a mutual trust; and
  (3) a basic understanding of how decisions are made, at what levels they are appropriately made, and who is accountable for the decisions;

Encourages broad participation by students and faculty in decision-recommending and decision-making activities, particularly in areas directly affecting campus life;

Work toward greater specificity of formal organizational structures, and appraisal of the effectiveness of those structures;

Attempts to maximize the use of informal communication, information, and influence structures;

Recognizes and utilizes the special identity and diverse resources that students and faculty bring to the college community;

Attempts to utilize procedures in resolving conflicts as opportunities for learning and self-development.[13]

Certainly, all of these points would make sense for the social agency as well as for an institution of higher learning.

Formal and Informal Relationships in the Social Work Agency

In the social work agency, people function and relate their activities to other persons on two levels: the formal level prescribed by the organization and the informal level created by interpersonal interaction.

Albers, in discussing the formal hierarchical organization, says, "The management hierarchy ranks and relates positions and persons. . . . It represents simultaneously a decentralization and centralization of decision-making. Decisional responsibilities are decentralized in the sense that they are dispersed among whatever number of executives is necessary to do the job. The work division involved in organized endeavor generally is applied to managerial work. But organization requires a coordination of effort if a common purpose is to be achieved. Two people who cooperate in pushing a stalled automobile will accomplish little if they push in opposite directions. Coordination is a necessary consequence of organization; and absence of coordination is disorganization. The ranking of executives in a hierarchy provides a means for coordinating management action. Conflicting and contradictory decisions can be resolved by executives at higher levels. Every executive below the chief executive is subject to planning and control decisions from higher levels. Proceeding from the bottom to the top of the hierarchy, decision-making responsibilities are centralized in fewer and fewer numbers of executives until the apex is reached. All persons in the organization, managerial and non-managerial, are required to respond to decisions from that point. The hierarchy sets the stage for cooperative executive action. Each executive is assigned some part of the total decisional burden. Executives at lower levels function within an area of discretion determined by executives at higher levels. They make decisions on their own initiative, but they are also required to respond to decisions from superiors. The decisional responsibilities at the various levels are differentiated by a process called 'departmentation.' The executives who occupy the basic positions in the hierarchy are generally assisted by staff and service personnel. Committees may also be used to perform decisional responsibilities and serve other purpose." [14]

Some writers on the subject of organization have tended to picture modern organization as rigid and static structures in which employees operate mechanically. The employees' human needs are modified to conform to the impersonal, static, hierarchical, unyielding nature of the organization. Current research findings refute many of these stereotypes. Students of modern organizations reveal that bureaucratic structures continually create conditions that alter the structure to suit the needs of the human beings in the situation. Modifications come about because human beings ultimately reject formal, rigidly prescribed patterns of behavior and relationships. The forms of patterns that are created represent a new element that is an integral part of the organization as is the formal organization. But as this innovation relates to the network of unofficial, informal, personal, and social interactions of members of the organization, it has an entity apart from the formal structure. People and their relationships are the primary emphasis of the informal organization.

Millett says, "Regardless of the formal structure of organizations in an administrative agency, there tends to develop an informal structure in an agency. These informal relations become an important factor in the internal power structure." [15]

The staff member's concept of the organization as a whole and the meaning it has for him grows largely out of his participation in the informal organization. Here he is a thinking, deciding, relating, acting human being, interacting with other human beings and causing modifications in the formal system that either contribute to or prevent effective unity in the total organization.

Essential Contributions of Informal Organization

Many authorities have pointed out that informal organization is essential to the operation of the formal organization because informality provides a means of communication, of cohesion, and of protecting the integrity of the individual. Thus, the informal organization becomes a valuable aid to the agency's operation if there are well-integrated, cohesive groups to which members belong. In addition, the informal group relationships that grow are characterized by subtle controls in the form of norms and role expectations that are sometimes binding on the members. The more cohesive the group, the stronger the controls. Because the individual finds so many need satisfactions in the informal group, he submits to its controls and attempts to encourage others to cooperate in terms of group norms. Unofficial group norms therefore become an inevitable part of the informal organization. These standards of behavior constitute the subtle pressure of the cohesive group that operate to bring the individual member into conformity with the group. In a sense, a social system is created by people through their thought and action, and the system is greater than the sum of its parts.

Barnard says, "One of the indispensable functions of informal organizations in formal organizations is that of communication. Another function is that of the maintenance of cohesiveness in formal organizations through regulating the willingness to serve and the stability of objective authority. A third function is the maintenance of the feeling of personal integrity, of self-respect, of independent choice. Since the interactions of informal organization are not consciously dominated by a given impersonal objective or by authority as the organization expression, the interactions are apparently characterized by choice, and furnish the opportunities often for reinforcement of personal attitudes. Though often this function is deemed destructive of formal organization, it is to be regarded as a means of maintaining the personality of the individual against certain effects of formal organizations which tend to disintegrate the personality." [16]

In the informal organization are certain factors that contribute to and are essential requisites for the emergence of group norms. There must be effective communication between participants in the informal group. To be effective, the informal group must relate individuals to each other in areas of basic values, ideas, orientations of life, as well as in social, economic, and physical contacts. Such informal relationships imply the existence of certain "feelings" of members for each other; in addition, the quality and quantity of these emotional factors are significant in establishing the kinds of communication that will facilitate the development of common norms. Once these are developed, their enforcement requires still stronger networks of communication between members in the group.

In addition, the group must have inherent in its totality sufficient rewards for adhering to these standards of conduct. These rewards are most often intangibles, such as group acceptance and support, feelings of belonging, and security. The prevalence of such supportive ties or bonds in what becomes a cohesive group is a worthwhile source of emotional strength for its members. More tangible rewards to the group are often realized in increased productivity, increases in salaries, promotions, special merit awards, and so on.

Baur says, "Informal systems tend to flourish where large numbers come together and turnover is low, and when the job itself requires communication and cooperation between employees. They are used to show the 'ropes' to new employees, transmit and receive information prior to its official release, amend and amplify information after its official release, aid workers in helping each other in emergencies. Informal groups are essential for organizational stability and can strengthen morale, reduce absenteeism and turnover, promote harmony and increase efficiency." [17]

When enough members in the group have common orientations toward the social conduct of its members, sufficient social pressure is generated to enable members of the group to exert control over individuals within the group. This is possible because the individual, like the group, has internalized the standards of the small society. He, therefore, has feelings of guilt about not living up to his accepted standards. Consequently, pressure that compels conformity comes both from without and from within the individual. The individual's conduct, therefore, is influenced not only by the motivating force of his own internalized value orientations but also by the pressure resulting from shared group values of the members. This constitutes an external pressure that operates over and above the individual's own thinking, attitudes, and values and constrain him to act or refrain from acting in a certain way. Blau, in studying twelve supervisory units of caseworkers in a public assistance office, discovered that if pro-client values prevailed in a group this factor affected the performance of duties of its members independently of the individual's own attitudes toward clients. This difference in attitude was demonstrated in the amount of casework service offered over against the group that was not pro-client oriented. Members in the former group were motivated to express social approval of these members who were service-oriented and social disapproval of those who were not. In response to those sanctioning patterns, individuals tended to modify their approach to clients. Most members of the agency did not have a callous attitude toward clients; by expressing anticlient sentiments, some were showing acceptance of what were the prevailing norms of their particular group. Blau defines these external influencing factors as "structural constraints" that are exerted on each individual by virtue of his participation in a group that shares common values and norms.[18]

Albers says, "Organizing and reorganizing involves far more than formally defined authorities and responsibilities. Indeed, formal organizing actually disorganizes in that it disrupts and in some instances destroys an informally organized social system. Such a system plays an important part in the process through which people cooperate in pursuing common purposes. The organizer should recognize this fact and retain as much social continuity as possible. Informal groups can cause serious cooperative problems by supporting personal goals that are contrary to organizational needs. In such situations an organizer may deliberately attempt to break up the informal social pattern. Some structural changes may be made specifically for this purpose. Another approach is to change the leadership and membership of informal groups by personnel transfers and forced resignations. This technique represents an attempt to create favorable changes in attitude through different combinations of personality." [19]

Thus, even though the agency is organized along logical, deliberate lines —the formal organization—informal patterns of staff behavior are of great importance. Vinter underlines this when he says, "Like the human personality, the agency must adapt to its environment, and may develop 'pathologies' in the course of doing so. Unlike the individual person, the agency organization is deliberately created as an instrument to serve designated ends. All features of its structure and action may be evaluated as they contribute to stated goals, and efficiency is the major criterion. Agencies are designed as rational administrative systems; personnel are assigned to positions with specified tasks, each to be performed in accordance with prescribed policies and rules. The totality of positions, tasks, and rules constitute the formal or administrative structure of an agency. Yet these official designs cannot govern all behavior within the agency. Individuals perform somewhat differently to comparable positions, rules can never anticipate every eventuality, and relations of friendship or rivalry develop among staff members. The unplanned patterns of behavior that emerge and persist constitute an organization's informal structure; they may largely complement and reenforce official designs, or they may subvert and conflict with formal norms and requirements. And finally, diverse consequences flow from specific administrative actions, only some of which are either known or intended. Thus, an administrative decision to institute a particular form of intake procedure may have far-reaching implications for clients, for staff members, and for other agency practices. Not all the ramifications of any decision can be anticipated in advance, or observed thereafter." [20]

Defining and Utilizing Purposes

Skillful social work administrators make wise and continuous use of agency purpose. It should be their primary point of reference. It should influence and guide their every move. As Urwick has pointed out: "Unless we have a purpose there is no reason why individuals should try to co-operate together at all or why anyone should try to organize them. This, however, is very easily forgotten. Once an organization is set up, a human group is in being, all the individual and personal motives which have induced persons to join the group, which keep them in the game and playing the game, assume great importance in their minds. Most of us suspect that the main purpose of the undertaking which employs us is to provide us personally with a job. . . . People derive social satisfaction from working together. And they build up, often unconsciously, a very elaborate code of behavior and loyalties, and affections and antipathies, which may have little or nothing to do with the formal organization of the undertaking, the official relationships which their superiors recognize. . . . Every organization and every part of every organization must be an expression of the purpose of the undertaking concerned or it is meaningless and therefore redundant." [21]

All social work administrators must engage themselves in goal identification and formulation. This point is made by Traxler when he says, "Since the major job of the administrator is the shaping of organizational goals and reconciling these with those of the people involved, it might help to identify goals that are universal to *all* organizations. These are: (1) to maximize the use of all facilities—economic and human, (2) to work toward a common purpose, (3) to sustain a long-range growth potential; and (4) to establish a position for the organization in the community." [22]

Speaking about administration of the public schools, Moore points out: "One of the most difficult but at the same time the most important means of binding an organization together and causing it to work in a given direction is through getting it to agree on and accept common goals. The primary function of the school administrator is developing goals and obtaining their acceptance. In this he functions at the highest leadership level." [23]

One test of the effectiveness of the social work administrator is the extent to which his every action gives support to and helps in the attainment of the basic purposes of the agency. In fact, agency purpose must be a central consideration and a guiding influence in the day-to-day doing of administrative work. Administrators, therefore, must be increasingly clear on the nature and meaning of purposes. They must give attention to the process by which purposes are determined, and they must give thought to the ways by which soundly conceived statements of purpose are utilized by everyone connected with the agency. It is equally important for administrators to give leadership to the process by which purposes are modified to keep abreast of changing conditions.

Barnard says, "The continuance of an organization depends on its ability to carry out its purpose. This clearly depends jointly upon the appropriateness of its action and upon the conditions of its environment. In other words, effectiveness is primarily a matter of technological processes. This is quite obvious in ordinary cases of purpose to accomplish a physical objective, such as building a bridge. When the objective is non-physical, as in the case with religious and social organizations, it is not so obvious. It should be noted that a paradox is involved in this matter. An organization must disintegrate if it cannot accomplish its purpose. It also destroys itself by accomplishing its purpose. A very large number of successful organizations come into being and then disappear for this reason. Hence, most continuous organizations require repeated adoption of new purposes. This is concealed from everyday recognition by the practice of generalizing a complex series of specific purposes under one term, stated to be 'the purpose' of this organization. This is strikingly true in the case of governmental and public utilities organizations when the purpose is stated to be a particular kind of service through a period of years. It is apparent that their real purposes are not abstractions called 'service' but specific acts of service." [24]

When purposes are clear, the social work administrator can mobilize, focus, and coordinate individual and group energy in terms of priorities logically stated and soundly developed. There is nothing more important than administrative leadership in the area of formulating and utilizing purposes, but as Selznick says, many administrators default in this area: "One type of default is the failure to set goals. Once an organization becomes a going concern with many forces keeping it alive, the people who run it can readily escape the task of defining its purpose. This evasion stems partly from the hard intellectual labor involved, a labor that often seems to increase the burden of already onerous daily operations." [25]

NOTES

1. Fremont Kast, "Systems Concepts and Organization Theory," in Preston P. LeBreton, ed., *Comparative Administrative Theory* (Seattle: University of Washington Press, 1968), pp. 151–152.
2. Henry H. Albers, *Principles of Management,* 3rd ed. (New York: John Wiley & Sons, Inc., 1969), pp. 74–75.
3. Bertram S. Brown, M.D., "Concepts Underlying the Development of New Patterns of Community Mental Health Services," in *Proceedings Seminar on Social Welfare and Community Mental Health,* March 1–4, 1966, sponsored by the National Health Council and the National Social Welfare Assembly, p. 24.
4. Louise A. Frey, ed., *Use of Groups in the Health Field* (New York: National Association of Social Workers, 1966), pp. 21–22.

5. Arlien Johnson, *School Social Work—Its Contribution to Professional Education* (New York: National Association of Social Workers, 1962), pp. 60–61.
6. Kast, "Systems Concepts and Organization Theory," pp. 147–148.
7. Harry J. Hartley, *Education Planning—Programming—Budgeting—A System Analysis* (Englewood Cliffs, N.J.: Prentice-Hall, Inc., 1968) pp. 41ff.
8. Thomas Dolgoff, "Power, Conflict and Structure in Mental Health Organizations—A General Systems Approach," *Administration in Mental Health,* Winter 1972.
9. Bernard J. Coughlin, S.J., "Interrelationships of Governmental and Voluntary Welfare Services," *The Social Welfare Forum,* 1966 (Published for the National Conference on Social Welfare by Columbia University Press, New York), pp. 82–83.
10. Eleanor K. Taylor, "The Role of the Administrator in Facilitating Change," *Report of the Cooperative Project on Public Welfare Staff Training, Vol. I, Learning and Teaching in Public Welfare* (Washington, D.C.: Division of Technical Training, Bureau of Family Services, Welfare Administration, U.S. Department of Health, Education and Welfare, 1963), p. 191.
11. Ralph W. Tyler, "Insights from Behavioral Sciences," *Faculty-Administration Relationships,* Report of a Work Conference, May 7–9, 1957, sponsored by the Commission on Instruction and Evaluation of the American Council on Education, pp. 35–36.
12. *Social Work Administration* (New York: National Association of Social Workers, March 1968), pp. 9–10.
13. Richard E. Hamlin, *From the Quadrangle,* Newsletter, George Williams College, Downers Grove, Illinois, February 1969. pp. 2–3.
14. Albers, *Principles of Management,* pp. 102–103.
15. John D. Millett, *Organization for the Public Service* (Princeton, N.J.: Van Nostrand Company, Inc., 1966), p. 105.
16. Chester I. Barnard, *The Functions of the Executive,* Thirtieth Anniversary Edition (Cambridge: Harvard University Press, 1968), p. 122.
17. E. J. Baur, "The Spontaneous Development of Informal Organization," *Hospital Administration,* Summer 1963, pp. 45–58.
18. Peter M. Blau, "Structural Effects," *American Sociological Review,* April 1960, pp. 178–192.
19. Albers, *Principles of Management,* p. 296.
20. Robert D. Vinter, "The Social Structure of Service," in Alfred J. Kahn, ed., *Issues in American Social Work* (New York: Columbia University Press, 1959), p. 244.
21. Lyndall F. Urwick, *Notes on the Theory of Organization* (New York: American Management Association, 1952), pp. 18–19.
22. Ralph N. Traxler, "The Qualities of an Administrator," *Hospital Administration,* Fall 1961, p. 42.
23. Harold E. Moore, *The Administration of Public School Personnel* (New York: The Center for Applied Research in Education, Inc., 1966), p. 33.
24. Barnard, *The Functions of the Executive,* pp. 90–92.
25. Philip Selznick, *Leadership in Administration—A Sociological Interpretation* (Evanston, Ill.: Row, Peterson, 1957), p. 25.

4 The Administrator and the Community

The social work administrator must have effective working relationships with the community. In recent years, administrators have found it necessary to devote more time to community affairs because of the many changes that have taken place. Fresh facts about community needs are called for. Deeper understandings of client feelings are required. Developments in social welfare planning are increasingly important to the individual agency. New patterns of citizen and client participation in policy-making have emerged. Agency public relations, always important, have taken on new significance. Pressure groups of various kinds have brought their weight to bear upon agencies. Programs of interagency cooperation have increased. Board members and agency executives now take more part in legislative and community action. The fact that social welfare services are frequently a product of the political process has been more and more recognized. For all of these reasons and many others, the social work administrator must be skillful in community relations.

Goldman says, "School-community relations define the mutual understanding of school program and community needs which exist between the professionals who work in the schools and the citizens who support them. These understandings are necessary if the school is to reflect the values of the community and also be a positive influence on the future directions of it." [1] Although Goldman is talking about school-community relations, his remarks apply to social agency-community relations as well.

As Hardwick and Landuyt say, "Administration as a dynamic social reality cannot escape the influence of the beliefs and philosophies of the environment in which it is practiced." [2]

85

The Administrator Must Know the Community

In connection with the community, the administrator needs to see and know it in great breadth and depth because the community provides sanction for the service and the necessary financial support. The administrator should be particularly clear about the relationship between the agency and the community. He should have knowledge of the sociocultural factors that exist and should know about the degree of integration between community groups and the extent to which they hold values in common.

Hungate says, "A knowledge of cultural forms in the community is necessary for the public welfare administrator. A lack of recognition of sociocultural factors and cultural differences may cause the administrator to institute procedures and techniques for achieving program objectives that are culturally unacceptable as goals for the community. The administrator cannot expect community groups to go beyond their cultural limitations; he must know the cultural meaning of what is being done to the social values of those affected. The administrator must be aware that welfare programs operate within several subcultures at the same time; that the public welfare agency does not exist in isolation; nor is the organizational behavior of individuals working as a composite within any agency understandable without a reference to their cultural values. The variable of culture is always interposed between the environment and the welfare agency, which, with its multiple programs, is in the midst of a rapidly changing society. As cultural and social values change, welfare programs must be constantly adapted to solve the problems of human need. However, the administrator is expected to develop welfare programs that consistently conform to the dominant values currently held by the community, even though, with shifting emphasis, these values are constantly changing." [3]

It is necessary for the administrator to make sure that the agency has up-to-date information and basic social facts about the community for use in policy-making and program-planning. In addition, the administrator is responsible for developing a method whereby the agency is constantly studying the emerging social needs brought about by community changes. Furthermore, sound communication lines must be maintained between the agency and other community organizations. The administrator has the responsibility to help see to it that the board members are representatives of the community. Additional responsibility is to see to it that new volunteers and staff are given a thorough orientation to the community and are helped to participate in the life of the community. It should be certain that job analyses include specific itemized references to the workers' responsibility for community participation and leadership. Programs of staff development and in-service training should include material on the community. The administrator should work out with the board and the staff a statement of policy on community relationships, and he should represent the agency in total community planning and coordination.

In an earlier publication, the author listed ten questions designed to test the extent to which the agency's administrative processes are socially related to the community.

1. To what extent does the agency have up-to-date information and basic social facts about the community for use in policy-making and program planning?
2. To what extent does the agency have a method of arriving at an understanding of emerging social needs brought about by community changes? Consider, for example, the implications of such material as the following, stated by an administrator who is describing the area where a youth-service agency is at work: "It's an area of new homes, vast suburban tracts, many of them very picturesque as they are carved out of the hills. There is much mobility into and within the area and many people travel long distances to employment. Urban Redevelopment is very strong in the older sections. There are three separate public school systems in the area, as well as many parochial schools. Two Junior Colleges are here. Children are bussed long distances to school in some places. Some are on half-day sessions. There is continuous increase in school population with new schools and additions to old ones always under construction. At the present rate, a 55 per cent increase is indicated in school population in the next ten years. A tremendous adult education program is provided. A large Americanization program is conducted both in adult school and high school. Public transportation is very limited. What there is, is to the metropolitan centers and none between areas."
3. To what extent are sound communication lines maintained between the agency and other community organizations?
4. To what extent are board members representative of the community?
5. To what extent does the orientation of new volunteers and staff include orientation of the community and planned participation in the community?
6. To what extent do job analyses include specific itemized reference to the individual's responsibility for community participation and leadership?
7. To what extent does the agency make a conscious effort to see itself as the community sees it?
8. To what extent do staff development and in-service training programs include material on the community?
9. To what extent does the agency work with other agencies in common service projects?
10. To what extent does the agency participate in total community planning and coordination? [4]

The Administrator and Public Relations

The social work administrator, the staff, and the board find themselves involved with a number of groups that are important in the public relations of the agency. In his writing about school-community relations, Campbell and Ramseyer specify five such groups.[5] These groups include the constituency of the agency, other agencies serving in the same or related area, community planning bodies, state and national organizations, contributors and supporters of the agency, and the community at large.

The U.S. Office of Education observes that "The role of the administrator in relation to the community needs to be clarified, too. While it may be true that the successful administrator does not require the experience of long years of teaching, it is also becoming more important than ever befor that he be a 'teacher' in respect to the community at large, that he have an acute awareness of the social structure within which schools operate and be able to communicate the needs of the schools to the community upon which the schools depend and which they serve. Together with this ability, of course, there is a need for the administrator to be knowledgeable about the socio-political environment, so that he may successfully appeal to the proper agencies for support of his programs." [6]

Effective Public Relations for Community Groups

In their book on effective public relations for community groups, the Levines present a broad and inclusive definition of public relations. They say, "Public relations is as simple as a thank-you note and as complicated as a four-color brochure. It is as specific as writing a news release and as general as sensing community attitudes. It is as direct as a conversation between two people and as broad as a television panel show reaching thousands of people. It is as inexpensive as a phone call to an editor or as costly as a full-page advertisement. It is as visual as a poster and as literal as a speech." They also say, "Public relations is a term often used but seldom defined. In the broadest sense, public relations is good work publicly recognized. There is no secret public relations formula that can be applied to a group to make it respected and successful. Public relations is the group itself saying, 'This is who we are, what we think about ourselves, what we want to do, and why we deserve your support.' Public relations is not an end in itself, nor will it enable a group to gloss over its own deficiences. If the group is not doing 'good work,' that is, if it is not filling a real need for its members or for the community, if its program is uninteresting, or if its goals are unrealistic, public relations can help, of course, by being sensitive to community opinion and reporting it accurately, by pointing out the areas in which the group is failing, and by suggesting ways to improve. But the group with problems must try to solve them before its public relations will improve. If, however, the program is sound, if the membership agrees on basic values, if the group is performing a necessary function in the community, public relations can be an invaluable aid in achieving specific goals and in winning general community support." [7]

The Administrator and Social Welfare Planning

A major task of the social work administrator is to relate the agency to the on going social welfare planning program of the community. Because social welfare planning is changing rapidly, it becomes necessary for the administrator to see the goals of his agency in relation to the emerging goals of the social welfare field. Although most agencies tend to deal with specific needs and problems, there is a trend toward more generalized services.

Gurin and Perlman, in discussing social welfare planning and social planning, say, "The boundaries of social welfare as a field have always been hard to define, and the ambiguities grow as time goes on. Additionally, social welfare has dealt with specific disabilities of individuals or groups rather than with failures of the basic institutions of society. Social welfare planning has therefore been focused primarily on the more adequate provision of services to meet specific disabilities. The major exception is the field of social insurance where social workers have played a role along with other disciplines but not as the dominant professional group. This focus on disabilities has long been identified as the 'residual' approach to social work or social welfare, and there has been an equally long drive toward moving the field to more 'institutional' approaches which would give it a place within the normal social fabric. One prong of this drive is the attempt to provide social welfare services of a specialized character on a more general basis—to obtain greater coverage of the population—by building them into other institutions, such as the school system and the employment services, and indeed, into the economic system itself. Beyond this lies the still largely unexplored territory of prevention of a more fundamental character, which would involve the revision of patterns of community life in ways that would reduce the incidence of problems requiring services. To state the problems in these terms is to indicate how far away such ultimate goals remain from the reach of existing knowledge. It seems clear that social welfare planning cannot be adequate if it is limited to a narrow range of service programs, if only because planning in broader areas is required both to secure adequate provision of services for current problems and to avoid future ones to the extent that knowledge permits. There is still no clear approach, however, to the specific roles and responsibilities of social welfare within the larger framework." [8]

Administrative Choices, Client Needs, and Pressure Groups

Administrative choices and decisions should always be made in terms of what is best for the client. Often the administrator finds himself at the center or vortex of competing value systems. Value systems may be at variance within the agency and within the community. Here the social work administrator tries to get these variations looked at and understood and sufficiently reconciled to bring about effective service. Even though compromise is needed and even though it may be impossible to secure complete agreement, the administrator keeps working on this matter and tries to create the best possible program of services for clients. How the administrator reacts when faced by failure, frustration, and even defeat is extremely important.

Goldman observes: "A key administrative position in the public schools is that of principal. As the 'man-in-the-middle' posed between central administration and the teaching staff, the principal must put into operation the policies of the school district while at the same time he must meet the personal and professional needs of the teachers. While at times these factors may be congruent, at other times they are in conflict. The position of principal incurs other conflicts as well. While the central administration and the teachers hold certain expectations of the principal, community groups may have other views which further complicate the life of the principal. Moreover, the principal's professional organization may set expectations which are in conflict with all the groups mentioned above. It is into this cauldron that many 'mere' men are thrust." [9]

The social work administrator as he strives to meet the needs of his clients may find that pressure groups in the community make it difficult if not impossible for him to provide the programs and services needed. Social welfare and education share a common problem in that they are often subject to the pressures of the community. Melby, writing about education, see these pressure groups as sources of possible support: "The complex structure of pressure groups in the modern community is seen by many administrators as a body of critics to be appeased, yet different approaches could also convert these groups into resources to be utilized. The pressure groups are most often people who really care about education. Were greater use made of them they would realize more than they do now the complexity of many educational problems. Beyond this their contributions to education would be outstanding. What our school administrators have been taught in their preparation may equip them to deal with these persons and agencies in the community which they control, but increasingly the success of the administrator depends on the way he relates to persons and agencies he does not control. Here compassion, willingness to listen, a cooperative spirit, respect for the feelings of others will be more important than a commanding posture and a cocksure manner. It is also likely that in the years ahead it may be more important to be in communication with labor, the poor and the minority groups than with the Chamber of Commerce and the exclusive clubs." [10]

Administration and Citizen Participation

A fundamental tenet of social work administration is citizen participation. The skillful administrator involves citizens in policy-making, resource provision, and need determination. However, in large and complex communities, it is not easy to develop an effective program of citizen participation.

As Coughlin points out: "In the small societies of the past, citizen participation was relatively easily carried out through the immediate interrelationships between individuals, families, primary and secondary groups. The size and complexity of modern society, however, have removed the individual from his previous strategic position for discovering welfare need, and for the planning, servicing, coordinating, and accounting for welfare programs. In medieval and early colonial times, welfare need was easily discovered by every citizen who strolled into the marketplace; welfare services were so simple that planning and coordinating required little ingenuity; and one could scarcely evade accounting to a public to which one was known on a first-name basis. Today, things are changed. Discovery of real need is not as easy since real causes are remote and buried in a complexity of social values and institutions; planning and coordinating must be of a multiplicity of services, the totality of which is intended to strike at the complexity of the causes of need; and accountability is through impersonal institutions through an impersonal public." [11]

One of the major changes in recent years has been the emergence of a national policy in connection with a number of federal projects that declares it to be essential that the persons who live in a community have a voice in the project. As Piven points out: "new objectives and strategies are being associated with resident participation in the anti-poverty projects. Three interrelated objectives can be identified: (1) Fostering the participation of low-income people in a variety of local associations. (2) Enhancing the effective influence of low-income people on the policies and practices of institutions that serve the low-income community. (3) Establishing the conditions for effective individual and family life by altering the social context of individual behavior. These objectives for resident participation reflect the concern of the poverty programs with political problems pertaining to democratic participation and influence, as well as concern with the social welfare problems to which the programs are principally addressed." [12]

Related to the matter of resident participation is the fact that more and more agency executives, staff members, and board members are themselves becoming active in programs designed to improve the lot of the disadvantaged.

Brodsky reports that "The professional staffs of thirty-five Centers in thirty cities were described as being 'very active' in community planning and action groups concerned with the problems of the disadvantaged. The staff of twenty-eight additional Centers in as many cities were described as 'active' in such community groups. Only nine Centers reported no staff involvement.

"Generally, staff involvement has meant active participation by the Center's executive director. Center professionals have been appointed to serve on mayors' committees concerned with disadvantaged youth, or serve in an advisory capacity to local anti-poverty agencies. There are numerous instances of outstanding professional leadership given by Center staffs to local anti-poverty agencies.

"Forty-eight Centers in forty-five cities reported that some of their board members were 'active' or 'very active' in community planning and action agencies. Many board members tended to serve as individuals rather than as formal representatives of the Center." [13]

Mogulof asks: "What is a competent community?" He says, "For one, it is a place where the leaders are of the people and are a power in effecting the decision of all those agencies that provide resources to that community. In low-income communities, it is the place where the neighborhood representatives know how to deal with the police and courts, how to make their public schools aware that the price of the continued failure of their youth will be high, and where the welfare department, housing agencies, and so on know they are not dealing with a supine mass. Do such communities exist? Probably not, but that they must is clear, especially while the United States has a large 'underclass' dependent for most of its resources and opportunities on the decisions of public agencies." [14]

The Emerging Concept of Community Control

The National Federation of Settlements and Neighborhood Centers has taken formal action on the matter of community control and has issued the following statement:

STATEMENT ON COMMUNITY CONTROL

Definition

Community control means substantial policy-making power by local residents over the programs of an institution which provides services to the local community. The concept is broad enough to include significant numbers of total representation of local residents on boards of service agencies and also various other ways by which users of services obtain administrative accountability by those in charge of programs.

Community control also means the power of local people to influence those institutions which are organized on a non-local basis but which deliver services locally. This implies some form of delegation of power or the development of a partnership arrangement with representative community groups.

It also means that local community groups have the right and need the necessary resources to engage in social action on problems that people face in their locality, and to enter into coalitions with other groups to act on problems that transcend neighborhood boundaries. Such problems obviously include income and housing in poor areas of cities. Local pressure is often needed as the impetus for city, state, and national action.

Community control should be democratically representative of the interest groups of the community.

Position

NFS will support local moves toward greater community participation and control, as broadly defined. We recognize the variations in local situations—limitations posed by funding patterns, inflexible corporate structures, and the lack of skill or experience of local people in some places in agency management—but we believe that member houses of NFS should look upon growing community interest in agency control as a timely opportunity to realize principles of local democracy which have long been a part of settlement philosophy.

We therefore urge settlements to act on their own initiative to transfer control to or share it with local residents in new and creative ways. Within its limited resources NFS will assist member houses in making such changes.

We reaffirm our general belief in the value of services by board members from outside the local community and note that their role is especially justified when they act as advocates and communicators in addition to other helpful services. The expanded concept of the work of board members from the larger community, which is evident in many places, is consistent with the idea of community control, insofar as it provides added resources for effective action on local problems.[15]

Administrators and the Political Process

Although actual records of the amount of time spent are not available, it is evident that the administrator devotes considerable energy to the matter of interpreting his agency to political and governmental bodies. He does this to create an understanding of his agency and to get financial support for its programs. As Hungate says, "Administration of public welfare is one of the political processes of government. Although there is some flexibility within the programs, administration of welfare activities is thoroughly dependent upon and must interact with all other political processes. Therefore, provision of welfare services at an optimum level is contingent upon the attitudes of public welfare administrators toward public affairs and, in turn, the attitudes of public officials toward welfare. Because the legislative authority for welfare services is derived from political activity, it is in relationship to public affairs that public welfare administration tends to differ most decisively from administration of a voluntary agency." [16]

Millett remarks, "Every administrator is a participant to some degree in the political process. As an administrator he is expected to give advice to the chief executive and to the legislature about desirable policy and program, about desirable scope of activities, and about the desirable authority (organizational and otherwise) needed to accomplish assigned purposes." [17]

NOTES

1. Samuel Goldman, *The School Principal* (New York: The Center for Applied Research in Education, Inc., 1966), p. 63.
2. C. T. Hardwick and G. F. Landuyt, *Administrative Strategy* (New York: Simmons-Boardman Publishing Corporation, 1961), p. 324.
3. Joseph I. Hungate, Jr., *A Guide for Training Local Public Welfare Administrators* (Washington, D.C.: U.S. Department of Health, Education and Welfare —Administration, Bureau of Family Services, Division of Technical Training, 1964), p. 109.
4. Harleigh B. Trecker, *New Understandings of Administration* (New York: Association Press, 1961), pp. 92–94.
5. Ronald F. Campbell and John A. Ramseyer, *The Dynamics of School–Community Relationships* (Boston: Allyn and Bacon, Inc., 1958), pp. 19–21.
6. Harold Howe II, *The People Who Serve Education* (Washington, D.C.: U.S. Department of Health, Education and Welfare, 1969), p. 8.
7. Howard and Carol Levine, *Effective Public Relations for Community Groups* (New York: Association Press, 1969), pp. 15, 17–18.
8. Arnold Gurin and Robert Perlman, "Current Concepts of Planning and Their Implications for Public Welfare," in David G. French, ed., *Planning Responsibilities of State Departments of Public Welfare* (Chicago: American Public Welfare Association, 1967), p. 17.
9. Goldman, *The School Principal*, p. vii.
10. Ernest O. Melby, "Needed: A New Concept of Educational Administration," *The Community School and Its Administration,* July 1965, p. 3.
11. Bernard J. Coughlin, S.J., "Interrelationships of Governmental and Voluntary Welfare Services," *The Social Welfare Forum,* 1966 (Published for the National Conference on Social Welfare by Columbia University Press, New York), pp. 83–84.
12. Frances Piven, "Participation of Residents in Neighborhood Community Action Programs," *Social Work,* January 1966, pp. 74–75.
13. Irvine Brodsky, *The Jewish Community Center and the Urban Crisis* (New York: National Jewish Welfare Board, 1968), p. 13.
14. Melvin B. Mogulof, "Involving Low-Income Neighborhoods in Antidelinquency Programs," *Social Work,* October 1965, p. 56.
15. *Statement on Community Control,* National Federation of Settlement and Neighborhood Centers (New York, February 27, 1970).
16. Hungate, *Public Welfare Administrators,* p. 45.
17. John D. Millett, *Organization for the Public Service* (Princeton: D. Van Nostrand Company, Inc., 1966), p. 135.

5 The Administrator and the Staff

Most social work administrators agree that they carry major responsibility for seeing to it that their agencies are well staffed. As Friedlander says, "Competent, reliable, conscientious personnel is the most important factor in social agency administration as it is in other professional services, medicine, nursing, law and teaching. Only a well-trained staff of adequate size can perform social services as required for the welfare of the people. In this sense adequate staff means economy, because too few or untrained workers cannot perform qualified social work which is necessary to achieve the social agency's objectives. Personnel policy of the social agency demands three basic elements: 1) clearly formulated written standards of employment for specific positions, based upon competence: 2) provisions for fair-dealing on grievances; and 3) delegation of final authority to the executive in dealing with matters of competence and discipline." [1]

With reference to the public schools, Moore observes: "The strength and effectiveness of a school system is largely determined by the adequacy and quality of its staff. Recognizing this fact has led the total administrative process to be greatly concerned with personnel policies and practices." [2]

Pomeroy points out: "It is through the worker that the client typically relates to the agency. Thus, the worker not only can be viewed as a participant in a two-way relationship (between him and the client), but also as a link (albeit a mediating one) in the relationship of the client to the agency." [3]

Administrative Responsibility Shared with Staff

Many people carry administrative responsibility in the social agency. The chief executive is one; the department heads and supervisors are

95

others; then there are special staff people such as heads of business, finance, and buildings. The chief administrator is responsible for the entire work of the agency and is responsible for all of the people on the staff. Therefore, he has more complex relationships and a much greater degree of authority. The administrator must delegate work assignments to other people and must serve as a supervisor and a coordinator. Administrators are closer to the policy-making realm than are subadministrators.

As a workshop group pointed out: "Every social welfare agency exists to give one or more services; but in order to produce those services, many facilitative or supporting activities must be carried on. These include the activities of the executive and supervisors, board and staff meetings, financial operations, record keeping, and a host of other activities. Administration may be regarded as the sum of the facilitating and supportive activities which are not themselves service activities but which are necessary and incidental to the production of the service. Administration is the 'effectuation' of service. And, from this point of view, not only the executive but every member of the board, every member of the staff, every volunteer has a relation to and is a participant in administration. There is no such thing as a 'pure service' job. Every staff member carries on administrative as well as service activities—dictation, keeping records, attending staff conferences, conferring with supervisors, etc." [4]

As Hungate says, "Within the organization, the administrative process is performed in some way by every individual. The director may be the one 'executive' for the program, but he's not the only one engaged in the practice of administration. . . . Within the sphere of their activity, all staff members perform administrative tasks; thus all program activity involves administration. Many persons who have the responsibility to direct and manage some phase of agency activities are not aware that they are engaged in administration. The administrative aspect of each job may not be readily distinguishable: (1) The typist must organize, plan, and direct the typing of records, and set schedules for getting out letters and for a variety of other clerical functions. (2) The supervisor of casework must direct the activity of the assigned workers, and many administrative considerations are evident in assignment of cases to specific workers. (3) A portion of the worker's time is spent in administration of the case load. Many case workers have been heard to exclaim that they do not want to be placed in administrative positions, but want only to see clients and 'do casework.' Analysis will show that the caseworker in many agencies is one of the most facile of administrators. No one would deny that mangaging a case load of 50-150 clients requires abundant administrative skills. Thus, administration permeates the whole structure. Everyone using personal judgment and skill to perform an assigned duty effectively is constantly solving individual problems of administration." [5]

The Administrator's Attitude Toward and Relationship with the Staff

The social work administrator is the professional leader of the staff. His major responsibilities include helping the staff to set goals, achieve high standards of work productivity, and provide high-quality services to clients. Administrator attitudes toward staff should express faith in their ability to do the job. As Clapp says, "Given two agencies with reasonable similarity in respect to the competence of its individual members, what makes one lethargic, apathetic, and erratic in its course and performance and the other purposive, energetic, and reasonably creative in its performance? I suspect that at the root of the causes may be found a fundamental difference in at least two respects—the presence or absence of a deep faith within the key administrators in the latent intellectual and emotional reasonableness of human beings and rejection or acceptance of the desire to reform people as contrasted with the willingness to let them reform themselves. I believe that one's beliefs and convictions about these two variables lie close to the heart of whatever may be the administrative art. A more limited and suggestive hypothesis might be something like this: the key to the performance of an organization is the positive willingness of individuals to spend and apply their energies, single or in groups, to the tasks committed to their hands. How to elicit within and among the farthest reaches of an organization the positive self-induced desire, intent, and energy to decide to act is the central problem of administrative leadership." The social work administrator seeks to promote the growth of his staff, for as Clapp says, "The highest purpose of administration is to build processes which encourage and promote the growth of human talents, especially the talent to select progressively richer ends or goals and more effective means to achieve them." [6]

Tead elaborates on this theme when he says, "My considered judgment is that for long-time success, the best administrative leaders are those who have socially justifiable purposes and who enlist loyalty to them by provocative creative appeals to those groups involved. This is the essence of *democratic* leadership in that the effort is consciously being made to achieve the institutional goals while trying simultaneously to assure that those implicated are realizing and actualizing themselves *as* they labor and *through* their labor for the corporate good. The development or realization of the personalities of the followers has always to be one-half of the dual goal of the leader, the other half being to assure that the institution's purpose is well served by the integrated labors of all." [7]

The social work administrator has a role to play in helping the staff to understand the heritage of the agency. In writing about the job of the school principal, Goldman makes a point that is pertinent for social agency administrators as well: "In his role as administrator, the principal works with his staff to preserve and transmit to present and future generations the accumulated heritage of the past. This tends to provide a certain stability to the on-going activities of the school. By lending stability to the program, the principal can instill a feeling of security and trust in those who work with him. By resisting impulsive action or hastily conceived 'instant change' the principal can contribute to diminishing the feelings of insecurity among staff members and in this way obviate a major cause of entrenched resistence to change." [8]

The Administrator and Work Productivity

As a goal-setter for the staff, the administrator has much to do with determining work output or productivity. As Argyris says, "The leader seems to exhibit realistic goal-setting ability. He tends to set his goals just high enough so that effort is required to achieve them, but not so high they are unattainable." [9]

Likert says, "To achieve and maintain high performance, it is necessary that the subordinates, as well as the superiors of an organization, have high performance goals and have their work well-organized. Subordinates are unlikely to set high performance goals for themselves and organize their work well if their superiors do not have much aspiration for each salesman and for the whole office. A superior with high performance goals and excellent job organization is much more likely to have subordinates who set high goals for themselves and organize their work well when he uses group methods of supervision and applies the principle of supportive relationships effectively than when he does not." [10]

The administrator is thus a key person in work productivity. Increased productivity and job satisfaction of all members of the work group appear to be related to the administrator's activity in developing in the employees a feeling of self-confidence and security in the way the agency is managed. The administrator must be able to demonstrate adequate control over the formal organization in order to win the allegiance of his staff. The administrator must command the respect of the workers in order to contribute to the development of cohesive ties that bring about unity. The absence of such bonds produces strains and tensions that find expression in more critical attitudes toward the administrator.

A workshop group reported: "Basically, administration is a process that involves working with other people. Wherever there is administration, there are people; the administrative process involves primarily working relationships with others. Thus, (a) equipment, procedures, records are important only as they relate to human beings; they exist and have significance only insofar as they are used by people to facilitate the achievement of the goal of giving services; (b) the fabric of administration is woven from the multi-colored threads of *human relationships*. The executive, the sub-executive, the supervisor, the social worker, the office manager, the typist, the janitor, the maid—these are people, each with a job to be accomplished within an overall agency program, and as each works at his job, he does so in relation to the work being done by every other member of the staff within the total program. The relations are 'there' because the people are 'there'; wherever there are people associated in an enterprise, there are relationships." [11]

Likert says, "The principle of supportive relationship is a general principle which the members of an organization can use to guide their relationships with one another. The more fully this principle is applied throughout the organization, the greater will be the extent to which (1) the motivational forces arising from the non-economic motives of members and from their economic needs will be harmonious and compatible and (2) the motivational forces within each individual will result in cooperative behavior focused on achieving organizational goals. The principle is stated as follows: The leadership and other processes of the organization must be such as to ensure a maximum probability that in all interactions and in all relationships within the organization, each member, in the light of his background, values, desires, and expectations, will view the experience as supportive and one which builds and maintains his sense of personal worth and importance." [12]

The social work administrator tends to become a model for the staff. The way he carries on task activities has a considerable influence on those around him. Task behavior, as discussed by Moment and Zaleznik, has an element of leadership in it that is of great importance: "Task behavior involves the individual in an aggressive mode of action. By thinking and weighing ideas, his own and others, he becomes committed to the points of view that he must formulate and assert, both forcefully and confidently, if he is to work with conviction. He seeks to influence other persons, to change and modify their points of view, which involves him in competitive activity. To assert and to compete opens the individual to aggressive behavior from others. If he is functioning in task activity, the individual has to be able to take competitive behavior from others; this includes criticism, evaluation, and attack. One of the main characteristics of task-oriented behavior is the release of energy and its direction on to a problem-solving situation and at the same time the absorption of energy display resulting from the direction of energy by other persons." [13]

The Staff Member as a Part of the Agency

The social work administrator must strive to understand the staff member as an individual *and* as a part of the agency.

Bennis calls attention to the fact that "individuals who come to work for the organization bring into the system some needs which they desire to have satisfied on the job and certain expectations about the job they are to perform. On the other hand, the organization has certain needs to be fulfilled and a set of expectations to be fulfilled by the people who work for it." [14]

It is the task of the administrator to help staff members become integrated with the agency even though their loyalties may be in conflict at the outset.

As Green observes, "when the problem of conflicting loyalties is considered in its broad perspective, it is essentially one of reconciling the professional workers' need for autonomy and the organization's need for employees to be integrated within the complex of its activities. For the social worker, autonomy means maintaining professional standards, developing a creative and resourceful approach to practice, and finding opportunities for professional development and research activities. For the organization, integration involves maintaining administrative standards and the rational coordination of activities, together with the development of responsibility and loyalty in the employee. As the professional social worker needs the resources of the organization, and as the latter needs the skill of the professional worker, there is considerable motivation to find some accommodation to the interests of both." [15]

What the Professional Social Worker Wants from Administration

A prominent factor in the social worker's choice of employment is the kind of administration provided by the agency. What kind of administration do professional social workers want? *First,* they want an administration that makes it possible for them to practice their profession, that is, to make use of their knowledge and skill in professional service to people. *Second,* they want an administration that allows them to make decisions about client needs based on their professional judgments. *Third,* they want to be accepted as responsible professional persons who can be depended upon to carry out their work assignments with competence and commitment. *Fourth,* they want opportunities for growth plus new responsibilities and challenges as their experience warrants. *Fifth,* they want an administration that both permits and encourages them to contribute their practical knowledge and experience to the process of problem-solving and policy-determination. Utz says, *"The administrative staff should share fully and frankly with the casework staff the problems and issues confronting the agency as soon as they are identified and their dimensions are assessed.* Sharing such knowledge clears the air, removes a shroud of secrecy, and releases staff energy that might otherwise be consumed in speculation and anxiety. Furthermore, it provides a challenge to staff members who are capable of assuming some of the responsibility for seeking solutions to the problems and dealing with the issues." [16] *Sixth,* they want an administration that is constantly striving for high standards of professional service. *Seventh,* they want an administration that provides strong and sound leadership.

Taylor says, "A major function of the executive is the provision of sound leadership to his staff. There are many problems in this area that can give rise to stress. There is the matter of individual as opposed to group decisions and the thorny problems surrounding the manipulation and engineering of consent." [17]

Eighth, they want an administration that respects and seeks to implement the nationally agreed-upon personnel standards and practices.

The National Association of Social Workers says, "As a member of the profession, an administrator has the responsibility to acquaint the governing body of the agency with NASW standards for personnel policies and salaries. These include providing opportunity for employees to bargain collectively with management, if they so choose. Job descriptions should state clearly which positions are considered managerial and are therefore excluded from the collective bargaining unit.

"If the majority of employees in an agency determine that a union is their preferred method of carrying out their program for recognition and ultimately their collective bargaining activities, the first consideration should be whether the union should be a craft or an industrial union. In making this choice, the employees should explore, among other factors, what kind of a union would best facilitate conditions for good professional practice and which would be most effective in improving working conditions and salaries in social agencies.

"Useful methods in achieving recognition and in collective bargaining include exploration, education, persuasion, negotiation, enlistment of influential allies, representation by council, presentation through news media, use of professional mediators, and arbitration." [18]

The Staff Member's Responsibility to Administration

Social workers are responsible to administration in many ways. Their professional ideals and ethics are the foundation for responsible behavior on their part.

The National Association of Social Workers declares: "Social work is based on humanitarian, democratic ideals. Professional social workers are dedicated to service for the welfare of mankind, to the disciplined use of a recognized body of knowledge about human beings and their interactions, and to the marshaling of community resources to promote the well-being of all without discrimination.

"Social work practice is a public trust that requires of its practitioners integrity, compassion, belief in the dignity and worth of human beings, respect for individual differences, a commitment to service, and a dedication to truth. It requires mastery of a body of knowledge and skill gained through professional education and experience. It requires also recognition of the limitations of present knowledge and skill and of the services we are now equipped to give. The end sought is the performance of a service with integrity and competence.

"Each member of the profession carries responsibility to maintain an improved social work service; constantly to examine, use, and increase the knowledge on which practice and social policy are based; and to develop further the philosophy and skills of the profession." [19]

In discussing the methods by which the school social worker discharges his responsibility to administration, Nebo lists: "1. Demonstration of the value of the service by his work and changes in children; 2. Initiation and participation in case conferences involving both school and community personnel; 3. Planned conferences with both principals and superintendents or their delegated representative; 4. Participation in curriculum-planning committees and other committees; 5. Participation in orientation meetings, PTA functions, faculty meetings, and meetings of groups outside the school to interpret his function, and also to further a general understanding of children; 6. Submission of monthly and annual statistical and narrative reports to the superintendent and other key administrators; 7. Preparation and distribution of specially prepared written material. In summary, the school social worker can be of value to administration by: 1. Understanding the role of social work as it operates within an institution whose primary function is to educate children, and focusing his goals on this educational function; 2. Understanding the over-all educational philosophy, practices, and policies of his school district and of the individual buildings he serves; 3. Understanding, respecting, and using lines of authority, responsibility, and communication as they operate within the school district and within individual buildings; 4. Working closely with teachers, principals, and other school personnel on individual cases, sharing appropriate information with them, and utilizing their knowledge and skills; 5. Maintaining cooperative relationship with representatives of other special services within the school, and, with administrative leadership, participating with these representatives in a mutual delineation of each person's responsibilities and in a recognition of overlapping elements in their roles; 6. Understanding the functions, policies, and procedures of community agencies and interpreting them to the school; and interpreting the school's functions, policies, and procedures to the community; 7. Attending faculty meetings, serving on committees and assuming other appropriate responsibilities which will promote his integration with the faculty." [20]

Code of Ethics of the Social Worker

The code of ethics of the social worker must govern his behavior in all of his relationships. As the National Association of Social Workers states:

This code of ethics embodies certain standards of behavior for the social worker in his professional relationships with those he serves, with his colleagues, with his employing agency, with other professions, and with the community. In abiding by it, the social worker views his obligations in as wide a context as the situation requires, takes all the principles into consideration, and chooses a course of action consistent with the codes' spirit and intent. The code of ethics includes the following:

I regard as my primary obligation the welfare of the individual or group served, which includes action for improving social conditions.

I will not discriminate because of race, color, religion, age, sex, or national ancestry, and in my job capacity will work to prevent and eliminate such discrimination in rendering service, in work assignments, and in employment practices.

I give precedence to my professional responsibility over my personal interests.

I hold myself responsible for the quality and extent of the service I perform.

I respect the privacy of the people I serve.

I use in a responsible manner information gained in professional relationships.

I treat with respect the findings, views, and actions of colleagues and use appropriate channels to express judgment on these matters.

I practice social work within the recognized knowledge and competence of the profession.

I recognize my professional responsibility to add my ideas and findings to the body of social work knowledge and practice.

I accept my responsibility to help protect the community against unethical practice by any individuals or organizations engaged in social welfare activities.

I stand ready to give appropriate professional service in public emergencies.

I distinguish clearly, in public, between my statements and actions as an individual and as a representative of an organization.

I support the principle that professional practice requires professional education.

I accept responsibility for working toward the creation and maintenance of conditions within agencies that enable social workers to conduct themselves in keeping with this code.

I contribute my knowledge, skills, and support to programs of human welfare.[21]

Authority and Administration

It is widely recognized that authority is inherent in every social work job. Authority goes with the function, the task, and the position. It is also agreed that the amount of, or degree of, authority varies with the position held and is specific to the given position. In every case, authority implies knowledge, experience, and a degree of competence. It also implies trust, responsibility, and acceptance by people. Thus, in social work, authority is widely distributed throughout the enterprise. It is shared by a large number of people. Insofar as the social work administrator is concerned, it is necessary for him to make substantial use of his authority of competence. It is used to design and set limits on individual and group responsibility. It is used to establish methods, procedures, and policies. It is used to foster coordination and to create agency unity and wholeness.

Albers says, "Organized executive action is impossible without authority. . . . Power and authority are closely related to concepts. Power may be defined as the capacity to change individual or group behavior. . . . Power is present when an individual or group is able to affect the activity of another individual or group. It gives rise to behavior that differs from the behavior that would have occurred otherwise. The power that evolves from a managerial position is usually categorized as authority. People with authority have power, but power does not always denote authority. A subordinate may have no authority, but he can have a great deal of power. The 'authority of position' is the power (or authority) that a person has by virtue of his superior position. Subordinates normally accord authority to those who occupy higher hierarchical positions. This authority is to a great extent unrelated to the particular person who occupies the position. Authority would arise even though the occupant does not have the personal capacity to create power." [22]

Walton says, "By authority we mean simply the power and the recognized right of the administrator, enforced by whatever sanctions he may employ, to make decisions necessary for the coordination of the activities of persons working within the organization. The authority of the administrator to coordinate is similar to the teacher's authority to teach." [23]

Administrators may have certain feelings about authority and may have difficulty in accepting the fact that they must use the authority vested in them and in their position. Problems may arise from misunderstandings and from the failure on the part of administrators to spell out precisely the degree of authority involved in the various positions in the agency.

To summarize: 1) authority is inherent in every job; it goes with the function, the task, the position held. 2) The amount or degree of authority, its specific nature, varies with the particular job. 3) Authority implies knowledge, experience, and is both earned and conferred. 4) Authority is distributed, shared, and is best regarded as authority *with* people rather than authority *over* people. 5) Authority implies trust, responsibility, and acceptance by people. 6) Authority is essentially positive; in fact, it is very useful, even essential. 7) All of us need the help of authority, few people can function long without it. Therefore, the administrator uses authority to define and set limits on individual and group responsibility. He uses it to establish methods and procedures and policies for performing work and to foster coordination and agency wholeness.

A Survey of Staff Attitudes

Social work administrators are frequently lacking in information as to how staff members really feel about their jobs and their agency. Although the administrators try to keep the lines of communication open, staff members may be reluctant to reveal their feelings.

In a hospital, an employee attitude survey was conducted by a university research agency. The findings as reported in the following newspaper account indicate that social agencies as well as hospitals can learn much from such a formal study.

Hartford Hospital is the first medical institution in New England to use an attitude survey program to keep up with its employees.

A year and a half ago, the 2,800 employees each spent an hour filling out questionnaires of the Industrial Relations Department of the University of Chicago.

Hospital personnel director Robert C. Gronbach reports the reason behind the program is to have truly "participative management." Workers are asked to make suggestions and take part in the constant realignment of duties.

Gronbach said Hartford Hospital started with generally good morale and has improved it. Nurses are asked to answer 93 questions, "agree," "don't know" or "disagree." Other workers answered 78 items. The unsigned sheets were then sent to Chicago for tabulating.

The hospital's mean score was 61 per cent favorable replies—the exact mean the Chicago quiz found after testing 100,000 industrial firms, and well above the mean among hospitals using the survey.

Key to making the survey work, Gronbach said, is follow-up and feedback. The University of Chicago supplies a management development program to teach supervisors to make use of the survey results. A "workbook" comes with the test scores and each department head goes over the questions and answers with his personnel.

What did Hartford find besides a few personal gripes and attacks on individuals?

It found that communications were poor—within and especially between departments. It also found that coordination was often absent so that time and money was wasted.

It found that pay was generally good—much better than other hospitals surveyed. But the nurses said that scheduling of shifts was unsatisfactory.

Employees had a page on which to write criticisms and ideas—responses that were sent unread to Chicago and then typed up and returned to the Hospital. Many of the ideas, reports Gronbach, have been put to good use.

Employees now have a formal Employees Council that meets once a month. It is made up of 35 representatives from the more than 40 departments within Hartford Hospital. This group discusses specific issues and files reports with management. Management has agreed to discuss any personnel proposals with the Council, first.

A year from now, another attitude survey will be made. In the meantime, department supervisors are attending conferences to improve their techniques, antiquated equipment has been replaced, coordination has been improved and 140 other suggested changes have been implemented.[24]

Delegation of Responsibility to Staff Members

The skillful social work administrator learns how to delegate responsibility and authority to members of his staff. In fact, delegation is a necessity as Albers points out: "Delegation becomes necessary when the work load of an executive position exceeds the physical and psychological capacity of the executive. The delegation process reduces the executive work load, but it also adds to the work load by increasing the number of subordinates or span of management. This process can continue until the work load that evolves from an increasing span of management exceeds the executive's capacity to carry the burden. Additional levels of management become necessary when this limit is reached. The superior's responsibility is not absolved by the act of delegation. Delegation involves taking a risk on the capability of subordination. This risk cannot be entirely avoided, but it can be mitigated by exercising some degree of supervision over the activities of the subordinate. Decentralization is greater or less to the extent that executives are willing to delegate important decision-making responsibilities and exercise a minimum of supervision and control." [25]

Clegg, in analyzing his experience in public welfare administration, places much importance on delegation when he writes: "The successful executive does not do anything himself which can be done as well or better by some member of his staff. The Welfare Administrator who is to follow this admonition needs to examine critically his daily activities to ascertain if he is performing unnecessary and useless tasks. The proper delegation of authority is one of the keys to successful administration. Its accomplishment requires constant study and reconsideration. The wise executive attempts to surround himself with staff who are the most competent available. He may be successful in employing assistants who are his equal or superior in management phases. This is a promising situation, for it permits the executive or administrator to operate the organization at a high level of performance and to bask in the light of the talents of those who surround him. It is quite obvious that it will be of no avail to acquire competent staff unless they are permitted sufficient delegated power to perform at maximum and to develop their personal talents." [26]

Differential Use of Staff

Increasingly, social work administrators are making differential use of staff, defined by Barker and Briggs as "a social work organization's allocation of its functions to the organization members who are considered most capable of fulfilling them efficiently." [27]

As Epstein points out: "Making maximum use of professional staff time in productive direct work with clients occupies high priority in the administration of social services. Need for improved methods in use of staff is intensified by the shortage of trained caseworkers, the increasing demand for social services, and their increasing cost. Advances in diagnostic and treatment knowledge and in administrative techniques are making some older methods obsolete and in need of revision and up-dating." [28]

In an interesting report on how one agency made differential use of staff, Epstein cites the administrative assumptions that were made at the start of the project. They are: "(1) Structure was considered a prerequisite for the full use of technological knowledge in social work, as in other disciplines. (2) Job specialization was viewed as a way to produce expertise in a particular segment of agency function, permitting some use of less-trained staff, thus lowering some costs. (3) Job specialization in a closely structured administrative design was believed to require disciplined staff performance and a system of job coordination which must be built into the work process and is not achievable by supervision alone. (4) It was considered to be primarily an administrative responsibility to design, install, and control the systems used, rather than depend on independent staff initiative for improvisation and implementation. It is this element of sole administrative responsibility, which, when combined with consistent teaching in supervision, builds the work process both into the system and individual workers' performances. (5) It was considered professionally valid to construct empirical classifications of the caseload so as to obtain a practical working base for differentiating case assignments among different categories of staff." [29]

In describing one differential work assignment system, Epstein says, "The characteristics of this staff-use plan may be stated as follows: (1) Professionally trained, fully qualified casework staff to be used as exclusively as possible at their highest level of skill. (2) Adjunctive personnel to be used maximally to enable the casework personnel to attend fully to their particular role. A full array of essential services will thus be made available, raising the level of all services. (3) Job descriptions that accurately portray existing duties and differences between categories to be made explicit in writing. (4) Casework assistant personnel to be developed. It was found expedient to change the job title of 'case aide' to 'casework assistant' because deprecating connotations seem to have grown up around the former title. Casework assistants are never to be made to assume full professional responsibility for diagnosis or outcome, but to be offered readily accessible professional supervision at all times. Conversely, caseworkers are expected to assume professional responsibility, using supervision to develop knowledge and technique for diagnostic clarity and treatment efficiency. (5) Volunteer personnel to be used maximally on assignments tailored to be within the limits of their knowledge and skill, their duties also to be defined explicitly, and never to be assigned without immediate access to professional supervision. (6) Work-simplification devices to be developed to reduce time spent on clerical duties and to standardize and economize on repetitive professional procedures." [30]

Epstein went on to summarize the results of this special project on differential use of staff in the following words: "In conclusion, the project reported here has demonstrated that a structured, differential use of staff can be developed and can increase staff productivity and impact on the social problems for which the agency assumes responsibility. The basic elements of the administrative design described here are explicit role clarification among the different types of personnel; built-in safeguards against demands in excess of defined areas of staff competence; assumption of administrative responsibility for classifying and making decisions on key areas of caseload characteristics, focus, and content of services to be offered." [31]

In developing patterns of staff usage in differential terms, social work administrators must take into account not only their agencies but the profession as well. Barker and Briggs accent this point when they say, "Differential use of staff to meet the needs of clients better is a joint responsibility involving agencies, which must be clear regarding job specifications and delineation based on agency role and client needs; the profession, whose obligation is to establish and/or redefine the legitimate status positions for various levels of personnel; and education, which must retool and design educational programs along the whole continuum based on new designations and roles." [32]

Job Satisfaction and Staff Retention

In his significant research on job satisfaction and staff retention in social work, Weinberger studied a number of variables and concluded that while income was of course important and necessary it was not a vital factor in job satisfaction.[33] Rather, he found that professional climate and agency atmosphere where workers could practice their profession and be free to innovate were most vital. Also he found workers got greater satisfaction in small rather than in large agencies and suggested that the large agencies find ways to organize their workers into small units. Professional autonomy was found to be significant in terms of job satisfaction and retention. Not surprising was the fact that workers placed high value on adequate physical facilities, including privacy in offices where work could be carried on in a professional confidential fashion.

NOTES

1. Walter A. Friedlander, *Introduction to Social Welfare*, 3rd ed. (Englewood Cliffs, N.J.: Prentice Hall, Inc., 1968), pp. 205–206.
2. Harold E. Moore, *The Administration of Public School Personnel* (New York: The Center for Applied Research in Education, Inc., 1966), p. 1.
3. Richard Pomeroy, *Studies in Public Welfare: Reactions of Welfare Clients to Social Service* (The Center for the Study of Urban Problems, Graduate Division, Bernard M. Baruch College, The City University of New York, undated), p. 69.
4. *Proceedings of Workshop on Social Agency Administration, Leadership and the Social Welfare Executive*, Richmond Professional Institute—School of Social Work, Richmond, Va., April 12–14, 1967, p. 2.
5. Joseph I. Hungate, Jr., *A Guide for Training Local Public Welfare Administrators* (Washington, D.C.: U.S. Department of Health, Education and Welfare—Welfare Administration, Bureau of Family Services, Division of Technical Training, 1964), pp. 10–11.
6. Gordon R. Clapp, "The Social Scientist and the Administrative Art," in Leonard B. White, ed., *The State of the Social Sciences* (Chicago: University of Chicago Press, 1956), pp. 395–396, 397.
7. Ordway Tead, "Reflections on the Art of Administration," *Hospital Administration*, Winter 1959, pp. 10–11.
8. Samuel Goldman, *The School Principal* (New York: The Center for Applied Research in Education, Inc., 1966), p. 92.
9. Chris Argyris, *Executive Leadership—An Appraisal of a Manager in Action* (New York: Harper and Brothers, 1953), p. 23.
10. Rensis Likert, *The Human Organization—Its Management and Value* (New York: McGraw-Hill Book Company, 1967), p. 63.
11. *Proceedings of Workshop*, p. 3.
12. Likert, *The Human Organization*, p. 47.
13. David Moment and Abraham Zaleznik, *Role Development and Interpersonal Competence* (Boston: Harvard University, Graduate School of Business Administration, Division of Research, 1963), p. 158.
14. Warren G. Bennis, "Problem-Oriented Administration," *Hospital Administration*, Winter 1960, p. 53.
15. A. D. Green, "The Professional Worker in the Bureaucracy," *Social Service Review*, March 1966, pp. 82–83.
16. Cornelius Utz, "The Responsibility of Administration for Maximizing the Contribution of the Casework Staff," *Social Casework*, March 1964, pp. 138–139.
17. Graham C. Taylor, "Executive Stress," in Alan McLean, ed., *To Work Is Human—Mental Health and the Business Community* (New York: The Macmillan Company, 1967), p. 158.
18. *Guidelines in Labor-Management Relations* (New York: National Association of Social Workers, March 7, 1968), p. 3.
19. *Standards for Social Work Personnel Practices* (New York: National Association of Social Workers, 1968), p. 7.
20. John C. Nebo, *Administration of School Social Work* (New York: National Association of Social Workers, 1958), pp. 34–35.
21. *Standards for Social Work Personnel Practices*, pp. 7–8.
22. Henry H. Albers, *Principles of Management*, 3rd ed. (New York: John Wiley & Sons, Inc., 1969), pp. 255–256.
23. John Walton, *Administration and Policy-Making in Education* (Baltimore: The Johns Hopkins Press, 1959), p. 104.
24. David H. Rhinelander, "Hartford Hospital Notes First in Attitude Survey Program," *The Hartford Courant*, February 26, 1967, p. 24.

25. Albers, *Principles of Management,* pp. 188–189.
26. Reed K. Clegg, *The Administrator in Public Welfare* (Springfield, Ill.: Charles C. Thomas Publisher, 1966), pp. 71–72.
27. Robert L. Barker and Thomas L. Briggs, *Differential Use of Social Work Manpower* (New York: National Association of Social Workers, 1968), p. 53.
28. Laura Epstein, "Differential Use of Staff: A Method to expand Social Services," *Social Work,* October 1962, p. 66.
29. Ibid., pp. 66–67.
30. Ibid., p. 68.
31. Ibid., p. 72.
32. Barker and Briggs, *Social Work Manpower,* p. 270.
33. Paul Weinberger, "Job Satisfaction and Staff Retention in Social Work," National Association of Social Workers *News,* March 1970.

6 The Administrator and the Board*

The social work administrator is responsible for working with and giving leadership to the board of his agency. The board may be either policy-making or advisory.

In this country, from its very beginning, there has been a great tradition of citizen participation and volunteer service in community affairs. Cohen calls citizen participation "the backbone of democracy."[1] Service on boards is a part of this system of personal responsibility for meeting social welfare needs. Seider sets it in a broad framework when she says, "Volunteers are a traditional and integral part of the American social welfare system. . . . The specific duties assigned differ from agency to agency. . . . These may be classified as: (1) identifiers of human conditions or problems requiring social welfare services; (2) initiators and makers of policy in agencies created to prevent, control, or treat the social condition; (3) contributors of service based on knowledge, skill, and interest; (4) solicitors of public and voluntary support; (5) spokesmen and interpreters of agency program and problems in which they are directed; (6) reporters of community reaction, critical or positive, to the agency's program; and (7) collaborators in community planning activities for the purpose of modifying or designing services to meet changing social conditions."[2]

As was reported in a national survey, "volunteer work, in general, can be divided into three types: executive and policy-making, administration, and direct service. The job of the board volunteer is essentially advisory or policy-making, as it has been traditionally. Such volunteers are found

---

* Most of the material in this chapter appeared in Harleigh B. Trecker, *Citizen Boards at Work—New Challenges to Effective Action* (New York: Association Press, 1970).

not only on the boards of voluntary and non-profit agencies but also participating in such community services as school boards, planning, and other local government operations. Administrative volunteers may be engaged primarily in fund raising, but their functions may also include assisting in management or supervising other volunteers. In some private agencies, volunteer members control personnel policy, set salary standards, and negotiate union contracts. Service volunteers give direct assistance to the agency client." [3]

Administrative Philosophy and the Board

As Millett puts it, "Administration is not and cannot be a one-man show. No enterprise can be performed by one person, unless it is the most simple of endeavors. Administration usually involves the cooperative efforts of many persons. Indeed, administration is a system of people working together, it is a pattern of cooperative activity in which the specialized talents of various individuals are brought together to achieve a common purpose. By definition, I am disposed to say that administration is a team operation." [4]

As has been stated previously, the social work administrator must have a philosophy that is basic to the carrying forward of the work of his agency. The following concepts are offered as a summary of that philosophy.

1. *The concept of the work group:* Social welfare services are carried on by groups of people working together to solve problems, to make decisions, to establish legislation, to create policy, to determine needs, to develop programs and procedures. These *work groups* include the board, the staff, various committees, community groups, and others. Some of these groups are established by the legal instruments of the agency, namely, the articles of incorporation, the constitution, or the by-laws. Some of the groups are special ones set up to deal with special problems. Each group, whether it be regular or special, has authority, responsibility, and limits as granted by the legal articles or the appointing authority. While each group is similar to every other group, each group is also different. Some groups are made up of direct service participants, and some are made up of representatives who are a number of steps removed from the services being rendered. Boards usually fall into this category, but increasingly, service participants and recipients of service are being included on boards.

2. *The concept of leadership:* The various work groups mentioned above require leadership if they are to accomplish their assigned tasks. None of these groups is leaderless. All of them require the efforts of people, particularly prepared and particularly competent to enable them to understand their jobs and get them done. These leaders are both profes-

sional workers and volunteers. The methods they use should be essentially democratic.

3. *The concept of the leadership team:* In most community agencies, leadership is given to these work groups by teams of persons. The usual team consists of the professional worker and the lay or volunteer worker. By this is meant the chairman of the board of education and the superintendent of schools; the chairman of the board and the social agency administrator; the library board and the professional librarian. This team pattern proceeds across the agency structure with committee chairmen frequently teaming up with related staff members and so on. Teamwork is the heart of democratic administrative leadership. In fact, the way the social work administrator and the board president work together does much to set the tone of the entire organization.

4. *The concept of structure:* In every community agency, there are work groups simultaneously going about their affairs. Thus, it is necessary to arrange these groups into a form of organization or structure that will show people as being interconnected and in communication with one another. Out of the continuous relatedness and communication of these work groups comes the totality of the agency or organization.

5. *The concept of time and timing:* As the professional and volunteer team provide leadership for the work groups, the work groups go through a cycle that can be plotted on a time continuum. Each session of the work group requires different leadership as the group becomes better able to fulfill its task role. Each session of the work group produces a product, and subsequent sessions grow out of what has been accomplished before. The leadership needs of the work group change, making it necessary for the leadership team to redefine the ways in which it will work. Leadership roles are dynamic and changing just as work groups are dynamic and changing.

6. *The concept of coordination:* Because the many work groups are engaged in a variety of tasks and are usually at different stages in their progress, they must coordinate their several separate efforts if maximum output is to occur. The task of providing the impetus for this coordination and the mechanisms for its occurrence are primary in the portfolio of the social work administrator and the board president. Coordination skills are also paramount in key leaders such as board presidents and social work administrators.

7. *The concept of reporting, decision-making, and implementation of decisions:* As the many work groups carry forward their endeavors, it is necessary to prepare reports for transmittal to the parent authority. Then decisions must be made and plans prepared for the implementation of the decision. In all agencies, especially in large ones that have scores of work groups, the questions of when to report, what to report, and to whom

to assign follow-up are of great importance. Having done this, a new cycle of activity gets under way.

Functions of the Administrative Board

The functions of the administrative board can be summed up in this fashion: 1) To establish the legal or corporate existence of the agency, whether it be under the auspices of government or voluntary efforts; 2) To take responsibility for formulating general objectives, policies, and programs; 3) To inspire community confidence in the program because of the competence and dedication of the board members as active trustees of the agency; 4) To assume responsibility for the provision of adequate finances and to be accountable for the expenditure of funds; 5) To provide conditions of work, personnel policies, and staff. The boards are particularly responsible for the selection and evaluation of the administrator; 6) To understand and interpret the work of the agency to the community; 7) To study, know, and interpret general community needs to the agency staff; 8) To relate the services of the agency to the work of other agencies and to concentrate upon the improvement of community conditions; 9) To conduct periodic evaluations of agency operations with a view toward improving and strengthening the amount and quality of work that is done; 10) To provide the continuity of experienced leadership so that major staff changes will not weaken the agency.

Writing from his perspective as a social work administrator, Schmidt lists nine responsibilities of the board: "1) Attaining the goals or purposes of the agency . . . making certain that the established goals are being pursued and advising when the goals need changing because of changed conditions. . . . 2) Creating the structure . . . the board has the responsibility of seeing to it that the agency's legal structure is proper and that it continues to remain so under all state and federal laws. . . . 3) Providing the necessary facilities . . . needed by an agency to conduct its activities . . . 4) Employing the executive . . . select, fix compensation, establish duties, delegate to him the necessary authority to administer the work of the agency, evaluate his work, relieve him of his duties if necessary. . . . 5) Fixing the policies. . . . It is the duty of the board to prescribe the services to be provided as well as the basic policies for the administration of these services. . . . 6) Setting the budget and providing the finances. . . . The obligation rests upon the governing board to set the budget and thereby establish services. . . . 7) Checking the operation. . . . The board must check the operations periodically and see to it that all is going well. . . . The trustees of an agency are accountable to the public for their stewardship of the agency. . . . They must know that the services are provided as they have directed. 8) Interpreting the services . . . is a special concern of the members of the governing board. . . . 9) Participating in community planning. . . . The board has a clear duty to participate in community efforts to plan and raise funds for health and welfare operations." [5]

The Minnesota Department of Public Welfare has an excellent handbook for county welfare board members. In it it states: "In reviewing the role of the county welfare board it is necessary for the board as a group and as individual members to understand the legal basis for the composition and organization of welfare boards in the State of Minnesota . . . the law clearly states that it is the welfare board that has the responsibility for administering the public welfare program in Minnesota. Consequently, welfare board members must have an understanding of public welfare programs and services even though the board hires professional staff to carry out these responsibilities. First of all, it is incumbent upon the welfare board member to have some knowledge of public welfare and the social problems which exist on a state and nation-wide basis, as well as doing everything possible to increase his understanding of the needs of his own community and the social services which are required to alleviate or correct the social problems existing therein. Board members need to learn about the way in which their board is organized. They should learn about its chief functions and the way these functions should be performed so that an effective welfare program will be carried on in their community." [6]

The Administrator at Work with the Board

The way the agency board and the administrator work together is of tremendous importance. This fact holds true in all fields of community service and in all types of agencies, governmental and voluntary. In thousands of social welfare agencies, work is done by two groups of people. There are the hundreds of thousands of volunteer board members who enter into or offer themselves for service by their own free will and without remuneration. Working along with these volunteers are professional staffs who have acquired special knowledge as a result of professional education and experience. They are engaged in social work as a means of livelihood. They have been hired to guide, advise, and work with the boards. There is a general agreement that both groups of workers are needed and have important tasks to do. Certain assumptions underlie the way they must work together if the goals of the enterprises are to be achieved.

First it is assumed that the volunteer board members and the professional workers of the agency constitute a leadership team. They are partners in a common task. In discussing the concept of partnership and shared responsibility, one agency states: "Leadership in the Y.W.C.A. is both volunteer and employee. Volunteers bring to the Association not only their own individual skills, abilities, and often accumulated Y.W.C.A. experience but a broad knowledge of the community as well—its resources and organizations, its patterns of life, its feelings, its tensions, its values, its sources of pride. The contributions of the employed leaders include individual skills and experience, knowledge of specialized resources for program and administration, an objective way of looking at the community and the Y.W.C.A. with understanding and insight, and concentrated time for the work." [7]

Second, it is assumed that professionals and volunteers have specific responsibilities as well as common and shared responsibilities. Both groups are fundamentally motivated by a common interest in and a wish to serve people. As for the professional workers, their primary role is that of carrying on or providing the program of professional services that the agency is set up to offer. For the volunteer workers, their chief responsibility is generally thought of as that of providing the conditions under which the agency may render the best quality of service. To a great extent, there is an overlapping of responsibilities between professionals and board members. This will be elaborated upon later in the discussion of policy-making.

Third, it is assumed that communication is of the utmost importance as board, staff, and administrator work together. They must be in continuous communication about the major concerns of the agency if they are to define, understand, and carry their separate and combined responsibilities.

Fourth, it is assumed that volunteer board members and professional workers have much to learn from one another. In fact, their learnings are continuous as board members glean insights from the problems faced by staff and as staff develop a grasp of the feedback from the community by the board.

If the above assumptions are correct, what is meant by the term "role" when used in connection with either the professional or the board member? In this context, role means a set of tasks that the individual is expected to perform in the defined agency situation. In other words, it is a work role. A work role is a function allocated to a particular person. In the social agency, role has the dimension of the task or what is expected of the person, and it has the further dimension of responsibility as to how the task will be done and in what time span. The concept further assumes that persons so entrusted with tasks will have the competence necessary to fulfill those tasks. Furthermore, to define the role of the professional worker, it is necessary to define the role of the volunteer because what they do is so interrelated.

Admitting the fact that there are many variables of agency size, situation, community conditions, purposes, and so on, it is likely that the professional staff member will frame his role by selecting items from the task needs of the organization. Because the professional social worker is prepared by education and experience to bring professional knowledge and skill to the job, it is right to assume the exercise of professional skills in providing service to people. The employing agency has hired staff precisely for this reason. Consequently, a major role would seem to be that of doing work of the agency. Because the board is the policy-making group that decides what work is to be done, it can be assumed that policy-making is its primary role. Every board member, thus, must be committed to a partially predetermined role. But because the agency is dynamic and changing, purposes, policies, and programs are also in a constant state of flux. This means that the professional worker has the further task of bringing to the policy-making board information needed to arrive at sound policy judgments in terms of either formulation or revision. Thus, the professional worker cannot be removed from the policy-making process because he must carry the role of helping the policy-making group to arrive at the best possible decisions. The way in which the worker fulfills this policy participation role varies with the position occupied. Obviously, the agency administrator has a great responsibility in this realm, which would not be so for the beginning junior staff member.

So the role of the volunteer board is policy determination. The board must determine policies regarding purpose, program, personnel, finance, public relations, and the like. But board members bring to the agency general life experience rather than specific professional education. Out of their general experience they have the responsibility to study and understand and interpret community needs for service. They must know the history, purpose, programs, policies, and prevailing procedures of the agency. They must seek constantly to evaluate the work of the agency to assure that policies are not only being carried out but that they are achieving the agency goals. But they cannot do this alone. They must do so in cooperation with the executive and staff. There must be a coming together of insight, experience, wisdom, and professional expertise. Policies, of course, are voted by the board, but no board can make wise judgments without the contribution of the staff members who have the firsthand experience with the services being rendered and the clientele being served.

A review of literature on the role of the social work administrator in his work with the board shows that the following points are frequently discussed. 1) The administrator instruments the policies of the board. 2) The administrator prepares reports, budgets, personnel recommendations, program plans, and other information to keep the board well informed. The administrator reports on needs in the agency and in the community that indicate that changes in services may be required. 3) The administrator is the liaison between the board and the staff and other agencies. 4) The administrator is responsible for a program of in-service training to improve services. Help is given to board members to develop their skills both within the agency service and externally in community relations. 5) The administrator is a key person in helping the board to understand its job and perform its tasks. However, the administrator does not seek to dominate or control the board. 6) The administrator interprets policies and actions of the board in the agency and in the community. 7) The executive helps in the selection of board members but, of course, does not make the final selection.

Administrators Describe Their Role with Their Boards

In an interview study, a number of social work administrators were asked to describe their role with the boards as they saw it and tried to carry it out. All of them stated that it was their responsibility to carry out the decisions of the board and to translate the board's policies into action. The majority felt that they were suppliers of information to the board as aides to the making of policy decisions. They felt that data such as reports of operating experience, service statistics, and the like were essential to effective board decision-making. Approximately three-fourths of the administrators interviewed saw the supplying of information as only a subsidiary part of their major role, namely, that of supplying leadership for the board to help it develop policies, provide resources, and make the agency more valuable and useful to the community. They agreed that it was their continuing task to stimulate the board to devote time and attention to the major problems of the agency. They assumed that it was their job to encourage the board to develop its powers of judgment and discrimination in the always vital area of policy-making. Recognizing the inevitable gap between the board and persons served, these administrators stressed the fact that they had a key job in helping the board to understand the program of services being offered. They saw themselves as interpreters of changing conditions in the community and as the initiators of program changes based upon revised policies.

The same administrators reported that they carried an important liaison role between the board and the staff. This role frequently had dual aspects, helping the board members become more aware of problems encountered by the staff in providing services (and staff problems in general) as well as interpreting staff attitudes and thinking; helping the staff to understand board thinking and attitudes. Other administrators reported that it was a major responsibility of theirs to work with individual board members to help them to develop their capabilities and to enable them to make the maximum possible contribution to the agency. Some administrators stated or implied that it was their role to bring and interpret the values, standards, and principles underlying good practice in their field of service.

As the interviewed administrators described their role, certain words appeared again and again. The most frequently used words were to stimulate, to interpret, to guide, to motivate, to integrate, to initiate, to direct, to advise, and to suggest. Two-thirds of these administrators used several of these words denoting a philosophy of active leadership insofar as their work with the board was concerned.[8]

In another study, the author discovered that social work administrators saw their role with the board growing out of ten major areas of executive leadership responsibility that they felt had to be exercised in the total work of the agency. They stressed that they took responsibility for planning and coordination, helping to formulate clear plans and then coordinating the work of various individuals and groups within the structure of the total agency; facilitating communication, keeping the channels open within the organization; presenting knowledge of the total agency so that various groups would develop understanding; providing an organized work environment in which group and individual tasks are defined, carried forward, and coordinated; helping to develop clear assignments of responsibilities for board and staff members; analyzing tasks in terms of their relevance to specific aspects of program; studying, understanding, and interpreting the community situation in which the work of the agency takes place; establishing and maintaining effective working relationships with the groups to which defined tasks have been assigned; making continuous and creative use of the purpose of the agency with the board, the staff, and the community; providing opportunities for individuals to experience creative growth in their jobs.[9]

The Administrator and the Chairman of the Board

The way the board chairman and the agency administrator work together is a major factor in agency operation. If their relationship is a good one, they can be fairly sure that they will set a pattern for other relationships throughout the agency. If it is a poor one, this also will be influential.

The administrator and the board chairman are the persons who make up the primary leadership team. To lead effectively, they must have: 1) An understanding and acceptance of and a deep commitment to the basic values of the agency; 2) Substantial knowledge of the professional services that the agency is rendering to people; 3) A strong identification with the fundamental purposes of the agency. Administrators and chairmen are continuously engaged in establishing effective working relationships with the people. Getting work done to accomplish agency purposes is primarily a matter of motivating people to their finest and highest levels of achievement.

As one observes effective board chairmen at work they seem to have certain basic characteristics. *First,* they are well informed about the work of the agency; they have the facts; they know what they are talking about because they have spent long hours studying the work of the agency they represent. *Second,* they care deeply about the work of the agency; they couple competence and concern with commitment. *Third,* they see the connection between conditions that exist in the community and the need for the agency to provide services. *Fourth,* they know how to work within and through their organization and in cooperation with other organizations that have similar goals. *Fifth,* they have a sense of history and a grasp of the processes of orderly, democratic change. *Sixth,* the effective chairman is generally aware of what is happening in the field and strives to keep up with new developments and new trends.

What are some of the major responsibilities carried by the leadership team of the administrator and the board chairman? A partial list would include: 1) They are responsible for giving leadership to the continuous process of identifying community needs. 2) They are responsible for giving leadership to, defining, and realizing agency purposes. 3) They are responsible for giving leadership to provisioning the agency in terms of financial resources and other forms of support. 4) They are responsible for giving leadership to the development of program and services. 5) They are responsible for giving leadership to the development of a form of organization and structure that will support the program. 6) They are responsible for giving leadership to the continuing process of policy formulation and reformulation. 7) They are responsible for giving leadership to the evaluation of the agency. 8) They are responsible for giving leadership to the change process.

However, in carrying these responsibilities, the chairman and the administrator clearly cannot do everything themselves. They must work with and through many persons in creative and productive ways. The work of the administrator and the board chairman is thus seen as a process of working with people in ways that release and relate their energies so that they use all available resources to accomplish the purpose of providing needed social welfare services and programs. People, resources, and purposes are thus brought together by the administrator and the board chairman in a continuous dynamic process. The administrator and the chairman, as the primary leadership team, are seen as working with people to establish and maintain a system of cooperative effort with the total agency as the point of focus. Because many people must carry separate and specific tasks if the agency is to do its work, and because they inevitably see only a part of the picture, the job of seeing the whole agency and providing overall leadership falls to the administrator and the board chairman.

The board chairman and the administrator are also responsible for community leadership. This means the taking of initiative in helping people know about, understand, and hopefully be in support of the important work that the agency is doing. It also means sharing leadership with other agencies that have like goals and that have a reasonable similarity of values and convictions as to what kind of a community it should be.

Of great importance in assessing the relationship between the executive and the board chairman is the extent to which they truly trust each other and have confidence in each other. When trust and confidence prevail, it is apt to permeate the institution and be reflected in the other essential team relationships among staff members and committee chairmen and the like. Here it is basic that board chairmen and administrators see their leadership as being essentially helping, enabling, and supporting so that an increasing number of new leaders will be developed year after year. Thus, board chairmen and administrators must maintain many relationships simultaneously. They must make more decisions and more complicated decisions.

While the administrator is in no sense "supervised" by the board chairman, the chairman and the board do have the responsibility to evaluate the work of the executive at periodic intervals. Regular evaluation rather than crisis evaluation is of great importance. The executive has a right to know how the board views his work, and the board has the responsibility to share its views with him.

The Administrator, the Board, and Policy-making

One of the crucial responsibilities of the board and the administrator is that of policy-making. While there is a widespread agreement that it is the job of the board to make policy and the job of the administrator to carry it out, there is ample evidence to support the thesis that it is not so simplistic as it sounds. In fact, the process of policy-making is so involved and so complicated today that it often looms as an area of conflict and confusion. As Stein pointed out: "We have been told in no uncertain terms that policy determination is the responsibility of the board alone, that policy execution is the responsibility of the executive and staff, that the executive is ultimately responsible for the results of agency programs. Nearly everyone understands these points, and yet boards and executives have had trouble ever since there were boards and executives. It is not, of course, only in social work that problems arise. Every field has its own version of the same *concerns*." [10]

Perhaps a part of the problem is caused by the fact that persons are not clear on the meaning of the term "policy." A look at a number of definitions reveals a variety of meanings. One national youth agency declares: "A policy is an established course of action to be followed in recurring situations. . . . Policies serve many purposes. They point the way for developing plans, solving problems, and attaining objectives. They provide the framework for carrying out the work and the means by which the board can delegate authority and still maintain control. They permit uniformity and consistency of action throughout the council. For example, in dealing with a question covered by a policy affecting troops, all personnel concerned are able to handle the question in the same way. They bring about quick and effective decisions. Without a governing policy it would be necessary to refer each case as it occurs to the board for decision. When there is a policy, the detection can be made at the point of occurence without delay." [11]

In the field of education, one writer defines the role of the board as "legislative, that is, the establishing of policies and the role of the superintendent as administrative, or the carrying out of policies. By definition, policies are principles adopted by the board . . . to chart a course of action for its administrator and to define the limits within which he shall exercise judgment and directions. Essentially, policies are a guide to the what, why, and the how much of desired educational operations." The same authority goes on to say that "rules and regulations, as distinguished from policies, are the detailed directions necessary to put policies into effect. They are more likely to be formulated by the administrator with the informal approval of the board than to be initiated or formally acted upon by the board itself. Essentially, rules and regulations provide a blueprint as to the how, the who, the when, and the where of actual educational practice. Procedures are working rules, or bylaws for the board itself as it regards its organization, meetings . . . order of business, minutes and the like." [12]

With brevity and focus, Faatz said agency policies are written statements "which express the purpose, intentions, conditions under which the agency effectuates the service for which it was created." [13]

Reid says, "The board's responsibility includes establishing the basic policies of the agency and constantly reexamining and modifying those policies." [14] Sher agrees that "the board has a profound responsibility, in partnership with administration, to establish policies dealing with such matters as determining priority in offering service. Equally important, it should join with other enlightened people in the community to determine ways and means of making such services available to the total community on a broader community and governmental level." In addition, Sher observes: "If policies are to be wisely fashioned, they must stem from a basic grasp of the agency's purpose within the community and of the extent to which that purpose is met by the agency." [15]

Sorenson says, "Policy formulation and planning are the responsibility of both board and committee members and of professional staff. . . . Policy determination is the responsibility of the board alone. . . . Policy execution is the responsibility of the executive and his staff." [16]

There is increasing evidence to support the notion that while the board must determine what the policy is to be a great many people should be involved in working with the board to help it understand how to make wise policy decisions. Surely the administrator and the staff have a great deal to contribute. But what about the persons being served by the program, some would say that clients should have no part in the policy process; yet how can the policy be in tune with the views of the constituency unless they too are involved? There is a rising tide of feeling that policies should not be made by remote boards and then simply imposed upon persons on a "take it or leave it" basis. As Jennrich declared: "All persons affected by policy should have some part in creating it, and any social agency that operates under the hoary concept that the board alone makes policies and the staff alone carries them out, should be well on the road to extinction. Ideally, on major policies, neither the executive nor his board nor staff should make final decisions, since the community that picks up the check for these costly services should be involved. Only as we work toward responsible participation and integration of policy-making and operations can we have a dynamic agency." [17]

In his study of voluntary social welfare agencies, Kramer isolated five variables that influence the extent to which the will of the board or the executive would predominate the policy process. "1) The organizational structure of the agency; its size, complexity, and degree of bureaucracy. 2) The character of the agency's services or program, whether they are technical or highly professionalized in content or conceived as residual or institutional in character. 3) The type of policy, e.g., programmatic, housekeeping, professional, ideological, or fiscal. 4) Aspects of the board member's status and relationship to the agency, such as the duration of his membership, degree of financial responsibility and contributions, role as a consumer of agency services, or participant in its program; the number of his other organizational affiliations and his social status in the community. 5) The executive's professional status and duration of employment . . . the executive exerts a greater influence than the board member in the policy process to the extent that these variables are maximized." [18]

What are the sources of data, information, opinion, thinking, and feeling that must be considered in the important task of policy-making? Beyond the defined purpose of the agency, it seems necessary to recognize that other things enter into policy-making. *First,* there is the matter of specific community characteristics and conditions that will influence what services should be provided, to whom they are to be given, and how they should be conducted. *Second,* there is a major source of policy material in the operating experience of the agency critically reviewed and evaluated. *Third,* suggestions from persons served, clientele, and general constituency represent a vital source of data and expression both regarding need for policies and how they should be stated. *Fourth,* current best practice as revealed by study and research in the field should be considered. *Fifth,* interagency cooperative projects often provide useful material for policy determination. *Sixth,* special committees such as professional advisory groups may offer experience particularly pertinent to a given policy problem. *Seventh,* agencies that are a part of a national organization may receive much help from communicating with their parent body.

Many Persons Involved in Policy-Making

The process of policy determination consists of a series of steps or phases in which many persons play a part. The board, the administrator, the staff, the constituency, and the community must all become involved. Any one of these groups or individuals within them may feel, recognize, and express the need for a stated policy to guide some phase of the work of the agency. The policy process thus can begin at any point. When the need is recognized and accepted by the board, responsibility for fact-gathering and preliminary formulation of tentative policy must be assigned. The assignment can be made to the administrator and the staff, or it can be made through a board committee, or it can be made to a joint committee of board, staff, and constituency. In any event, as a matter of principle, those persons to be affected by the policy should participate in the presentation of facts, suggestions, and ideas prior to the first formulation. Although they may not be legally responsible for the ultimate decision, their views are important if the final policy is to be understood and followed.

Ordinarily, it is wise and helpful to prepare a trial formulation of a new policy and give consideration to the implications of it before it is enacted. Thought must be given to the effect of the policy on persons served, program, budget, staff workload, and community relations. It is time well spent to check up on the impact of the policy in advance of adoption. In some situations, a new policy may be tried out on a time-limited basis before it is permanently enacted. When a policy has been adopted, it is vital that a timetable be established for its review and a decision made as to who will be responsible for the review. When major policy changes are to be made, time must be devoted to advance interpretation of them as a way of preparing the persons affected by them. As a general rule, policy-making should proceed in an atmosphere of openness and sharing with maximum participation on the part of the people involved. Good policies grow out of a process of participation on the part of many individuals and groups. They are evolutionary and flow out of operations to a great extent. Policies are tools for the board, the administrator, the staff, and the constituency to use. Policies should be positive statements clearly offered as helpful tools for those who follow and implement them.

In summary, good policies should be based upon and develop out of the agency purpose. Adequately evaluated facts are the essential ingredients in policy formulation and reformulation. Persons affected by policy should share in the creation of it. There must be an organic unity and consistency among the various policies of the agency, and the relationships between policies and purposes should be apparent. Although the board has the legal responsibility for the final determination of policy, the entire agency should participate in the process leading up to the final decision. Policy-making, planning, and operations are integrally related and cannot be disassociated. New policies should grow out of the evaluation of the effectiveness of old policies. The carrying out of policies in the spirit of their intent is an integral part of the administrative responsibility of the administrator and the staff.

Problems of Administrators and Boards

In some agencies, the administrator and the board seem to have difficulty in working together. There seem to be problems that must be dealt with. *First,* there is the problem of confusion between board and administrator as to respective roles and responsibilities. In some situations, the board and the administrator seem to be working at cross-purposes and getting in one another's way. The most serious problem seems to center around the differences between policy determination, which is the primary legal responsibility of the board, and administration of policy, which is the job of the administrator and the staff. When clarity is lacking with reference to these functions, there are bound to be many situations where major difficulties can arise. *Second,* in far too many agencies, particularly the large ones, there is inadequate communication, slow communication, or even breakdown in communication between the administrator and the board. Under these circumstances, the board is not fully informed as to what is going on, and as a result, it is out of touch with current policies, programs, and procedures. Consequently, it may work at cross-purposes and with a considerable waste of energy. *Third,* sometimes administrators feel that board members are not doing a good job of interpretation in the community. They feel that they are not utilizing their normal and natural community contacts to tell the story of the agency effectively and to build growing public understanding. This same charge is sometimes stated by board members who feel that the administrator as the first-line representative in the community fails to capitalize on opportunities for good public relations. *Fourth,* in some cases, the board fails in its responsibility to do a regular, comprehensive evaluation of the work of the administrator. The administrator does not know where he stands. In some instances, the failure to evaluate periodically has resulted in very serious problems. *Fifth,* in some cases, the administrator does not really want the help of the board and prefers to operate as a one-man agency.

Problems of the kind listed above are in no way new, unusual, or universal. Every situation is different, and no one situation will have all of these problems, but most situations have a chance of occasionally having some of them. When these problems exist, they result from reasons that can be enumerated. For example, agencies have not given enough thought and study to the matter of board-administrator relationships. They have tended to assume that good relationships develop automatically without any particular planned effort. This is not true. Some agencies have not been careful enough in choosing the administrator, and they have not been careful enough in choosing board members. Consequently, incompatability results.

When the administrator and the board are working in harmony, the agency can be seen and felt as united. The responsibility for achieving this unity is shared by both parties.

NOTES

1. Nathan Cohen, *The Citizen Volunteer* (New York: Harper & Row, 1960), Chap. 3.
2. Violet Seider, "Volunteers," *Encyclopedia of Social Work* (New York: National Association of Social Workers, 1965), pp. 830–836.
3. *American Volunteer*, Manpower/Automation Research Monograph No. 10, April 1969, p. 7. U.S. Department of Labor, Manpower Administration.
4. John D. Millett, "National Conference of Professors of Educational Administration," *The Community School and Its Administration*, Vol. IV, No. 1, September 1965, p. 2.
5. William D. Schmidt, *The Executive and the Board in Social Welfare* (Cleveland: Howard Allen, Inc., 1959), pp. 39–50.
6. *Handbook for County Welfare Board Members* (St. Paul, Minn.: Division of Field Services, Minnesota Department of Public Welfare, n.d.), p. 23.
7. *The Board and the Executive Director* (New York: National Board, Y.W.C.A., 1953), p. 6.
8. Harleigh B. Trecker, *Social Agency Boards—An Exploratory Study* (School of Social Work, University of Connecticut, 1958).
9. Harleigh B. Trecker, "Understandings of Administration," *Y.W.C.A. Magazine* (June 1960).
10. Herman D. Stein, "Board, Executive, and Staff," *Social Welfare Forum 1962*. (Published for the National Conference on Social Welfare by Columbia University Press, 1962), p. 217.
11. *The Council Manual*, Copyright © 1960, 1969 by Girl Scouts of the U.S.A., p. 23. Used by permission.
12. Edward M. Tuttle, *School Board Leadership in America*, rev. ed. (Danville, Ill.: The Interstate Printers, 1963), p. 107. Reproduced by special permission of the author and copyright owner, Edward Mowbray Tuttle.
13. Anita J. Faatz, *The Nature of Policy in the Administration of Public Assistance* (Pennsylvania School of Social Work, University of Pennsylvania, Philadelphia, 1943).
14. Joseph H. Reid, "The Board's Responsibility," in *The Board Member of a Social Agency* (New York: Child Welfare League of America, Inc., 1957), p. 26.
15. David Sher, "Boards Must Do More Than Manage," in *Making Yours a Better Board* (New York: Family Service Association of America, 1954), pp. 36–38.
16. Roy Sorenson, *The Art of Board Membership* (New York: Association Press, 1950), p. 30.
17. Lorraine H. Jennrich, "Social Policy Comes from Knowing Families," in *Making Yours a Better Board* (New York: Family Service Association, 1954), p. 34.
18. Ralph M. Kramer, "Ideology, Status, and Power in Board-Executive Relationships," *Social Work*, October 1965, p. 114.

7 Constituency and Community— Partners in Administration

One of the newest developments in social work administration is the extent to which agencies are seeking to involve the persons they serve in the administration of the agency. While it is true that social agencies have always had some kind of a relationship with clientele or constituency, the trend in recent years has been to make this relationship more meaningful and truly dynamic.

Traditionally, the private agencies have been voluntary nonprofit corporations essentially owned and operated by upper-class individuals who made possible a wide range of services through their leadership, financial support, and so forth. This is not to say that their motives were evil. In fact, the opposite was the case. But power, especially in boards, rested with the managerial, professional, and entreprenurial segment of the society rather than with the people served. The federated financing movement after World War I really brought corporate business interests into the financing, planning, and decision-making. In fact, agencies seemed to be controlled by remote "downtown" forces. When government became more involved in the human services, public agencies were dominated by a top-down hierarchial power approach.

Challenges to the "system" grew when in 1964 the Economic Opportunity Act became law and the Office of Economic Opportunity was required by law to assure "maximum feasible participation" of neighborhood people in program development. This same requirement was written in to the Model Cities Act of 1966 and in subsequent related legislation. It became evident that the earlier distinction between "providers" of services and "recipients" of services was no longer possible. Proponents of the new system of client involvement spoke of it as the democratic way, with inputs of actual experience combining with services and creating an indispensable new area of knowledge. They added that the wider the participation, the stronger the agency and the more realistic the evaluation of its services. Opponents claimed that client involvement was too time-consuming, that it was impossible to get real representation, and that administrative control and authority would be weakened.

The Importance of Participation

Yet it soon became evident that client and community participation was basically helpful to agency administration because: 1) Clients have a contribution to make out of their experience and knowledge in the real-life situation. 2) They have a right to a role in policy-making because they are most affected by the policy. 3) They have skills to contribute as a supplement to professional know-how. 4) They are in the best possible position to evaluate the agency. 5) They are people who basically want to take on responsibility.

Many of the institutions of society are undergoing a similar surge of interest in, even demand for, relevant participation on the part of persons served. Colleges, universities, public schools, churches, government agencies are all engaged in one way or another in restructuring their services so that a greater share in governance is allocated to the clientele. The power to make decisions once reserved exclusively for the board has now shifted to include staff and constituency in appropriate ways. Thus, the social work administrator must develop his skill in working effectively with the persons the agency serves.

In field after field, the importance of broad participation has been accented. In community organization and planning, the matter of citizen participation has received extended treatment. Gurin and Perlman offer a brilliant discussion of the theory of participation and raise a number of fundamental questions. They say:

In the social welfare field, planning and community organization have been closely linked, particularly at the local community level. The common element is citizen participation, a concept that holds a firm place, historically, in all types of social welfare activities. In theory, the responsibility for setting goals and developing plans lies with the responsible policy-making bodies of the community and the professional role is one of serving these groups and enabling them to achieve their objectives. So much has been written on this subject in recent years, that we feel no need to review the different concepts of planning roles that have been put forward. Let us assume it has been demonstrated that the so-called enabling role is never pure, and that it is intermixed with elements of expertness and leadership. There remains the issues of *what* citizen? Participation in *what?* These questions need further discussion. Citizens' participation involves both the development of plans, including setting goals, and the implementation of plans. There has always been interest in developing citizen participation in both areas. Each presents its own problems. On the level of formulative goals and policies, it is not always clear where the responsibilities should be. Even in areas where the responsibility is fixed by legislation, as in the case of boards of education or departments of public welfare, there is room for discretion in the extent to which this responsibility will be shared by others, at least in an advisory capacity. Since there is no such single entity as a "community," it becomes necessary to locate and choose the people who are to engage in these roles, and to develop a rationale that will provide the criteria for such selection. The engineering of participation, hopefully democratic, therefore becomes a major planning function in itself. The tendency to stress direct participation by citizens in formulating the policy of operating agencies obscures the fact that the basic structure for participation in a democratic society is the governmental system, whereby citizens participate in formulating policy, not directly, but through their representatives. In major issues of social welfare, such as taxation, income maintenance, and provision of general services for the entire population, the crucial decisions are legislative. For policy to be established, the will of the people must be transmitted through the actions of those who make the laws. The function of community organization and social action is in large part to influence the lawmakers. That function is widely distributed through society. Administrators in charge of executing programs are a major element in policy formulation, and much of their planning is inevitably directed toward influencing the lawmakers to enhance and improve the programs for which they carry responsibility.[1]

Because it is evident that the agency constituency has a function beyond that of merely accepting services, the administrator must understand the place of constituents in the total administrative process of the agency. Among the many contributions of the constituency are: *first,* they can be helpful in pointing out the needs that must be met; *second,* constituency can give expression regarding the kinds of programs or services that are most likely to meet these needs; *third,* constituency can participate helpfully in the process of policy formulation and reformulation; *fourth,* constituency can become a vital resorce for agency interpretation and support; *fifth,* constituency can assist the agency in evaluating the quality of its work and can suggest ways of improving the services.

As Carlton says, "It seems to me that every voluntary social service agency today should seek the participation of those who use its services, its consumers, in formulating policy and judging program. . . . The reality is that no matter what the service may consist of, even though it involves the most highly technical, professional care, such as surgery in a hospital, the voice of the recipient of the services, patient, client, neighbor, local resident, consumer—whatever he's called—must be piped to management loud and clear. I state this categorically because the evidence of functional breakdown is so clear when his voice is not heard." [2]

Obtaining Significant Participation

It is interesting to note that one study revealed little real participation on the part of welfare clients. Schwartz and Chernin made a study of the participation of recipients in public welfare planning and administration. They found "that public welfare agencies had had little experience with client participation other than at the level of the caseworker-client relationships." They felt "that experimentation in recipient participation in welfare agency programming could profitably be initiated at local levels by group discussions with recipients and subsequent appointments of recipients to advisory committees. The results of this study further indicate that the incorporation of welfare recipient opinion into welfare agency planning might have a beneficial effect on the operation of these agencies and could stimulate new responses in welfare recipients by making them more aware of themselves as contributing members of society." [3]

In a brilliant paper, Fortin writes about the importance of client or consumer input in the field of children's protective services. He says, "When we ask the question of why client or consumer input into an agency such as the Children's Protective Services, we must remember that as a group, as well as individually the agency reflects certain beliefs that are in some relationship to the larger social and political system. The question of client participation is quite involved in how that belief system interlocks with the larger social order. Frankly, consumer input has and will probably continue to be a threat to the balance of that relationship since the ideology which supports that input is in relative conflict with the predominating values of society. [Thus great social changes are required.] Some are in the areas of *Leadership*—We must be careful of what we are leading. Leadership means representing *client group interest* also. This principle is necessary so that we do not fall into the recesses of professional elitism. In order to represent adequately we must have contact with the group. It also must be recognized that the interest of the staff and the client community may at times vary, or conflict; this calls for meaningful problem solving rather than neglecting client interest for short term staff goals. *Participation*—Members to the organization must be re-interpreted to include the client community. *Communication*—This includes the client community's right to know. *Morale*—This is a reflection of the ease or disease of the participation of the client community with the organization: Emphasis on the administrator's role of trouble-shooter, ombudsman for client and staff affairs." Fortin goes on to say that consumer input will only be effective if it is meaningful and he draws upon Louis Crown's excellent article, "Meaningful Consumer Participation—A Challenge to the Social Agency Administrator," which appears in *Social Work Administration—A Resource Book* published in New York in 1970 by the Council on Social Work Education and edited by Harry Schatz. "To be meaningful participation must: 1. Be representative of the *consumer* and the *community* served. 2. Be significant *numerically,* not mere tokenism. 3. Be representative of the various *sectors of society* affected by the agency (racial, ethnic, economic, and where appropriate age-related). 4. Be included in the *decision-making* process from the early stages of *planning* through *program development, delivery of service* and *evaluation.* 5. Permit *ease of access and attendance* at meetings by those less able to participate conveniently (subsidization, appropriate scheduling, provision of transportation, day care, etc.). 6. Provide adequate orientation, information, and *in-service training* as to the duties, rights, responsibilities and options of the participant role at various levels. 7. Encourage *increased involvement* of those concerned and afford the opportunity for growth to *higher levels of influence.* 8. Incorporate policies of recruitment and rotation to permit continual involvement of new participants." [4]

The Poor as a Constituent Group

The passage of the federal Economic Opportunity Act of 1964 in Section 202 (a)(3), dealing with community action programs, states that the program must be "developed, conducted, and administered with the maximum feasible participation of residents of the areas and members of the groups served." [5] This mandate from the Congress has had a profound influence not only on the antipoverty projects but also on many different kinds of community services.

A number of authorities have begun to do evaluative research on the "maximum feasible participation" concept. For example, in his research, Kramer describes four modes of resident participation by the poor in Community Action Programs [CAPs] financed by the Office of Economic Opportunity. He says, "The first mode of resident participation involved the process of . . . decision-making in which the poor were cast in the role of policy-makers as voting members of the governing board of directors. In this capacity, the representatives of the poor were regarded by OEO as essentially members of a tripartite coalition, along with the major governmental and voluntary welfare agencies, and the leadership of important elements in the community such as labor, business, religious, and minority groups. . . . A second mode of resident participation took place on the neighborhood level and was linked to the first through the elected representatives to the CAP's board of directors from the target area. The core process was one of program development; here the poor were initially viewed primarily as consumers who could give useful advice and suggestions to those responsible for the planning and delivery of social services. According to this view, a concern with resident participation was akin to market research and the quest for a high-quality service or product. . . . Resident participation was thus seen as a means of securing reliable feedback from clientele. . . . The third type of resident participation was the most radical and controversial of all, and for many persons the possibility of increasing the power of the poor was either the most objectionable or the most encouraging feature of the CAP. According to this view, the poor were an underdeveloped political constituency that needed stimulation and nurturing. It was assumed that the 'powerlessness' of the poor perpetuated poverty, and only as low-income persons were organized and mobilized as an effective pressure group could they begin to influence city hall, the schools, and the welfare and housing bureaucracies. In addition, it was believed that the social service agencies upon whom the poor were dependent would be more likely to change if they were prodded by their clientele. Since the poor lacked the resources necessary for interest group bargaining in urban politics, OEO was expected to support the development of indigenous organizations in low-income areas through which the poor could overcome their traditional disengagement and begin to assert their influence in the community decision-making processes from which they had been excluded. Within OEO a militant faction of the staff interpreted their congressional mandate so as to justify 'organizing the poor' to become a more powerful force in changing the policies of community institutions affecting their lives. . . . Another approach was represented in a series of variations on what was essentially a community development model whereby the poor were to be organized around social service issues directly affecting them with the objective of improving their daily living conditions and at the same time gaining skills in decision-making and in exerting influence. . . . The fourth and perhaps least controversial way in which the poor could participate was through employment as aides or in other non-professional roles which were defined as 'new careers' in educational, health, welfare, legal, and correctional agencies.

"Employment was originally regarded as the primary, perhaps sole form of resident participation. The rationale for employing the poor, apart from its obvious economic profit, was based in large part on an indictment of the professionalism and 'credentialism' of the educational and welfare systems and their failure to come to grips with the causes of poverty." [6]

Sylvester offers a penetrating discussion of the reasons why the poor must become more involved in all social welfare programs, and he suggests several important roles for the poor as constituent groups:

The demands upon the bureaucracies are consistent, varied and competing. All too often that pressure group which is most vocal or best organized sees its demands gratified, despite contrary national priorities. Therefore, the poor must press their interests constantly, not just at the top of the bureaucracies, but up and down the line at every level of decision. Almost every interest in this country has, within the Federal establishment and most State and Local governments, people who in addition to their regular duties, understand and represent its specific point of view. In the Labor Department many officials are from the unions and the labor movement. Similarly, the Office of Education is inhabited by educators from the establishment. They are present in the daily dialogue that takes place while policies are developed, decisions are made and procedures promulgated. But there are no poor anywhere and very few blacks where it really counts.

Now, partially as a result of OEO and the Poor People's Campaign, some correction is taking place. Commitments to include representatives of the poor on a wide range of governmental advisory committees are being implemented. This is no easy task, considering the fact that HEW alone has nearly 500 of them.

Representation of the poor on committees is not the answer in itself. I should like to propose at least three other devices. These proposals are based on the notions that our institutions, in their present form, have some, but not all, of the ability to serve the poor; that these institutions are not going to adjust rapidly to the current need; and that it is more feasible to supplement their current capability than to try major overhauls and restructuring. I believe that all the foregoing supports these premises.

First, cohesive constituencies, capable of bringing about change within the framework of the service institutions themselves must be created. These constituents would serve to balance off the well-entrenched interests which do not represent the ultimate client population. Such creation will be slow—perhaps almost evolutionary. . . . Secondly, these same constituencies must operate to bring about changes in the constraints and parameters within which the institutions function. This too will be slow developing. The real rules of institutional practices are highly sophisticated, more often than not hidden, and almost quite different from those on the books. An excellent example, at least at the national level, concerns the relation between the excutive branch and the legislative branch, the latter being a particularly complex and almost unfathomable bureaucracy. It is, however, very effective in its own way. This relationship is carried on in such a way as to make it almost impossible for the citizens of this country, rich or poor, to determine with any certainty exactly where the root of a problem lies. And yet, this knowledge is absolutely essential if the democratic process is to have real meaning. The poor and black, of course, are doubly handicapped. The shell game of who did what to whom and when and why leaves the unsophisticated little idea of where the pressure points are and no idea of when to apply the pressure . . . all of this compounds the difficulty for any concerned constituency which attempts to change the external framework and to gain helpful allies in the effort. . . . Third, is the need to develop a series of new public and private institutions to span the gap between the poor and the black and the large existing institutions. These new institutions should operate at the local level and should serve to shortstop and resolve many problems at that level. They should serve as conveyances into the existing institutions and they should train their clients in how to operate successfully with the existing institutions. This is not proposing anything really new—insofar as the total institution scene is concerned. What is suggested in large part is an adaptation of techniques tried in other areas, to the problems of the poor and the black. Nor is any great increase in bureaucracy meant. These new institutions ought to be accommodated out of the continuing expansion of existing institutions—particularly state and local governments.[7]

As Piven points out: "The anti-poverty project itself is a potential arena for resident participation. This has lately become something of a public issue and several different organizational forms of participation are being recommended: (1) Residents should participate on policy-making structures—ordinarily the board—either on the city-wide or local level. These residents are regarded as representatives of the resident population in the areas served. It is this kind of participation that has usually been associated with the legislative mandate for 'maximum feasible participation of residents.' A certain proportion of the seats on these structures are allocated to residents, with different schemes—elections, appointments, or conventions—for selecting them. These arrangements have often been the occasion for tugging and hauling among various groups, local and city-wide, for controlling influence. (2) Residents should participate as staff. These programs, generally referred to as the employment of indigenous or nonprofessional workers, are among the most widely used of the poverty program strategies. (3) Residents should be formed into active constituent groups. These groups are sometimes recommended as a program resource for professional staff, providing feedback for program evaluation, or they may be regarded as pressure groups that properly influence the project in its activities." Piven then raises some fundamental questions: "Whatever patterns developed in the anti-poverty projects for resident participation will reflect answers to two sets of questions: (1) Who should participate? In what action should they participate? Where should this participation be located in the organizational structure? What conditions should govern this action? (2) How can participation by the specified group, and in the prescribed forms, be elicited and maintained; i.e., what are the effectuating mechanisms for the forms of participation prescribed by the answers to the first set of questions above?" [8]

The welfare rights movement born in the mid-1960s has become a force of some importance in the social welfare field. As Paull points out: "The new welfare rights movement is a recent organizing attempt by public assistance recipients to protect their civil rights and improve conditions in the welfare system. Starting with isolated client groups that are generally coalescing, this movement is a spontaneous combustion of the festering grievances and indignities of welfare clients—the rock bottom of the nation's poor." In evaluating the rise of the welfare rights movement, Paull then says, "Social workers as individuals have been aiding the organizing efforts of the new group, but professionals have not been the prime movers, and taken as a whole, professional response has not crystallized. Two interesting questions are raised, however, by the development of the new movement: (1) What will be the response of social workers who are also administrators, supervisors, or otherwise within the structure maintaining the public programs? (2) How will social workers in a community organization and the profession as a whole respond to a movement that is controlled by clients, reserves no endowed status roles for the professional, and frequently collides with the professional operating in the program under attack? The public responses of social workers in administrative and leadership roles of public agencies so far offer no clear-cut answers to the first question. Some have welcomed the protest, explained the nature of their own limited authority to the groups, and helped them to identify the appropriate sources for change. They have managed to fulfill their institutional stewardship responsibilities while leaving no doubt of their support for change. Others have developed a defensive stance and have justified the existing system. For the profession as a whole, the issue has not been sharpened as yet to confrontation and decision." [9]

In reviewing their experiences with organizations of welfare clients, Rabagliati and Birnbaum say, "It seems clear that a neighborhood-based organization of welfare clients acting alone can do very little to change the welfare system. A nation-wide organization of welfare clients now exists which hopes ultimately to put such pressure on the total welfare system that it will ultimately have no change. It remains to be seen what changes such an organization will bring about. Although it would probably extract from the welfare system much more than is now given to clients, such a strategy also tends to overlook the possibility that repressive measures will be taken against individual clients as well as against the agency that sponsors such welfare organizations." [10]

Client Complaints and Pressures

Among the complaints registered by clients of social welfare agencies is that they are often treated routinely rather than as individuals. In addition, they complain of excessive red tape complicated by obsolete rules and regulations. Frequently, they see the agency as an inflexible instrument unable to meet their particular needs. Now and then, because services are poorly organized, the client feels that he is getting a "run-around" because jurisdictions between agencies are confused. Very often the client feels that he is treated with indifference and abruptness because workers are so frequently under pressure. In addition, the client sometimes feels that the staff is not really interested in his problem and is more interested in the problems of other people. Of course, a major complaint is the inadequacy of welfare grants, which are frequently so low that clients cannot live at even a minimum standard of decency and health.

Client pressure groups have emerged in a number of cities. The protest demonstration, the sit-in, and other tactics have been used. Administrators have had to cope with these disruptive pressure tactics. In one state, policy guidelines have been formulated by the central administration of the state welfare department. These guidelines are reproduced below.

CONNECTICUT STATE WELFARE DEPARTMENT

GUIDELINES FOR EMERGENCY CONDITIONS
IN DISTRICT WELFARE OFFICES DURING DEMONSTRATIONS

1. It shall be a policy of the State Welfare Department to seek out and initiate, wherever possible, positive avenues of communications between the Welfare recipient and the Welfare Department.

2. Meetings with Welfare recipients will be encouraged at neutral meeting sites.

3. If meetings with Welfare recipients cannot be accomplished at a neutral meeting site, the meeting will be held in a meeting room separated from the office area.

4. In the event of a demonstration by an organization of Welfare recipients or any other organization protesting Welfare policy every effort will be made by the Welfare administration to persuade the group to meet with the Department at a neutral meeting site or in one of the aforementioned meeting areas.

5. If the group refuses to meet with the administration under these conditions, the Welfare employees will be vacated from the interview and reception areas in the inner office area.

6. The doors to the inner area will be locked to prohibit admission of any demonstration group.

7. In all situations where it is known that groups are preparing to gather or when they have gathered in District Office waiting rooms or interview areas and are threatening to sit in or invade staff work areas, the District Director is to advise the local police chief and request that he be prepared to provide protection for staff and assure the orderly behavior of such groups.

If it is evident that groups gathered in District Office waiting rooms and interview areas are about to attempt or are attempting to gain access to staff work areas, the District Director is to advise such a group that he will request the assistance of the local police department to prevent access. If the group persists in attempting to enter off limit areas assistance from local police will be immediately requested.

Should the demonstration group gain admission to the staff area and present a clear and present danger to the safety and well-being of the staff, administrative action will be taken to assure that the health and safety of the employees is safeguarded.

If it is clearly indicated, the District Director, shall with the approval of the Chief of the Bureau of Social Services, instruct the staff to leave the work area.

On the basis of such factors as the size and composition of the group, their attitude, the time of the day, and the condition of the work area, the District Director is to advise staff through whatever means available, of the time that the staff is to return to work. No leave is to be charged against an employee when released under these conditions by the District Director.

The District Director may request the stationing of uniformed security officers within District Offices at any time it is clearly indicated. Durational approval may be granted considering the intensity and frequency of the demonstrations and the capability to physically secure the District Office.

The Need to Work Together

Ortof discusses "the need for board, staff and the users of agency services to find new ways of communicating and working together. If we are really to become relevant and change our view, we must simultaneously understand that the sponsors, whoever they may be, public or private, and the professionals—whether they are trained or untrained—and the users of the service, cannot all be jaunty, jolly partners in an enterprise. We must face the fact that these different estates have different angles, different perceptions, different views, different needs, and that indeed there is not peace and harmony between and amongst these estates. There has to be conflict, clash, controversy, and differences. Those of us who would rather see everything peaceful and quiet will never truly and honestly engage and join the issues, or the sponsors, the ones who give the funds; or the staff of the agency, either trained or untrained; nor the users of the service. Our experiences, whether we be lay or professional, should make us realize that the categories mentioned above do not see the service, nor the function of the agency in the same way. There are differences and if we pooh-pooh them and sweep them under the rug and try to find mental hygiene approaches for working everything out, it may very well continue to lead us nowhere with respect to steps forward and programs. My experience in the last three years of working with the poverty program has only sharpened my awareness of this situation, and, in my opinion, we must come to terms with it and not be frightened by it. Controversy, conflict, and differences must be accepted as a beginning basis for making our agencies more relevant through changing their function and truly involving the users of the services." [11]

Out of his rich experience in the juvenile delinquency area, Mogulof observes:

Projects must make clear to those involved what their function is and what authority they have with regard to developing policy. The poor may be involved in policy groups as representatives of the different groups the project seeks as constituents. Or groups of target area residents may be involved on an ad hoc or continuing basis for the purpose of advice and/or sanction. The difference between advice and sanction in dealing with neighborhood representatives is critical. In many of the delinquency projects, neighborhood groups were established on levels subordinate to the projects' top policy group. In some instances the program planners wanted to develop and test ideas by using target area residents as advisors. However, members of the locally based group thought (or were led to think) that they had the authority to sanction as well as to give advice. Sometimes demonstration projects were not honest with neighborhood residents because they thought they could engineer their consent without giving any real sanction over policy. Often, of course, they were successful. When they were not successful and yet did not intend to have policy sanction rest with a local group, neighborhood residents often became hostile to the project. Whether or not neighborhood representatives are to have policy sanction must be decided individually by each community. But it *must* be decided and this decision must be communicated to those involved. Needless to say, it is easier for neighborhood groups to accept a decision denying their right to sanction policy when their representatives are part of the project's top policy echelon. This does not mean that projects ought to deny sanctioning authority to local groups. In a specific community, target populations may be the most relevant source of power for a project and any program decided upon that did not have the sanction of significant target community groups could not be implemented.[12]

The systems approach discussed at length in Chapter 3 is harmonious with the client participation approach.

The Federal Management Improvement Conference Panel 2 discussed "Applying the Systems Approach to Management" and reported: "We agreed the word 'system' should be defined as an assemblage or combination of things or parts which form a complex interrelated whole. We acknowledged that a system may, in turn, be built of subsystems, but there is no system unless there is a meaningful relationship between parts. . . . The systems approach involves a large element of managerial common sense and the use of competent people who have enough analytical skill to identify relationships, to define the systems, and to plan for their integration into an overall management system best suited to the needs of the particular organization, functioning in a particular environment, and charged with a particular mission." [13]

Schools of Social Work should likewise review their systems of governance. In his discussion of governance of the professional school, Kraft says, "Although specific governance structures will vary and depend on unique attributes in individual professional schools, the basic principles that ought to apply in designing the structure are easily stated: the professional school should be governed according to strictly democratic procedures with shared power among all constituencies, limited tenure in administrative posts, and provision for due process and grievance machinery to handle all academic complaints. The rationale for including all the constituencies in this framework of governance is based as much on reasons of productive efficiency as on reasons of theoretical justice. As human beings raised in a democratic tradition, we feel it to be a self evident truth that it is just to give people a voice in matters affecting their everyday life and work and we are quick to see injustice when people who have such a voice suddenly find themselves without it." [14]

In Summary

Pifer observes that "Public policy is in essence the entire body of goals, plans, directives, and procedures, both domestic and foreign in their thrust, through which the common, or general interest of the nation is advanced. The formal enactment of public policy, which of course takes place at all levels of government, is the responsibility of elected or appointed officials operating within a constitutional framework and accountable through representative political institutions. While it is expressed in a multiplicity of detailed laws, regulations, executive orders, judicial decisions and other forms, it rests ultimately on certain broad principles, most notably those expressed in the Declaration of Independence and the Constitution. The processes which lead up to formal enactment of public policy in this country are incredibly complex. It is a deliberate part of our system that these processes are thrown open to wide citizen participation, involving input from, and interaction among, elected and appointed officials, political parties, the communications media, industry, trade associations, trade unions, professional associations, citizen action and many other groups, and, finally, the charitable sector with its wide range of private non-profit organizations. This intricate pre-enactment process serves not only as an instrument for the development of public policy but also as a means of mediating and reconciling the claims of conflicting interests in the society." [15]

It would be poor judgment, even unthinkable, for the modern administrator who has an eye to the future if there were no plan for "opening up" the agency and sharing power and control with the community, especially with those who are being served or who use the agency. Of course, the functions, roles, and responsibilities of various groups must be spelled out quite clearly and expectations stated in advance. Decision-centers must be clearly designed in terms of competencies required. Oviously, professional judgment is needed for certain things, but equally obvious is the fact that the professional functions better when full knowledge of the client and community situation is taken into account.

NOTES

1. Arnold Gurin and Robert Perlman, "Current Conceptions of Planning and Their Implications for Public Welfare," in David G. French, ed., *Planning Responsibilities of State Departments of Public Welfare* (Chicago: American Public Welfare Association, 1967), pp. 19–20.
2. Winslow Carlton, "Agency Policy—Who Makes It—Who Controls It?" in

Twenty-Fifth Board Members' Institute Report (New York: Federation of Protestant Welfare Agencies, 1967), p. 3.

3. Jerome L. Schwartz and Milton Chernin, "Participation of Recipients in Public Welfare Planning and Administration," *Social Service Review,* March 1967, pp. 13, 22.

4. Alfred J. Fortin, "What Are We Doing in Protective Services About Client Input?" December 1974. Unpublished paper, School of Social Work, University of Connecticut, West Hartford, Conn.

5. "Economic Opportunity Act of 1964," Public Law 88–452, 88th Congress, S. 2642, August 20, 1964, p. 9.

6. Ralph M. Kramer, *Participation of the Poor–Comparative Community Case Studies in the War on Poverty* (Englewood Cliffs, N.J.: Prentice-Hall, Inc., 1969), pp. 6–18.

7. Edward C. Sylvester, Jr., "The Limited Response of Governmental Institutions to Rapid Social Change—and Some Alternatives," in "Achievements and Challenges," *The H.E.W. Forum Papers,* Second Series, 1968–69 (Washington, D.C.: U.S. Department of Health, Education and Welfare, 1969), pp. 31–33.

8. Frances Piven, "Participation of Residents in Neighborhood Community Action Programs," *Social Work,* January 1966, pp. 79, 80.

9. Joseph E. Paull, "Recipients Aroused: The New Welfare Rights Movement," *Social Work,* April 1967, pp. 101, 106.

10. Mary Rabagliati and Ezra Birnbaum, "Organizations of Welfare Clients," in Harold H. Weissman, ed., *Community Development in the Mobilization for Youth Experience* (New York: Association Press, 1969), p. 1351.

11. Murray E. Ortof, "Agency Policy—Who Makes It—Who Controls It?" in *Twenty-Fifth Board Members' Institute Report* (New York: Federation of Protestant Welfare Agencies, 1967), p. 8.

12. Melvin B. Mogulof, "Involving Low-Income Neighborhoods in Anti-Delinquency Programs," *Social Work,* October 1965, pp. 53–54.

13. *Proceedings of the Federal Management Improvement Conference,* September 21–22, 1974, Washington, D.C., Executive Office of the President—Office of Manpower and Budget.

14. Ivor Kraft, "Governance and the Professional School," *Journal of Social Work Education,* Spring 1975, p. 72.

15. Alan Pifer, "Foundations of Public Policy Formation," *1974 Annual Report,* Carnegie Corporation of New York, p. 3.

8 Effective Administrative Communication

The social work administrator must understand the importance of establishing and maintaining good communication channels within the agency and between the agency and the community. The administrator has primary responsibility for seeing to it that people are in communication with one another all of the time.

Based on their research, Ronken and Lawrence say, "The administrator needs primarily to be concerned with facilitating communication in the organization. This is a different way of thinking about the job of the administrator from one that is commonly encountered. Administrators frequently think of their job as being one of solving problems, formulating policy, making decisions, delegating authority and checking up to make sure that their subordinates are living up to their delegated responsibilities. It follows from their concept of their job, that they spend considerable time in making value judgments about their subordinates and trying to find the individual who was to blame for some trouble, in giving orders to subordinates and in trying to please their superiors so that they will give favorable judgments. On the other hand, could not the administrator more usefully hold the following assumptions about his job? 'I am best performing my job when I am maintaining the conditions for clear and candid communication with my associates. If I am doing my job well, it will follow that my associates and I, in fact, will be spending our time defining, clarifying and solving our mutual problems.' Instead of thinking it was up to him, the administrator, to supply the answers, the administrator would then be searching with others for answers in the situation itself." [1]

141

Definition of Communication

Communication has been defined by many authorities. For example, Albers says, "Communication may be defined as the transfer of meaning from one person to another through signs, signals or symbols from a mutually understood language system." [2]

Bellows says, "Communication determines quality and climate of human relationships and pervades work activity throughout an organization. Communication is intercourse by words, letters, symbols or messages; it is interchange of thoughts, opinions or prejudices; it is a way that one organization member shares meaning and understanding with another. It is a two-way channel for transmitting ideas, plans, commands, reports and suggestions among all appropriate tasks with an organization. It is the link that unites executives, employees and customers in a common enterprise and establishes a liaison between business, government and the public." [3]

Tead says, "Communication, beyond its techniques, is always the touching of mind to mind, of person to person, whether it is one man to a thousand diverse individuals, or one man to thirty in a single department. This process can be many things, including conversation, interview, dialogue, visual impress—all if they yield an interaction of one personality upon another. Hopefully the interaction will be affirmative and new agreements will be achieved. *Active consent is the important end.*" [4]

The Administrator and the Communications System

The social agency as pictured in Figure 7 is a system of inputs, relationships, and outputs. The administrator as the central person in the system is responsible for seeing to it that the various persons within the agency are so organized that a communication system is always operating. As Hungate says, "Communication is a primary administrative tool; thus purposive communication must be studied in relationship to functional aspects of administration. Communication occurs in all organizations, whether or not it is purposefully considered by the administrator. However, it becomes more effective when it is given clarity by having a specific purpose. The broad purposes of communication are: (1) to secure action or cooperation; (2) to solve problems and facilitate decision-making; and (3) to keep all elements within the administrative structure informed. The purposes of administrative communication include: (1) to clarify what is to be done, how, and by whom; (2) to reinforce identity with agency purposes; (3) to transmit problems, suggestions, ideas; (4) to report progress; (5) to promote participation; (6) to promote social interchange or provide recognition. When communication fails, frequently it is because the originator did not have the specific purpose of the communication clearly in mind and did not know precisely enough the results to be

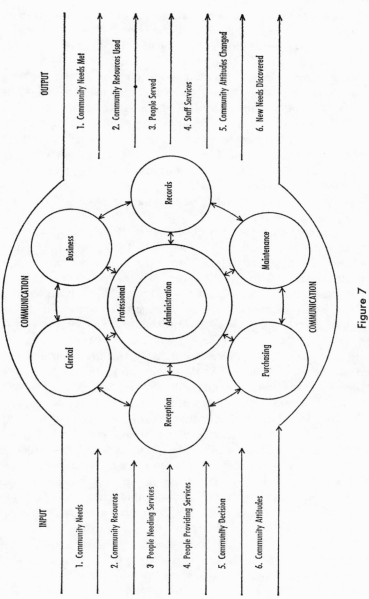

Figure 7
Social Agency Inputs and Outputs

achieved. Communication must be thought out clearly and logically and have a sharply defined purpose." [5]

In establishing the system of communication, the administrator must ask and answer these questions. 1) Who are the communicators, or who must be in continuous communication in our agency? 2) What is the content of communication, or what is it that must be communicated? 3) Why is this content being communicated, or what is the goal or reason for communicating this material? What decisions will it enable us to reach? 4) When must this content be communicated in terms of total timing of agency operations? 5) How should this content be communicated, or what means or methods of communicating do we have at our disposal? 6) Where are the channels or networks, both formal and informal, in our organization that should be used to facilitate communication? The ways and means of communication must be based upon a clear understanding of the purposes sought, the nature of the material to be communicated or solicited, and, of course, the persons involved.

With reference to the communication system, Clegg says, "One of the necessary qualities of the successful executive is the ability to communicate ideas and information. In a welfare office, the dissemination of information is of utmost importance. Welfare programs are governed by laws and regulations which tend to be voluminous and which are subject to frequent change. It is a rare month when some change does not occur in regulations which alters welfare policies and procedures. The Welfare Administrator should treat the subject of communications with the importance it merits. He should express his ideas with clarity and precision and be able to get to the heart of what he wants to say or write. Having mastered these essentials, he should organize and develop an efficient system of communications within his department and devise methods to test systematically and periodically the effectiveness of the system itself." [6]

The test of the communication system is the extent to which the staff really works together, for, as Ronken and Lawrence say, "In order to do their jobs effectively . . . people must learn to perform their technical operations, but they must learn also to work with one another—to communicate effectively with each other and with their superiors. This process of learning how to communicate involves not merely the words that people use but even more the meanings that people assign to the spoken words. And each individual brings to the communication process certain personal equipment in the form of attitudes, expectations, feelings, and social skills or the lack of them. These factors must be taken into account by the administrator whose responsibility it is to develop teamwork in his organization, or to protect a functioning group against the disruptive effects of change." [7]

As the chief architect of the communication system, the administrator must consider the communications he is receiving from others. Evaluations must be made of the material, and as Albers says, "The executive should look beyond words in listening and reading. He should attempt to evaluate the information he receives from subordinates and others by asking himself questions. Are these the real facts? Does the communicator have direct access to the facts? To what extent is he relying upon information received from others? Does the message contain purely subjective judgments that may vary from person to person? In what respects may the message reflect individual or group vested interests? To what extent might the personality of the communicator have given the message a particular bias? These and similar questions can be helpful in determining the distortion that may be present in a message. Although deliberate distortion may also be involved, the present discussion is concerned with non-deliberate distortions evolving from semantic problems. In other words, the person doing the communicating is not consciously aware that the message is distorted." [8]

Agency Structure and Communication

The structure of the agency should facilitate communication. Unfortunately, in the large hierarchical agency, communication is often slow and incomplete. There are many decision centers and many types of information that must be passed along. As Albers sees it, "The management hierarchy may be viewed as a structure of communication centers through which decisional and control information is transmitted to and from the performance level. The volume of information that flows through this system is closely related to the extent to which decision making is centralized. Decisions made at the apex of the hierarchy involve more communication centers than those originating at lower levels. Too much centralization can easily overload the system and create bottlenecks in the flow of information. This problem is amplified with increases in the size of the management hierarchy, and it may significantly reduce the speed of decision making and the ability to adapt to dynamic operating conditions. A further difficulty is that information is frequently distorted as it passes through a long maze of hierarchical positions." [9]

In Chapter 9, which deals with organization, the matter of structure will be examined with criteria for facilitating communication spelled out.

Criteria of Effective Communication

Some of the criteria of effective communication are: 1) The purpose of the communication must be clear and must be understood by the person making it and by the person receiving it. 2) Both spoken and written material must be as clear as possible and subject to one and only one interpretation. If it is not possible to be this precise, every effort should be made to reduce the number of exceptions or options that are left open at the point of interpretation. 3) Effective communication is a series of consistent acts. In other words, subsequent communications are consistently related to earlier communications and avoid the hazard of nullification. 4) Good communication is adequate to accomplish its purpose; it is neither too much nor too little; it has a sharp focus and is selective as to content. 5) Good communication is timely in that thought is given to the timing at point of issue and the readiness on the part of the recipient. 6) In good communication, thought is given to the channels to be utilized and to the distribution so that the right persons will receive the material. This usually requires a system that will make for not only downward and upward communication but for lateral communication as well.

NOTES

1. Harriet O. Ronken and Paul R. Lawrence, *Administering Changes* (Cambridge: Harvard University, Graduate School of Business Administration, 1952), p. 315.
2. Henry H. Albers, *Principles of Organization and Management,* 2nd ed. (New York: John Wiley and Sons, Inc., 1965), p. 71.
3. Roger Bellows, "Communication and Conformity," *Personnel Administration,* September-October 1960, pp. 21–28.
4. Ordway Tead, "Reflections on the Art of Administration," *Hospital Administration,* Winter 1959, p. 14.
5. Joseph I. Hungate, Jr., *A Guide for Training Local Public Welfare Administration* (Washington, D.C.: U.S. Department of Health, Education and Welfare—Welfare Administration—Bureau of Family Services, Division of Technical Training, 1964), p. 24.
6. Reed K. Clegg, *The Administrator in Public Welfare* (Springfield, Ill.: Charles C. Thomas, Publisher, 1966), p. 79.
7. Ronken and Lawrence, *Administering Changes,* p. 291.
8. Albers, *Principles of Organization,* p. 442.
9. Ibid., p. 193.

9 The Changing Organization—Models for Planning and Coordination

The social work administrator must have skill in the areas of organization, planning, and coordination. While all social workers must also function effectively in these realms as well, their efforts tend to concentrate on their respective jobs. But for the administrator, the point of focus is the *total agency*. The administrator must be responsible for the overall organization of the agency and must lead the overall planning process; in addition, the administrator must coordinate the efforts of the entire staff, the board, and others.

As Vasey says, "When a law is enacted establishing a program, machinery must be provided for making the authorized services available, and a structure must be created. This structure may be located in an existing agency, or it may require establishment of a new organization. The outlines of the organization at any rate must be specified in the law. Procedures must be set in motion for this recruitment, selection, and employment of staff. The agency must be organized into divisions, sections, and units, each performing some particular part of the work. In the agency of today, specialization of function is a common feature of organization as the services rendered demand more and more technical skills and processes. The administrative process must be developed to insure the flow of work and the coordination of activities of the organization so that the purposes of the program will be fulfilled. The relationships of boards of advisory or governing committees to the agency executive and to the political authority must develop, as well as that of executive to staff. Personnel policies and procedures must be established, and responsibilities of staff positions clearly delineated." [1]

147

What Is Organization?

A review of the literature of administration reveals that organization is defined in various ways. Usually, emphasis is placed on the formal structural arrangements created between people so that they can work together to accomplish their purposes. As Millett says, "Organization for public service is people working together for a common purpose. People working together create a reaction system, a behavior pattern of individual and group relationships. Organization is supposed to establish relationships among people in terms of work assignments, duties, and responsibilities. But organization does more than this. It provides opportunities and limitations, it encourages ambitions and frustrates the role some individuals believe they should achieve. In spite of political and technical considerations organization quickly becomes also a problem in human relations." [2]

Friedlander affirms the fact that organization is the means by which staff members' duties are defined and clarified: "Setting up the organizational structure of the agency leads to a distribution of duties to the members of the staff with a clear definition of responsibilities concerning their work, delegation of authority, and supervision; a description of staff and line services, and the establishment of standardized operations. It includes the delegation of everyone's authority, so that each member of the staff knows exactly what his assignment and responsibilities are." [3]

Pfiffner and Sherwood say, "The formal structure of an organization represents as closely as possible the deliberate intention of its framers for the processes of interaction that will take place among its members. In the typical work organization this takes the form of a definition of task specialties, and their arrangement in levels of authority with clearly defined lines of communication from one level to the next." [4]

Peterson relates organization to purpose as he observes: "Organization is the act of putting into systematitc relationships those elements essential to the satisfaction of purpose. Organization serves as a facilitating agency in the achievement of a purpose." [5]

Barnard also sees purpose as one of the elements in organization when he writes: "An organization comes into being when (1) there are persons able to communicate with each other, (2) who are willing to contribute action, (3) to accomplish a common purpose. The elements of an organization are therefore (1) communication; (2) willingness to serve; and (3) common purpose. These elements are necessary and sufficient conditions initially and they are found in all such organizations. The third element, purpose, is implicit in the definition. Willingness to serve, and communication, and the interdependence of these three elements in general, and their mutual dependence in specific cooperative systems, are matters of experience and observation." [6]

In a rich and penetrating discussion of how to keep organizations healthy, Gardner lists nine "rules," including the importance of having a program for developing the skills of people in the organization and the continuous search for new blood. He points out the importance of the climate or feeling tone of the organization and suggests it should be such that the individual's needs will always be a central concern of administration. Gardner emphasizes the importance of built-in evaluation processes and urges organizations to look at themselves critically and honestly. He calls for flexibility of structure and for change as it is needed. In addition, there must be a well-developed system of internal communication. He warns against the organization becoming overburdened with rules and procedures that are outmoded and have to be reviewed continuously. He specifies vested interests as a deterrent to organizational health and urges guarding against the development of such a phenomenon. He says the self-renewing organization must always be interested in what it is going to become rather than only in what it has been. Gardner places strong weight on human motivation, conviction, and morale. After all, individuals make the organization function and stay healthy and self-renewing. The way they are treated is of the utmost importance.[7]

Models of Organization

The way in which a social agency is organized always reveals its conception of its purpose, the values it treasures, the relationships it deems important, and the nature of its day-to-day activity.

There is today no perfect form of organization, but it is evident that many agencies are no longer satisfied with what they have in the way of structure. Many are undergoing modification and change.

The well-established *bureaucratic hierarchy* is one model of organization that persists in many places. It may be visualized as a sharply pointed pyramid. Coming more and more into being is the modified hierarchy in which the pyramid is flattened somewhat, and professional services are decentralized by means of smaller working units. More talked about than practiced is a collegial or professional team model of organization that in a sense replaces the bureaucratic hierarchy and seems more compatible with the rendering of professional services.

Of course, the bureaucratic hierarchial model of organization is clearly the most prevalent because of its long history growing out of an essentially authoritarian society that had its early beginnings in the monarchy, the central church, and the military. Many people say the bureaucratic hierarchy works as a model of organization, so why question it. They see the importance of goal-setting, power, authority, and decision-making located at the top of the pyramid with lesser amounts delegated down the line. They believe in a highly stratified, departmentalized operation that makes a continuous use of the division-of-labor principle. They believe that the communication flow should essentially be from the top down, and barriers are then established against lateral communication. They advocate the bureaucratic hierarchy because they say it makes for uniformity of procedures and equity of treatment and people always "know where they stand." They claim that it is neat, efficient, orderly, accents control, and minimizes conflicts. Responsibility is clearly pinpointed, and people are generally comfortable in the system.

Critics of the strict bureaucratic hierarchial model of organization question the claims of efficiency and argue that the system really works slowly and is encumbered with red tape. They see it as being inflexible and non-adaptive. They claim that real power and control are too remote from the people doing the work and the people who need the services. They see it as a form of organization that stifles creativity and individual growth. Innovation is very hard to promote in the bureaucracy.

Those who are flattening out the pyramid and modifying the strict bureaucratic hierarchy have developed what might be described as the *modified bureaucratic hierarchy*. This model still retains much central administrative control, but in terms of service delivery and professional "on-the-spot decision," decentralization has become much more acceptable. The lines of communication from the top to the bottom are shorter. Special work teams or task groups can be created to provide special services. Lateral communication is emphasized with planned opportunities for staff conferring across rather than up and down lines.

The *collegial or professional team model* is coming to the fore in a number of places. Here emphasis is placed on a group of professional colleagues organized in a collaborative lifestyle that prizes well-used channels of communication. Mutual trust is basic. Everyone understands how and where decisions are made and the involvement of people is clearly stated as a goal before the decision is even made. After the decision is made, accountability can be assigned with clarity. This model works for clear delegation of responsibility and authority with continuous built-in evaluation of how well the responsibilities are being carried. It maximizes informal communication and develops clear information and influence systems. It recognizes special resources in the agency and the community, and it stresses the growth of the persons involved.

Hierarchy, Bureaucracy, and Power

The prevailing organization of large social welfare agencies is often hierarchical, bureaucratic, and often power-dominated. These elements must be understood, for if the administrator fails to recognize them serious problems may arise.

Moore observes: "Every organization is a hierarchical system in which each individual, with the exception of the man at the top and the people at the very bottom, operates within an interacting triad of relationships in which some people are viewed as being in higher positions to him, some as being in lower, subordinate positions, and some as being at the same level. Dealing with these various levels and modifying behavior in appropriate ways in terms of the hierarchical system is one of the important skills of the executive. He has to learn how to get things done through the boss, how to approach him at the right time, how to avoid getting a definite *no,* how to sell ideas to him, how to motivate him, and so on. The executive who doesn't have these skills doesn't get much done. Every executive has to be a promoter of ideas; he has to be selling all of the time. By the same token, the executive has to learn how to deal with subordinates as well as with those at his own level. With his subordinates, he has to learn how to see the sometimes unpopular notion of work; he has to learn how to translate organizational ideas into goals that have meaning to those under him; he has to learn to balance the impersonal demands of the organization against the personal needs of his people. Above all, he has to learn how to deal with people in sympathetic but not emotionally involved ways. He has to avoid the sense of guilt that haunts many executives who cannot bring themselves to ask others to get the job done. He has to learn to exercise the power given him without projecting his own emotional needs into the situation. Any power position is potentially tyrannical, and the individual with power has to be either self-disciplined or, of necessity, outwardly controlled." [8]

In his discussion of administration as a social process, Getzels says, "Let me say then that we may conceive of administration structurally as the hierarchy of subordinate-superordinate relationships within a social system. Functionally, this hierarchy of relationships is the locus for allocating and integrating roles and facilities in order to achieve the goals of the social system. It is here, in these relationships, that the assignment of statuses, the provision of facilities, the organization of procedures, the regulation of activity, and the evaluation of performance takes place." [9]

Because bureaucracy is a prominent feature of all governmental organizations, it is necessary that one understand the characteristics of it. Weber says, "The distinctive characteristics of the bureaucracy are: 1) The organization operates according to body of laws or rules, which are consistent and have normally been intentionally established. 2) Every official is subject to an impersonal order by which he guides his actions. In turn, his instructions have authority only insofar as they conform with this generally understood body of rules; obedience is due to his office, not to him as an individual. 3) Each incumbent of an office has a specified sphere of competence, with obligations, authority, and power to compel obedience strictly defined. 4) The organization of offices follows the principle of hierarchy; that is, each lower office is under the control and supervision of a higher one. 5) The supreme head of the organization, and only he, occupies his position by appropriation, by election, or by being designated as successor. Other offices are filled, in principle, by free selection, and candidates are selected on the basis of 'technical' qualifications. They are appointed not elected. 6) The system also serves as a career ladder. There is promotion according to seniority of achievement. Promotion is dependent upon the judgment of superiors. 7) The official who, in principle, is excluded from any ownership rights in the concern, or in his position, is subject to discipline and control in the conduct of his office." [10]

But as Green points out: "often the professional worker may see the requirements of the bureaucracy as impediments to service. The emphasis on procedure, the fact that so many public welfare programs are limited by law, the public accountability of the organizations supported by taxes— these factors stimulate insecurity and rigidity which may clash with the standards of service the social worker professes." Green elaborates as he observes: "when organization requires standards of eligibility for service, the client is automatically categorized. This process conflicts with the social worker's goal of unlimited service to the particular client on the basis of his individual needs. This problem is accentuated in those settings in which the administrative framework was established long before professional social workers were employed by the organization—e.g., in many public aid and correctional settings. The statutes under which the bureaucracy operates set patterns which are not easily modified by 'experts' who move into a structure that is already well-established." [11]

Quite often the administrator has very little chance to change his organization because much of the structure is mandated by higher authority. As Millett says, "Organization for public service establishes a structure for the exercise of administrative power. This structure and this exercise of administrative power are usually subject to determination in the first instance by the political organs of decision-making in our government, and then subject to periodic review by the legislative, executive, and judicial branches of government. This situation necessarily means that organization for public service is a political problem." [12]

In a brilliant discussion of "the good bureaucrat," Pruger suggests that even though the social worker is a helper, organizer, and so on, the bureaucratic role must also be assumed at times within complex organizations. However, this need not be interpreted negatively, provided that the worker understand legitimate authority and the importance of clear rules of procedure. Pruger also emphasizes that the worker does have options even in a bureaucracy and should seek for those options that are most helpful in meeting client needs. He further suggests that the worker must understand the organization structure and help to create one, not in terms of mere administrative convenience, but one that will help to meet client needs imaginatively and creatively. [13]

Creating the Effective Organization

The job of the social work administrator is to create an *effective* organization, effective in the sense that purposes are achieved insofar as possible. As Miller and Form have observed, the theory of organization may be simple, but there are always problems in making the organization work: "The theory of formal organization is . . . quite simple. It holds that throughout the organization there is a strict definition of authority and responsibility. Similarly, there is an equally precise definition of the function of every department. . . . Formal organization is necessary to achieve organizational goals. It is necessary because it is by nature impersonal, logical, and efficient. . . . Although formal organization is designed to subject production to logical planning, things never seem to go 'according to plan.' This is evidenced by the many 'problems' managers encounter. They find that no matter how carefully they organize, despite the concern in anticipating problems, unanticipated ones always arise. For these eventualities formal organization offers little guidance because it is created as a guide-post for the routine, the typical, and the foreseeable." [14]

Communication problems seem to rank high in many large social welfare agencies. These problems may result from the rigid, steep hierarchy so common among massive governmental operations. Albers observes that a flat structure is apt to reduce communication difficulties: "A flat structure has fewer hierarchical levels, thereby tending to reduce the 'administrative distance' between top and bottom levels. The concept of administrative distance has reference to the understanding and intimacy which characterizes the relationship between persons at different levels of the organizational structure. Too much administrative distance can create communication difficulties. . . . Many hierarchical levels or 'layering' increases impersonality and reduces understanding between higher and lower levels. The personal touch is lost and informal ties become tenuous." [15]

By grouping functions in departments, it is possible for the administrator to create specialized units that can have a high degree of autonomy. Barnard observes: "the bases of specialization or organizations (and of individuals also) are five: (a) the place where work is done; (b) the time at which work is done; (c) the persons with whom work is done; (d) the things upon which work is done; and (e) the method or process by which work is done." [16]

Albers, in his discussion of work division, says, "Departmentation divides the work of the organization into semi-autonomous units or departments. The consequence of departmentation is a delineation of executive responsibilities and a grouping of operating activities. Every level in the hierarchy below the apex is departmentalized, and each succeeding lower level involves further departmental differentiation. The activities necessary to achieve the organizational objective are a basic consideration in organizing. The nature of such activities may differ significantly with such diverse objectives as making steel, waging war, selling insurance, and educating students. However, the types of departmentation have general applicability and can be applied in many different situations. The types most commonly used are as follows: (1) Functional, (2) Product, (3) Service, (4) Territorial, (5) Time, (6) Equipment, and (7) Alpha-numerical." [17]

As Hungate says,

There is no one absolutely correct organizational structure for a welfare agency. However, in planning the "best" structure to facilitate the particular program being administered and to make "the policy" effective, the following should be considered: (1) Organization provides framework and environment; the goal of organization in a welfare agency is to create a situation in which workers can meet the objective of the program most effectively. Therefore, some type of formal organization must be established to carry out the purposes of the agency program. (2) The organizational chart is an abstraction of administration. It represents an ideal organization of authority, and functions as a description of actual operations. How far these operations depart from "the chart" will vary with the complexities of the function being performed. However, if the actual organization departs too widely from the formal chart, the program may be moving informally rather than by adequate planning under a responsible director. (3) The objectives of organization should be clear and, to be effective, must be positive considerations—that is, the orientation should be toward constructive achievement rather than preventive or defensive measures. (4) All individuals within the organization influence the program, and in turn the organization molds and influences the activity and responses of individuals. It follows that any new program that changes established organizational lines and relationships may produce emotional reactions. It is difficult to compensate for losses of prestige, authority, or independence of action if these have been considered the prerogatives of individuals within the organization. In this connection it is helpful if a system of recognition and incentives can be made an integral part of organizational structure. (5) The organizational structure should be established on the premise that the people being served have a *right* to the services of the agency. However, the right is based on the law establishing the program rather than in the need of the client. (6) The more programs in functional services a single organization involves, the more differences are encountered and the more the administrator must coordinate and integrate all aspects of service. (7) The organization must not be allowed to become an end in itself but must be a means for achieving agency goals.[18]

The key to organizational effectiveness rests in the quality of the personnel being organized. As Likert says, "The productive capability of a human organization can be illustrated by thinking of two firms in the same business. Both are of the same size and have identical equipment and technology. One, however, produces more and earns more than the other, because its personnel is superior to the other's with regard to such variables as the following: (1) Level of intelligence and aptitudes. (2) Level of training. (3) Level of performance goals and motivation to achieve organizational success. (4) Quality of leadership. (5) Capacity to use differences for purposes of innovation and improvement, rather than allowing differences to develop into bitter, irreconcilable, interpersonal conflict. (6) Quality of communication upward, downward, and laterally. (7) Quality of decision-making. (8) Capacity to achieve cooperative teamwork versus competitive striving for personal success at the expense of the organization. (9) Quality of the control processes of the organization and the levels of self-responsibility which exists. (10) Capacity to achieve effective coordination. (11) Capacity to use experience and measurements to guide decisions, improve operations, and introduce innovations." [19]

Criteria of Adequacy for Structure and Organization

When the administrator stands back a bit and looks at the structure of the organization in terms of its adequacy, it is hoped that the structure is no more extensive than is needed to support properly the work of the agency. Every effort should be made to keep structure at a minimum with simplicity rather than complexity the goal. In addition, a good structure is economical to manage from a time, money, and leadership standpoint. When structure is well constituted, there is an orderly flow of work through the agency; there is a uniformity of procedures and a regularity and equity of services. Adequate structure clarifies areas of responsibility for the individuals and groups so that they know what they are to do and how their work relates to the work of others. Good structure shows the relation of the agency to the community with which it is working. Satisfactory structure provides for an orderly grouping of the various duties and tasks that must be performed and that enables specialized professional tasks to be departmentalized and decentralized. Adequate structure brings about continuous two-way communication, both vertical and horizontal, and tends to stimulate interaction. When structure is indigenous to the agency that it is designed to serve, it creates unity rather than separation and helps to bring about real coordination and integration. Structure must provide for broad participation in policy-making on the part of the many groups that make up the agency. This calls for a reasonably rapid transmission of information up and down and across agency lines as well as the elimination of isolation of various units. Flexibility is a criterion of good structure along with periodic review and evaluation. In a very real sense, *agency structure must grow and develop out of process* and must be considered equally dynamic with purpose and program. Perhaps good structure can be summed up with these three words, *simplicity, economy,* and *flexibility.*

Some Emerging Trends

Lippitt [20] has some stimulating things to say about organizations and their leadership. He claims that new organizational models are emerging to replace the bureaucratic hierarchy because clients, consumers, and the general community wish to have a larger role in agency affairs. He observes that the newer organizational models are accepting the fact that a central task of administration is the utilization of *all* human resources and talents; development of people has become a major concern of administrators, and the bureaucratic form is not generally responsive to this need for personal development because it tends to keep people in their places in little "boxes." He goes on to say that the old obedience expectancies of organization are being replaced by a mutual negotiation system of relationships, and order-giving does not work like it once did! The new approach to organization stresses access to all vital information and accents communication of such information. It rests on a philosophy of basic trust in people. Lippitt observes that the new approach to organization stresses understanding and includes a wide range of agency relationships because of the interdependence of private and public agencies, federal, state, and local. He stresses the fact that the new organizational format tried to achieve a balance between centralization and decentralization with such things as purchasing and maintenance centralized and service delivery decentralized. He says that the new organizational modes make creative use of conflict and that stress, even confrontation, sharpen the agency's awareness of the legitimacy of its service. Also the new organizational models make increasing use of flexibly formed special task groups to deal with special problems. In addition, the new organizational models stress accountability and quality control because increasingly the consumer, the client, and the taxpayer or giver are holding the agency responsible for the quality of its work. He indicates that there is increasing use of general systems concepts and more attempts made at organizational conversion in terms of total systems.

The Responsibility of the Administrator for Planning

The social work administrator has a continuing responsibility for giving leadership to the process of planning. A good plan indicates what is to be accomplished, who is responsible, what are the resource requirements, and what are the methods of evaluation and review. As Seider observes: "Planning in a direct-service agency such as the state department of public welfare takes the form of (1) the projection of program and concomitant administrative support to meet anticipated future goals; (2) planning for the coordination of the multiple categorical service programs, internal and subject to the direct authority of the department; (3) planning for the coordination of specialized departmental services and programs with those of related public and voluntary agencies and organizations; (4) planning for the initiation of new or changed services operating under the aegis of the department; (5) planning of new or changed community resources to be operated under other auspices; and (6) planning for societal changes through changing the environmental or social institutions causing or contributing to social breakdown or blocks in the fulfillment of individual and community potential. Although these types of planning may have different goals, and use differing constellations of staff and community involvement, they generally are carried out through the use of one or more of three interrelated and progressively more complex community work processes: interorganizational exchange, mobilization of community support, and change of community resources." [21]

Hungate says,

The prime requisite of planning is relevance. The following considerations should be borne in mind during the planning phase of any welfare program: (1) The plans devised should be geared to the provision of service—not just to meet the legal requirements of compliance with State and Federal standards. (2) Plans to achieve program objectives are *substantive;* those for the organizational structure are *procedural.* Substantive planning calls for formulations of broad issues confronting the program, whereas procedural planning reflects concern for day-to-day details. (3) A program is a unit of planned purposive action. Program planning is the preparation for program activity, and purposeful activity to achieve goals must be preceded by adequate planning. (4) Agency planning should directly involve all agency personnel who will be closely affected by the plans developed, and should be integrated with all phases of the agency administration. (5) Plans to achieve the objectives of the welfare program should be: a. consistent with immediate and anticipated human needs. b. soundly rooted in agency philosophy and consistent with the philosophy of the welfare professions. c. based on accurate, imaginative statistical and community research. d. flexible; flexible enough to allow for the unexpected; consistent with available or providable funds and personnel; acceptable to the community. e. communicable; simple enough to be interpreted easily to the staff and to the public. f. progressive; designed to improve, strengthen, or focus the service in such a way that each planning point leads to improvement of performance or sharpens relationship to needs. (6) The concept that plans are always geared to purpose must be stressed pervasively. Plans cannot be calculated without a knowledge and thorough understanding of agency purpose. (7) The range of maneuverability in relation to achieving objectives is always a factor in planning. Capability and creativity are enhanced by flexibility in planning; plans that impose a strict uniformity are certain to result in rigid, unimaginative approaches to welfare. There must be a certain degree of uniformity in any program, but there should be left enough room for adjusting the plans to new ways of doing the job, and to the individuals who are expected to make the program effective, as well as to statutory requirements, cultural conditions, and society's goals. (8) Agency achievements are concrete manifestations of objectives well planned.[22]

Steps in Planning

In his work on comparative administrative theory, LeBreton offers a model of the planning process that consists of the following fourteen steps:

1) Becoming aware of a possible need for formulating a plan.
2) Formulating a precise statement of the objective of the plan to be prepared.
3) Preparing a broad outline of the proposal or plan.
4) Obtaining approval of the proposal.
5) Organizing planning staff and assigning responsibility.
6) Determining the specific outline of the plan.
7) Establishing contact with all cooperating units.
8) Obtaining necessary data.
9) Evaluating data.
10) Formulating tentative conclusions and preparing tentative plans.
11) Testing components of tentative plans and making adjustment where appropriate.
12) Preparing the final plans.
13) Testing the plan and making adjustments where necessary.
14) Submitting the plan for approval.[23]

Moss says, "Planning in the social service department in the hospital includes consideration of both the over-all purpose and plans of the institution and the specific goal and plans of the social service department. The social service department must be identified with the over-all objectives in the hospital in which it operates. The structure and functions of the institution will largely determine the planning of the social service department; that is, the planning of program and formulation of policy must reflect the fact that social service is only one part of the total medical care program. The objectives of the institution may change according to the needs of the community or within its own organization. Planning is, therefore, a dynamic process and responds to changes in the institution, in the community and in the social service department, itself. . . . In addition to planning the social work services in the hospital, the social work administrator has a responsibility to participate through appropriate channels in planning hospital policies and procedures and to contribute his knowledge along with other administrative staff in planning specific programs, such as home care program or a program for care of premature infants. The administrator of the social service department can contribute to hospital planning the philosophy of social work concerning the rights of the individual, his awareness of the social needs of patients and his knowledge of their reactions to existing policies and procedures. The extent of social service participation will depend upon the acceptance of the team concept in planning by the hospital administrator or the department head responsible for over-all planning." [24]

Osborn stresses the importance of broad participation in planning: "If each person caring for any aspect of agency program has an opportunity to share in a manner appropriate to this function, in the promulgation of the plan and in the subsequent evaluation process carried on under it, agency administration and programs will in all likelihood be greatly strengthened." [25]

The Responsibility of the Administrator for Coordination

Coordination is one of the continuing responsibilities of the social work administrator. Coordination is an activity that interrelates the various parts of the agency so that it functions as a whole. Walton says, "Coordination is referred to as the activity that allocates and directs various persons, functions, specialities, and spaces with a view to their reciprocal relations in such a way that they contribute maximally to the accomplishment of an organization's purposes." [26]

Georgopoulos and Mann say, "Organizational coordination is defined as the extent to which the various interdependent parts of an organization function, each according to the needs and requirements of the other parts and of the total system." [27]

Simon distinguishes between procedural and substantive coordination: "Coordination may be exercised in both a procedural and a substantive sense. By procedural coordination is meant the specifications of the organization itself—that is the generalized description of the behaviors and regulations of the members of the organization. Procedural coordination establishes the lines of authority, and outlines the sphere of activity and authority of each member of the organization. Substantive coordination is concerned with the content of organization's activities." [28]

Based on many years studying human organizations, Likert notes that "At least four conditions must be met by an organization if it is to achieve a satisfactory solution to the coordination-functional problem. (1) It must provide high levels of cooperative behavior between superiors and subordinates and especially among peers. (2) Favorable attitudes and confidence and trust are needed among its members. (3) It must have the organizational structure and the interaction skill required to solve differences and conflicts and to attain creative solutions. (4) It must possess the capacity to exert influence and to create motivation and coordination without traditional forms of line authority. (5) Its decision-making processes and superior-subordinate relationships must be such as to enable a person to perform his job well and without hazard when he has two or more superiors." Likert goes on to specify a major ingredient of effective coordination: "To perform the intended coordination well a fundamental requirement must be met. The entire organization must consist of the multiple, overlapping group structure with *every* work group using group decision-making processes skillfully. This requirement applies to the functional, product and service departments. An organization meeting this requirement will have an effective interaction-influence system through which the relevant communications flow readily, the required influence is exerted laterally, upward, and downward, and the motivational forces needed for coordination are created." [29]

NOTES

1. Wayne Vasey, *Government and Social Welfare* (New York: Holt, Rinehart and Winston, 1958), p. 257.
2. John D. Millett, *Organization for the Public Service* (New York: Van Nostrand Reinhold Co., a Division of Litton Educational Publishing Inc., 1956), p. 102.
3. Walter A. Friedlander, *Introduction to Social Welfare,* 3rd ed. (Englewood Cliffs, N.J.: Prentice-Hall, Inc., 1968), p. 203.
4. John M. Pfiffner and Frank P. Sherwood, *Administrative Organization* (Englewood Cliffs, N.J.: Prentice-Hall, Inc., 1960), p. 18.
5. Elmore Peterson, E. Grosvenor Plowman, and Joseph M. Trickett, *Business Organization and Management* (Homewood, Ill.: Richard D. Irwin, Inc., 1961), p. 27.
6. Chester I. Barnard, *The Functions of the Executive,* Thirtieth Anniversary Edition (Cambridge: Harvard University Press, 1968), p. 82.
7. John M. Gardner, "How to Prevent Organizational Dry Rot," *Harper's Magazine,* October 1968.
8. David G. Moore, "What Makes a Top Executive?" in Robert T. Golembiewski and Frank Gibson, ed., *Managerial Behavior and Organization Demands* (Chicago: Rand McNally and Co., 1967), pp. 331–332.
9. Jacob W. Getzels, *Administrative Theory in Education* (Chicago: Midwest Administration Center, University of Chicago, 1958), p. 151.
10. Max Weber, *Theory of Social and Economic Organization,* trans. Henderson and Parsons (London: William Hodge and Co., Ltd., 1947), pp. 329–334.
11. A. D. Green, "The Professional Worker in the Bureaucracy," *Social Service Review,* March 1966, p. 72.
12. Millett, *Organization for the Public Service,* p. 28.
13. Robert Pruger, "The Good Bureaucrat," *Social Work,* July 1973.
14. D. C. Miller and W. H. Form, *Industrial Psychology* (New York: Harper and Row, 1951), pp. 159–160.
15. Henry H. Albers, *Principles of Management,* 3rd ed. (New York: John Wiley & Sons, Inc., 1969), p. 113.
16. Barnard, *The Functions of the Executive,* pp. 128–129.
17. Albers, *Principles of Management,* p. 120.
18. Joseph I. Hungate, Jr., *A Guide for Training Local Public Welfare Administrators* (Washington, D.C.: U.S. Department of Health, Education and Welfare —Welfare Administration, Bureau of Family Services, Division of Technical Training, 1964), pp. 19–20.
19. Rensis Likert, *The Human Organization* (New York: McGraw-Hill Book Company, 1967), p. 148.
20. Gordon Lippitt, 100th Anniversary Annual Forum of the National Conference on Social Welfare, Atlantic City, May 1973.
21. Violet M. Seider, "Organizing the State Welfare Department for Community

Planning," in David E. French, ed., *Planning Responsibilities of State Departments of Public Welfare* (Chicago: American Public Welfare Association, 1967), p. 37.

22. Hungate, *A Guide for Training*, pp. 21–22.
23. Preston P. LeBreton, "A Model of the Administrative Process," in *Comparative Administrative Theory* (Seattle: University of Washington Press, 1968), p. 170.
24. Celia R. Moss, *Administering a Hospital Social Service Department* (Washington, D.C.: American Association of Medical Social Workers, 1955), pp. 12–13.
25. Phyllis R. Osborn, "Meeting the Needs of People: An Administrator Responsibility," *Social Work*, July 1959, p. 75.
26. John Walton, *Administration and Policy-Making in Education* (Baltimore: The Johns Hopkins Press, 1959), p. 86.
27. Basil Georgopoulos and Floyd Mann, *The Community General Hospital* (New York: Macmillan Co., 1962), p. 273.
28. Herbert A. Simon, *Administrative Behavior: A Study of the Decision-Making Processes in Administrative Organizations* (New York: The Macmllan Co., 1955), pp. 140–141.
29. Likert, *The Human Organization*, p. 158, 167.

10 Administration and the Decision-Making Process

Social work administrators, like all administrators, have a major responsibility for the decision-making processes of their agency. They must understand the meaning of decision, the types of decisions, and the steps in the process of decision-making. They must know who to involve in the decisions that must be made. They must be willing to make difficult decisions, and above all, they must strive for decision-making that enhances the purposes of the agency and furthers the meeting of client needs. Albers makes the point that "An important function of executives is decision-making or choosing from alternatives. Decision-making is partly a matter of planning organizational objectives and the methods that will be used to achieve them." [1]

Morris observes: "Large organizations can be managed not by a single brain but through coordinated decisions made by many. Just how decisions are to be thus delegated and the resulting actions coordinated is the central question in organization design." [2]

The Meaning of the Term "Decision"

A number of authorities have developed helpful definitions of the term "decision." For example, Albers says, "Decision-making may be narrowly defined as the making of a choice from among alternative courses of action. More broadly, decision-making also involves all of the actions that must take place before a final choice can be made. Probably the most important of these is to determine whether something needs to be done. This aspect of decision-making is similar to the initial steps in a scientific investigation. Neither decisional nor scientific endeavor can begin unless

162

there is a problem that requires solution. . . . After a decisional problem has been identified, alternative strategies for the solution of the problem may be developed. This aspect of decision-making generally involves both the questions of ends and means. Are the ends presently sought by the organization appropriate in terms of changing environmental conditions? Are the means now being utilized adequate for existing or changed ideas? The final step in decision-making is to make a choice from among two or more alternatives. Strictly speaking, at least some of the alternatives must appear to be equally appropriate. If such were not the case, there would be no real problem of choice. The best alternative would be obvious and automatically eliminate the other alternatives." [3]

Gore says, "The term 'decision' may refer to the choice of picking up the telephone ('I decided to answer the phone'); it may just as well refer to a momentous and unprecedented international act. . . . Generically, decision refers to the consideration of the consequences of some act before undertaking it. Purposive behavior, behavior organized by means of goals projected by individuals as a means of meeting their needs, tends to extend beyond the resources of a behavioral system. In this situation, the decision becomes a mechanism for selecting both goals to be undertaken first and those that must wait. One of the meanings that decision has come to have is a choosing, not between alternative courses of action, but between alternative goals, each offering benefits prized by someone." [4]

Thompson and Tuden say, "Choices from among alternatives seem to be the end-point of decision-making, but the term 'decision' will not be confined simply to ultimate choice. Rather, 'decision' will refer to those activities which contribute to choice, including recognizing or delimiting and evaluating alternatives as well as the final selection. Thus an individual may have responsibility for making final choices on behalf of an organization, but if others help him delimit or evaluate alternatives, we will not decribe that individual as the decider." [5]

As Walton observes: "Administrative decisions contain three elements. First, there is a continuing element of purpose that gives direction to the decision about means. Second, there is the actual decision about the choice of means to accomplish the accepted purpose. And third, there is usually a concomitant value choice in the selection of means that does not materially affect the end." [6]

Hungate says, "A decision is a specific course of action selected from the alternative courses available. It provides a way to design action to solve a problem. The setting for decision is a human situation, and an understanding of the human elements is necessary to the problem-solving process. A problem must be confronted, fully grasped, and understood in all of its behavioral complexities before a decision can be made. A decision cannot be effective unless it is accepted by those to whom it applies. . . . The acceptance must come (1) from those within the organization who will be called upon to implement the decision, (2) from the public groups affected by the decision, and (3) from the superiors of the administrator making the decision. By the same reasoning, a decision must appear right and correct to those who are expected to accept it. . . . Decision-making rests upon the assumption that there is adequate competence and skill available to implement the decision effectively; decisions are of no consequence unless there is a probability that they can be carried out. No decision rests in isolation. Any decision has effect upon other areas not specifically covered by the particular decision; therefore, carrying out decisions is a matter for participation by all organizational staff. Decisions are made at all levels and by all personnel within an organization." [7]

Types of Decisions

When one reviews the number and types of decisions that must be made by an agency in the course of its work, it is evident that there are many variations and differences. Some decisions are simple: other decisions are complicated and far-reaching. As Gore says, "Decision serves so many purposes in the processes of an organization that it is difficult to characterize their functions in a word or a phrase. Most frequently they serve as devices for triggering action, but they may serve as both blueprints for and catalysts of action in a single stroke. Major decisions set off such rambling discussions that they serve many more objects than can be counted. Like radiation, some of the effects of a sustained decision process may appear only long after the process has run its course." [8]

Simon says, "Decisions are programmed to the extent that they are repetitive and routine, to the extent that a definite procedure has been worked out for handling them so that they don't have to be treated de novo each time they occur. . . . If a particular problem recurs often enough— a routine procedure will usually be worked out for solving it. Decisions are nonprogrammed to the extent that they are novel, unstructured, and consequential. There is no cut and dried method for handling the problem because it hasn't arisen before, or because its precise nature and structure are illusive or complex, or because it is so important that it deserves a custom-tailored treatment." [9]

Steps in the Decision-making Process

A number of writers have analyzed the decision-making process and have come to the conclusion that it is a step-by-step matter.

Jensen and Clark say, "Regardless of how the procedure is viewed or defined—decision-making or administrative process—it is a process involving sequential steps. These are orderly stages in a continuum, however, interrelated; that is, one cannot start with the resultant and work back-ward; the direction is toward the resultant. . . . One very significant component of the procedure lies in the deliberate phase of the procedure, the recognition of the problem, gathering and organizing facts and data, weighing alternatives, and eventually coming to a point of decision on a course of action to be taken. To stop at this point, which unfortunately happens in some cases, totally ignores the implementation and assessment of the continuum." [10]

Griffiths says, "In practically any discussion of the process of decision-making, steps similar to the following will be presented and described:

1) Recognize, define, limit the problem.
2) Analyze and evaluate the problem.
3) Establish criteria or standards by which a solution will be evaluated or judged as acceptable and adequate to the need.
4) Collect data.
5) Formulate and select the preferred solution or solutions. Test them in advance.
6) Put into effect the preferred solution.

"The preparation for making a particular decision becomes known, and the decision-maker goes through a process of defining and limiting the problem. He attempts to state the problem in terms of either his goals or the goals of the enterprise, and he also attempts to state the problem in such a way that he can grasp its significance." [11]

In discussing White House decision-making, Sorenson says, "It is not hard to state the ideal, but it is hard to state it with conviction. Theoretically it would be desirable to take, for each important decision, a series of carefully designed, carefully spaced steps, including ideally the following: First: agreement on the facts; second: agreement on the overall policy objectives; third: a precise definition of the problem; fourth: a canvassing of all possible solutions, with all their shades and variations; fifth: a list of all the possible consequences that would flow from each solution; sixth: a recommendation and final choice of each alternative; seventh: the communication of that decision; and eighth: provision for its execution. In these ideal and mechanical terms, White House decision-making sounds easy, if somewhat elaborate. It is simply the interaction of desire and fact —simply a determination of what the national interest requires in a given situation. But unfortunately it is neither mechanical nor easy; nor, it should be added, is the amount of care and thought devoted to a particular decision necessarily proportionate to the formality and regularity of the decision-making process." [12]

Participation in Decision-making

In professional social work administration, it is important for many people to have a part in the decision-making. In the large social welfare agency, there are many decisions to be made, and it is impossible for the administrator to make them alone. As Cleveland says, "[The] extent to which each individual is personally responsible to others is most noticeable in a large bureaucracy. No one person 'decides' anything; each 'decision' of any importance is the product of an intricate process of brokerage involving individuals inside and outside the organization who feel some reason to be affected by the decision, or who have special knowledge to contribute to it. The more varied the organization's constituency, the more its decisions affect 'the public,' the more outside 'veto groups' will need to be taken into account. But even if no outside consultations were involved, sheer size would produce a complex process of decision. For a large organization is a deliberately created system of tensions into which each individual is expected to bring work ways, viewpoints, and outside relationships markedly different from those of his colleagues. It is the administrator's task to draw from these disparate forces the elements of wise action from day to day, consistent with the purposes of the organization as a whole." [13]

Bennis says, "The leader does not abdicate from the tough decisions of management but attempts to deal with them by exploring with his group or organization the facts at hand, involving his people directly with the solution of the problem. His style is problem-oriented leadership and relies not solely on oganizational power or status but rather on situational demands. . . . He tries to mobilize his people, to activate them to explore mutually the job or problem that has to be accomplished. He does so by communicating the problem, by insisting on involvement and participation, and by jointly working on the problem. His is management by objective, not management by control." [14]

Millett observes: "If communication is to be a two-way street in an organization, then various persons and groups must be invited to participate in the decision-making process." [15]

Administrators who believe in the importance of involving people in decision-making have to decide *which* persons to involve in which decisions and at what time and in what ways.

Ripley points out in discussing hospital administration: "It is unwise . . . to think everyone must contribute to all decisions, because many of the personnel may be incompetent to make such decisions. For example, the housekeeper cannot be expected to express a valid opinion of the candidate for the hospital fiscal officer, and the chaplain is not qualified to advise on the purchase of x-ray equipment." [16] Similar observations can be made with reference to the social welfare field. The criterion of competence is basic to the choice of who should participate in what decisions.

The Administrator's Role in Decision-making

Decision-making is often difficult and always hard work. The administrator is at the center of the decision-making process and is ultimately responsible for the decisions made. Barnard offers a penetrating analysis of the problems of the executive along with suggestions on how to cope with the inevitable strains of the job: "The making of decisions, as everyone knows from personal experience, is a burdensome task. Offsetting the exhilaration that may result from correct and successful decision and the relief that follows the terminating of a struggle to determine issues is the depression that comes from failure or error of decision and the frustration which ensues from uncertainty. Accordingly, it will be observed that men generally try to avoid making decisions, beyond a limited degree when they are rather uncritical responses to conditions. The capacity of most men to make decisions is quite narrow, although it is a capacity that may be considerably developed by training and especially by experience. The executive is under the obligation of making decisions usually within approximately defined limits related to the position he has accepted; and is under the necessity of keeping within the limits of his capacity if he is continuously to discharge this obligation. He must, therefore, to be successful, distinguish between the occasions of decision in order to avoid the acceptance of more than he can undertake without neglecting the field to which his position relates. For the natural reluctance of other men to decide, their persistent disposition to avoid responsibility, and their fear of criticism, will lead them to overwhelm the executive who does not protect himself from excessive burdens of decision if he is not already protected by a well regulated and habitual distribution of responsibilities." [17]

When the administrator has developed an agency structure and organization that are working effectively, there are many decision-making persons and points. Under these circumstances the administrator does not have to make all the decisions, but as Thompson and Tuden point out, his role "is to *manage* the decision process as distinct from *making the decision.*" [18]

Griffiths and his colleagues sum it up by saying, "1) The role of the administrative staff in an institution is to create an organization within which the decision-making process can operate effectively. The organization should permit decisions to be made as close to the source of effective action as possible. 2) The administrative staff of an educational institution should be organized to provide individual staff members with as much freedom for initiative as is consistent with efficient operation and prudential controls. Hierarchical levels should be added to the organization with caution, and only when deemed imperative to maintain reasonable control over the institution. 3) The administrative functions and the sources of decision-making in an institution should be organized to provide the machinery for democratic operation and decentralized decision-making. 4) The purpose of organization is to clarify and distribute responsibilities and authority among individuals and groups in an orderly fashion consistent with the purposes of the institution. The structure of the institution is determined by the nature of its decision-making process and the organization of the institution should be established to provide for the most effective operation of this process. 5) An institution should be organized with a unitary source of decision-making at its head. Authority and responsibility delegated by the chief administrator should result in a unitary pattern of decision-making levels all subordinate in the institution. 6) The administrative organization, by its very structure, should provide for the continuous and cooperative evaluation and redirection of the organization from the standpoint of adequacy (the degree to which goals are reached) and efficiency (the degree to which goals are reached relative to the available resources)." [19]

NOTES

1. Henry H. Albers, *Principles of Organization and Management,* 2nd ed. (New York: John Wiley and Sons, Inc., 1965), p. 71.
2. William T. Morris, *Decentralization in Management Systems* (Columbus, Ohio State University Press, 1968), p. 3.
3. Henry H. Albers, *Principles of Management,* 3rd ed. (New York: John Wiley and Sons, Inc., 1969), pp. 78–79.
4. William J. Gore, *Administrative Decision-Making: A Heuristic Model* (New York: John Wiley and Sons, Inc., 1964), p. 19.
5. James D. Thompson and Arthur Tuden, "Strategies, Structures and Pressures of Organizational Decision," in James D. Thompson, ed., *Comparative Studies of Administration* (Pittsburgh: University of Pittsburgh Press, 1959), p. 196.
6. John Walton, *Administration and Policy-Making in Education* (Baltimore: The Johns Hopkins Press, 1959), p. 52.
7. Joseph I. Hungate, Jr., *A Guide for Training Local Public Welfare Administrators* (Washington, D.C.: U.S. Department of Health, Education and Welfare —Welfare Administration, Bureau of Family Service, Division of Technical Training, 1964), pp. 55–56.
8. Gore, *Administrative Decision-Making,* p. 113.
9. Herbert A. Simon, *The New Science of Management Decision* (New York: Harper and Row, 1960), pp. 5–6.
10. Theodore Jensen and David L. Clark, *Educational Administration* (New York: The Center for Applied Research in Education, Inc., 1964), p. 53.
11. Daniel E. Griffiths, "Administration as Decision-making," in Andrew M. Halpin, *Administrative Theory in Education* (Chicago: Midwest Administration Center, University of Chicago, 1958), pp. 132–133.
12. Theodore C. Sorenson, *Decision Making in the White House* (New York: Columbia University Press, 1963), pp. 18–19.
13. Harland Cleveland, "Dinosaurs and Personal Freedom," *Saturday Review,* February 28, 1959, p. 38.
14. Warren G. Bennis, "Problem-oriented Administration," *Hospital Administration,* Winter 1960, p. 64.
15. John D. Millett, *Organization for the Public Service* (Princeton: D. Van Nostrand, 1966), p. 116.
16. Herbert S. Ripley, M.D., "Human Problems in Hospital Administration and

the Care of Patients," in Preston P. LeBreton, *Comparative Administrative Theory* (Seattle: University of Washington Press, 1968), p. 247.

17. Chester L. Barnard, *The Functions of the Executive,* Thirtieth Anniversary Edition (Cambridge: Harvard University Press, 1968), pp. 189–190.
18. Thompson and Tuden, "Strategies, Structures and Pressures," p. 209.
19. Daniel Griffiths et al., *Organizing Schools for Effective Education* (Danville, Ill.: The Interstate Printers and Publishers, Inc., 1961), pp. 71–72.

11   Administrators and Policy Determination

Administrative leadership is responsible for developing and guiding the process of policy determination for the agency. A policy is a stated course of action adopted and followed by the agency in doing its work. Policy in action becomes practice. While many persons are involved at various points in the policy-determination process, the administrator has a special role as does the agency board (see Chapter 6).

It is the function of the administrator to develop and present to the board proposals concerning policies, taking into account community, constituency, and staff thinking and consensus. Then it is necessary for the administration to assist the board as it makes policy decisions. Once the policy decision has been made, it is the job of the administrator to administer the policy effectively with the staff.

Policy Defined

A policy is a stated course of conduct, a statement of intentions. Agency policies are written statements formally adopted by the board or legal authority and made public so that persons will know the conditions under which services will be rendered. The community, the constituency, and the staff should be clear on the nature and purpose of the specific policy and its interpretation. Policies are tools of administrators, staff, and constituents to use in providing service. Good policy statements are positive affirmations of what the agency exists to do and how it is to be done. Policies give focus and direction to the work of the staff, especially in terms of decision-making. As Griffiths points out: "An effective set of policies should indicate *who* is to make a decision, *what* the decision is to be concerned with, and some information as to *how* the decision is to be made. Members of an organization should have the security which well-written policy affords them. One of the chief causes of confusion in the network of human relationships in an organization is the lack of clear policy." [1]

Areas Where Policies Are Needed

Policy determination within a framework of defined agency purpose tends to evolve in a number of interrelated categories. *First,* there is a need for policy regarding whom the agency is to serve and the kinds of services to be offered. To a great extent, the legislative body determines broad purposes and eligibility policies for public agencies, but there are many details of service policies that must be worked out at the agency level. Policies regarding evolution of services and termination of services are also needed. *Second,* policies are needed in the area of personnel. These include standards of employment, salaries, workloads, promotion, and evaluation. *Third,* the area of financial arrangements requires policy formulations especially when fees for services are charged. *Fourth,* the area of community relationships should have policy pronouncements to guide the agency in its work with other agencies. In addition to these broad policy areas, the agency must work out procedures that constitute uniform ways of carrying out operations. Ordinarily procedures are chiefly internal and do not require the breadth of participation in formulation necessary for policies.

The Policy-Determination Process

In Figure 8, policy-making is presented in a series of steps. Policy-making in social work administration is a process through which communities, constituencies, staffs, and boards with the leadership of social work administrators contribute facts, experiences, views, and preferences so that statements of intention will be adopted by the board and will be implemented by administration and staff to achieve the agency goals of services to people uniformly provided.

In Specht's model of stages of policy formulation, he identifies eight stages. They are: 1) identification of the problem, 2) analysis, 3) informing the public, 4) development of policy goals including the involvement of other agencies, 5) building public support, 6) legislation, 7) implementation and administration, 8) evaluation and assessment. [2]

In working out professional social service policies, the staff must be given an important role. The same principle applies in all professional fields. With reference to policy-making in the public schools, a commission said, "Teachers should play a major role in initiating and formulating administrative and policy decisions. In the interest of the advancement of

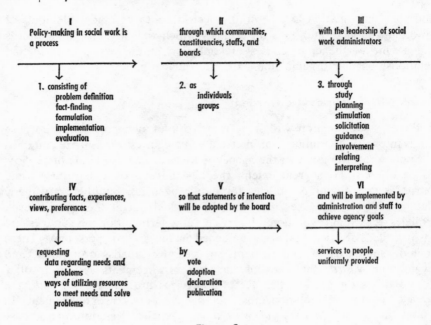

Figure 8
The Policy-making Process

education, the staff should seek such a role and the superintendent should welcome it. Most school policies and administrative plans are successful only insofar as they foster improved interaction between teacher and pupil, for classroom instruction is the most important function of the school. Policy-making and administrative direction which ignores the professional knowledge of specific situations are likely to result in poor policies and poor directives. Decisions should therefore reflect the pooled intelligence of the professional staff. In the interests of education this is a necessity, not a mere matter of professional courtesy." [3]

Moore and Walters, in their work on personnel administration in education, say, "Policy formation by the staff, subject to approval by the governing board, is a responsibility of the entire group, and those that are affected by a given policy should have a part in its development." [4]

Based on her experience in hospital social work, Moss says, "Direction in a social service department is facilitated when established policies and procedures are set down and made available to the entire staff. To operate on the basis of a separate decision on each situation would become a complicated and trying ordeal for director and staff alike. When it becomes necessary to change an established policy or procedure, everyone should have a common body of knowledge and a common starting point. Where the staff is informed of the reason for a new procedure before it becomes a directive, they accept it more readily. Consultative direction, in which the staff participated in planning for and formulating the actual instruction, produces more cooperative effort and professional growth on the part of the staff." [5]

Utz says, *"The administration should make provision for the staff to participate in policy formulation.* This undertaking is particularly challenging for both the administration and the staff. The challenge for the administration lies in deciding what kinds of policy formulation the staff can participate in appropriately and in being clear about the issues at stake. The challenge for staff members lies in learning how to participate effectively. Effective participation requires the caseworker to behave quite differently from the way he behaves in casework practice, where 'the waiting game' is the appropriate one. He must be prepared to state his views promptly. The administration has a responsibility to give casework staff members guidance and direction in how to prepare themselves in how to participate responsibly in policy formation. Their eventual responsibility in this sphere can be discussed with potential staff members during employment interviews, and later it should be brought up for discussion in supervisory conferences. Moreover, although it is not appropriate to encourage the expression of differences for its own sake, the atmosphere of the agency should be conducive to the kind of free expression in which genuine differences in opinion can be aired. Along with this it is important to realize that in a complex agency operation refinement and progress come more from the combination of one person's bits of ideas with another's than from one person's 'pearls of wisdom.' " [6]

Lack of clarity about roles and responsibilities is one of the usual problems in the policy-making process. While various groups must participate in the process of defining the policy, only one group, usually the board, can adopt policy legally, and only one group, usually the professional staff, can carry out policy. Writing from the hospital field, Hennessey says, "In a hospital there is an apparent conflict surrounding policy-making represented by these three observations: (1) the legally responsible group in the hospital, charged with legislating policy, is the board of trustees; therefore, these men must be the policy-makers. (2) The essential activity of the hospital is medical care for the sick, a specialty of physicians; therefore, they should determine the policies of the organization. (3) The person most knowledgeable about all phases of life in the hospital, the only full-time professional with wide perspective, is the administrator; therefore, he should decide policy. The fact of multiple interest and involvement in policy-making causes the process to be complex and ambiguous. In this sense it is like policy processes in the federal government implying a balance of contending powers. Thus, the relationships among the three principal groups have a crucial effect on hospital policy." [7]

Hungate says, "There are a number of problems inherent in the policy-making process." He lists:

(1) *Policy Too Strictly Defined.*—The tendency to think of policy in terms of law, charter, or legal order has created a problem in the failure to focus upon policy as a facilitative device of administration to accomplish established objectives. Administration, all too frequently, is not seen clearly in the policy role. The administrator may consider himself as an executor of policy with no part in formulation, but legal mandates only establish the broad general limits of policy. The administrator must assume the responsibility for policy within the realm of legal prescription. (2) *Policy Too Rigidly Detailed.*—The attempt to cover every detail of agency service in a policy directive can pose serious problems. Policy must be sufficiently flexible to allow for some variation as unique situations are encountered. Detailed policy that spells out with excessive rigidity every phase of operation undermines worker confidence. Attempts to ensure uniformity of attention to details can produce stagnation and stultify imaginative efforts. Details are necessary in certain instances, but they can become the center of concern at the expense of good service. (3) *Emotional Subjectivity of Individuals.*—Emotional involvement in the policy process is a problem which must be considered. It is not easy to carry out a policy that impinges upon emotions or is contrary to beliefs. The administrator may not face the policy decision at all if what must be decided causes too severe discomfort. (4) *Variety of Training and Experience Levels.*—Policy formulations for a widely diverse staff are exceedingly difficult. With a fully trained staff more flexibility and discretion can be permitted at the point of application of the broad policy. For the less experienced workers policy formulations need to be more elementarily stated. A heterogeneous staff produces problems in the policy process. Obviously administration faces a difficulty in meeting a wide range of competences. (5) *Variety of Disciplines.*—If an agency has a staff composed of several disciplines it is difficult to find generally acceptable frames of reference for the policy decisions. Each discipline's particular professional expertise may stoutly defend its own interpretation of policy as it pertains to its own realm of practice. (6) *Segmentalized Participation.*—An individual may invest only a part of himself in the organization, leaving the remainder of himself to work outside of the policy controls of the program. The part of the policy which is in accord with his beliefs he supports, but he segments himself and simply ignores the elements he disagrees with, or leaves them to chance. (7) *Geographical Distances or Socialization of Work Load.*— The policy process faces problems if units widely separated geographically are implementing the same policy without close coordinating efforts. The distances between program specialization can also create difficulty. If work assignments are narrowly specialized by units the problem of finding conformity in policy and assuring uniformity is greatly increased.[8]

Principles of Policy Determination

In an earlier publication, the author summarized some general principles of policy determination:

1. Policy must be based on and develop out of agency purpose.
2. Policies must be soundly based on adequately evaluated facts and experience. Persons affected by policy should share in the creation of it.
3. Policy implies focus and direction for the achieving of the agency purpose.
4. Unity and consistency between the various policies of the agency and between policies and purposes are essential.
5. Although the board is responsible for the *enactment* of policy, the entire agency should participate in the policy-formulation process.
6. Policy should relate the agency purpose to the realities of the community setting (including other agencies, special needs, etc.) and of the agency's own facilities and resources.
7. Policy-making, planning, and operations are integrally related and cannot be separated.
8. New policies should develop out of an evaluation of the existing policies in practice as they are systematically reviewed and studied.
9. Thorough knowledge of policy on the part of every staff member is essential. It is the administrator's responsibility to make policy statements available to staff in written form.
10. Policies should be expressed in position forms; expressed in this way their constructive use is emphasized.
11. The carrying out of policies in the spirit of their intent is a major responsibility of administration.
12. Conflict between statement of policy and actual practice is a signal to the administrator of a need to evaluate both.[9]

NOTES

1. Daniel E. Griffiths, "Administration as Decision-making," in Andrew M. Halpin, *Administrative Theory in Education* (Chicago: Midwest Administrative Center, University of Chicago, 1959), p. 140.
2. Harry Specht, "Casework Practice and Social Policy Formulation," *Social Work,* January 1968, p. 44.
3. Educational Policies Commission, *The Unique Role of the Superintendent of Schools* (Washington, D.C.: The Commission, 1965), p. 12.
4. Harold E. Moore and Newell B. Walters, *Personnel Administration in Education* (New York: Harper and Row, 1955), p. 19.
5. Celia R. Moss, *Administering a Hospital Social Service Department* (Washington, D.C.: American Association of Medical Social Workers, 1955), p. 39.
6. Cornelius Utz, "The Responsibility of Administration for Maximizing the Contribution of the Casework Staff," *Social Casework,* March 1964, p. 139.
7. John W. Hennessey, Jr., "The Administrator and Policy Processes," *Hospital Administration,* Fall 1965, p. 66.
8. Joseph I. Hungate, Jr., *A Guide for Training Local Public Welfare Administrators* (Washington, D.C.: U.S. Department of Health, Education and Welfare —Welfare Administration, Bureau of Family Services, Division of Technical Training, 1964), pp. 93–94.
9. Harleigh B. Trecker, *Group Process in Administration* (New York: Association Press, 1950), pp. 275–276.

12 Financial Resources and Administrative Accountability

Every administrator is concerned about the financing of the agency. Funds have to be secured from either legislative appropriation or from private giving or fees charged clients. Administrators must determine what needs are to be met and how the budget must be set up to meet these needs. They have to interpret budgetary needs to various groups who decide how much will be appropriated. In addition, executives must control the spending of the budget in terms of the law, and in relation to the declared objectives. They must pay attention to sound business practices and must be ready to be held accountable at all times. Furthermore, they must evaluate the results of the spending program in terms of the objectives that have been set up. Most administrators would agree that securing, spending, and evaluating the use of funds is most important in their work. As Friedlander says, "The mobilization of the financial resources of the agency depends upon its nature and structure. In public agencies, the administration of the budget requires negotiations for the allocation of funds with the Federal, state or local government; in private welfare organizations, money from special campaigns or the Community Chest is relied upon for funds. Budget controls guarantee that the money received is spent economically and in accordance with the policies and rules of the agency. Budgeting also describes the allocation of the funds available to the branches and divisions of the agency so that each of them can operate most effectively." [1]

Large amounts of money are now needed to finance existing social welfare programs. As new programs are authorized and as the nation grows in population, more funds will be required. Programs are possible only when money is available. Held says, "Since every governmental program is only as extensive as the money put into it, the place where the decisions

—whether rational or not—over how to divide up the national effort are most apparent, is in the federal budget. The budget is the central expression of how the government's finite resources will be allocated, the terms of the annual cease-fire, as it were, within the executive branch, between the competing claims of different advocates for more money for defense, or agriculture, or new welfare programs." [2]

The Budget and Its Preparation

The agency budget is the annual estimate of the financial needs of the organization for the year to come. It is one of the most important documents in the agency. Its preparation is a demanding task. Its utilization is a matter of trusteeship. Wildavsky says, "In the most literal sense a budget is a document containing words and figures, which proposes expenditures for certain items and purposes. The words describe items of expenditure (salaries, equipment, travel) or purposes (preventing war, improving mental health, providing low-income housing), and the figures are attached to each item or purpose. Presumably, those who make a budget intend that there will be a direct connection between what is written in it and future needs. Hence, we might conceive of a budget as intended behavior, as a prediction. If the requests are granted, and if they are spent in accordance with instructions, and if the actions involved lead to the desired consequences, then the purposes stated in the document will be achieved. The budget thus becomes a link between financial resources and human behavior to accomplish policy objectives. Only through observation, however, is it possible to determine the degree to which the predictions postulated in the budget document turn out to be correct." [3]

A first step in budget preparation is to look again at the purposes of the agency and the needs it is designed to meet. Then a decision is made as to what resources are required to achieve the purpose. As Wildavsky says, "In the most general definition, budgeting is concerned with the translation of financial resources into human purposes. A budget, therefore, may be characterized as a series of goals with price tags attached. Since funds are limited and have to be divided in one way or another, the budget becomes a mechanism for making choices among alternative expenditures. When the choices are coordinated so as to achieve desired goals, a budget may be called a plan. Should [the administrator] include a detailed specification of how its objectives are to be achieved, a budget may serve as a plan of work for those who assume the task of implementing it. If emphasis is placed on achieving the most policy returns for a given sum of money, or on obtaining the desired objectives at the lowest cost, a budget may become an instrument for ensuring efficiency." [4]

How the administrator regards the budget and its preparation is crucial to the matter of who he involves in the preparation process. Clegg says,

"The preparation of the annual budget is one of the most important tasks performed by the Welfare Administrator. The budget sets the pattern for what can be accomplished by the department in the fiscal year which the budget covers. The budget also acts in a limiting manner, for that which is not anticipated in its preparation cannot be initiated and accomplished during the year." [5] Moss comments on the budget of the social service department in the hospital: "The social service director is responsible for helping to plan the departmental budget and for administering it during its period of operation. Obtaining capital and income for the social service department may be a serious problem in hospitals where the values of the social service activities have not been recognized. However, the social service department is a segment of the hospital program, and its method of obtaining funds must be the same as that used by the hospital itself. The director of the department will play little or no part in raising of funds, but in preparing and administering the budget of his department he is participating in the assembling of financial resources." [6]

Heads of departments and other key staff members have a contribution to make to the budget preparation process. As Clegg says, "While the actual preparation of the budget may be centered in a few individuals, it is helpful to enlist the estimates of personnel in the department who are close to a particular operation. For example, the supervisor of Aid to the Aged may have a first-hand knowledge of trends which will be helpful. When staff members are called upon for estimates, they develop a better knowledge and understanding of the budget than they would otherwise. This, also, is in a small way an opportunity for administrative growth in the supervisory level and should be considered for that reason." [7]

When the budget estimate has been drawn up, it must be presented to the boards of the voluntary agency or to the executive branch of the governmental agency. The administrator, often assisted by department heads and fiscal officers, must interpret the budget request pointing out why the funds are needed. Wildavsky makes some interesting points about the several purposes served by budgets when he says, "It should now be apparent that the purposes of budgets are as varied as the purposes of men. One budget may be designed to coordinate diverse activities so that they complement one another in the achievement of common goals. Another budget may be put together primarily to discipline subordinate officials within a governmental agency by reducing amounts for their salaries and their pet projects. And a third budget may be directed essentially to mobilizing the support of the clientele groups who benefit by the services that the agency provides. Nothing is gained, therefore, by insisting that a budget is only one of these things when it may well be all of them or many other kinds of things as well." [8]

In stating and discussing the services to be provided if the budget is adopted and funds provided, the administrator is committing the agency to a course of action that must be faithfully pursued. As Clegg points out: "Regardless of who does the actual work of [budget] preparation, the director of the Welfare Department is held responsible for it. He may take credit for its accuracies, but he must also answer for its deficiencies. He must present it to the board of local supervisors or commissioners charged with the responsibility of adjusting it, and he must return to that same governing board to request additional funds for any deficiencies which may occur." [9]

Budget Management and Evaluation

Living within the budget becomes the responsibility of the administrator once allocations have been made. Controls have to be set up on a monthly basis, and care must be taken to see to it that expenditures conform to the intentions expressed under the budget that was prepared and submitted. When budget adjustments must be made, approval has to be sought from higher authority, especially if the changes are major in scope. If deficiency appropriations are required to meet emergencies or unanticipated needs, these requests must go through the regular process.

Schottland makes a point about the power and responsibility of the administrator who controls the budget. He says, "Too frequently, the fund allocation process is looked upon as one in which the legislative body appropriates the funds. As we have pointed out, however, administrative decisions may be as important as legislative appropriations. Decisions made prior to submission of budgets to the legislature usually set over-all feelings while the subsequent decisions of budget officers or administrators may curtail expenditures or channel them into certain program areas rather than others. In many jurisdictions, considerable flexibility is given administrative officials in expending appropriated funds. Occasionally, legislative committees will appropriate additional sums and leave to the discretion of administrators their allocation to programs. In effect, this relegates a fund allocation role to administrators." Schottland observes in addition: "Many of us are beginning to learn that good laws may be sabotaged by inadequate appropriations, and good programs may be hampered by bad administrative decisions; that sound administrative decisions may be useless if inadequate fund allocations prevent their implementation or that even adequate fund allocations may be ineffective if their proper use is blocked by inept administrative decisions." [10]

In recent years, the federal government has developed what has become known as Program, Planning, Budgeting Systems (PPBS). [11] This approach has merit and helpful features for the administrator. As Greenberg says, "PPBS starts with the assumption that an organization rarely finds its resources adequate to finance all of the valid programs which are urgently needed. The program, planning, budgeting systems approach deliberately pits one program proposal against another—or more properly against all the others—and tries to assess the relative merits of each in achieving the organization's objectives. . . . Its practitioners hoped to achieve those gains through its use: First, to find some ways of achieving 'order' when faced with tons of data about large numbers of people, complex activities, interrelated programs, high powered demands for money, et cetera. Second, to make rational decisions wherever it is appropriate to be rational and to identify the value decisions which need to be made—and their consequences. . . . There are several basic operations in PPBS. The more you observe them, the closer you come to achieving the full potential of the method. These elements are: 1. Keep your eye on the 'end product'—not just on the specific activity; 2. Take a long-range view, looking five or even ten years in the future—rather than just a year-to-year review; 3. Identify alternative courses of action—and if none exists invent some; 4. Analyze each alternative course of action in terms of both its contribution toward achieving the 'end product' and its costs; 5. Keep tabs on what is happening in the system; and 6. Be flexible." [12]

Cost-Benefit Analysis

Another approach of considerable value to the administrator who wishes to evaluate the extent to which the budget is achieving its objectives is the "cost-benefit" method. Levine says, "By 'cost-benefit' is meant the relationship of the resources required—the cost—to attain certain goals—the benefits. It is based on the economic concept that many executive decisions involve the allocation, or best use, of limited resources among competing requirements. The allocation of available resources is determined by a comparative analysis of the current system with presumably practicable alternative systems. Thus conceived, cost-benefit analysis is a tool for the administrator confronted with the need to make choices among viable competing programs designed to achieve certain objectives. It is not a substitute for the educated judgment of the decision-maker. Rather it provides a package of relevant information on which to base certain kinds of decisions. Also, it does not favor the 'cheapest' or even the 'best' program, but the optimal program in terms of the available resources—money, trained personnel, facilities." Levine goes on to point out: "As generally used, cost-benefit analysis provides the administrator with a package of information to assist him in making a choice among alternative programs which are competing for that scarce resource—even in an affluent society—money. Actually the uses to which such an analysis can be put by administrators vary with the level of the administrator. For the local administrator it can serve as a guide to the improvement of project operations: to remind him of the objectives and to raise the question of whether project operations have strayed from the original objectives of the program. For the administrator of a state or national program such an analysis provides the basis for choice among programs to accomplish either the same or other important objectives in terms of the relative returns on investment." [13]

When one considers the fact that expenditures for social welfare are generally modest when compared with expenditures for defense, it can be argued that the nation receives a substantial return from whatever it invests in the welfare of its people. Because the returns are intangible and often hidden, it is difficult to make the public understand how important it is to help people with special needs. The administrator faces a never-ending task of interpreting the need for and importance of adequate resources for the work of his agency.

Financial Accountability and the Administrator

It must be emphasized that the administrator is finally accountable for carrying out the trust that goes with the acceptance of funds for human service purposes. Administrators are accountable to the appointing authority, to the staff, to the clientele, and to the public whether they be taxpayers, contributors or both. It is important for the administrator to be clear about all financial responsibilities and obligations, and these should be so described in the job specifications of all administrators. The contract or letter of appointment should go into these matters so that there will be no misunderstanding. Administrators are responsible for submitting regular financial reports to the board or the governmental authority and to the staff as well. There should always be an "open set of books" as well as an open administration.

It should be pointed out that the administrator is not the only person responsible for securing the financial resources needed by the agency. Actually, many people share in this responsibility. But the administrator should have leadership in *developing a plan* for securing resources from government, private contributions, federated financing bodies, fees for service, grants, and contracts. Of course, this is largely a matter of spelling out with clarity the objectives of the agency and the specific program needs. In addition, the administrator must take leadership in *developing a plan* for securing the resources from these various possibilities, and this is a matter of delegation, assignment, and follow-up. Having developed a plan and having secured resources, the administrator must then take leadership in determining with others how resources secured or committed are allocated or budgeted for specific agency functions. It then becomes necessary for the administrator to take leadership in the control, evaluation, and assessment of the extent to which *all* resources are used as they were promised and intended.

Much time goes into the cycle of budget-securing. There is the preparation of the request for funds for a stated period and from stated sources. This requires a review of program and objectives and input data from department heads, clients, and the community. Of course, the budget or finance committee is heavily involved. Then comes the submission of the budget request to various bodies, and this is a matter of written and oral interpretation, provided budget hearings are the practice. The cycle continues with the receipt of funds by allocation, and in turn, these must be properly distributed within the agency in terms of specific programs. Following this is the problem of continuous accountability and evaluation to assure that funds are being used properly.

In going through this cyclical work, it is, of course, necessary to look at current expenditures and past expenditures so as to make a future estimate of needs. It is also necessary to project program goals for the period ahead. This may mean a continuation of present programs, the launching of new programs, or the cutting back of programs. In any case, the budget will be a reflection of these kinds of decisions. Also, there is a great deal of estimating in terms of costs, and the best one can do usually is to anticipate known legal increases such as Social Security taxes and probable inflationary trends. Then fixed expenditures have to be studied in the areas of personal services such as salary and fringe benefits; contractural services such as telephone, fuel, and so on; consumable supplies; and equipment, either new, replaced, or repaired. Major capital budget requests for facility expansion require the same kind of cyclical process.

Because it is highly unlikely that any agency will receive all of the funds it needs to do all of the things it would like to do, administration has to have a plan for setting priorities and making the best use of what is available.

Some of the major issues faced by the country are the redefinition of social needs in modern society and the redefinition of governmental roles at various levels. There is also the role and responsibility of government with reference to the voluntary agencies.

Greene describes the changes that are going on in the field of private philanthropy in his thoughtful piece, "A Farewell to Alms." [14] He indicates that tax-supported programs are more and more thought of as the major source of revenue for the human services and sees a probable decline in private giving because people are being asked year after year to pay more in federal, state, and local taxes and thus feel that their contributions to private causes must be held steady or even curtailed. Corporate society also has to redefine its role, and as always, there must be greater clarity as to the responsibility of the individual in terms of individual needs.

NOTES

1. Walter A. Friedlander, *Introduction to Social Welfare*, 3rd ed. (Englewood Cliffs, N.J.: Prentice-Hall, Inc., 1968), p. 203.
2. Virginia Held, "PPBS Comes to Washington," *The Public Interest*, Summer 1966, p. 104.
3. Aaron Wildavsky, *The Politics of the Budgetary Process* (Boston: Little, Brown and Co., 1964), p. 1.
4. Ibid., pp. 1–2.
5. Reed K. Clegg, *The Administrator in Public Welfare* (Springfield, Ill.: Charles C. Thomas Publisher, 1966), p. 52.
6. Celia R. Moss, *Administering a Hospital Social Service Department* (Washington, D.C.: American Association of Medical Social Workers, 1955), p. 31.
7. Clegg, *The Administrator in Public Welfare*, p. 53.
8. Wildavsky, *The Politics of the Budgetary Process*, p. 4.
9. Clegg, *The Administrator in Public Welfare*, p. 52.
10. Charles I. Schottland, "Administrator Decisions and Fund Allocations in Social Welfare," Social Welfare Reprint Series 22, Brandeis University, The Florence Heller Graduate School for Advanced Studies in Social Welfare. Reprinted from *Economic Progress and Social Welfare*, ed., Leonard H. Goodman. Published for the National Conference on Social Welfare by Columbia University Press, 1966, pp. 65–66, 85–86.
11. Held, "PPBS Comes to Washington."
12. Martin Greenberg, "Program, Planning, Budgeting Systems," *Research Reports*, Council of Jewish Federations and Welfare Funds, New York, N.Y. Paper presented at the Annual Meeting of the National Conference of Jewish Communal Service, Atlantic City, N.J., May 26, 1967, pp. 1–2.
13. Abraham S. Levine, "Cost-Benefit Analysis and Social Welfare Program Evaluation," *The Social Service Review*, July 1968, pp. 174, 182.
14. Wade Greene, "A Farewell to Alms," *The New York Times Magazine*, May 23, 1976.

13 Agency Evaluation for Change and Growth

In this chapter, attention will be given to the evaluation of administration, the role of the administrator in providing leadership for the process of change, and ways of facilitating the growth of administrators and staffs.

The Importance of Evaluation

There are many reasons why it is important to evaluate administration. The quality of administration has a considerable influence on the quality of services rendered. Because the agency is held in trust by the community, it has a moral obligation to appraise the extent to which it is fulfilling its role. The community has a right to expect that the agency will evaluate itself. As Coughlin observes: "A social welfare agency is a public trust. Unlike a profit-making business or industry, but rather like a university, a welfare institution springs out of the culture and value and needs of the community, and offers to the community its service. In turn, it is financed and supported by the community, so that in a certain real sense the right to ownership is the community's, even though direct administrative responsibility is in the hands of a private group." [1]

The changing nature of the community and the changes in social service programs make administrative evaluation increasingly important.

A superintendent of schools underlines the importance of evaluation in the following local news story:

Burch Asks Board, Officials to Evaluate His Performance
By Carol Giacomo

WEST HARTFORD—Paul R. Burch concluded his first full year as school superintendent here by asking the Board of Education and his administrators to evaluate his performance—in writing.

It is believed to be the first time here—and possibly one of the few instances in this area that a superintendent deliberately made himself vulnerable to formal criticism by his staff and elected overseers, school officials said.

Burch had the results of the standard evaluation form interpreted by someone he described as "an individual outside the system in the field of education" so he could benefit from an "impartial" analysis, he said.

Burch did not make the results of the evaluation available for publication. But he agreed to discuss his reasons for the evaluation, an experiment he described as "humbling" and "worthwhile," and which he plans to continue using each year.

One reason demonstrates his political acumen. Burch, who has been with the system more than 25 years and through several administrations, said his predecessors complained after their firing that they were unaware of the great opposition against them building up in the school board and the community until it was too late.

Now, Burch said, while he is still fairly new in the office he wants to begin identifying trouble spots and begin correcting things "where I can."

Contending "The effectiveness of my performance can best be judged by those with whom I work," Burch said he also wants to know how his colleagues judge him.

"The point is that people have been given a chance to express pent-up feelings," he said, "if things I'm doing negatively affect the performance of a professional [educator] then the result is harmful to the system and students.

"All of us like to think we're perfect, but we're not," said Burch.

The evaluation, a three-page form Burch learned about while at an educators' conference, was distributed in early May to school principals, central administrators and the school board.

It included such questions as how the superintendent gets along with the board, how he presents himself in public and how he handles the business and financial affairs of the system.

Burch said he only asked respondents to indicate their level within the organization [principal, for instance] so he could get a reading on whether he was relating better to one group than another and why.

Board of Education Chairwoman Elizabeth K. Steven said the results of the evaluation as a whole were "very favorable" of Burch's performance. She termed it a "great measure of the man that he would initiate the formal evaluation of himself when it was not required.

"I can't praise him enough for doing it," she said. The procedure is particularly significant now, Mrs. Steven said, since state law now mandates school systems to devise a formal and sophisticated method of annual evaluations for all school personnel below the rank of superintendent.

"It has a real relation to the evaluation process we're trying to develop in the whole system," she said. "His attitude is that evaluation is to improve performance and really find strengths and weaknesses, not just to axe someone."

But a teacher suggested that it was significant Burch did not also ask the teaching staff to evaluate him.

Burch said he was "basically pleased" with the results because respondents "took it seriously" and "distributed their comments across the scale." But he admitted that in at least one case, a respondent expressed strong feelings against him.

Burch reported the results of the evaluation to the school board during an unannounced closed meeting last Monday.

He said he plans to analyze the results further in an effort to decide whether he wants to "move in the directions" suggested by some of the respondents in some areas.

He would not elaborate.

Burch said he would recommend other superintendents use a similar evaluation and would also be suggesting school principals here devise a process whereby teachers can similarly express their feelings about the leadership in a particular school building.[2]

Continuous and regular evaluation of administration is of significant benefit to the agency as a whole. It gets a picture of itself and sees points where it needs to be strengthened. It becomes more flexible and more able to modify its administrative practices.

When an agency evaluates its administration, it sets the tone for evaluation elsewhere. If it never looks at administration, it is less likely to attempt appraisal of other aspects of its work.

Evaluation is valuable to administrators because they need to know how well they are doing their jobs. When they know their strengths and limitations, they can work out programs of personal growth and self-improvement. Furthermore, administrators get a real sense of satisfaction when accomplishments are revealed through evaluation.

It would be the unusual administrator who did not question at one time or another whether or not his administration is really the "cup of tea" desired. Perhaps it would help if administrators were to ask such questions of themselves as:

1. Do I really like to assume so much responsibility for the problems that arise day after day?
2. Am I succeeding in dealing with these problems and growing in my ability to cope with them?
3. Am I constantly tuning up my listening operation so I really hear what people are saying?
4. Do I really like taking action even when disagreeable tasks come to the fore?
5. Am I spending my time working with people, or have I allowed myself to become bogged down with paper, things, and trivia?
6. Am I successful in recruiting and retaining able staff?
7. Am I using *all* of the resources at my disposal?
8. Am I critical of myself in a self-evaluative way, always seeking to improve my methods?
9. Do I help staff produce the best in services through creating a climate in which morale is turned into high motivation?
10. Am I enjoying my job and growing with it?

Criteria and Standards of Evaluation

A vital step in the evaluation of administration is the formulation of criteria and standards to be used by the person who is making the evaluation. This is not easy, for, as Moss says, "Social workers have sometimes been guilty of resisting standardized procedures in administration. The importance of individualization which is the primary tenet of casework, is often misconstrued when applied in administration. It is applicable in administration but the unit individualized is not always a person. Often it is a form of organization in relation to a function to be performed. One of the differences between business and social work is that of measurement. The social service department in the hospital does not operate on a profit motive that can be translated into financial gain. Its activities are essentially cooperative rather than competitive. It, therefore, has difficulty in evaluating the degree of success of its service, since for the most part success consists of enabling the persons served to achieve personally satisfying and socially useful lives within the limits of their illness. The skills of professional personnel which make this result possible are not often easily interpreted." [3]

In spite of the difficulty in formulating and applying criteria, more and more agencies are publishing helpful guides.[4] Gladieux lists eight elements of good administration of welfare: "1. A sharp distinction between the legislative powers and policy leadership of the governing board and the executive authorities of the chief administrator; with scrupulous observance of these respective roles by both parties. 2. Well-understood goals and well-defined programs arrived at through a process of intensive planning based on a perceptive evaluation of changing conditions and need. 3. The provision of a sound structural organization which divides the work to be performed into manageable functional units based on purposes to be served. 4. The clear fixing of administrative responsibility and the delegation and redelegation of authority to points of competence in the hierarchy. 5. The establishment of coordinating and control mechanisms at the level of a top responsibility and the provision of effective processes of consultation and decision-making. 6. A system of personnel management which recruits and maintains a staff corps that performs to the limit of its capacity and that is satisfied as to the equity and justness of its conditions of employment. 7. The provision of a rational budgetary and fiscal system that scrupulously controls expenditures and assures the balanced allocation of resources. 8. Sound business practices which take advantage of the multifarious and striking advances of modern management in procedural and mechanical techniques." [5]

Administrative Yardsticks for Evaluation

A workshop group listed twelve administrative yardsticks:
1. The agency's objectives and functions should be clearly defined. 2. The agency's program should be based upon actual needs; it should be limited in scope and territory to a field in which the agency can operate effectively; it should be related to the social welfare needs, patterns, and resources of the community; it should be regarded as dynamic rather than static; and the program should change to meet changing needs. 3. The agency should be soundly organized. This would include a clear distinction between policy-making and execution; cooperative and creative relationships between board, executive, and staff; unity of command, that is, administrative direction by a single executive; logical allocation of functions in accordance with a general plan of administration; clear and definite assignments of authority and responsibility; and effective coordination of all organization units and staff members. 4. Staff members should be employed on the basis of qualifications for their job. Staff personnel should be adequate in quantity and quality to the needs of the agency. Employees should be paid adequate salaries. The agency should operate on the basis of good working conditions and sound personnel policies. 5. The agency should be located effectively from the standpoint of its function; it should have adequate space, and equipment and supplies should be adequate in quantity and quality to its needs. 6. The agency's funds should be regarded as trust funds, to be administered in a sense of stewardship to those from whom the funds are received and to the community. The agency should operate on the basis of an annual budget; it should have an adequate accounting system; its accounts should be audited annually by a competent disinterested professional accountant; the sources of funds and methods of money raising should be appropriate to the nature and needs of the agency. 7. The agency should maintain adequate records. Records should be accurate, as comprehensive as necessary for the purpose yet as simple as possible, filed so as to be readily accessible when needed, and properly protected and safeguarded. 8. Clerical and maintenance services and facilities should be adequate in quantity and quality and efficient in operation. The agency should have an office or organization manual as a textbook for new staff members and a handbook of operation. 9. The agency should avoid isolation and should be an active and contributing participant in the social welfare services of the community. It should have constructive working relationships with appropriate local, state, and national bodies. 10. All who are connected with the agency should develop attitudes and methods of working which will build sound public relations. The agency should have a definite program of education and interpretation. The agency should seek to develop a constituency which will have a real understanding of the needs which it is trying to meet, and of its objectives, services, and problems. 11. The work of the agency should be characterized by a basic desire to serve human beings; an understanding of the individual whom it seeks to serve, and of their needs; a spirit of freedom, unity, and democratic participation in a common adventure in human service; and a sense of creativeness, movement, and growth. 12. At appropriate inter-

vals, probably once a year, the agency should put itself to the test of self-appraisal which would take stock of such matters as the successes and failures of the past year, the present status of the agency and its program, its performance as measured by objectives and established criteria, its strengths and weaknesses, its current problems, and the next steps that it ought to take.[6]

Criteria of Administrative Effectiveness

In an earlier volume, the author presented criteria that might be used in an evaluation of the effectiveness of administrative leaders.[7] These criteria have been revised and are offered below:

1. Effective administrative leaders advance the organization toward its goals of providing high quality programs and services. Barker and Briggs say, "Without a clear notion of what the organization's function is, there can be no way of determining whether manpower deployment has achieved its optimum level, but defining this function is an impressive challenge. This is so because every organization has many different functions, some of which are continually being modified, many of which are inconsistent with other functions, and most of which are not clear to the organization members. Furthermore, for every function there is a variety of possible means that may be used to fulfill it, and these different means must also be identified. Organization members may compete among themselves for the institution of means that are relevant to their own capacities. Pressures from a variety of sources, including other organizations, present barriers to the fulfillment of functions. Finally, members of the organization continually change in their capacities and interests and are subject to outside pressures that require behavior of them that may not be in harmony with the organization's functions." [8]

2. Effective administrative leaders have a deep and growing understanding of the culture and character of the agency. Moore's discussion of business organizations has pertinence for social agencies as well: "Each company has a history, a way of doing things, a set of conventions, customs, and social habits that constitute its character as a business. Executive development in many organizations represents a kind of acculturation process whereby the young executive is taught how this particular company operates—what its way is, what its character is, what kinds of things it will do, what kinds of things it positively will not do, what its policies, common symbols, ceremonials, and heroic figures are. The difference between the young immature executive, the fellow who doesn't know his way around, and the older one is often simply a difference in the degree of acculturation that has occurred. The latter knows the ins and outs of the organization, how to get things done, what symbols and conventions to invoke under varying circumstances; he looks, speaks, and acts the part. The other man doesn't even know how to write a letter; he doesn't know

business parlance, the lingo; he is unaware of all the sacred cows around the organization; he has no sense of the tempo of the place, how people dress, how they act, and how they get things done. There is an uneasiness about him because he has not yet learned the culture, symbols, and values of the organization. The culture or character of a business and the understanding that executives and employees within the organization have of this culture are important controls. As a consequence, determining the character of an organization, which really means determining who you are, where you are going, and how you operate in this complex world, is likely to absorb a great deal of the attention of top management." [9]

3. Effective administrative leaders give vigorous, continuous, and stimulating leadership to the people with whom they work.

4. Effective administrative leaders establish and maintain cooperative, productive working relationship with their community and with their regional and national affiliate groups.

5. Effective administrative leaders achieve a balance in relationships with the board, the staff, the constituency, and the community.

6. Effective administrative leaders state and project challenging goals for the period ahead and encourage people to work toward these goals. As Dimock puts it, this calls for an administrator "who can rise above his daily tasks and see his institution with a fresh eye; he is the one capable of providing energy and drive and preventing the onset of decline. Unfortunately, many administrators are limited to trouble-shooting, to the settling of immediate and often petty crises, and to keeping their noses to the grindstone; as a result, they have no time or energies left over to devote to questions of morale, inspiration, and vitality." [10]

7. Effective administrative leaders strive to create a sense of organization wholeness and unity. They place accent on the importance of coordination of human effort.

8. Effective administrative leaders strive to establish good channels of communication within which all members of the organization feel free to contribute their thoughts and energies. This makes for the growth of a responsive staff with high morale.

9. Effective administrative leaders give evidence of getting satisfaction out of their work and try to see that others also receive satisfaction.

10. Effective administrators plan their work carefully, they review their accomplishments and their shortcomings, and they set goals for themselves.

11. Effective administrators think ahead. They concentrate attention on forecasting trends and needs so that the organization will not get caught short.

12. Effective administrators predict and anticipate behavior. As a result of their sensitive timing, they avoid creating situations that arouse misunderstanding and conflict because people are not ready.

13. Effective administrators make good choices in terms of priorities and sequence of items that need to be done at a certain time.

14. Effective administrators select competent and qualified people and see to it that they are clear on their duties and responsibilities. They surround themselves with the best people they can get.

15. Effective administrators delegate responsibility to people and show faith in the ability of the people to carry through successfully the assignments they have accepted.

16. Effective administrative leaders keep people informed about plans, changes, problems, and other important areas of knowledge needed by the total work force.

17. Effective administrators seek to understand the continual changing force of the community, the nation, and the world and keep in mind their overall responsibility to their community.

18. Effective administrators exhibit a spirit and attitude that is buoyant, hopeful, positive, and contagious because they know this is an important factor in helping other people achieve their maximum potentials.

19. Effective administrative leaders have worked out a theory and a philosophy of administration grounded in conviction about democratic values.

20. Effective administrators are oriented toward the future and have learned how to facilitate change within their organization.

21. Effective administrators know how to handle the unexpected, emergency, crisis situation and know how to deal with the inevitable pressure of work. They are flexible and adaptable and give evidence of being able to respond to the challenge of the moment.

22. Effective administrative leaders concentrate attention upon the growth of persons and the development of leadership. As has been pointed out: "The continued vigor of any institution is dependent in large measure upon its ability to provide a continuous supply of creative leadership to its critical points of control." [11]

23. Effective leadership places emphasis on research and evaluation as means of helping them discover better ways of performing their tasks.

24. Effective administrative leaders spot emerging problems and move in on these problems before they become seriously advanced.

25. Effective administrative leaders know how to release the energy of people. As Schlesinger says, "The true test of an administrator may be, not his ability to design and respect organization charts, not his ability to keep within channels, but his ability to concert and release the energies of men for the attainment of public objectives. It might be argued that the essence of successful administration is: First, to acquire the ideas and information necessary for wise decisions; second, to maintain control over the actual making of the decision; and, third, to mobilize men and women who can make the first two things possible. . . ." [12]

26. Effective administrative leaders handle the mechanics of their job with confidence and dispatch.

27. Effective administrators are conscious of the importance of careful and close control of all finances.

28. Effective administrators build good understanding of the services and programs their agency offers through wide and continuous interpretation.

29. Effective administrative leaders make good use of technical resource experts to provide special help on special problems.

30. Effective administrative leaders have worked out a thoughtful program of self-development, including reading, participation in conferences, seminars, and the like.

Questions to Guide Administrative Evaluation

When an evaluation is made of the structure, organization, and administrative processes of the agency, such questions as the following may serve as a guide:

1. Are all unit roles, that is, board, staff, constituency, and so on, clearly defined and understood?
2. Are all overall policy and operating decision centers clearly identified and understood?
3. Are there well-established channels of communication, horizontal and lateral, formal and informal?
4. Are there adequate means and mechanisms for continuous coordination of all groups working in the agency?
5. Are there ways of getting steady in-put from the service population and from the community?
6. Are there continuous ways of interpreting the work of the agency as a means of securing the understanding, participation, and support of both clientele and community?
7. Is the responsibility of the chief administrator clear to all?
8. Are there appropriate delegated responsibilities to assistant administrators and to staff?
9. Are there provisions for program evaluation?
10. Is there a built-in way of reviewing the structure of the agency on a periodic basis?

In his excellent checklist for top administrators, Goodner offers six items of major importance. He says the administrator must identify problems quickly and concisely and must have well-developed skills in problem-solving. He goes on to say that the administrator must have a clearly developed system for making systematic and widely understood decisions. Communication is next on his list, and everyone involved in the agency must have all the information he needs at the proper time. Goal-understanding is likewise listed as of major importance, and objectives must be clear to everyone in the agency. Goodner also emphasizes the importance of priority-setting and utilizing resources accordingly. In addition, he calls for a complete understanding of the evaluation processes used with the staff and administration. While he makes no claim that this is a complete list, it is obvious that all of the points are important.[13]

The Administrator's Role in Facilitating Change

The social work administrator must assume considerable responsibility for facilitating change. *First,* he must be expert in diagnosing and determining the need for change. This is another way of saying that he locates agency problems and spots points at which changes are needed in the agency's operations. *Second,* the administrator must be an expert in assessing the motivation, the capacity, and the readiness on the part of people to change. *Third,* the administrator must have an understanding of his own motivation for change, his own capacity to change, and an awareness of what change is going to do to him. All too often administrative staffs expect other people to change without being willing to change themselves. *Fourth,* the administrator must have skill in selecting appropriate change objectives and in relating those objectives to a time span. Changes that might be suitable at one time are not necessarily suitable at another time. Changes that require months to accomplish are different from changes that may require years to accomplish. *Fifth,* the administrator has the responsibility of choosing the appropriate type of helping role within the change situation. He may take leadership in gathering, collating, and interpreting needs factual materials. He may give leadership to the formulation of change plans and objectives. *Sixth,* the administrator must establish and maintain a helping relationship or helping role in the change process. He must be willing to modify his role as new and different needs emerge.

As Vasey has pointed out: "The concept of social welfare in the United States of America is not constant but rather it alters with changing conditions. Most recently, social welfare has been defined as encompassing the development and administration of (1) social insurance, (2) social assistance, and (3) other social services designed to strengthen family life and to provide care and protection for special groups such as children, the aged, and mentally, socially or physically handicapped persons." [14]

As Titmuss says, "The inescapable fact, regardless of whether we like the world as it is today, is that we are all living in a period of startlingly rapid change. In the past, economic and social changes were affected only at the price of immense hardship. The amount and rate of change under way today, and affecting all countries in varying degrees, may in some areas be less crudely evident in strictly economic terms but the consequences as a whole may be no less profound—though more subtly expressed—in generating social frustration and psychological stress. In other respects, economic and industrial changes dominate the problems of societies in transition. In all countries, the question of 'how to live together in society' is made more insistent by the widespread and pervasive effects of technological change. Yet little is known about how all these factors of change are affecting levels of poverty and need, patterns of family living, and community relations. Change, however induced, cannot take place without people being hurt. In consequence, new and different social needs are constantly arising, many of which are (or should be) the direct concern of social workers and social welfare programs. To identify and meet these needs and to minimize and prevent the hardships caused by change, social policy should be better informed. More and better data about the human condition, constructive and critical, should be at the disposal of policy-makers and administrators." [15]

Critics of society's institutions frequently levy the charge that the human services are not changing fast enough to meet the new needs and rising demands for service. As Marien says, "Although there is evidence of a trend toward humanistic organization, it is also clear that organizations—especially those facing little competition—have not changed fast enough to meet demands for new services and the growing norm of participation. Indeed, every public institution is under attack today for obsolete personnel, structure, and processes: Police and welfare departments, schools and colleges, planning agencies and post offices, foreign policy-makers and political parties, churches and labor unions, the construction and transportation industries, Congress and state legislatures, hospitals and mental hospitals, and prisons and courts. Ironically, the institutions most responsive to human needs—those producing toothpaste, tires, and television sets—are probably the least important to our 'progress' or survival." [16]

Specht feels that at least some of the blame for failure to change rests with the administrators: "The basis for institutional policy change is in some problems identified as an unrecognized or unmet need in the community, a need the originator of the policy goal believes that the institution is responsible for meeting. The perception of the problem and the institution's responsibility are related to the political, economic, social and institutional forces that come to bear on the perceiver; what is perceived to be a problem will depend on the institutional position of the initiator. So, for example, it is possible that concerns for institutional maintenance might guide the perceptions of professional administrators more than their feelings of responsibility for providing better service to clients." [17]

The administrator must realize that every agency is always undergoing change and that in every agency there are forces that resist change. Likert says, "Every organization is in a continuous state of change. Sometimes the changes are great, sometimes small, but change is always taking place. The conditions requiring these changes arise from both within and without. As a consequence, there is never-ending need for decisions which guide adjustments to change. The adequacy of these decisions for meeting an organization's current and developing internal and external situations determine the well-being, power, and future of that organization. We are coming to recognize with increasing clarity that the capacity of an organization to function well depends both upon the quality of its decision-making processes and upon the adequacy of the information used. Sound decisions require accurate information about relevant dimensions of the problem as well as correct interpretation of that information. If the information available for decision-making is inaccurate or is incorrectly interpreted, the diagnostic decisions are likely to be in error and the actions taken inappropriate." [18]

Dalton, Barnes, and Zaleznik say, "The forces for change represented by tension and the desire for change must be mobilized, however, and given direction. Those forces acting to resist change in some given direction must be overcome, neutralized, or enlisted. In an organization, unless there is to be protracted resistance, someone must gain the acceptance and possible support of individuals not seeking change and even of those who feel threatened by it. The initiator of change gains support and overcomes resistance in proportion to his power and the relevance of his power to the objectives of the organization. His power in turn stems in large measure from the multiple resources of authority attached to his position in the structure." [19]

The social work administrator who takes leadership in the change process is helped by Kahn and Katz, who list four suggestions for facilitating change: "(1) In every attempt to create change, specify the target for change—change in individual behavior, in individual personality, in some interpersonal relationship, in family arrangements, or whatever it may be. . . . (2) Remember that no method of change is uniquely powerful and appropriate to all situations. Learn to use more than one approach, to judge the indicators favoring one or another. Above all, learn to use them in combination. . . . (3) Learn to work with the natural groups in which the individual functions—family, friends, organizations, work groups. Use them to learn of his life situation from observers besides himself, and use them to reinforce and secure and assist the process of change. . . . (4) Social workers [should] acknowledge the importance of and attempt to utilize . . . direct systematic changes—changes which involve altering formal procedures, policies, and structural arrangements." [20]

While it is true that no one knows nearly enough about how to facilitate change, some studies have been enormously helpful. As Ginsberg and

Reilley put it, "Effecting change in large organizations is primarily a question of alterations in the behavior of various groups who carry major responsibility. Top management must recognize, therefore, that its success in carrying out the major changes will largely depend on how well it mobilizes the psychological forces that can facilitate acceptance of the new and how well it diminishes those forces which reinforce people's adherence to the existing pattern. The major approaches available to management are effective communication, the control of anxiety, and the learning of new skills." [21]

There is substantial argreement that when staff members are involved in the change process and in the decision to change there is a much greater chance that the change will be accepted. As Guest notes: "Controls imposed by persons at the top of the hierarchy do not assure either efficiency or the cooperation of subordinates. There must be some kind of involvement from below which makes it possible for subordinates to accept changes and even to initiate a certain amount of change themselves. Put in the form of a general hypothesis: In a complex organization tension and stress will diminish and performance will improve with the introduction of social mechanisms which permit those in subordinate positions to participate in making decisions affecting their present and future roles in the organization." [22]

Dalton, Barnes, and Zaleznik agree: "In instances of successful change, there is a movement over time toward increased self-regard as the person finds himself capable of making the changes in behavior or attitude. He experiences a sense of accomplishment, a relief from tension, and a reintegration around a new pattern of activity and thought." [23]

As administrators evaluate the change process in their agencies, they come to realize that change in one part of the organization is likely to call for changes in other parts. As Kahn and Katz observe: "The degree of control and regulation of the activities of an organization cannot be changed at one level without affecting the whole organization. In fact, there is a characteristic of the properties of a system. If we are dealing with an organizational or system variable, we are working with something which applies to the entire organization. Change of such organizational characters is regarded as inherently difficult because it means changing so much and of course, this is correct. What is overlooked, however, is that less ambitious attempts to modify organizational processes by working with non-organizational variables is definitely more difficult from the point of view of organization outcome, though it may entail less effort on the part of the change agent." [24]

Administration has to understand the feelings of individuals who will be affected by agency changes. This requires a thorough knowledge and a careful evaluation of the effect that change will have on the total organization before action is taken. As Selznick says,

The art of the creative leader is the art of institution building, the reworking of human and technological material to fashion an organism that embodies a new and enduring view. The opportunity to do this depends on a considerable sensitivity to the politics of internal change. This is more than a struggle for power among contending groups and leaders. It is equally a matter of avoiding recalcitrance and releasing energies. Thus winning consent to new directions depends on how secure the participants feel. When many routine problems of technical and human organization remain to be solved, when the minimum conditions for holding the organization together are only precariously met, it is difficult to expend energy on long-range planning and even harder to risk experimental programs. When the organization is in good shape from an engineering standpoint, it is easier to put ideals into practice. Old activities can be abandoned without excessive strain, for example, the costs of relatively inefficient but morale-saving transfer and termination can be absorbed. Security is bartered for consent. Since this bargain is seldom sensed as truly urgent, a default of leadership is the more common experience. On the same theme, security can be granted, thereby releasing energies for creative change, but examining established procedures to distinguish those important to a sense of security from those essential to the aims of the enterprise. Change should focus on the latter; stability can be assured to practices that do not really matter so far as objectives are concerned but which do satisfy the need to be free from threatening change. Many useless industrial conflicts have been fought to protect prerogative and deny security, with but little effect on the ultimate competence of the firm. If one of the great functions of administration is the exertion of cohesive forces in the direction of institutional security, another great function is the creating of conditions that will make possible in the future what is excluded in the present. This requires a strategy of change that looks to the attainment of new capability more nearly fulfilling the truly felt needs and aspirations of the institution leadership.[25]

The individual is likely to react positively toward change when he feels that it will strengthen the organization and his important place in it. As Dalton, Barnes, and Zaleznik say, "Increasing self-esteem also appears to be an integral part of the phenomenon of behavioral and attitudinal change. Interestingly, moving toward greater self-esteem seems to be a facilitating factor not only in establishing new patterns of thought and action, but also in unfreezing old patterns. Abandoning previous patterns of behavior and thought is less difficult when an individual is moving toward an increased sense of his own worth. Movement along this continuum is away from a sense of self-doubt toward a feeling of positive worth, from a feeling of partial inadequacy toward a confirmed sense of personal capacity. The increased sense of one's own potential is evident all along this continuum, not merely at the end." [26]

Lowenstein and his colleagues make some interesting observations growing out of their research on the management of organizational change. They are aware of the complexities and uncertainties involved in all organizational change and suggest that it is vital that workers be given certainty that their jobs are safe. When job duties have to be changed because of agency reorganization, the process should be handled carefully and fairly. Workers should have a voice and a choice in the new duties that they may be asked to take on. There should be full worker involvement in the entire reorganization process. Then, of course, there must be special efforts made to retrain workers whose roles are to be altered considerably. Clients likewise must be involved in learning how to use the new system of services. Lowenstein and his colleagues urge incremental and gradual change so that the impact will be spread over a period of time because sudden changes are always disruptive.[27]

Principles of Institutional Change

The best formulation of principles of institutional change was prepared by Sorenson and Dimock. They developed ten principles as a result of their extensive research:

1. Policy making or legislation by the official Board of Directors is a developmental process in planned change. Policy control by citizen groups is a cardinal principle of institutional life. Technical contributions by staff are essential in proper combination with citizen policy control. Keeping these two factors in proper relation through periods of change is important, and it is not easy. Neglect of either principle blocks permanent change. The hard fact in policy making is that voting by a board does not necessarily change the attitudes, habits and practices of the organization. A new policy must be undergirded with enough understanding, commitment, and ability to carry it out or it will be only a good resolution on the books. This means that some change must actually take place before official policy becomes really governing policy. . . .

2. Planned change in an institution takes time and occurs by stages. Only insignificant changes are effected quickly. A considerable span of years is required to change attitudes, generate motivation, create new methods, materials, and facilities, get new habits for old, and establish new ways as accepted policy. Willing it, voting it, exhorting for it, does not bring significant change. Recognizing in advance that it will take time and projecting some scheme of stages (even though they cannot be firmly scheduled) has strong advantages. It relieves anxieties on the part of the participants, thereby lessens resistance and encourages positive attitudes toward the undertaking. It saves the administrative leadership from frustration arising from trying to accomplish everything all at once, releasing them to take each stage in stride. It also insures against certain failure if too short a time expectancy is assumed.

3. Planned institutional change must reckon with the strength and resilience of established patterns. If this were not so, institutions would die more easily. It is a common observation that ten years, and often twenty years, of mismanagement do not kill an old organization. The complex attitudes and habits in all the parts hold an agency together and cause it to persist even when administrative leadership is lacking or blundering. This fact, which protects an institution

and which permits its body to live on even when the head is missing, is what makes changing an institution so difficult and so slow. . . .

4. Determined and persistent administrative leadership is required for planned institutional change. Because the whole agency is involved, in all its policy-making, administrative, financial, building, personnel, and program aspects, it is not possible for the executive officer to delegate program modernization to some staff member. Unmistakable commitment by the board and the executive to achieving the planned change is essential to give the effort the force of full "company policy." The administrative leadership must be continuing, persistent yet patient, and confident rather than sporadic, intermittent, easily discouraged with blocks, resistances, and time consumed, or threatened by hostility and failures. . . . The executive's job is always a twofold one: to administer change and to achieve cooperation in organization. These tend to pull in opposite directions. There is conflict between newer ways and newer policies that can be voted on and declared quickly and the old habits of men and institutions which change slowly. Beyond a certain point the processes of change cannot be hurried. Management involves a wide gamut of interpersonal and inter-group relations. It is not a technical but a human matter. Change without attention to cooperation in the social system is, ultimately, to fail to change. . . .

5. Planned institutional change precedes from centralized to distributed operations and from external to internal motivation. At the outset, administrative leadership supplies the initiative, sets up meetings, does the bulk of the document formulation, enlists participation and cooperation, and gets the early steps in motion. In this early stage it is necessary as well as inevitable that such operations as get under way are centralized and that for most of the staff and constituency the motivation for the project is chiefly external, that is, in the administrative leadership. This does not mean that they are not for it, but that they have not participated in and agreed to, the decision, or that they are not anxious to see it succeed. But such commitment is permissive, not propulsive, in the early stages. As the project proceeds, the involvement of staff, advisors, and officers becomes deeper. Satisfactions come from new ways of doing things. As new skills are gained, confidence, security, and further commitment to the new ways develop. They are then more ready to take responsibility and leadership in their own branch and group. Persuading and training others speeds the process of internalizing motivation. . . .

6. Planned change in an institution calls for detecting and dealing with blocks. There will be blocks in the form of specific difficulties, fallacies in early assumptions, resistance, and specific need for additional processes and skills. It is impossible to foresee the whole route, the detours, the engine trouble, the poor roads and obstacles, or the number of miles ahead. No complete map or report of road conditions is available in advance. Knowing and accepting the fact that there will be difficulties is some preparation for them. Skill in diagnosing them as they arise grows with practice. The reasons for resistance to change must be discerned beneath the symptoms. Remedies for some difficulties must await more insights and motivation in the persons. Some problems call for administrative changes; some, for additional training; others, for revision in materials and methods; and still others yield with some catharsis or talking it out.

7. Institutional change is basically in persons and human relations. Institutional change is personality change. An organization is the sum of the attitudes, habits, and practices of the people in its leadership. Therefore, the deeper the institutional changes desired, the deeper the changes must be in staff. Logically, institutional change could come quicker if the re-education of the staff came first. Practically, this is not possible. Staff realization of the need for change comes enroute, as they become more involved. The need for staff re-education comes only as the need for it is discovered by them in the process of undertaking program change.

8. Administrative changes go with program change. As new ways of work are tried, blocks become apparent which are involved in building design or building usage, staff organization and assignments, and finance. Again, it would be logical to tackle these essentials first. But such changes usually require the pitchfork of necessity. New ways of working, when blocked by older administrative arrangements, generate readiness for undertaking difficult changes in structure, finance, and buildings. Budgets, organization, buildings, and administrative procedures are means to ends. They exist to support functions. When functions change, the means must change. However, so devoted do people become to the outer forms of structure, budgets, and buildings that their continued operation almost becomes ends. Functions are squeezed and adjusted to the inherited forms, rather than the forms being adjusted to changes in functions. When people come to care most about the vital functions, they are ready to change the inherited forms. This is what happens at the stage in planned change where the inherited structure, budget, and buildings get in the way of what people are enthusiastic to do. Changing the institution is a by-product of changing what the institution does. A new concept of function with its goals and methods set new directions. The blueprint for institutional change grows out of changes in function. Program changes fashion changes in every other part of the institution.

9. Institutions have not been changed until the changes have been consolidated, rooted, or established as normal. This is the fact too often overlooked in short-term experiments. No matter how sound or how effective has been a short demonstration, the institution itself will be relatively unchanged by the novel interlude unless the new is rooted in regular procedures and habits as established in normal ways. This means that enough people must understand and approve the changes. The new ways must be established as policy in the organization. And the new practices must be established in harmony with the new policies as normal operating habits. The "new" must no longer be new. It must have become the usual.

10. Institutions have not really changed until the members are undergoing a different experience. Real institutional change is not petty manicuring of the externals or just rearranging machinery or even in exciting professional exercise by the staff. Real change is measured at the heart, in the experience of the members for which it exists. Until that happens, all else is prelude.[28]

Growth of Administrators and Staffs

One of the vital areas of need in all social agencies is an educational program designed to further the growth of administrators and their staffs. If persons are to develop their skills and achieve higher levels of competence, they must engage in programs of study developed by the agency or by a group of agencies or by institutions of higher education in cooperation with the agencies. As Clegg points out: "Welfare departments should have an on-going training program for all employees who are working in the social service program. The program should be designed to increase the competency of the staff, and to provide a continuing training program for efficient operation of new programs and changes in existing programs. The programs must take into consideration the levels of performance of administrative, social work, technical and clerical staff, and be geared to upgrading performance at all levels." [29]

What is involved when the social work administrator seeks to develop his skills and competences? *First,* he should accept the fact that this is an individual matter. No two administrators have exactly the same needs at any given time. Consequently, each administrator should frame his own program by self-development. *Second,* to formulate such a program, the administrator must analyze the job he is doing and focus upon the skills required to do it well. He will discover that in some areas he is strong and in other areas less so. *Third,* as discussed earlier in this chapter, evolution of the agency will reveal points where improvements are needed. *Fourth,* the administrator must try to set aside time for reading and for attending conferences, institutes, workshops, and seminars. In so doing, he sets a tone for the agency and encourages others on the staff to do likewise. *Fifth,* the administrator can learn much about the community by participating actively in community affairs. *Sixth,* in his supervision of his key aides, the administrator can locate areas of development important for all. In addition, he can spot persons who show good potential for growth and the ability to assume more complicated administrative tasks. *Seventh,* by participating in research efforts, the administrator has the opportunity to learn much about the extent to which his leadership of the agency is resulting in good achievement. *Eighth,* by formulating a comprehensive program of in-service training, the administrator locates common growth needs of everyone who works for the agency.

Staff Development and In-service Training

Many agencies have directors of staff development and in-service training who are responsible to the executive. As Clegg says, "Staff development is a widely used term which relates to any process or program whereby an agency or department seeks to improve staff performance during the period of time they remain with the agency or department as employees. It includes all efforts to increase knowledge through planned instruction, reading or academic training, technical skills basic to job performance and improvement in work habits and attitudes. It includes training on the job and participation in training activities outside the scope of regular working hours. . . . All supervisory staff must share responsibility for staff development. Much of the encouragement and necessary inspiration for participation in staff development programs will spring from supervisory conferences with individual employees and from group discussions in unit meetings." [30]

As Schroeder says: "Staff development is important because it serves to strengthen an agency and provides for improvement of staff services to clientele. In order for educational activities to be successful within the agency, it is essential that this belief be implemented by administrative sanction and support, by planning for this part of the program as systematically as for the other necessary parts of the program. Four principles are identified as basic to the planning of an educational program: 1. Staff development should be continuous and ongoing. 2. Staff development should be planned. Plans should include the educational assessment of staff members, which, along with the needs and problem areas in the agency, forms the basis for the formulation of objectives. Educational objectives should always be service oriented. 3. A variety of techniques can be used in carrying out the educational program. The particular combination of agency needs, staff needs, and immediate goal will determine which techniques are applicable at any particular time. 4. Staff development must be an integral part of the total program." [31]

Taylor and associates observe that: "To be successful, a staff development program must ensure—1. identification of training needs on a long-term and current basis for groups of staff as well as for individuals; 2. use of the administratively planned and implemented methods of training available within the State agency and its subdivisions; 3. use of educational resources outside the agency in accordance with the special needs of individual staff members; and 4. establishment of policies concerning the rights and obligations of personnel with respect to training and technical and professional education, the educational requirements for various positions, training, leave for short-time study, and attendance at professional conferences and meetings." [32]

In her brilliant formulation of criteria and guidelines for the evaluation of in-service training, Heyman sees the agency's administrative structure and policy as basic: "In-service training is an essential component of administration. . . . The goals, content, and methods of training are necessarily determined by the continually developing and shifting agency goals and programs. In addition, training holds implications for organizational change. Frequently, the need for organizational change is identified during in-service training by the trainers themselves and brought to the attention of program administrators. Frequently, organizational change is identified as a result of the training through the trainee's increased knowledge and skill and appropriate attitudes toward the client. The trainee reflects these changes in a new perception of his job which in turn may call for structural and policy change within the agency. To implement the integral relationships between in-service training and administration, there is a constant flow of intelligence between them. This is made effective by locating the position of Director of Staff Development among the policy-making staff positions of the agency." [33]

The principles of social work administration, which are summarized in the next chapter, can be used as a guide for the formulation of educational programs.

NOTES

1. Bernard J. Coughlin, S.J., "Interrelationships of Governmental and Voluntary Welfare Services," *The Social Welfare Forum,* 1966 (Published for the National Conference on Social Welfare by Columbia University Press, New York), p. 95.
2. Carol Giacomo, "Burch Asks Board, Officials to Evaluate His Performance," *The Hartford Courant,* Sunday, July 13, 1975, p. 2B.
3. Celia R. Moss, *Administering a Hospital Social Service Department* (Washington, D.C.: American Association of Medical Social Workers, 1955), p. 57.
4. In this connection, the National Federation of Settlements and Neighborhood Centers has prepared a checklist for rating neighborhood centers entitled, *Measuring Up!* (1967). Also the Midwest Region of the National Jewish Welfare Board has developed, *A Guide for Creating Tools for Program Evaluation* (1968).
5. Bernard L. Gladieux, "Management Imperatives for Welfare Administrations in the Future," New York: National Social Welfare Assembly, December 12, 1957, p. 4.
6. *Proceedings of Workshop on Social Agency Administration—Leadership and the Social Welfare Executive,* Richmond Professional Institute—School of Social Work, Richmond, Va., April 12–14, 1967, pp. 27–28.
7. Harleigh B. Trecker, *New Understandings of Administration* (New York: Association Press, 1961), pp. 193–197.
8. Robert L. Barker and Thomas L. Briggs, *Differential Use of Social Work Manpower* (New York: National Association of Social Workers, 1968), p. 57.
9. David G. Moore, "What Makes a Top Executive?" in Robert T. Golembiewski and Frank Gibson, ed., *Managerial Behavior and Organization Demands* (Chicago: Rand McNally and Co., 1967), pp. 330–331.
10. Marshall E. Dimock, *Administrative Vitality* (New York: Harper and Row, 1959), p. 59.
11. *Professional Administrators for America's Schools,* 38th Yearbook, 1960 (Washington, D.C.: American Association of School Administration, National Education Association), p. 143.
12. Arthur M. Schlesinger, Jr., *The Age of Roosevelt—The Coming of the New Deal,* Vol. II (Boston: Houghton-Mifflin Co., 1959), p. 522.
13. Jack Goodner, "A Checklist for Top Administrators," *College Management,* May 1974, pp. 22–24.
14. Wayne Vasey, *Government and Social Welfare* (New York: Holt, Rinehart, and Winston, 1958), p. 10, quoted from "Social Welfare Administration in the United States," a report prepared at the request of the United Nations for incorporation in its international study of social welfare administration.

15. Richard M. Titmuss, *Commitment to Welfare* (New York: Pantheon Books—A Division of Random House, 1968), pp. 42–43.
16. Michael Marien, "Irrepressible Revolt," *New Republic,* February 22, 1969, p. 31.
17. Harry Specht, "Casework Practice and Social Policy Formulation," *Social Work,* January 1968, p. 45.
18. Rensis Likert, *The Human Organization* (New York: McGraw-Hill Book Co., 1967), p. 128.
19. Gene W. Dalton, Louis B. Barnes, and Abraham Zaleznik, *The Distribution of Authority in Formal Organizations* (Cambridge: Harvard University, Division of Research, Graduate School of Business Administration, 1968), pp. 114–115.
20. Robert L. Kahn and Daniel Katz, "Social Work and Organizational Change," *The Social Welfare Forum,* 1965 (Published for the National Conference on Social Welfare by Columbia University Press, New York), pp. 179–181,
21. Eli Ginsberg and Ewing W. Reilley, *Effecting Change in Large Organizations* (New York: Columbia University Press, 1957), p. 60.
22. Robert H. Guest, *Organizational Change—The Effect of Successful Leadership* (Homewood, Ill.: Dorsey-Irwin, 1962), pp. 153–54.
23. Dalton, Barnes, and Zaleznik, *The Distribution of Authority,* p. 132.
24. Kahn and Katz, "Social Change," p. 179.
25. Philip Selznick, *Leadership in Administration* (New York: Harper and Row, 1957), pp. 22–28, 33–43, 62–64, 149–154.
26. Dalton, Barnes, and Zaleznik, *The Distribution of Authority,* pp. 129–130.
27. Edward R. Lowenstein et al., "The Management of Organizational Change: Some Findings and Suggestions," *Public Welfare,* Winter 1973.
28. Roy Sorenson and Hedley S. Dimock, *Designing Education in Values—A Case Study in Institutional Change* (New York: Association Press, 1955), pp. 204–210.
29. Reed K. Clegg, *The Administrator in Public Welfare* (Springfield, Ill.: Charles C. Thomas Publisher, 1966), p. 105.
30. Ibid., p. 107.
31. Dorothy Schroeder, "Basic Principles of Staff Development and Their Implementation," in *Staff Development in Mental Health Services,* ed. George W. Wagner and Thomas L. Briggs (New York: National Association of Social Workers, 1966), pp. 45–46.
32. Eleanor K. Taylor, Eulene Hawkins, and Hilda P. Tebow, *Administrative Approaches to Staff Development in Public Welfare Agencies,* (Washington, D.C.: U.S. Department of Health, Education, and Welfare, Social and Rehabilitation Service, 1968), pp. 16–17.
33. Margaret M. Heyman, *Criteria and Guidelines for the Evaluation of In-Service Training* (Washington, D. C.: U.S. Department of Health, Education and Welfare, Social and Rehabilitation Service), pp. 5–6.

14 Basic Principles of Social Work Administration

In this concluding chapter, the principles of social work administration will be presented. In a sense, the chapter is a summary of the book in that the principles grow out of what has been discussed in Chapters 1 through 13.

Principles Defined

One dictionary declares that a principle is "an accepted or professed rule of action or conduct" and "a fundamental, primary, or general law or truth from which others are derived" and "an adopted rule or method for application in action." [1]

White says that "a principle must be understood to mean a hypothesis so adequately tested by observation and/or experiment that it may intelligently be put forward as a guide to action, or as a means of understanding." [2]

Barr and associates observe that "a principle is a verbalized statement of an observed uniformity relative to some class of objects. . . . Principles —that is, general rules or laws, concepts, fundamental truths, generally accepted tenets—are the means by which we proceed from one situation to another. . . . Principles may arise from either critically analyzed experience or from systematic investigation." [3]

The principles of social work administration are generalized statements for use by the administrator as he does his job. These statements of good practice in administration have grown out of observation, analysis, and research. They are separate ideas, but they are also interrelated and, taken as a composite, constitute a philosophy of administration.

The Importance of Principles

Administrators who have an understanding of basic principles and who use these principles to guide them in the action they take are behaving professionally. They make choices and decisions not in terms of technique but rather in terms of broad beliefs as to what social work is, the values that undergird it, and the purposes it serves in society. Professional skill rests upon one's knowledge of how people behave and how they work together.

The social work administrator who is guided by principles works planfully and consistently. Methods and goals are closely related. There is a drive for excellence in work that encourages others to perform to the best of their ability. When confronted with situations where values are in conflict, decisions are made in terms of what is regarded as being best for the clients. In evaluating the work of the principle-oriented administrators, the long view is taken rather than the short view.

Principles are the most useful tools the administrator has. They are tools for the analysis of problems, the determination of goals, the choice of methods, the assignment of responsibilities, and the evaluation of results. When the administrator pays serious attention to principles, his efforts are creatively productive in terms of the growth of persons and the advancement of the agency to high levels of accomplishment.

Basic Principles of Social Work Administration

The eighteen principles that are offered and discussed below represent the author's formulation. It is hoped that they will be useful and will lead administrators to their own formulations of principles as they see them.
1. *The Principle of Social Work Values.*

In social work administration, the values of the profession are the foundations upon which services are developed and made available to persons who need them. The administrator and everyone in the agency responsible for providing service must accept these values and be guided by them.

Central to this principle is our belief in the dignity and worth of all people and in their right to participate in making decisions about matters that affect them. Administrators who accept social work values and are guided by them believe deeply in freedom of expression and respect the rights of individuals in this regard. The human personality is considered to be the prime source of energy and influence in administrative work. The way administrators accept individuals as persons and release their energies and talents is reflected in the tone of the agency and in the way it does its work. The individual and his needs are always the primary concern of the administrator. Administration is responsible for the individual's basic well-being. An essential attribute of social work administration is the realization by all individuals of their full potential to serve society through participation in the purposeful work of the agency. The administration is obligated to find ways by which individuals can achieve self-realization. What happens to people is always of central importance.

2. *The Principle of Community and Client Needs.*

In social work administration, the needs of the community and the individuals within it are always the basis for the existence of social agencies and the provision of programs. The administration along with the others who make up the agency must accept the fact that the meeting of needs is their primary obligation.

The principle of community and client needs implies that the administrator will seek always to understand the condition out of which needs arise and that he will work to remove such conditions insofar as is possible. The administrator will have a method of studying the community to discover points of stress and will anticipate emerging needs to be better prepared to meet them. He will seek to relate the agency to all of the forces making for the enrichment of community life and the strengthening of community services. The administrator will be an active participant in the community development process.

3. *The Principle of Agency Purpose.*

In social work administration, the social purposes of the agency must be clearly formulated, stated, understood, and utilized. The administrator, along with others, makes decisions and takes action in terms of the extent to which the decisions and actions will further the achievements of the stated objectives of the agency.

The administrator who recognizes the need for consciously formulated specific objectives for the agency becomes a purposeful leader who influences the course of the agency in terms of agreed-upon goals. Skillful administrators make wise and continuous use of agency *purpose*. It should be their primary point of reference. It should influence and guide every move they make.

The administrator, therefore, must be increasingly clear about the nature and meaning of purpose. Leadership must be given to the process by which purposes are determined and utilized.

When purposes are clear, the administrator is able to mobilize, focus, and coordinate individual and group energy in relation to priorities logically set up and systematically implemented.

4. *The Principle of Cultural Setting.*

In social work administration, the culture of the community must be understood inasmuch as it influences the way needs are expressed, services are authorized and supported and utilized by people who need them. The administrator must have an ever-increasing knowledge of the culture of his community.

Every social agency exists in a cultural setting that in itself is always changing. The beliefs, views, values, prejudices, experiences, and feelings of the people in a given situation constitute the basis for their behavior. The administrator who recognizes this fact seeks to sharpen an awareness of the nuances of cultural determinants and diligently tries to work in ways that will utilize the cultural strengths in his setting. Programs and services should be in harmony with the prevailing cultural forms and should be carried forward in ways that support the growth of positive cultural change.

5. *The Principle of Purposeful Relationships.*

In social work administration, effective purposeful working relationships must be established between the administrator, the board, the staff, and the constituency. The administrator must concentrate attention on helping people relate to him and to each other so that their joint efforts will result in a program of services.

This principle assumes that it is both possible and necessary to create the conditions under which effective relationships may develop. It assumes that the team-work character of effective working relationships can be experienced and felt. Effective working relationships grow out of the mutual acceptance of the administrator and others in the agency who seek to cooperate and work in harmony. The quality and strength of the administrator's relationships with people determine in large measure the extent to which they will be motivated to their highest levels of productivity. Relationships based on acceptance, cooperation, mutual respect, shared responsibility, and broad participation are the foundation of democratic administration.

6. *The Principle of Agency Totality.*

In social work administration, the agency must be understood in its totality and wholeness. It must be seen as a living instrumentality made up of interrelated parts that constitute a system of energy output and resource deployment to meet defined needs and render defined services through the united efforts of people.

The administrator must strive to create a sense of unity in the agency and must strive for balance, continuity, stability and relatedness so that the impact will be as efficient as possible.

When the administrator accepts the totality of the agency and sees it in its wholeness, his leadership and energy output are distributed across the spectrum of ongoing programs to the advantage of all and the favoritism of none. Resources are properly allocated and services are appropriately underwritten in terms of their value to the agency as a whole and the needs of the people to be met.

The approach of wholeness and total agency understanding and development makes for unity and reduces the forces of devisiveness. The administrator more than any other person must regard the agency as a totality.

7. *The Principle of Professional Responsibility.*

In social work administration, the administrator is responsible for the provision of high quality professional service based on standards of professional practice that have been carefully formulated and rigorously applied.

The professional social work agency is made up of persons who have specialized knowledge and skill that they have acquired by means of professional education and experience. It is the task of the administration to help provide the conditions under which professional people can render professional services. The way the agency is set up and regarded as a system of *professional responsibility* is largely determined by the administrator, who is a major model of professional behavior to be followed by colleagues. It is scarcely possible to develop a staff that behaves with professional judgment and skill unless the administrator exhibits the highest form of professional, responsible leadership. The accountability of the administrator is basically to the clientele, who need the professional services the agency is designed to provide.

8. *The Principle of Participation.*

In social work administration, appropriate contributions of board, staff, constituency, and community are sought and utilized through the continuous process of dynamic participation structured and encouraged by the administrator who seeks to involve people in agency decision-making and problem-solving.

This principle is based on the dual proposition that agency members have both the *right* and the *responsibility* to take part in the administration of the agency. *Participation* is a key concept in the democratic process. It assumes that the product that emerges from the joint efforts of many competent people is superior to what any one person can produce alone. In addition, the issues of administrative situations come alive when people are involved in solving problems and in making decisions. Furthermore, decisions made this way are more certain of implementation. It is the interaction of persons with each other that makes the agency a corporate force for furthering the agreed-upon objectives.

9. *The Principle of Communication.*

In social work administration, open channels of communication are essential to the complete functioning of people. The administration is responsible for creating the communication channels and for seeing to it that they are kept open and utilized to the fullest possible extent.

Communication is, of course, basic to the principle of participation. Unless people are in communication with one another, there can be no organized human effort. Unless the communication is focused on objectives, problems, and tasks to be done, it will be random and will not produce the agreements required. The social work administrator, therefore, has a responsibility to give direction to the communication efforts of the people for whom he is responsible. In addition, the administrator must be in communication with board, staff, constituency, and community and must constantly assess the extent to which communication skills are being effective.

10. *The Principle of Leadership.*

In social work administration, the administrator must carry major responsibility for the leadership of the agency in terms of goal attainment and the provision of professional services.

In the leadership role, the administrator by example, by stimulation, and by encouragement and support seeks to create a climate where innovation is sought and regarded as essential to the ability of the agency to meet changing needs with the utmost of effectiveness.

Good leadership is basic to all productive group experience. In social work administration, it is apparent that the administrator carries a heavy leadership responsibility that must be taken seriously. In leadership of the agency, the administrator skillfully solicits the contributions of his board, staff, constituency, and community and creates new patterns of synthesis from these contributions. High but reasonable goals are set forth and offer direction and guidance to people who join in efforts to achieve these goals. The administrator encourages others to develop and display their leadership abilities and provides opportunities for them to assume progressively more responsible roles in the agency.

11. *The Principle of Planning.*

In social work administration, the process of continuous planning is fundamental to the development of meaningful services. The administration must give leadership to the planning process and must enable others to plan their work as individuals and in relation to the total task of the agency.

The principle of planning assumes that the agency must have some method or system for determining policies and programs and that the administrator is a key element in the formulation and operation of the planning mechanisms and processes. Sound administration is necessarily planned action rather than sporadic or haphazard. When action is planned, it has a logical quality about it. There are steps that can be taken in a serial way in the planning process, and each phase of the plan being made grows out of previous moves. Planning does not guarantee the complete success of every venture, but without planning, most ventures have little chance of succeeding. The skill of planning is an essential quality for the social work administrator.

12. *The Principle of Organization.*

In social work administration, the work of many people must be ar-

ranged in an organized manner and must be structured so that responsibilities and relationships are clearly defined.

The administration is responsible for developing the form of organization most suitable for the kind of agency it is. He must check on the effectiveness of the organization in terms of maximum energy release and output focused upon the tasks of service provision.

The principle of organized human effort is fundamental to both individual and group accomplishment. When administration is viewed as a process of interaction and as a situation within which interpersonal relationships provide the energy for the agency to use in pursuing its goals, it is clear that the administrator must concentrate upon organizing for productivity. Unless there is good organization, energy will be wasted and efficiency will become illusive if not impossible.

13. *The Principle of Delegation.*

In social work administration, the delegation of responsibility and authority to other professional persons is essential inasmuch as no one executive can possibly perform all of the specialized tasks that must be undertaken.

The administrator delegates work assignments and responsibilities to colleagues in terms of their competence and then assumes that they have the authority to make decisions within defined realms and according to agreed-upon policies and practices.

The act of delegation is symbolic of the confidence shown by a person who trusts someone else to carry a responsibility. When one delegates a task, it is assumed that the person to whom it is assigned has the ability to perform it. This implies that when personnel are selected to do various jobs they meet qualifications essential to the doing of the work. Delegation is itself a matter of administrative judgment. The decision to delegate or to retain a task is one of the vital ones an administrator makes in all day-to-day work.

14. *The Principle of Coordination.*

In social work administration, the work delegated to many people must be properly coordinated so that specific contributions are brought to bear upon the major tasks of the agency and that all energy is rightly focused upon the mission to be accomplished.

The administrator as the central person around whom and with whom work gets done must understand and give leadership to the continuous process of coordination of effort.

The larger the agency, the more work divisions it has; the more specialized its delegation format, the greater is the need for coordination. Coordination must take place on divisional and departmental levels and must occur within the agency as a whole and between the agency and community. Without effective means and processes of coordination, the agency administrator cannot hope to integrate the contributions of the many people who carry specific parts of the total agency load.

15. *The Principle of Resource Utilization.*

In social work administration, the resources of money, facilities, and personnel must be carefully fostered, conserved, and utilized in keeping with the trust granted to the agency by society.

The administrator as the custodian of resources is responsible for seeing to it that they are properly controlled and carefully accounted for.

It is assumed that for an agency to serve people it must have sufficient resources, and these resources must be economically deployed. The administrator keeps an inventory of all resources, and he projects the resource requirements essential for the expansion of services when it becomes necessary to meet new or changed needs. The skill with which the administrator extracts maximum value from the resources at his disposal is a matter of signal importance.

16. *The Principle of Change.*

In social work administration, the process of change is continuous both within the community and within the agency. The administrator has the responsibility to guide the change process and to assist people to implement necessary changes democratically decided.

The world, the community, and the agency are always changing. In the well-administered agency, the director seeks to guide, to influence, and to direct the change process along lines that will enhance the contributions of all concerned. Planned institutional change becomes a matter for the continuous and wide involvement of board, staff, constituency, and community, with the administrator taking major responsibility for leadership. As new needs arise, new services are offered. As new patterns of administration are required, they are developed consciously and planfully. Change becomes a goal of innovation and growth.

17. *The Principle of Evaluation.*

In social work administration, continuous evaluation of processes and programs is essential to the fulfillment of the agency's objectives.

The administrator, the staff, the board, and the constituency have roles to play in the evaluation process, with the administrator assuming primary responsibility for guiding it.

It is assumed that evaluation is not only desirable but necessary if one is to know the extent to which objectives have been achieved. Administrators must evaluate their own work as well as the work of others. The climate within which evaluation flourishes is open, critical, secure, and future-oriented. The ruts of routine operations are avoided when regular evaluation procedures assess the continuing advisability of programs, procedures, and policies and when there is a willingness to subject every act to thoughtful appraisal and scrutiny.

18. *The Principle of Growth.*

In social work administration, the growth and development of all participants are furthered by the administrator who provides challenging work assignments, thoughtful supervision, and opportunities for individual and group learning.

The growth needs of persons can and must be met by administration. In so doing, the administrator helps each person to render greater service to the agency, and in addition, he enriches the life experience of the person concerned.

The growth of the administrator is essential if skills and competence are to broaden. Consequently, he seeks experiences that will widen his horizons, deepen his insights, and make firm the grasp he has over himself and his duties.

Learning and growth are essential to life. Without them, there can be no progress and no fulfillment.

When one reflects on the eighteen principles listed above, it should be apparent that social work administration is a coming together of ideals and methods deeply rooted in the values of the profession of social work. As Moss says, "Effective administration requires a fusion of ethical and operational principles. Neither is sufficient without the other. Individuals attain their richest fulfillment through participation in democratically organized and effectively productive enterprises. Democratic organization and effective production are the twin and inseparable goals of successful administrators." [4]

As social work administrators continue their vital labors in service to people, they will discover that *what* they do is less important than *how* they do it. They will learn that administration has many rewards, the greatest of which is the fact that through their efforts people have been helped to a fuller life.

NOTES

1. *The Random House Dictionary of the English Language* (Unabridged Edition) (New York: Random House, 1966, 1967), p. 1144.
2. J. M. Gaus and Leonard D. White, *The Frontiers of Public Administration* (Chicago: University of Chicago Press, 1936), p. 21.
3. A. S. Barr, William H. Burton, and Lee J. Brueckner, *Supervision—Principles and Practices in the Improvement of Instruction* (New York: Appleton-Century-Crofts, 1938), pp. 32–33.
4. Celia R. Moss, *Administering a Hospital Social Service Department* (Washington, D.C.: American Association of Medical Social Workers, 1955), p. 9.

PART II

THE PRACTICE OF
ADMINISTRATION

Cases, Papers, and Documents for Study

The materials that are included in this section of the book are offered as brief examples that may be useful in the teaching of social work administration either in schools or social work or in social agency staff development programs. They have been tested in the classroom and in numerous institutes throughout the country. Naturally, names and agencies and locations have been disguised, and editorial changes have been made to further the anonymity of the case material. However, they are real situations or combinations of real situations. Most of these documents have never before been published. In selecting these particular materials from the many that have been turned in by students and practitioners, an effort has been made to offer a variety of settings and problems.

The cases do not necessarily represent either good or poor practice of social work or social work administration. Instead, they are offered to illustrate some of the problems of administrative leadership at work. The questions at the end of each example may serve as a springboard for group discussion.

CASE 1

Successful Administration Is an Art

Constance H. Keene
(Used with Permission)

My main assumption is that the administrator of a structure is the most influential element in and to that structure. That the person in charge of the institution determines what that institution will be and what direction it takes in light of his administrative ideology and the principles that he employs. I shall briefly trace the development of the most pervasive administrative ideologies, and then emphasize some administrative principles that I believe to be of particular importance in the art of administering. In conclusion, I shall cite particular problems that did occur in a clinic because of the failure of the staff to consider these principles of effective administration.

Administration has been defined comprehensively as the capacity to coordinate many, and often conflicting, social energies in a single organism, so adroitly that they shall operate as a unity. Brooke Adams in *The Theory of Social Revolution* also suggests that the administrative ability is possibly the highest faculty of the human mind. All of the activities of our modern institutions embody and reflect the purposes and ideas of their members and especially their leaders. Theories on procedures of operation greatly determine what form the institution structure will employ and what the pervasive attitudes of the staff will be.

How did philosophies of management develop, and upon what were they based? Scientific management was conceived in America about 1911. The major concern was on structure and technology—the definition, measurement, and planning of the work process. Frederick W. Taylor's thinking and methods had great impact on the organization. He was an engineer and a "fact-hunter," whose influence resulted in a more formalized management structure and more specified jobs and greatest stress on efficiency. His philosophy separated the planning, thinking, and imagining from the moving, doing, and acting of one's job. The effect was demeaning and degrading to the worker who was relegated to the status of an unthinking animal. Responsibility was commensurate with authority. This philosophy caused a wave of resistance from the workers, reflected in subtle forms, such as slow-downs, sabotage, and pegged production. At higher levels, "Taylorism" affected a tight authoritarian structure with overlapping, confused areas of authority and responsibility. Formalization and restriction of communication resulted in depersonalization of relationships. Varieties of specialists on the white-collar level caused problems of coordination of activities.

By the late 1920s, American administrative philosophy became more people-concerned. There developed an awareness of human social and psychological needs in the place of employment. Intangibles were recognized as being casually related to production. If workers were involved in the planning and decision-making relevant to their jobs, better performance was affected. This more participate approach involved the idea that the group was almost a substitute for authority because pressure of loyalty and commitment tended to be strong. Furthermore, people tend to support strongly what they help to create. Acceptance of this philosophy was retarded somewhat by the managers' fears of loss of control and coordination problems generated by many small groups operating rather autonomously. However, this approach had greatest impact on the higher administrative levels.

In the 1950s, organizational philosophies embodied the image of the gray flannel suit, characteristic apparel of the statistician and the engineer. In certain respects, judgment and experience were deemphasized by the computer. New tools for measuring and analyzing were developed. More complex decisions were handled more efficiently because technological advances enabled administrators to get more comprehensive information to key points more rapidly. The blue-collar worker was reportedly able to turn over to the machine many of the routine, monotonous tasks, thus creating cheaper, easier ways of doing their jobs. However, the lives of managers were complicated by additional problems of interrelating and estimating. Higher executives were confronted with new kinds of analytic methods, involving areas never before subjected to analysis that tended to cause greater psychological pressures.

Philosophies of administration in the 1970s are being greatly influenced by research that is providing verifiable, stable, accurate information on techniques of management. The information is particularly relevant to administration of agencies concerned with human needs and services. Administrative ideals and principles are particularly revealed through the organizational structure. In spite of evidence that, with few exceptions, highly productive departments are found to be using management systems that apply an "interest" in their employees' approach, many organizations are clinging tenaciously to their old, familiar hierarchical structures.

Traditional hierarchical structures employ a man-to-man, superior-to-subordinate, pyramid-shaped structure. The entire process of policy formulation is that of issuing orders, delegating responsibilities down the vertical, rigid channels, checking, and controlling. Most important, this approach severely limits the integration of the needs and desires of the members of the organization. Good, effective communication is almost an impossibility.

A democracy professes to value conserving and enhancing the personality of all people. It emphasizes respect for the integrity of the person and helping persons to develop a sense of worth through working toward worthy ends. Ideally, the institutions of our society should reflect these values in their philosophies. The collegial structure whose principles emphasize collaboration and cooperation is most compatible with these values. This approach allows the individual to more fully realize his potentialities for the betterment of himself, his organization, his community, and ultimately the nation.

Administrative principles I believe to be particularly important in the art of administering, which is concerned in establishing effective working relationships with and between people, in line with the highest principles of ethics of one's profession, are:

1. Supportive relationships should be developed as fully as possible. Staff morale and resulting output to the community are largely dependent upon feelings of cohesiveness. Cooperative relationships produce favorable attitudes of trust and confidence among members. Greater satisfaction from accomplishment is attained when peers and superiors work together toward a common end. Informal meetings in which ideas and techniques can be freely shared can promote feelings of greater commitment to the group and to one's supervisor and inspire individuals to more effectively utilize their own abilities.

2. Use of formal authority should be limited. An administrator should be sensitive to the needs of others and able to exert influence and create motivation and coordination without depending upon the form of line authority. The assumption that when an organization buys a man's time and energy, it obtains control over his behavior, is no longer valid. Evidence implies that the issuance of edicts often produces apathy, alienation, and hostility in the subordinate and competition and conflict among peers. Areas of responsibility should be delegated with respect to the special capabilities of the staff members, and accountability should be clearly defined, as simple and direct as possible, providing for an orderly flow of work that minimizes chances of blockages. Ambiguous responsibilities and conflicting expectations breed misunderstanding and dissension. Each staff member needs a clear perception of his role and status. The values and purposes of the agency need to be continually restated.

3. Communication must be encouraged. Administrators should provide the structure and interactional skills to solve differences and conflicts and to attain creative solutions. Issues must be clarified and investigated factually. When informal, well-defined, widely known, and accepted channels of communication are kept open, problems can be solved at the point of disagreement in lieu of their developing into irreconcilable conflict and formal grievances. Rigid structures tend to force staff members to depend upon unrecognized informal channels and finagling to accomplish their task. The relationship of superior to subordinate should enable the individual free expression of needs and encouragement toward good performance. Trust, honesty, and confidence encourage effective, open communication and inhibit misconceptions both within the agency and between the agency and the community.

4. The decision-making process should include all those whom the policy will directly affect, especially those involved with its implementation. The area of collective responsibility proposes that when everyone in the organization is encouraged to feel a positive and creative stake in its success task accomplishment is significantly more successful. The organizational ends and individual aspirations become a cooperative whole because each individual has contributed to the clarification of

aims and to the determination of policy. Supervisors direct and maintain the groups' focus on important issues. Agencies are involved in the process of continuous planning, which gives action a logical quality. Authority is cumulative, and the decision by an administrator is only a moment in a process that has involved the functioning of many people.

5. Individual potentials of staff members should be recognized, utilized, and respected. Staff effectiveness depends greatly upon the members' ability to exercise his initiative, originality, and judgment. It is necessary to create a climate where staff growth and development is encouraged by evidence of trust and confidence in individual ability. Impersonality tends to create self-centeredness and separation from the agency. Opportunities for upward mobility promote optimism, and staff feelings of worth are increased by compensations for extra time and effort in the form of credits, money, awards, and so on. Staff development and in-service training are a part of this concept.

6. The adaptability of an agency is tremendously important. Evaluation is necessary periodically to enable administrators to know to what extent agency objectives are being achieved. Poorly functioning agencies can survive for years. Ineffectual policies are inhibiting. As the needs of the constituents change and the needs of the staff members change, the agency should be flexible enough to be able to respond accordingly. In a climate that is open, critical, secure, and future-oriented, effective review and assessment are possible. Changes are often indicated when points of stress develop. In determining the causes, it is important to constantly consider the feelings of staff members and constituents. Conflict situations can be utilized to effect constructive changes. Individual creativity and innovations are essential to an agency's ability to meet changing needs with utmost effectiveness.

In an attempt to stress what problems can develop in institutions that do not successfully employ these principles of administration in their daily patterns of functioning, I shall use a relatively small out-patient clinic department of a city hospital as my role model. Information has been obtained by interviews with the doctors who served as chief residents.

The oral surgery department has a full-time staff of five members, consisting of one chief resident, one first-year resident, one intern, and two specially trained assistants. Eighteen attendings are also affiliated with this program along with the head of the department. This clinic is unique in many respects. The head of the department has his own private practice, located near the hospital, and is in the hospital regularly only on Friday mornings. He is in the hospital sporadically when important cases need his attention or when staff problems develop. The assistants in this department are under the jurisdiction of the general nursing service, although their job responsibilities make it impossible for them to abide by the regulations pertaining to the regular nursing shifts and routines. There has been a change of emphasis from a general dental service to a specialized oral surgery service. Patient load has increased dramatically from 950 patients to 3,029 patients. Although more involved operations are performed in the hospital operating rooms, less severe operations are performed in the clinic itself.

In assessing the problems encountered by the oral surgery department in its efforts to provide an efficient, effective service, we may view these problems from the standpoint of the community, task, and psychosocial dimensions described in the diagram of Administrative Process in Trecker's *Social Work Administration*.

It is useful to be aware of the view of the hospital as a social system made up of interacting parts and small subsystems that interact with each other and in relation to the whole. Any significant influence will cause all of the parts to shift and move through a series of new positions and relationship patterns, eventually establishing a new and different balance. I see this oral surgery department as functioning predominantly as an autonomous unit, yet being dependent upon and working interdependently with other subsystems and within a total system where partially conflicting goals and interests create stresses and strains that negatively affect its effective functioning.

High on the list of job frustrations of each of the doctors was the matter of patient fees. There are certain discrepancies between goals of efficiency and economy stressed by the hospital and the professional values of the oral surgeons. Patients who come to the clinic characteristically have little money and are under the impression that they will receive adequate care at a minimal cost. The hospital fees are comparable to private doctors' fees and in some cases even higher. Also, for those who are receiving public assistance, there are definite restrictions on what will be paid for, which limits the ability of the doctor in making decisions regarding the best possible treatment for the patient. Postoperative examinations are particularly necessary in this department. Again, because of high hospital fees, many patients are discouraged from this necessary follow-up care.

The intern and the residents are involved in the hospital for the purpose of obtaining training and experience in their field. The ethics of oral surgery profession stress adequate occlusion as a necessary function. Reductions or extensions of the patient's jaw-prognathisms or of the upper pallet are in certain cases mandatory for the patient's well-being. The hospital, however, considers this cosmetic surgery, and in cases where the patient is unable to financially afford this procedure, preadmissions procedures often screen out these cases, thus depriving the individuals of treatment and depriving the doctors of important training and experience.

Another problem greatly stressed by these doctors was that of conflicting demands upon their two assistants. These women are classified and paid in terms of being general dental assistants. However, they also function as receptionists and assistants in the operating room. They cannot work according to the regularly allotted hours, for on certain mornings they must set up for an operation by 7:30 A.M., and many afternoons they must work overtime assisting one of the doctors in an operation in their clinic office. The hospital nursing service states that they cannot compensate the assistants in money because of budget pressures and that their erratic schedules upset the business office. Thus, the assistants must formally adhere to regular hospital policy. The only possible compensation allowed them is in terms of taking hours off, if taken within the week in which the hours are accumulated. It is extremely difficult for the doctors to schedule hours-off because the assistants are so necessary to the clinic's effective functioning. Great social and psychological stresses are caused as the chief resident, in the role of advocate, wrestles for adequate compensation for these two staff members. We are reminded of findings on what employees want most in a job, the first two priorities being pride in their job and in their institution and adequate pay. Our services are no better than the personnel who staff them. Good, qualified staffs are often demoralized in such a hospital setting.

In some cases, the responsibilities of the doctors are not clear. There are no clear-cut criteria for what cases will be covered, for example, by oral surgery rather than E.N.T. The result is that the doctors' familiarity with one another greatly determines to which department a case will be assigned. Staff prejudices develop between departments, which further impedes the doctors' ability to give their patients the most efficient, effective care.

Communication problems of this department are complicated by the fact that the head of the department is not a full-time member of the hospital staff, functioning in and according to the routines of the hospital setting. His affiliations with hospital staff, other than those in his own department, are limited as is his ability to fully understand and empathize with the three doctors under his supervision who are functioning exclusively in this rather confused hospital atmosphere.

As social workers, it is important that we be aware of administrative principles and procedures that characterize the various institutions of the helping professions not only to better prepare us in making more realistic decisions as to job choice but to better prepare us in functioning effectively in the agency with which we affiliate.

QUESTIONS

1. What elements go into making administration an "art"?
2. What have been some of the major historical changes in administration?
3. Evaluate the six major points the author makes.

4. What changes would you make in the way the department she describes operates?

CASE 2

Administrative Problems at a Methadone Maintenance and Treatment Program

In my last job, I acted in the function of a social worker/mental health worker for the Methadone Maintenance and Treatment Program, a program of the Health Department in a city of about 83,000. The program's effectiveness and efficiency suffered from the problem of low staff morale and allegiance to the program. What I would like to examine here are: the origins of the problems, its effect on interpersonal relations within the agency, on staff effort and allegiance to the program, on patient program involvement, and the attempted resolution by employees and administration.

The city is a manufacturing town surrounded by some of the wealthiest suburbs in the country. These suburbs are growing rapidly, siphoning off upper-income families and excluding those unable to afford large homes on acre and half-acre lots. Between 1970 and 1975, the non-Spanish-speaking white population in the city reached a plateau, and the black and Spanish-speaking went from 15 to 20 percent of the population, while in the suburbs, which grew by about 15 percent in the same period, the black and Spanish-speaking populations actually shrank from 2.5 percent to less than 2 percent of the population. Industry was shifting from labor intensive jobs to those requiring higher levels of skill, and these workers were commuting from outside the city, so there were increasingly fewer jobs for the unskilled left in the city. Housing vacancy rates were among the lowest in the entire country.

By the end of 1971, it was obvious, both nationally and locally, that drug abuse was a problem. It was estimated that there were about 1,000 hard-core opiate and opoiod addicts in the four-town greater city area who were not being served by the available drug-free treatment programs, either because they didn't meet program age criteria, because the programs didn't meet their particular needs, or because the addicts were unable to meet the costs of the available drug substitution programs. The medical director of the Alcohol and Drug Dependence Division (ADDD) of the Department of Mental Health informed the city's director of health that it would be advisable to establish a methadone treatment program and that funding from his department could be counted on, although Law Enforcement Assistance Administration (LEAA) funds were also a possible funding source. Eventually, LEAA funds were secured to cover the majority of costs, but they were to decrease 25 percent per year (including one ex-

tension) so that by fiscal 1976 the LEAA money would be phased out while city funding would have to cover the total cost.

While the Democratic party has traditionally controlled the city government, it has had to appeal to the strong conservative element in the community, especially the Taxpayers' League and its political arm, the Conservative party, whose representatives appear at all the budget request hearings of the Board of Estimate and Taxation. The city government therefore gave very little financial support to so highly controversial a project as the establishment and continuance of the Methadone Maintenance and Treatment Program (MMTP), so from the beginning, the funding of MMTP was in trouble. This attitude was also present in the other three towns of the four-town area, who, although by state mandate MMTP would have to serve patients from their towns, felt that any drug problems could be handled by the facilities available to them, and so refused to contribute financially to the running of the program. In spite of later proof that approximately one-fourth of the patients came from these towns, the attitude was maintained that hard-core addicts come from the inner city and not from suburban communities.

Requirements were established to ensure that the program, aimed at adult hard-core addicts as a last treatment of choice, reached only those who had no alternatives. A patient had to be at least twenty-one years old, although a few nineteen- and twenty-year-olds, already on methadone programs, were accepted as transfer patients. There had to be at least a two-year history of continuous addiction, because experimenters and persons not yet addicted would not benefit from the program due to the addicting nature of methadone. There had to be at least two prior serious attempts at rehabilitation in other modalities, for which records were obtained, in order to determine that a person could not better be served through another treatment method. A patient had to have the symptoms and the scars indicative of his stated drug use. He had to pass a physical and a screening by program staff to ensure motivation.

The variety of reasons for applying for treatment are those found in any program: wanting to look good for an impending arrest, trial, or probation officer; family or marital pressure; because a habit was getting too big to support even with illegal means; because of a scarcity of heroin and the free drug was tempting to those afraid of detoxification; being tired of hustling; and the rare psychological leap of having looked at oneself, decided on a different life, and made the effort to achieve it.

MMTP opened its doors to treat patients on October 9, 1972. Although it was a branch of the Health Department, the program was not located in the new city Health Department building for several reasons. One was fear by Health Department staff, particularly the director, of the kinds of behavior that might be expected from patients in this new building. Another was that the location of the Health Department in the middle-class section of the city would be inconvenient for the majority of the patients, who were expected to come from the lower-income areas of the central city and from south city. Quarters were therefore found for the program in the middle of the urban renewal area of south city, in a rundown building occupied downstairs by the local antipoverty agency and later by the redevelopment commission as well, and in the other half of the second floor by Legal Services offices. The building was located across the street from a flophouse hotel and a block and a half from the main drug pushing area in south city, while the shops on the street tended to have fly-by-night tenants who went in and out of business quickly.

As initially funded, the program was to treat 50 patients. By the end of December 1972, there were 54 patients on the program, 64 by the end of December 1973, 81 by the end of June 1974, and an average of 73.4 in calendar 1975. This was due in part to a policy decision to accept patients from an area of the state that was not covered by a catchment area, thereby effectively increasing the population of the total catchment area to about 200,000. Funding did not increase proportionately, but rather remained the same the second year and has decreased each year since.

The staff structure of MMTP consists of Dr. L., the medical director, who puts in one-sixth time because of other duties as director of health for the city, with only four hours spent at the clinic each week; Andrew P., the program administrative director, who directs the counseling staff and overall running of the clinic; the social worker, formerly full time, since September 1975 part time, who makes educational-vocational referrals, maintains statistical records for the state and federal inspecting agencies, makes medical and collateral agency referrals, and maintains a caseload of patients for counseling, especially those with more serious psychological problems; the two ex-addict counselors, who maintain individual and group caseloads; the three part-time nurses, who dispense medication and also assist the patients with minor medical problems or refer them to the medical director; the pharmacist, who contracts with the medical director to prepare the medication; the full-time secretary, who maintains the files, the billing, the schedules, and so on. The nurses and pharmacist are directly responsible to the medical director, although they are in closer contact with the administrative director, while the rest of the staff are responsible to the latter, and ultimately to the medical director. Dr. L., as medical director, per state law, is responsible for all clinical decisions; while as city director of health, he takes ultimate responsibility for the administrative decisions and can overrule the program administrative director. Dr. L. is a former general practitioner, who went back to school and got his MPH degree after his appointment as city health director twelve years ago. Since then, he has gotten a new Health Department building and state and federal funds for many new health programs that are generally unavailable even in larger cities in the state. He is on friendly terms with all the political leaders in the four parties that exist in the city, and they are usually accommodating to Dr. L. He was the medical director of one of the three competing drug-free programs in the city as well, until the program closed in 1975 due to staff problems, that is, falsification of inpatient census records by the executive director in order to meet their funding criteria, a staff member sexually involved with a female minor patient, and several staff members arrested together with several patients for smoking marijuana. With these problems, the hostility between Dr. L. and the state Alcohol and Drug Dependence Division medical director, which before had been centered around Dr. L.'s antagonism and passive-aggressive attitude toward compliance with state requirements, and had been covert, became open.

Andrew P., the administrative director, is a former priest with a masters degree in counseling, who had never worked at any agency before, other than at his former parish church, which was located in one of the suburbs in the four-town area. He and Dr. L. developed the protocol and original budget request for the establishment of MMTP. He had enjoyed that, but he had found little satisfaction in the job since then because the day-to-day administration of the program did not appeal to him. He stated, however, that at his age (approximately fifty) it would be hard for him to find another job that would pay him as well as this one ($16,000 per year) with his lack of experience. As a result, he preferred to do direct therapy with patients, provided no case supervision, although that was specified as part of his job, and abdicated responsibility for decisions to either Dr. L., or to me, in day-to-day matters. This abdication of responsibility to the mental health worker extended even to my appointment to fill out the director's federal year-end reports and to the preparation of most of the material for the justification aspects of the budget requests.

When I heard about the opening for a social worker/mental health worker at MMTP in July 1973, I was under no illusions as to the situation there, other than the illusion that I would be able to change things. Having worked at a collateral agency, I had heard of some of the previous worker's problems at MMTP. The first worker, an MSW, had left after two months, and my predecessor, a BA in Psychology with two years' experience at another methadone program, was leaving after five months; the counselors were apathetic about their work; the nurses had little to say about the program that was good, were constantly in conflict with other staff members about boundaries of authority and professional independence, and were threatening to quit. The state ADDD inspection team had visited in April, and no measures had been taken to deal with the serious deficiencies they had found, and because of which final approval of the program was being withheld. Most important, the patients were expressing much dissatisfaction with the program and were showing little inclination to do more than what was minimally required, and that with extreme reluctance.

The facilities were rundown, sanitary conditions were almost nonexistent, and supplies were frequently hard to come by. The counselors who carried the burden of the treatment counseling load had to share an office, the social worker/mental health worker's office was a passageway to the medication room and the medical director's office, until Dr. L. ordered the worker out of even that because there was too much noise when he was in his own office. Meanwhile, Dr. L. had a private office that, although it was used for only four hours per week and had no medical equipment, he refused to allow anyone to use in his absence, and the administrative director and his secretary each had a private office.

The two ex-addict counselors, who each had at least a three-year history of drug counseling work in other programs, carried heavy caseloads and responsibility in direct work with the patients. Yet they carried no real authority within the program, were very poorly paid ($7,200 per year), had little reason to believe they would receive pay increases, and were not encouraged to take part in further professional education. Patients who were legally required to participate in group or individual counseling for a minimum of one to one and a half hours per week often refused to participate because the counselors had no capacity to confer or withhold privileges. This was due to what might be called the Good Guy Syndrome on the part of Dr. L. Because of a basic attitude of contempt toward addicts, leading to an encouragement of their dependency needs, and which he allowed to show in staff meetings, Dr. L. frequently encouraged patients to act out by granting requests for special privileges in the face of contrary recommendations by staff and records of continued drug use, arrests, failure to participate in counseling. These decisions were often made with no explanation to the staff. The patients joked about how the doctor could never say no, just like themselves, and knew that unless they directly defied staff to try to do anything about having circumvented them, the doctor would give them what they wanted. Staff decisions in which he had participated were, according to the doctor's own guidelines, supposed to be reported to a patient as a staff decision, but patients reported that Dr. L. had told them, "I voted for your request, but the rest of the staff turned you down." Or, contrary to his own rules, patients would inaccurately report their medication dosage, and let it be known that Dr. L. had given it to them.

The counselors, mental health worker, nurses, and administrative director felt that their professional integrity was violated, that all authority was stripped from their positions. The response was apathy on the part of the counselors. To what end should they try to work, when they were undermined by the medical director, so that their counseling carried no credibility with the patients. They were glad just to hang on to their jobs until something better came along. Eventually one counselor left to take a similar position in another methadone program with a $2,000 per year increase in salary, and three other counselors came but left within six months because of the untenable position in which they found themselves regarding their professional integrity.

When the nurses tried to bring their conflicts with the counseling staff to the attention of the administrative director, Andrew P., in early 1974, and demanded a meeting with the rest of the staff, they were labeled troublemakers by him, and he felt very threatened by them, as he did whenever he felt any female challenged his competence. An attempt was made by the nurses and myself to discuss the situation, but without the support and cooperation of the counselors or administrative director, there was little that could be done. Eventually, after a series of unsuccessful meetings between Dr. L. and the nurses, two of the three left, one quitting in April 1974, and one forced to resign in November 1974, both because of the unresolved conflicts.

When it became obvious that the conflicts between staff members were symptomatic of the problems at MMTP, rather than the cause, having haphazardly analyzed the problematic situation, and realized that it would be futile to think of trying to replace the administrators, while knowing that I was planning on leaving anyway, knowing that any changes or definition by the administrators of the sources of problems would be directed toward the lower staff members and not toward themselves, I chose to try to deal with some short-term goals. I decided that if there was to be any relief from the situation, several issues would have to be dealt with: 1) how to keep the program open in the face of threatened closure by the state ADDD inspection team and the seeming indifference of the administrators to the possible validity of their criticisms; 2) how to deal with the lack of clarity in job descriptions, boundaries of authority, and performance expectations and standards; 3) clarification of the expectations held by and required of the patients participating in the program; and 4) how to deal with the lack of unity and self-esteem among staff.

Several measures were initiated in May 1974 in the hope of altering the situation. First, suggestions were made concerning record-keeping (files instead of folders with loose material), and organization of patient treatment procedures (monthly progress evaluation, mutual goal-setting with the patient, clarification of request approvals and of requirements for privileges, plus enforcement of the legally mandated counseling participation requirement). Second, Dr. L. was privately approached to find out in what areas, and to what extent, staff had the right to make decisions, administratively and/or clinically, and to express the staff concern about the position they were in vis-à-vis their lack of credibility with the patients. The reaction was in hindsight predictable. Dr. L. stated that he was the director and that he had the final decision in all matters, that if the staff needed sanctions in order to deal with the patients, they were in the wrong job. Considering the conflict between the motivation of most patients and their need to learn to take responsibility for their actions and to expect realistic consequences for them, as stated in the program goals in the protocol, this seemed to be a rather inconsistent attitude. In addition, Dr. L. was questioned as to the responsibility of the mental health worker for the counseling program. During the first state ADDD inspection, after the worker joined the program in December 1973, the team assumed he had the responsibility for the program and criticized what they assumed were his failings in administering that area. Neither Dr. L. nor Andrew P. disabused them of this idea. However, when questioned about this responsibility, the directors assured the worker that Andrew P. was in charge and belittled the complaint of unfair treatment. When this was repeated a second time at the next semi-annual inspection in April 1974, the issue of accountability and job description was raised. That this occurred during an inspection and brought the internal staff conflict to the attention of the state team also raised this conflict from a covert to an open area of confrontation. This issue was therefore important to discuss in the conference. As it turned out, cooptation as a diversionary tactic was used; Dr. L. said that they were trying to divert some of the pressure by the inspection team; they knew that I would be able to take it; and after all, the team couldn't really do anything to me.

The third item with which Dr. L. was approached was the matter of expectations of and by the patients. Dr. L. agreed to a meeting at which the full staff, counseling and nurses, discussed the problem of the lack of patient participation in the program. The source of the problem was ascribed to the patients, not to the administration, and it was agreed that the federal regulations concerning minimum levels of participation in counseling would be enforced, although Dr. L. stated that it was nonsense and that he would go along reluctantly, preferring to consider individual cases. However, the suggestion that a patient council be formed to represent their interests by providing feedback concerning policy and procedural matters as well as complaints concerning treatment was voted down. The enforcement of the regulation lasted approximately one month, and even then was not complete, before the situation returned to the status quo.

The final initiative was in the area of lack of unity and self-esteem among staff. The counselors and I began to meet informally to discuss the situation at MMTP and to discuss ways to involve the patients in the program. We came up with several new ways to involve them after researching programs at other MMTPs. One area was redecoration of the clinic. We scrounged up paint, and some of the more artistic patients painted murals on several newly painted walls, while others had an idea wall on which to express themselves. We began to obtain free films for discussion from the public library, and a counselor was looking into films from the State Drug

Council at the time I left the program. This idea drew some of the people who were previously extremely opposed to group counseling into active participation. Finally, we began a psychodrama group, run under an out-side trained volunteer, with a counselor participating, which seemed to draw in still other patients. Recent inquiry has shown that the negative attitude of the administrators toward these initiatives has caused the film and psychodrama groups to end; the former because of objections raised to entrusting expensive borrowed Health Department equipment to the pa-tients and the ex-addict counselor running the group; the latter because of constant comments by the administrators in front of patients, belittling the group and its possible effectiveness, while officially denying any op-position, leading to the resignation of the volunteer leader.

Since my resignation in August 1975, I find that I have been unable to resolve the resentment and the sense of violation of my ethics and pro-fessional integrity. In checking with workers still at the clinic, the same complaints are being voiced, and the same resentments are felt as before, only focused, because there is an awareness of the source.

QUESTIONS

1. What is your evaluation of the staff structure in this agency?
2. What were the weaknesses in the way the administrative director conceived of his role and did his job?
3. What are the implications of excessive staff turnover?
4. Why are adequate facilities for a program such as this so important?
5. What were some of the problems caused by the behavior of the medical director?
6. What do you think of the efforts of the social worker to change and im-prove the situation?

CASE 3

Administration of a Day Hospital Affiliated with a Community Mental Health Center

The following is a short case record of the administration of a new day hospital project affiliated with a community mental health center in a rural county with a population of about 150,000 in the Northeast called Cler-mont County. The project was initiated and largely funded by the State Department of Mental Hygiene. However, details of planning were left to the Clermont County Mental Health Center, which had been founded about fifteen years previously. The director of the clinic, Dr. Hathaway, was a highly respected woman psychiatrist who had moved to the com-munity about four years previously, after her retirement from private practice in a large city one hundred miles away. Other members of the professional staff included a young clinical psychologist, Dr. Blake; a middle-aged psychiatric social worker, Miss Rivers; and several part-time psychiatrists. Dr. Hathaway chose not to delegate any authority in organizing the day hospital so that the other members of the staff were completely detached from the project and felt they had no investment in its success. Dr. Hathaway arranged to rent a separate facility near the Mental Health Center that had formerly been a three-floor residence for student nurses. She also undertook to decorate it, and the final product was a seven-room house with walls painted entirely a blue-gray color, with no window screens, pictures, or curtains. When questioned about the drab appearance of the day care center, she explained that she was opposed to screens, pictures, and curtains in homes and therefore certainly would not tolerate them in an institution.

The patient population comprised seven of Dr. Hathaway's patients, some private and some from the Mental Health Center, with an age range of twenty-two to eighty-one, and including a mentally retarded epileptic, two paranoid schizophrenics, one chronic simple schizophrenic, two patients with chronic brain syndromes associated with senility, and one patient with a depressive reaction.

The first new staff member Dr. Hathaway hired a young registered occupational therapist, Mrs. Rocco, who was commissioned to equip the hospital from a sum of $6,000 that had been placed in a special account. Unfortunately, Dr. Hathaway did not make clear to Mrs. Rocco that the $6,000 was not entirely for occupational therapy equipment and supplies, but also had to cover the purchase of three desks, a conference table, two file boxes, chairs, dictating machines, and an office typewriter. The result of this misunderstanding was that the day hospital opened with an elaborate shuffle board game but no woodworking tools or art supplies.

The week before the day center was to open, Dr. Hathaway interviewed and hired nine occupational therapy aides, most of whom were high school graduates with some college education, and a social work student, Miss Hall, who had just completed her first year of graduate training and had returned to her hometown for the summer vacation. One of the part-time psychiatrists at the Mental Health Center was assigned to work at the day hospital two hours each week.

The Clermont County Mental Health Center had no manual of policy and procedure, formal job descriptions, nor any provisions for in-service training or staff meetings. Miss Hall was not experienced enough to inquire as to what would be expected of her as social worker for the day hospital. Her first day at work was the day the day hospital opened. The case records were not made available to her until two weeks later, but she was told on the first day that transportation (with no provision for reimbursement) for all seven patients was her immediate responsibility. There was extended conflict between Dr. Hathaway and Miss Rivers as to who should supervise Miss Hall. Dr. Hathaway felt she should, as the day hospital was her project; Miss Rivers felt she should because she was a professional psychiatric social worker. Consequently, neither one communicated directly with Miss Hall during the first three days of the operation of the day hospital. The issue was resolved after three days because Dr. Hathaway left precipitously at that time on her six-week vacation. The policy of the Department of Mental Hygiene was for the clinical psychologist to assume administrative responsibility in the absence of the director, but Miss Rivers said that was "ridiculous," for social workers knew more about working with people than psychologists. Dr. Blake had recently given notice that he would be leaving the agency at the end of the summer anyway, so he did not argue with Miss Rivers over who the administrator of the two centers would be—and he never entered the day hospital again. Miss Rivers, meanwhile, was overwhelmed by the task of administration of both the Mental Health Center and the new day hospital, so the day hospital was vaguely left to Miss Hall, who was supervised for one hour each week and told not to try to handle any emergencies alone. The day-to-day functions actually proceeded quite satisfactorily until Miss Rivers suddenly took a two-week vacation without authorizing anyone to open the incoming mail, a task that had always been reserved to Dr. Hathaway and Miss Rivers.

By the time Miss Rivers returned from her vacation, the day hospital program was fairly well developed. Miss Hall led an informal discussion group with the patients and one O.T. aide from nine to ten, at which time Mrs. Rocco, the occupational therapist, arrived and supervised a well-structured program until noontime. The patients brought their own lunches at first, but as there was a kitchen up in the attic, they later decided among themselves to go dutch treat two days a week on a meal the women would prepare as an O.T. project. Miss Hall joined the group for lunch three days each week, at which time Mrs. Rocco conferred separately with her staff; the other two days Mrs. Rocco supervised lunch, and Miss Hall went out for an hour. Twice the patients organized a picnic. In the afternoons, after Mrs. Rocco left, the patients could either continue work on their projects, play games, or take short walks with an aide. Each patient was interviewed alone by Miss Hall weekly. Miss Hall took one group of patients home at 4 P.M., and another at 4:30, along with the aide who volunteered to remain with the second group in the interim. In two weeks of following this program, the only incident that occurred with regard to any aspect of the program was that one patient received a second-degree steam burn on her arm while cooking a pot roast for one of the luncheons. Miss Hall took her to the hospital emergency room, located on the same block as the day center, and after she was treated and returned to her home, held a group session in which the other patients relived the experience of the accident. The impression afterward was that there had been a definite group gain from the experience, for the patients had seen that the staff was capable of caring for them calmly and efficiently in the event of a crisis.

When Miss Rivers returned, however, plans for all future luncheons, picnics, and walks in the community were curtailed. Two reasons were given: one, that the day hospital was an institution, and if the patients were well enough to cook and take field trips, they should be discharged; and two, the risks of allowing patients to leave the day care building were too great, both in terms of private property and liability to the agency if a patient should thereby be injured. When this was communicated to the O.T. aides, they made the valid complaint that they really had no understanding of the purpose of O.T. projects. Miss Hall suggested that in-service staff training sessions be instituted immediately so that roles and tasks could be clarified before the threatened demise of the day care program. Miss Rivers termed this "senseless" because staff meetings had been tried once before at the Mental Health Center, and they didn't work. When Mrs. Rocco, the occupational therapist, realized how ineffectual Miss Hall was in implementing the total program, she pointedly expressed her exasperation and anger by suggesting that Miss Hall leave the day-to-day operation of the day hospital to her and instead spend her time finding the patients jobs, "like social workers usually do." In the face of this pervasive loss of morale, the program functions of the day hospital ground to a halt.

By this time the program was in its seventh week, and Dr. Hathaway returned from her vacation. However, Miss Hall was planning to leave the agency the next week, preparatory to returning for her second year of graduate training, which would take her out of the classification of case aide. Miss Hall felt overwhelmingly discouraged because she had expected to make a contribution to the day hospital program, but in the absence of proper role delineation and supervision, she had been unable to do so.

Nine months after the inception of the program, none of the patients had been discharged back into the community, although three had been committed to a full-time mental hospital. Only one new patient had been admitted. No innovations were made in the setting or the program; just as the regular staff members of the Mental Health Center had no investment in the success of the day hospital in the excitement of its organization, Dr. Hathaway did not have the time to continue her interest in it and be director of the main Mental Health Center, all in two and a half days per week. In short, the day hospital gradually faded away as it passed through the process of inadequate administration.

QUESTIONS

1. What is the role of the administrator of a day hospital such as this one?
2. How would you evaluate the organization of this new program?
3. Why did the day hospital fail in its mission?

CASE 4

Bureaucracy and Citizen Participation

Joan Onacki
(Used by Permission)

Bureaucracy is a dirty word to most people. They seem to have forgotten or never known that bureaucratic forms appeared in order to counter the excesses of earlier times. When advancement, recognition, status, and reward depended on the whim of a perhaps capricious leader, life was none too secure. That is not to say that organizational patterns are an invention of the twentieth century. Ancient China and Egypt had administrative structures. The Roman Empire exhibited many of the characteristics of bureaucracy, such as "chain of command, centralized direction, table of organization, specialization, formalization, and standardization of rules and regulations." [1]

With the Dark Ages, these relatively modern administrative concepts gave way to a return to power based on personal loyalties and law based on custom and oral tradition rather than on a written code. Formal administrative concepts reappeared in the sixteenth and seventeenth centuries particularly in France. The often attacked particulars of bureaucracy were a breath of fresh air in the labyrinth of government based on personality, cults, favoritism, and caprice. "Bureaucratic administration means fundamentally the exercise of control on the basis of knowledge." [2] If one is to exercise control, it is certainly better to exercise it on the basis of knowledge than on whim.

Max Weber is usually viewed as the first major theoretician of bureaucracy. But even before Weber, Hegel expressed his view of bureaucracy as a bridge between the state and civil society. Marx carried this idea further and saw the state along with the bureaucracy as instruments by which the dominant class exercised domination over other social classes. He felt that bureaucracy would wither away along with the state. [3] A modern version of Marxian thinking is found in an article by Sjoberg. [4] He says that because bureaucracy is based on middle-class values it is a device to keep the lower class in its place. From the New Deal to the Great Society, government has tried to solve social problems by expanding bureaucracies. As more problems arose, more bureaucracies were created.

Weber recognized that bureaucracy was (and is) a potential threat to freedom, but its efficiency, impartiality, and rationality were values of great importance. He described three types of domination—charismatic, traditional, and legal. Bureaucracy is the administrative apparatus of the legal type. [5]

To be a bureaucratic structure, Weber says an organization must evidence: a high degree of specialization, a hierarchical structure, impersonality, recruitment on the basis of ability, differentiation between private and official income, rules based on rational thinking.[6] It is the hierarchical concept with its accompanying implication of dehumanization and rigidity that is the basis of much of the criticism aimed at bureaucracy.

Although not always expressed in these terms, another large part of the criticism is actually directed at bureaucracy as an *end* in itself rather than as a *means* of accomplishing something. When dealing with a bureaucracy such as the Motor Vehicle Department, it is hard to avoid concluding that this organization has forgotten what its purpose is and is behaving as if the department itself is its own reason for being.

Michels puts forth this very idea in his "iron law of oligarchy." [7] He saw democratic movements coming in waves over the course of history. As soon as representatives are elected, they become more interested in preserving themselves than in serving their ideals. The leaders then control so many resources, such as communications, that the masses are powerless to influence the direction of their government. Michels sees democracy as impossible either within the organization or in the larger society. This brings up the controversy between those who see government bureaucracy destroying free enterprise and undermining democracy and those who feel that it is the capitalistic economic system that necessarily brings increasing bureaucracy and the decline of democracy.

Bureaucracy strives for efficiency and fairness. But there have been many other streams in the river of views toward organizations and their administration. Even a cursory glance at the card catalogue shows that an enormous amount has been written on bureaucracy. As this paper is just a beginning look at bureaucracy, I will make only the briefest mention of other organizational theories. Weber was looking at the whole society. As a humanist, he was concerned with problems of power. On the other hand, beginning with Taylor and the scientific management school, focus shifted to the individual, particularly the worker in a factory. Emphasis now seemed to be on scientifically determining how to boost the productivity of each individual. There is a sense of using people as tools. Even with Mayo's greater concern for the human elements, one still feels an aura of manipulation.[8]

Taylor and May are representative of the managerial tradition as opposed to the bureaucratic tradition of Weber. From a theoretical point of view, interchange between these two points of view—one starting with the individual, the other with society—would seem to be most valuable. And from the personal point of view, those of us who feel closer to one viewpoint need to be reminded of the other. I tend to think in more sociological and psychological terms. I care more about "the problems of organizational power and freedom." [9] But I must remember that not all individual needs can be met by rearrangements of society.

In this regard, I am interested in the philosophy of MacGregor in which he borrows Maslow's theories about human needs. MacGregor accused organizations of not recognizing the highest needs—those of self-fulfillment. He names "self-direction" as the key to realizing the full potential of human beings.[10] He wanted to see decentralization of power, delegation of responsibility, enlargement of the scope of most jobs, and employee participation built into organizations. MacGregor pointed out to management that employees would gain "prestige, knowledge and a sense of achievement," all of which, unlike money, are in unlimited supply.[11]

By looking at the process, the functionalists satisfy some people's needs to bring together the theorists of bureaucracy and of the managerial tradition. The functionalists recognize individual as well as organizational goals. They are concerned with such things as the informal organization, latent functions and unintended consequences. Although useful as a descriptive method, I find that for me this approach "reifies social reality." [12] It seems heavy with the values of "what is" rather than "what might be." We might sum up the organizational theories loosely by starting with Weber's seminal theories about bureaucracy and his concern with structure. This was followed by the scientific management school, which was concerned with technology. The human relations school focused on behavior. Now with systems theory, the emphasis is more holistic, an attempt to look at the process.

When the power inherent in bureaucracy is abused, a number of things manifest themselves. I was interested that the list of abuses of Mouzelis [13] sounds remarkably like our present national administration. These include overcentralization, big government (despite the new Federalism), authoritarian control, lack of democratic decision-making, and the excessive power of the executive over the legislative. If one adds to this list the tendency toward "internal unity in the face of external dangers," [14] one is tempted to see our national leadership as a bureaucracy in the perjorative sense.

There is no question that rather than the collegial model, the hierarchical model is part of the definition of bureaucracy. This can lead to the individual possessing very little real discretion. Hopefully, there will be increasing bureaucracies where individual needs and strengths are taken into account. Function follows form, but hopefully, form does not always dictate function, as bureaucracies are probably here to stay. We can only hope that they will consider their substantive aspects more important than their formalities.

I have come across one writer who defends bureaucracy rather vigorously. Anthony Downs [15] sees irony in the fact that bureaucracy is a term of scorn while it provides employment and makes critical decisions. He also notes that bureaucracy is criticized both for its monolithic power and its bungling. These would appear to be incompatible. He does not worry about bureaucracy as a threat to individual liberty because he feels that overall freedom is expanding and that bureaucracy is one cause of that freedom. He is aware that this trend could be reversed, but he does not believe it will happen in the United States. Downs's definition of bureaucracy is interesting because he sees it as nonmarket organizations whose outputs are hard to evaluate in dollar terms. This definition sets him apart from those who see bureaucracy as part of industry as well as government.

In this paper, I am chiefly concerned with the relationship between bureaucracy and citizen participation. Therefore, I am giving more attention to the relationships of a bureaucracy with the external world, rather than with its internal workings. I find I usually tend to think in organizational-sociological terms rather than individual-psychological terms. But nevertheless, I am fascinated by the internal problems. The basic one is the individual exercising his freedom in relationship to other people, which necessarily puts on some restraints. Another interesting problem is that of the divided loyalty felt by professionals. There is a real difference in their behavior depending on whether they see their loyalty as mainly toward the organization or toward their profession. In a hierarchical structure, it is difficult to deal with lateral affiliations inherent in the role of a specialist.

People not only work for an organization, they *are* the organization. Without any people, there would be no organization. Even the most rigid bureaucracy does not exist without people. The interaction of these people is of prime importance.

Citizen participation has been a popular phrase since the War on Poverty in the middle 1960s. I will be using the phrase in two ways. Sometimes referring to the particular federal requirements for citizen participation, but more often speaking to the general idea of citizens not only voting but having a continuing input into those organizations that govern them.

Citizen participation was written into the Economic Opportunity Act of 1964 because of a recognition that government was huge, impersonal, and unresponsive to the needs of many. These sound like criticism of bureaucracy rather than of elected officials. It is my contention that the discontent that led to the guidelines on citizen participation were in response to bureaucracy—red tape, slowness, unresponsiveness—rather than to the political arena. But what people found themselves up against was another bureaucracy. Through elections, indigenous people were given the illusion of being in the political action. Elections for the most part were not hotly contested and did not include large numbers of people. I consider true political expertise vital if heretofore neglected groups are to become contributors to the decision-making process. I do not consider that citizen participation under federal guidelines is a "real" political experience for most participants. Those elected to boards from the citizenry found that their role was advisory. They were excluded from important areas such as budget decisions.

I think there has been a real confusion as to whether people are playing a political game or a bureaucratic game. It seems as though it were politics, but I believe it is bureaucracy. As a resource person for the Interim Citizen's Assembly (ICA) in Hartford, I feel that the clearly stated guidelines for this group are probably being misread. The City Council retains all final power! The ICA is a group of twenty-four people that is writing bylaws, forming committees, and otherwise becoming organized. I wonder if it will become a bureaucracy?

The ICA is a formalization of citizen participation. All kinds of formal and informal citizen participation mechanisms are in operation now. Many of them revolve around client participation in agencies. Miller and Rein,[16] in an extremely interesting article, discuss the various reasons for participation—so that the poor would understand existing institutions (the implication being that the institutions are fine, the people aren't) and to provide jobs. But the poor were not interested in therapy. They saw a chance of getting in on the power. As agencies involve the poor more and more, they must learn from them as personnel and as policy-makers. Some of the professionals may find this hard to take. Social workers may also have difficulty working through their own ambivalence about power—which they often see as being in opposition to democracy. A further point is made that the system of a bureaucracy being accountable to elected representatives who are accountable to the people is imperfect. The agency must be directly accountable to the people. I find this almost a utopian point of view. Miller and Rein look for more democracy and more humanity in bureaucracy. They urge agencies not to surrender to efficiency as the highest social value.

It is not easy to get truly representative citizen participation. Providing resources and knowledge and building on existing alliances and on ethnic groups are some suggestions. Some even suggest that bureaucracies be created to deal with existing bureaucracies.[17] The vast subject of how to get citizen participation is not the subject of this paper.

I am also interested in the relationship between bureaucracy and citizen participation in the area of politics as well as in agencies. Elected officials set policies—more or less in accordance with their perception of what the electorate wants. Usually, bureaucracies carry out these policies, and their specialized knowledge gives them great power. Among their powers is the power to *not* act.

Elected officials—the City Council of Hartford—are the people who stand at the focal point of this conflict between citizen participation and bureaucracy. In some senses, they are mediators. They are the "elected instrument of the popular will and the policy making head of the bureaucracy." [18] It is a challenging place to be. Although I am leery of attributing too much positive value to conflict, I do think that the tension created in the place where citizen participation and bureaucracy come together can be dynamic, healthy, and creative. In the governmental area, this tension resides in the City Council (or mayor, and so on).

In my town, it has been interesting to watch a change in townspeople's attitudes toward our form of government. About ten years ago, we shifted from a Town Meeting to a Council-Manager form of government. The last few years have seen several controversies—among them Project Concern and low-income housing. Discontent with the decisions on these and other issues has created a small groundswell for a strong mayor form of government. Apparently, the people have felt that the more impersonal manager and his staff were not responsive enough.

Back in the days of ward politics, people knew where to go to get things done. Now with professional managers of government and councilmen elected at-large, people find themselves dealing with impersonal bureaucrats. It is interesting that in the 1930s it was the liberals who pushed, under the name of reform, for more professional, rational bureaucratic government. Now liberals demand citizen participation and the far left cries, "Power to the people."

Alford [19] discusses the conflict between and incompatability of bureaucracy and participation and comes to an interesting conclusion. He studies bureaucracy and participation as attributes of four Wisconsin cities. He concludes that modern political systems display a high degree of bureaucracy and of citizen participation. Traditional political systems show low bureaucracy and low participation. He favors the modern system because he feels that political decisions are then highly differentiated because the bureaucracies are responding to diverse but well-organized demands from outside. Communities with high bureaucratic and participatory levels are better able to act. They are more mobilized.

Before concluding, I would like to mention two other ideas that have occurred to me concerning bureaucracy and participation. We are traditionally a country that believes in rule by law, rather than by man. As bureaucracy amasses more power and interpretation and the carrying out of the law becomes more personal and further from the source, the danger to freedom is very real.

One of the problems around citizen participation is that vocal leaders often seem to prefer to address themselves to national rather than local issues. We must have people who are really concerned with and will work hard on local issues. Don't waste time fighting with Washington when City Hall is where energies should be directed.

Conclusions

In my opinion, bureaucracy is a tool, a way of doing something. Its fruits are many. A threat to freedom on the individual as well as on the governmental level is real. Rigidity and impersonality are evident far too often. Hierarchy is a part of the definition of bureaucracy, but somehow qualities of the collegial model must be integrated. Any administrative method must stress responsibility, interaction, process, the human qualities.

Citizen participation should not be viewed as a threat. Difficult times are ahead for organizations, but with careful recognition of the richness to be gained from a variety of inputs, the results should be better services to all people. And that should be our goal.

Elected officials stand in a crucial juncture of this interaction. If they make the mistake of seeing increased citizen participation as an unwelcome challenge, I think, in the long run those individuals will not last. Increased participation is resulting in increasing decentralization. As minorities, particularly black, increase in numbers in the cities, elected officials can expect a transfer of power to these groups.

I think social work has a unique contribution to make. Because of its background in both the psychological and the sociological fields, it can act as a bridge between these disciplines and create new theories of administration.

NOTES

1. George E. Berkley, *The Administrative Revolution* (Englewood Cliffs, N.J.: Prentice-Hall, 1971), p. 6.
2. Nicos P. Mouzelis, *Organisation and Bureaucracy* (Chicago: Aldine Publishing Co., 1968), p. 39.
3. Ibid., p. 8.
4. Gideon Sjoberg, "Bureaucracy and the Lower Class," *Sociology and Social Research,* April 1966.
5. Mouzelis, *Organisation and Bureaucracy,* p. 16.
6. Ibid., p. 39.
7. Ibid., p. 27.
8. Ibid., p. 168.
9. Ibid., p. 173.
10. Berkley, *The Administrative Revolution,* p. 17.
11. Ibid., p. 17.
12. Mouzelis, *Organisation and Bureaucracy,* p. 70.
13. Ibid., p. 53.
14. Ibid., p. 27.
15. Anthony Downs, *Inside Bureaucracy* (Boston: Little Brown, 1967).
16. S. M. Miller and Martin Rein, "Participation, Poverty and Administration," *Public Administration Review,* January–February 1969.
17. George Brager and Valerie Jorrin, "Bargaining: A Method in Community Change," *Social Work,* October 1969.
18. Robert R. Alford, *Bureaucracy and Participation* (Chicago: Rand-McNally, 1969).
19. Ibid.

QUESTIONS

1. What place does citizen participation have in a bureaucracy, and why is it important?
2. How should the administrator create greater citizen involvement in the work of the agency?
3. What must be done to combine the best features of the bureaucratic and collegial models of organization?

CASE 5

A Memorandum from the Superintendent to the Staff of the State School for Boys

TO: All Staff   July 22, 1976

FROM: Carl W. Wilson, Superintendent

I have been Superintendent for somewhat more than a month. When I agreed to take this position, I knew the following:

1. The situation was scandalously messy.
2. No one disagreed with point No. 1.
3. I had and would have the full support of Commissioner Hill, Deputy Commissioner Smith, and Director of Institutions, Mr. Carter.
4. I had a lot to learn in a very short period of time before acting decisively. I knew that in the first month I would be forced to make decisions I would regret, others I would feel far better about. In other words, the first month would be very difficult, and indeed it has been.

I have learned a lot about the State School for Boys, not so much as I would like or need to know, but enough to justify beginning a process of *drastic* reorganization that over time will create a more favorable climate for boys and staff.

What have I learned? I am going to list some of the major problems, and as I shall make clear below, these are the problems I shall ask you to think about and to come up with suggested solutions.

1. The amount of conflict, anger, and undercutting that exists between departments is without parallel in my experience.
2. For most people, their primary allegiance is to *their* department and not to the overall program for the boys. Each department has a piece of the action, which it considers more important than anything anybody else is doing. The major result is that boys are caught in the middle, and there is no coordinated program. As anyone with institutional experience would tell you, and as I am sure you know, the boys are fully aware of this infighting.

3. Most people spend a good deal of time blaming someone else or some other department for the situation we are in.

4. A lot of employees are unhappy in part because they do not feel that what they are doing is worthwhile. In other words, when your job is just a job and you regard it as no different than a factory job, you simply do not put out your best. What bothers me is that we are not only doing very little for the boys but we are doing even less to make employees feel that what they are doing is worthwhile. Employees will not change for the same reasons the boys will not change, *we have not provided them with the incentive to change.*

5. This place seems to be set up so as to see how boring and unstimulating one can make it for the boys. This place, particularly evenings and weekends, is like a tomb. If you cleared out all our boys and put here instead a group of bright, well-adjusted boys, I have no doubt with our present program that their level of boredom would soon provoke them to the same kind of behavior we see in our boys. Boys are bored and on edge and so are our employees.

6. The State School for Boys is isolated, in the most self-defeating ways, from the rest of the world. We want this community (and others) open to us, and this means we will have to be open to it and them. *We* don't own the State School for Boys. It is a public facility from which we have no right to wall the community off, except if we are doing, as has been the case, a lousy job.

I have developed a number of ideas about what might be done. None of them is simple or magical. There is no such thing as instant cure. My ideas would affect everyone, and it is precisely because they will have such effects that I am recommending the following.

1. I do *not,* at this time, wish to impose my ideas on the staff and employees. What I need to know is how you would deal with the problems I listed. I am not asking for gripes and complaints but *concrete ideas* about how we should change things so that we are serving the boys better than we now are. I am not asking for vague generalities about cooperation and communication. What I need are concrete steps that will get us out of the mess we are in.

2. I am going to set up groups whose task it will be to discuss the problems I listed and come up with a plan of action. These groups (about ten in a group) will meet twice weekly for two or three weeks.

3. I am asking four expert group leaders to act as leaders for the groups. They are from the University Psycho-Educational Clinic, and I can assure you of two things: they know institutions, and they are independent thinkers. Their job will be to keep you on the task of deciding what *you* think, recommend, and would get behind.

4. I have also invited Deputy Commissioner Hill and Director of Institutions Carter to participate in these groups. They will not be there to tell you what to think. *Anything they say will represent their personal opinions and should not be taken as official policy. Policy for the State School for Boys is primarily my responsibility, and I will discharge it. Mr. Smith and Mr. Carter know this, and I am delighted that they agreed to participate as individuals.*

5. These groups should conduct their discussion as if *any* change is possible. They are not to be bound by any existing departmental structure or practice or even policy. The State School for Boys will not change by nice words, pussy-footing, or token changes. The situation demands a lot of change.

I hope you take this responsibility seriously. I know that a number of you have good ideas, but they have not been "put on the table" for public discussion. This is your opportunity to do justice to *your* ideas. From this point on, we move forward and the more these groups face issues squarely, the more will the State School for Boys reflect what your consciences know needs to be done. We are here to serve boys, not ourselves.

QUESTIONS

1. What is your overall reaction to this memorandum?
2. If you were a staff member, what might some of your feelings be?
3. What do you think of the new superintendent's diagnosis of the problems?
4. Is it a good idea to bring in outside group leaders from the university? Why?
5. What do you think of the invitation to Mr. Smith and Mr. Carter to attend the meetings?
6. Do you agree with Mr. Wilson when he says, "Policy for the State School for Boys is primarily my responsibility?"

CASE 6

Incident at State Hospital

The following is the case record of an incident involving a large state psychiatric hospital. Although the incident concerned the entire hospital, it will be described from the standpoint of the administrative structure of one of the hospital's internal divisions.

The Hospital

The state has a number of psychiatric hospitals, each serving a designated geographic area. One of these, State Hospital, was founded at the turn of the century in the traditional manner for such institutions. Consisting of a number of two- and three-story brick buildings situated on a large "campus" outside of a small town, it had, at the time of its founding, a capacity of one thousand patients. The patients themselves were divided into "front wards" for those who seemed to be improving or from whom the prognosis was good, and "back wards" for chronic and severely disturbed patients.

At the time of the incident, the hospital's character and appearance had changed greatly. The town had grown to the edge of the hospital grounds. Many new buildings had been added over the years, and many professional services allied to the practice of institutional psychiatry had been incorporated. State now boasts a large, well-equipped occupational therapy building; augmented food, clothing and maintenance services; and training facilities for psychiatric residents, nurses, social workers, and psychiatric aides.

Even more important than the physical facilities is the growth and change in the philosophy underlying the administration of State. Administratively, the hospital's superintendent is directly responsible to the state director of Mental Health, who is in turn responsible to the governor. About a year ago, the decision was made by the director of Mental Health to begin implementation of some of the newer concepts in psychiatric hospital therapy and administration collectivized under the term "the open hospital."

The hospital was to be divided into three semi-autonomous units, each serving a part of the overall catchment area. Under the general administration of the superintendent, assistant superintendent, and chief of professional services (all three, psychiatrists), each of the three units would be administered by a unit chief and assistant unit chief, who could be directly responsible for psychiatric services carried on by staff and resident physicians.

The organization of the other professions (nursing, occupational therapy, social service) would be more complicated. Each of these professional services was to have a director, responsible directly to the superintendent. In each unit, there is an assistant director of nursing and a unit chief social worker, who were responsible both to their respective directors and to the unit chief. As can be foreseen, this dual responsibility was a source of tension when the system was put into effect. The occupational therapists would have no unit director; each worker was to be responsible directly to the unit chief and to his own director (again, a source of dual responsibility and tension).

This complicated administrative system can be seen as a compromise between the demands of the decentralized unit system, and the theory that each professional service should be autonomous in the hospital setting. As Magner puts it, "The crucial concept in developing an optimum climate for social work practice in the psychiatric hospital is that of autonomy— the autonomy of the social work department within the hospital setting." [1]

His claim is that the extent to which a department will contribute to the goals and purpose of the institution is dependent on the degree to which that department attains autonomy of role, function, and practice. Social work and nursing have achieved this autonomy, but at the price of a dualized responsibility with its conflicting demands and tensions.

At the same time, the patients were no longer to be segregated by type and severity of illness (the so-called front ward-back ward system) but were to be assigned to wards in rotating order of admission so that theoretically each ward would combine all degrees of illness and diagnosis. Only two exceptions would be made, for patients adjudged "criminally insane" and geriatric patients; these would be kept in their separate units as before.

It was decided to implement this planning, and a new superintendent with a reputation as a theorist in the field of community psychiatry and "the open hospital" was chosen. After some preliminary planning, the change to the "new system" was initiated, but not without opposition among the staff and community.

Among the staff, some of the opposition came about because of resentment: many of the personnel felt they had not been sufficiently included in the planning. Others felt that the therapeutic milieu of the hospital environment would break down with all kinds of patients on the same ward; still others felt uncomfortable and insecure in the face of such drastic reorientation.

In the nearby community, there was distress and fear over the "opening up" of State Hospital. Many citizens had always regarded the hospital, with its forbidding brick buildings situated in isolation outside of town, with fear and suspicion. The prospect of having "mental patients" allowed out of the buildings without restraint alarmed them; they felt that these patients would be wandering into town and posing a threat to the community. This fear went to the absurd length of suggestions from the community that all patients be required to wear distinctive clothing, or at least badges, so they could be easily identifiable if they did wander into town. The fear and opposition were serious enough, however, that the new superintendent felt it necessary, along with his other efforts at orientation of the community, to distribute printed cards with a telephone number (the hospital's) to be called if "suspicious or confused" persons were seen wandering in town.

In the internal administration of the north unit of the hospital, the "team approach" to patient therapy was theoretically in use. This called for the combined efforts of physicians, nurses and aides, occupational therapists, psychologists, and social workers on behalf of the patients. Representatives of each profession were assigned to a particular ward and worked with the patients as the requirements of the individual case dictated. The weekly ward meeting was to be the mainstay of coordination in planning and therapy; each patient was to be discussed, treatment planned and coordinated, and views regarding therapy and patient progress shared.

In practice, this team approach did not work efficiently for two basic reasons: 1) a serious shortage of professional manpower and 2) the fact that State is a teaching hospital.

The north unit consisted of nine wards (five for women, four for men), with an average capacity of fifty patients. To provide professional services for these 450 patients, there were three staff physicians (including the unit chief and his assistant, who are also charged with administrative duties) and two resident physicians, three social workers (including the unit chief social worker), and three occupational therapists. Nursing personnel seem adequate in numbers to provide "coverage" of each ward in three shifts, but not for fully individualized patient care. The psychologists were not assigned to wards but received referrals of individual patients for testing and/or therapy. These workers were accompanied by small numbers of student nurses and social workers, who were usually assigned individual patients rather than whole wards, and whose services were not materially helpful in the reduction of the workload of the full-time staff.

The effects of this shortage on the functioning of the "therapeutic milieu" were dramatic. The staff physicians (the theoretical "team leaders") did not have time to carry out the consultations that the team approach demanded due to the pressure of therapeutic and administrative duties. Ward meetings were taken up almost entirely with interviews of incoming patients for diagnostic notes and summaries. The unit chief, due to press of circumstances and his personal orientation to a more "traditional" system, had allowed an informal system to develop whereby he gave orders to be executed by the other members of the "team" and accepted full responsibility for the orientation of the "therapeutic milieu." Coordination between professions usually took place in informal "hallway conferences"; individual case conferences were rare. Much coordinating information, ironically, came from the patient himself, who kept the social worker, for instance, abreast of what the occupational therapist had planned for him.

Bernard and Ishiyama [2] have laid down two prerequisites for the effective functioning of the "psychiatric team"; 1) all factors, external as well as internal, must be a vital and positive part of the therapeutic program and 2) this orientation is too complex to be efficiently executed by any one person or profession. In the light of these insights, it seems evident that the "psychiatric team" in the north unit of State existed in theory, but not in practice.

The second reason for the breakdown of the team approach was the fact that the hospital was also training psychiatric residents, nurses, and social workers. Certain patients who presented unusual symptomatology or social situations were singled out and assigned to individual student workers. This practice worked to the benefit of the student (and usually the patient) but also had the effect of taking the patient out of what normal ward administrative structure there was, further complicating the communication process.

It should be noted that both these problems have been long-standing at State Hospital, antedating the administrative changes described above. The informal patterns of dealing with the problems, especially the lack of consultation and formal planning among all staff members, had become habitual by the time of the incident and contributed greatly to the ensuing difficulties.

The Incident

About nine months after the geographic-unit system was put into effect, a series of patient "escapes" brought State Hospital into newspaper headlines. It happens at times, of course, that patients leave a psychiatric hospital before the terms of their commitments have expired or without going through normal requested-discharge procedures. In hospital jargon, these patients "elope" or "go AWOL"; they are usually then listed as "requested discharge against medical advice."

During this three-week period, however, a number of patients who seemed inclined toward criminal acts, some of them under "police holds," left the west unit without permission. The first incident involved two men who had been arrested by the State Police for armed robbery and had been confined in west unit's only locked ward for psychiatric observation. They made their way out of the ward one afternoon, accosted a nurse who was walking to her car, kidnapped her, and took her car. About an hour later, they allegedly robbed a gas station, using a knife as a threat. They then came upon another car stalled on the highway, decided to steal it, and were apprehended by police in the act of trying to start the second car.

This incident would probably have gone by with relatively little notice were it not for the fact that two days later another man left the west unit and went to the home of his estranged wife, where he threatened to kill her. He also was apprehended by police a short time later.

The press, especially the *Chronicle,* began to pay close attention to the hospital. During the next two weeks, four or five other patients left west unit without permission. Although none was regarded as potentially dangerous and only one was under a "police hold," by this time every patient who left was headlined as "Another Escaped Mental Patient."

Stories and editorial comment began appearing in newspapers of cities miles away, and demands upon the governor for an investigation of the hospital were made. One or two locals of the American Federation of Labor issued statements calling for the dismissal of the superintendent and the director of nursing. The superintendent issued a public statement attempting to place the facts in perspective, but this was dismissed as an attempt to "whitewash" the incidents. The state's Mental Health Association issued statements deploring the biased reporting of the incidents, but these also received little notice.

As the "escape" incidents continued, the director of Mental Health announced that the governor had appointed a special commission to investigate the situation at the hospital and in the same statement laid the blame at the feet of the State Police, who, he said, had a habit of placing persons whom they had arrested, but against whom they did not as yet have sufficient evidence, in the hospital for "psychiatric observation." This statement received wide circulation, and the director of State Police was asked for a counterstatement, but he declined to communicate until after the investigation was completed.

During this period the only news the staff below the level of unit chief had of the situation was from the press; there was no official communication within the hospital regarding the incidents. The special commission came to the hospital and spoke to the administrative officials, but the only information the rest of the staff had about them was the fact that they were seen in the professional staff's dining room at lunch. Their report was sent to the governor the next day but was not published or communicated to the staff.

A few days later, three and one-half weeks after the original incident, the situation came to a head. The "night shift" of nurses and aides came on as usual at 3:00 P.M. At 7:00 P.M. that night, each ward received a telephone message from the superintendent's office: After the patients were in bed for the night, all wards in the hospital were to be locked until further notice. No patient was to be allowed to leave, even in the company of staff members, for any reason except medical emergency. No reason was given for the orders, nor any indication of how long the situation would last.

The next morning, the patients in north unit, which had had no "escapes," and who were only vaguely aware of the preceding incidents, reacted with resentment and agitation. As the personnel came on duty, they began bombarding the nurses with telephone calls, asking for information. The nurses could only respond that they knew nothing. Later in the morning they reported that the unit chief and assistant unit chief were making visits to each ward, inspecting records, and interviewing each patient individually. Every patient who had a "privilege card" (permission to leave the ward unaccompanied) was made to give it up, again without explanation. The loss of these cards, an important prestige item in the status system of the hospital, increased patient resentment, already exacerbated by the unaccustomed daytime crowding on the wards. Fistfights between male patients began to erupt. Some of the male patients who had been assigned to work in kitchens and dining rooms staged a strike; they refused to go to work as long as the wards remained locked.

Staff resentment among the nurses and aides was rising rapidly at the same time. Overburdened under normal circumstances, they were finding it increasingly difficult to deal with the agitation and resentment of the patients. They most keenly felt the absence of consultation or sharing of information with them before the orders were given. There was increased talk of resignation.

Finally, in midafternoon, a typewritten notice appeared on nursing service and social service bulletin boards to the effect that the wards had been locked and would remain so while each patient's legal status and possession of a "privilege card" was reviewed and necessary changes made.

The review was completed the next day. The wards were unlocked, some patients were reissued their cards, and the situation seemed about to return to normal, when without notice new changes in the ward arrangements were announced. Henceforth, each geographical unit, north, west, and southeast, would have a graded series of wards: one set was to be locked at all times with its patients carefully supervised, another set was to be locked but without the rigid patient control, and the rest were to be open. Patients would be assigned on the basis of legal status and the need for physical control of their behavior.

Staff opinion of this situation was divided. Those who had not agreed with the original opening-up of the hospital saw it as a fulfillment of their dire prophecies. Those who were personally inclined to the philosophy of the "open hospital" resented it as a return to an archaic kind of patient care. All were agreed that this system would result in the chronic, long-term patients gradually being congregated on one ward and, by implication, a return to the "back-ward" system.

In the two months since these administrative changes, only one "escape" from a locked ward occurred, and that patient was soon apprehended by hospital police. Shortly after the changes went into effect, it was announced by the hospital superintendent, in a statement to the press, that these changes were designed to stop such incidents as had occurred in the past. At the same time, the hospital police force was being expanded from five to ten men. After this announcement, public interest in the hospital subsided, and there were no further press reports.

Analysis

Interhospital communication and consultation: This seems to have been the most obvious point of difficulty and breaking down during the incident. The lower echelons of staff were not consulted and were provided with insufficient information during the incidents; this increased their resentment, which in its turn was communicated, however involuntarily, to the patients.[3] Two reasons for this situation could be put forward: lack of time and the developed pattern in which staff were given orders but not consulted. The governor was under considerable pressure to "do something about State." Although there is no direct evidence, one can surmise that he communicated this pressure through the director of Mental Health to the superintendent, demanding quick results. This, coupled with the order-giving pattern, could explain the lack of consultation but would not explain the lack of disseminated information.

The lack of information might be due to an attitude, because personnel had been functioning in the usual hospital situation without being included in interprofessional communication, that they did not need it now. It can only be concluded that this was a serious administrative mistake; the staff had already been resentful of the usual situation, and the incident confirmed the idea of many that the administration is autocratic and does not recognize the professional competence of others on the staff.

As Pfiffner and Sherwood point out,[4] people perform best in their assigned job positions in the hierarchy when they consider themselves full participants. This would be doubly true of persons who consider themselves "professionals" in their own right. The action of the hospital administration in disregarding staff consultation and preparation, as well as dissemination of information, did not fulfill this need, thus increasing staff resentment.

Result of staff shortage: At least a partial reason for the difficulties at State Hospital during the incidents was the already existing shortage of staff, which had led to certain undesirable patterns of informal organization and communication. This system of operation had evolved as an involuntary reponse to the staff shortages: the hospital must be kept functioning, and the evolved system met this need, however inefficiently. However, when a crisis developed, the shortage of staff showed itself in an acute disruption of routine functioning.

Sue Spencer[5] cites Hans Selye's observation that the healthy, vigorous agency can be distinguished from the stock or deteriorating agency by its use of resources; the agency that uses a disproportionate amount of its resources for survival "is eventually doomed." At State Hospital, the professional staff in north unit is totally committed in time and energy to staying abreast of the workload, with even the administrative head of the unit bearing a full load of frontline duties. There is no time or energy left to plan for development, research, or expansion, and none for coping with unforeseen crises.

Intergroup relationships: Trecker[6] lists in a diagram the various groups in the agency "matrix" with which the administration is concerned in a continuous and interlocking process. As applied to State, these groups would include professional staff, nonprofessional staff, volunteers, community groups, board and committees, and recipients of services. A strength of State is the fact that the hospital superintendent, already firmly committed to the practice and development of community psychiatry, is involved with community groups and boards and committees, as well as with the actual hospital work of professional and nonprofessional staff, volunteers, and patients. A weakness of the present functioning system is the fact that the administration has not yet been able to coordinate, in a significant and ongoing way, the processes within the hospital with those outside (community, board, and so on), nor to develop effective communication between administration and total staff. This leads to the complaint that "they give the orders and we carry them out." This situation leads one to postulate that Trecker's thesis, that a primary responsibility of the administrator is to create a productive working climate in which people function at their best, is not completely implemented at State.

This case study has been rather negative in tone because it has dealt with administrative structure that is not functioning with optimum efficiency, and with a crisis situation that has pointed up the deficiencies in the system. The basic problem (lack of interprofessional consultation and communication) and its basic cause (lack of sufficient manpower) are related of course, in a vicious circle. Professional persons will not, as a rule, work in a setting where they feel their competence and ability in planning are not recognized and utilized, and on the other hand, a viable "team approach" to patient care and therapy cannot be practiced where there is a serious shortage of professional staff.

The purpose of this study has been to point up and analyze these deficiencies, not to propose a plan for solution of the problems. However, in conclusion, it might be pointed out that Belknap's conclusions in his study of a large state hospital [7] would be informative. After examining the administrative problems of the hospital (not totally dissimilar to those at State), he suggests the reorganization of administrative structure so the authority organization, both internal and external, would become consistent with egalitarian team procedures.

NOTES

1. George W. Magner, "Autonomy: An Administrative Goal of the Department of Social Work in a Psychiatric Hospital," *Social Service Review* 37 (March 1963), p. 54.
2. Sydney E. Bernard and Toaru Ishiyama, "Authority Conflicts in the Structure of Psychiatric Teams," *Social Work* 5 (July 1960), p. 77.
3. For a discussion of communication of staff resentment to mental patients, see Alfred H. Stanton, M.D., and Morris S. Schwart, Ph.D., *The Mental Hospital* (New York: Basic Books, 1954), Chapter 17, "Morale and Its Breakdown: The Collective Disturbance."
4. John M. Pfiffner and Frank P. Sherwood, *Administrative Organization* (Englewood Cliffs, N.J.: Prentice-Hall, Inc., 1960), p. 362.
5. Sue Spencer, *The Administrative Method in Social Work Education* (New York: Council on Social Work Education, 1959), p. 24.
6. Harleigh B. Trecker, *Group Process in Administration* (New York: The Woman's Press, 1950), p. 14.

7. Ivan Belknap, *Human Problems of a State Mental Hospital* (New York: McGraw-Hill Book Company, Inc., 1956), Chapter 12, "Conclusions."

QUESTIONS

1. What is your evaluation of the way the changes were made at State?
2. What happens when staff is not involved in the decision-making process?
3. What is the difference between formal and informal communication?
4. What is involved in dealing with community pressure brought against an agency and an administration?
5. How could the problems that arose in the "incident" have been prevented?
6. What is your opinion regarding the author's analysis of the situation?

CASE 7

A Community Drug Program: A Case Study in Administrative Action

Four years ago, a medium-sized town in the East funded a small drug program that emerged from a citizen task force on drug abuse in the community. Drug abuse was defined as any use of illegal drugs or narcotics, and the operating assumptions included "marijuana leads to heroin," "only bad kids use drugs," and "drugs are sold by adult criminals (probably black) from the nearby city." The target population was seen as a fairly small group of adolescents who were "leading their friends and school mates astray." The explicit goals were to stop drug abuse through drug education and referral to regional health care agencies and counseling services. The implicit goals were to single out those abusing drugs and/or selling drugs and to apply sanctions from school, police, parents, or appropriate referral agencies.

The town has a population of 23,000, with about 3,000 of junior high and high school age. The proportion of those from eighteen through twenty-one drops off rapidly because there are no postsecondary educational facilities and little inexpensive housing for young people except in the parental homes. The town is predominantly white, middle class, middle income, and moderately conservative. Housing is almost entirely one-family and is scattered throughout the geographical area in a suburban pattern. An industrial area along the river, dividing the town effectively, separates one side from the other, the eastern section having a mild flavor of "wrong side of the tracks." The small commercial and public service center (including the library, Town Hall, high school, and some recreational fields) is not on the major routes of most residents. Minimal public transportation goes into the city, and no public transportation or even safe bike and walking routes go from one side of town to the other, much less through the center.

The community drug program was set up (without serious organizational thought) as a town department independent of the police and the school. It began with the hiring of one man, whose background was in public administration, journalism, personnel and development work for a community hospital, and settlement house work. A very modest program and staff budget were allocated from town funds and a three-room office was located in an old house next to the Town Hall. The first months were spent establishing relations with schools, PTAs, church groups, and local police through an educational format on drugs, that is, speaking, films, printed material, and so on (mostly with a "scare tactic" focus because little else was available). A telephone crisis line was developed through coordination with another suburban town and training provided to adult and high school age volunteers. Here the focus was on help for those with drug or drug-related problems instead of on frightening or punishing— and here the major direction began to change from the original goals set by the task force.

High school counselors involved in the crisis phone service began to see the complexity of issues concerning young people and the limitations of their work within the educational system. Many teenagers saw the school as their mortal enemy and were failing, dropping out, or even creating behavior problems in school in addition to using various drugs; others seemed to be tolerating school, some even doing well and still using drugs; and a lot of them expressed great unhappiness at serious difficulties with friends and family and with their own feelings about themselves. The misuse of drugs appeared to be widespread, unlike the original assumptions, and involved many different drugs; use ranged considerably around kind, frequency, and quantity. A nearby university research survey of drug use in towns of the area was releasing its findings about this time and confirming the picture emerging in our town.

The drug program director had been aware of this pattern of drug use for some time, but because his definition of the problem had been at variance with that of the task force, he knew his first job was to stimulate community awareness of the problem's complexity—that drug abuse was a societal phenomenon involving adults and adolescents misusing legal and illegal drugs in the midst of normative confusion and contradiction. Understanding and support were needed for an attack on the social problems and their consequent individual and family difficulties, and this would require a major change in the goals and activities of the drug program.

The word spread from those involved in the help line that young people wanting some nonpunitive assistance for themselves or friends involved with drugs had a resource *outside* of the school, which was not only hated by some but feared by most as administratively geared to police action— a fact announced as school policy at the time and felt by school counselors as a major restriction to their effectiveness. Despite a general suspicion that the program director might also "narc" (inform) for the police, some young people, alone or with friends or dragged in by parents, began to seek counseling. Adolescent discussion groups were formed, some family conflicts were helped, and some trust was established.

The Citizen Task Force on Drug Abuse had been reconstituted as an advisory board to the drug program, with most of its original membership remaining intact. The role of the board was the locus of some intragovernmental skirmishing as its power relationships with the program director and with the town's chief executive were being defined. Because the first selectman had the authority to hire the director and to recommend the program budget to the Board of Finance and town meeting for approval, the board's function was spelled out as "advisory." Its public opinion and political power remained considerable, as the board was both a feedback source from the community and an interpreter to the various constituencies represented by individual members. Particularly in the heated sociopolitical climate of the time, when more authoritarian than egalitarian measures were being loudly advocated by a vocal minority, the support and goodwill of the board were important to the elected chief executive of the town and to the program director at whose pleasure he served.

When original board members were replaced, for various attritional reasons, the drug program director carefully solicited new members of political value and with more sympathy to a recognition of problem complexity and to a multidirectional program involving counseling, alternative activities, and community involvement as well as education and referral. Hesitantly and cautiously, the board agreed to the addition of staff and some program expansion. Requests from PTAs for more presentations involving opportunities for discussion groups, similar requests from churches for leadership of groups on parenting, and even requests for classroom sessions on adolescent problems buttressed the case for increased staff.

With considerable imagination and ingenuity, the director hired six more staff members to carry out a variety of activities. These included a woman trained as a psychiatric nurse who did individual and group counseling and also brought special skills in physiology and pharmacology; a man trained as a community house worker—both worked part time for minimum wage because of their commitment to the need and other priorities in their lives; a women with social work training and wide political experience in the community to serve as staff trainer, community organizer, counselor, and assistant to the director—paid full time from funds allotted to the town by the federal government as a measure to combat high unemployment (therefore the salary was from other than the program's original budget); two male outreach workers skilled in youth programs were shared with a nearby town's YMCA for ten hours a week to develop recreational and alternative activities with young people in order to help them experience responsibility, rapid success, and some fun other than drugs; and a young ex-addict who was currently in a work-study plan at a community college to be a counselor and to bridge the defense of "how can you understand if you've never. . . ." The total staff cost to the drug program budget amounted to little more than a modest salary for one and a half people.

With the staff additions and improved relations with the school administrative and counseling personnel, small offices were manned in the high school itself with drug program staff available for crisis intervention, interpretation to teachers, "rap" sessions, and ombudsmen functions. The position of being in but not under the control of the school was difficult to develop and to maintain. The "host" agency often felt suspicious that its goals and those of the drug program were in contradiction—as indeed they were in terms of some socialization norms. Staff members were informal in manner and dress, encouraging egalitarian relationships rather than hierarchical and seeking to provide social and personal worth reinforcements on whatever possible level—a far cry from grades and large group discipline. The "obedient" lonely student was sought out as well as the one acting out; the failure and dropout were encouraged to relate to the successful student in noncompetitive discussions and short-term creative and recreative activities. Program participants, called "members" rather than "clients," did not have to "do dope" or "have problems" to gather for discussion groups, come to guitar-playing sessions at the Town Hall annex, or sing Christmas carols to shut-ins by the bus load. The only requirement was "no dope at the drug program"—for staff, kids, and adults alike.

The major thrust of the program had changed from labeling and separating out those who used drugs as "bad" and in need of "special" treatment to a multifaceted program concerned with all adolescents—and their parents and teachers—and in recognition of the many difficulties during this stage of growing up: the need for independence with boundaries, the opportunity to try something and be supported if it did not meet one's expectations, and the constant need to be liked and valued, especially in the midst of not so likable or estimable behavior. Adults and young people were encouraged to understand *each other's* problems in living together and not to "cop out" on the "generation gap."

To bridge the "generation gap," young people were appointed to the advisory board, counseling groups were co-led by a peer and a staff member, and parents and other adults were drawn into activity programs such as a summer arts-and-crafts festival of concerts, drama, and other creative presentations. The festival put into action a goal of greater youth involvement in and concern with the community itself, spinning off to youthful volunteers assisting the Recreation Department and Recycling Program, high school dropouts linking back into school via service as aides to elementary teachers, and a local motorcycle "gang" working with—not against—the local police in traffic duty for large concerts or ball games (an experience that has been mind-boggling to both). Once the police agreed to a special parking place for motorcycles, the "gang" had to be cajoled into being less tough than the police themselves!

These accumulated experiences became the basis for additional funding: a small federal/state Law Enforcement Assistance Administration (LEAA) grant and an increase from the town budget. A recent college graduate in psychology-sociology and a bright young high school "hippie" dropout were added to the staff (again part time or two for the price of one), one to focus on a developing juvenile delinquency program with the local police and Juvenile Court, the other to concentrate on peer counseling groups and musical activities plus interpretation of adolescents to adult groups, in tandem with an older staff member.

By this time, most staff members had received individual special training at the Drug Dependence Institute at the university, and the nine people plus several volunteers were concentrating on the best mesh and utilization of the varied training, backgrounds, skills, and experiences. The entire staff had been participating in a program-planning and -evaluation and in managing interpersonal relationships. The director functioned as the boundary setter, the overall policy-planner, the budget-manager, and personnel chief. He and his assistant were also responsible for the overall relationships with other community agencies, departments, and organizations, including the development of several new community organizations concerned with the growth and well-being of the town as a whole.

Through the LEAA grant, two consultants were employed to work with the staff on developing more precise evaluation methods and on group counseling skills with a more coherent short-term behavioral methodological approach. New techniques were practiced and learned by the staff as a whole as were methods of teaching and working with small groups. The experience and knowledge of each were shared as staff members also learned from one another. Each staff member also became involved in regional programs or task forces in an effort to coordinate and improve human services available to townspeople within the town and in the broader geographical area. Solid ongoing relationships grew with Family Service, Juvenile Court, the Adolescent Crisis Unit at the hospital, the regional Ys and Jewish Community Center, and the Drug Dependence Unit of the State Mental Health Center. Kids were leaving bikes near the Town Hall steps, the office lights burned late every evening, doors slammed, music played, paint spilled, picnics and touch football games enlived the parks—and there were fewer "bad trips." The town administration often wondered if an overdose in private might not be better than all the racket and rambunctiousness next door! Just about the time the drug program staff, members, and friends—with little to indicate who was whom—held a hot dog roast for the town employees, the department name was officially changed to the Youth Services Program, the major public recognition that the original goal had been discarded and the genuine problems were being faced by the community.

Two major strengths of the original Drug Program had occurred almost by happenstance. Administratively, the drug program had an independence from the other town departments, most specifically concerned with drug abuse—the school system and the police department; the former was focused on separating the abuser from the school population and the latter with carrying the one separated out of society in general. Neither agency was geared to perceiving drug abuse as a systemic problem of society and the abuser as a whole individual interacting painfully in societal systems with drug use as a "solution" to other problems.

The second major strength of the program was the choice of director with both considerable political ability and skill in working with young people as members of society. The former ability enabled him to understand and deal with the public pressures and the position of the mayor, and the latter helped him to be effective in the paranoidlike world of adolescents, especially those using illegal drugs. One suspects that it was the director's first quality that got him hired, but it was the second that got the program going.

The agency's independence from other town departments, while a source of strength in terms of program effectiveness, also meant that the drug program's position viz-à-viz other departments had to be negotiated. This required a good deal of formal and informal work on the part of the program's chief administrator and a good deal of his time during the first year of operation. The police needed reassurance that the drug program would not condone illegal acts or "harbor criminals" or in some way provide a "cop out" so that young people could escape the consequences of their actions. The issue of confidentiality between the staff and program members had to be spelled out and experienced over time before the police accepted the fact that the program would not act as an information source. The addition of a police officer to the advisory board and the interpretive-supportive work of the staff to police and to adolescents and their families, especially following arrests, helped define the relationship as separate but useful in some overlapping areas.

The relationship with the school system was even more complex. Except for a few counselors and teachers who saw the program as a referral source, the school administration was hostile and fearful—fearful that it might be the locus of an antischool "children's crusade" in an era of considerable student dissatisfaction and hostile toward an apparent conflict of values concerning dress, long hair, respectful behavior, group discipline, and so on. As a whole, the school was frightened at the drug abuse by students, uncertain what to do, and reluctant to face the widespread presence of drugs being used and sold within the school premises—never mind facing some of the reasons young people chose drugs to deal with their lives. Not until the program director produced the survey data by the university experts did the Board of Education confront the realization that drug abuse involved more than a few malefactors who should be dealt with by school expulsion and police action. It took more than a year for the school to agree to be a host agency for drug program workers during school hours. Unfortunately, as is often the case, drug-related crises that overwhelmed school personnel facilitated the use of school offices by the drug program staff. Effective crisis work and classroom presentations led to outreach work in cafeterias and the use of gymnasiums for informal recreational activities, but the administrative relationship continued to be tenuous and tentative. Without the power to control them, the school continued to be unsure how to feel about the "strangers" in its midst, especially adults who encouraged students to use their first names and to behave with more responsible assertiveness in school concerns. Student apathy or outright aggression seemed known and easier to deal with.

The drug program's first director, then, had the multiple task of devising a program to meet the original task force goals and, concurrently, to change and broaden the goals while bringing about a revised problem definition. Program, additional requests for service, new goals, and new problem recognition flowed back and forth, filtering through the advisory board, the town's governmental structure, adolescents and their families, and the community at large. The addition of staff and the application for and use of federal grant funds were further administrative functions and created additional administrative tasks.

The organization of a staff with equal status among staff members regardless of professional or paraprofessional background involved frequent all-staff meetings before a scheme of complementary authority and work was in full operation: each staff member was primarily responsible for several aspects of the total program; all other staff members would work under the direction of the one in charge of a particular activity. When Hank started a bicycle club, Mary carried out his instructions as an assistant; Hank in turn worked as a group counselor under the supervision of Mary. Helen was responsible for one high school building, and Charles checked with her before meeting with a certain student and guidance counselor there; Helen in turn cleared it with Charles before she gave a class on pregnancy and drugs in the other school building. The director's role was defined in a similar format, although he continued by necessity and agreement to be "more equal than others" in exchange for running departmental interferences for activities carried out by the staff.

The LEAA grant application process and implementation added new power and new tasks to the administration of the drug program. The recognition of value by state and federal agencies helped in relationships with local and regional departments and agencies, and the accountability requirements impetused the development of increased skills and more substantive evaluation procedures. After two years of operation, the program evaluation results were the firm basis of the next step: changing the name of the Drug Program to a title more descriptive of its new goals and multiple service activities. And the young people, with a father or two around as helpers, made a new sign—The Youth Services Center.

The assessment, diagnosis, and planned intervention for the drug abuse problem in our town was perceived from the beginning as involving the intertwining of values, knowledge, and the three major modes of social work in practice. The social diagnosis included the lag in school and family institutions in terms of current social change and the consequent stress felt by individuals and groups, especially the young entering such confusing maturity. The initial phase was primarily community organization geared toward developing community support and understanding for a more realistic problem definition and requiring multifaceted services. Roles included expert on drugs, advocate for the young, and broker-interpreter between families, children, and the institutions of school, church, government, and police. The drug program staff saw themselves as "change agents" concerned with effective strategies and institutional changes to help young people grow up with less need to abuse themselves with drugs or other life-threatening actions and with more support in the effort toward fulfilling their potentialities as responsible problem-solving adults. Individuals were seen as needing help from others in order to get "their heads sorted out" and then to grow in skills for living with the self-esteem needed to tackle choice and change in the years ahead. "Confidence and competence" became the goals for individuals and groups. One-to-one activity was often necessary in crisis or to explore specific conflicts; group methods were utilized for changes in behavior and attitudes on the part of adolescents, parents, teachers, and ongoing community groups. Community organization was the target strategy, both the beginning place and where the goal action was to take place—to put "confidence and competence into action" for self-in-society.

The Youth Services Program still gives off an aura of organized chaos—and hopefully it will continue to do so. The new goal is a *Community Service Program*, one that does not single out youth as the problem population but recognizes that everyone has problems in living at one time or the other and that all ages can be at the service of one another for the enhancement of our lives and the town as a good place to grow, learn, work, and live. Pie in the sky? Perhaps. The community is small enough, in the sense of the Greek philosophers, for voices to be heard from one end to the other. Now there are some listening to one another, talking with one another, and acting for and with one another. There seem to be fewer "strangers" in our midst.

QUESTIONS

1. What important administrative skills are revealed in this case?
2. As you trace the evolution of this program, what were some of the major steps?
3. To what extent was community readiness a factor in the success of the work?
4. What principles of good administration are illustrated in this case?
5. What next steps should be taken as the work moves ahead?

CASE 8

A Camp in a Crisis Situation

A camp is a world of its own—for three months of each year, many people choose to live in this isolated society. Our camp, one of the largest in the western United States, had its own system of government, forms of recreation, language, status structure, culture, traditions, mores, socialization process, and, of course, informal system.

Past experience in camping and in working with teenagers helped me into the position of director of the oldest unit in camp, the fifteen-year-olds, or "pioneers."

Probably the most important factor at this camp was the use of the group. The executive director, a social worker, had published articles concerning group techniques in training and problem-solving at camps. These methods were discussed, and we were taught different methods to make the group approach successful during staff training.

Camp Policy

The camp's policies were well defined, and the two-week training sessions helped clarify problem areas and socialize us for the remainder of the summer. The general philosophy was to make the children (the top level of administration always talked of "children"; most staff used the term "kids") aware of the values of living, working, and problem-solving in a group setting.

This case will focus on one major policy—the drug policy. The reaction by the total camp community will be studied. The policy is stated in this way: Camp *must* maintain a drug-free environment for these reasons:

1. Ideologically, we believe that hallucinogenic drugs, narcotics, and similar substances have *no* place in a community meant to focus on children's needs.
2. Pragmatically, we know that we have no right to ask parents to entrust their children to us without making this commitment.

Statements sent to both staff and campers and their parents leave no doubt that the use or possession of drugs will be "basis for immediate dismissal" of staff and cause to "send a camper home."

Camp Structure and Decision-Making

Before discussion of the drug incident, the administrative procedure deserves some analysis. For all practical purposes, the associate executive director does the physical work of overseeing three large camps. Each of the three camps has a camp director responsible to the associate executive director for the smooth-running of his camp. I worked in the largest of the three camps, where there were six units divided by age. Five units were approximately the same size, 180 campers. My unit, pioneers, was smaller, 85 campers. Each of these six units is administered by a unit director (UD). Unit directors have broad responsibility for control of their units. All unit problems flow toward them and from them to the camp director's level if they feel help is necessary. Other unit directors are usually brought in to solve major problems. The unit directors meet with the camp director both individually and in a group a number of times each week so that a constant problem-solving process develops. Group decisions, though, can be overruled by the camp director or the associate executive director.

Under the unit directors are program assistants (PA), who supervise groups of counselors. Program assistants are the lowest level of supervisory staff. They are expected to solve most day-to-day problems and to become involved in program. Next, of course, are the counselors, who provide direct service to the camper population.

Although the group is constantly stressed, the administrative model is hierarchical. Power is the key, and at camp, power is the ability to have one's decisions stand. So the higher one is in the structure, the more probable that his decision—whether good or bad—will become policy for all below him. Also, the top level has only to deal with a limited number of subordinates; for instance, the associate executive director has only to tell three camp directors what he expects done and a camp director has only six UDs to make demands of, but after that level, many more individuals become part of the process, and the imposition of any fixed rule or policy becomes something that must be accepted or lower level staff will ignore it and in some cases even work against the rule.

The Pioneer Unit

As mentioned, the pioneers made up the smallest unit in camp, but the pioneer unit is an elite group. The summer after being pioneers, a cross-country trip is offered for all who demonstrated true camping expertise. So pioneers are working for a chance to take the trip, but at fifteen years old, they have a number of personal stresses to cope with, especially adolescent peer structure.

Pioneer counselors are considered elites too. They are older and have experience at camp. They expect to take part in forming the unit's policies and above all want a "together" unit.

The unit has a small supervisory need with older kids and more mature counselors; therefore, the unit has only two supervisors. The supervisors share many responsibilities, but one does have final administrative authority. I had that role as senior program assistant (a traditional pioneer name, although I was really a unit director). The other supervisor was a program assistant. We both supervised counselors and took part in program whenever possible. As the head of a unit, I had the chance to become closer to my kids than unit directors in larger units.

The Drug Problem

Unlike many camp studies that deal with staff intervention into the problem of an individual child, this account will describe a problem that affected an entire unit.

The drug issue was a major item of the administration's presentation to kids and staff. As stated in their policy, the camp felt that drug abuse was wrong, especially when children were involved. Being sensitive to the demands of parents to keep the camp drug free, they did not want letters from campers going home with the mention of drug use in them. To emphasize the camp's strong stand, we, the supervisors, addressed our campers the first night of camp. We discussed individual and group rights, the dangers of lighted candles inside tents (a canvas tent can burn completely in less than a minute), and, of course, the rationale for the drug policy. All of these had been discussed earlier, before kids were even accepted for the pioneer program.

This was a six-week trip at camp, and most of the campers had been to our camp in the past. In a sense, this group was a sophisticated population. They knew the camp. They knew that physical punishment was never allowed and, also, knew that rarely was a camper sent home—the final step in the process when a camper broke all the rules. In their home environments many of these kids had experimented with drugs or at least had been exposed to drug usage, and although only fifteen years old, they were quite familiar with the many types of drugs.

For the first week of camp, there was no information about camper drug use; then at a unit director's meeting during the second week, it was announced that informal sources let it be known that some of the older kids were using drugs. That night the camp director spoke to all of the older units, once again emphasizing the camp's viewpoint on drugs. For the next few days, the camp director kept the pressure on the unit directors to develop a way for the kids to turn in any drugs they had. The camp director suggested putting a box in a central location in the unit and asking the campers to deposit any drugs in it. The unit directors were skeptical of this plan but agreed to it; we also asked our counselors to keep on the lookout for any signs of drugs.

The box plan did not work. For two days, the chance was available to remain anonymous and still turn in drugs. The box stayed empty, and different supervisors kept reporting that, according to the stories, drugs were still being used. The associate executive director met with the unit directors of the two oldest units and told us to get the drugs any way we could. We told him that we had no proof about usage, only rumors, and that individual kids would not violate their peer group to tell us who was using drugs. He demanded that we find the drug users.

That afternoon I began putting the pressure on the kids that I had heard or suspected might have drugs. I talked to a number of campers; most were offended that I suspected them and all denied any knowledge of drugs in camp. This first interrogation period began to hurt my relationship with the kids. Because I didn't discover anything, the administration wasn't pleased, and the kids began to view me as an administrator, not as their unit director and friend.

Drugs became the main topic for the next week. Because going directly to the kids didn't work, I began pressuring the counselors to watch their campers very closely and to report anything to me. There were fourteen counselors in the unit, and they said that it was harder for them to get this type of information and that if they pushed for it their kids would rebel. Most of them saw this as a minipicture of society, and we were becoming the police attempting to enforce our rules. The counselors understood my position but didn't think I should give in to the top level supervisors by pushing too hard. My relationship with the counselors stayed high, but this was a touchy issue.

During the next week, not much seemed to be happening with the drug problem; the administration even dropped the item from the unit director's meeting. Then it happened: A letter from a parent who had seen her son's letter to his brother. In the letter the camper described a "pot party" where the kids all smoked grass until very late one night. He also mentioned that the boys had the drugs. Naturally, the associate director called my assistant and me to his office because the boy was a pioneer. He had talked with the boy's mother and promised that no one would learn about the boy's letter to his brother. He felt that because the boys had the grass we should go after them. We discussed the boy and his friends. They all were in the same six-man tent. He told us to send the entire unit swimming, except the six boys, and then search all their belongings with them present. We refused, saying that we still had no proof, and we felt the letter was extremely exaggerated. We also doubted that we had the right to search their personal things and knew that if we did none of the kids would trust us for the remaining three weeks. At this point, the camp director said he would check their things with the associate director, and we could go with our unit to the lake. This still seemed unsatisfactory, but they were determined to find the drugs.

A few hours later when everyone went swimming except the six boys, the kids knew something was about to happen. We told them that the camp director had asked to see the group. The search turned up no drugs, only a large sum of money, each boy had some money, but the one boy had the most. He was accused of selling drugs to the other campers, and after a long period, it was discovered that the boys played cards every night for very high stakes. This too was against camp policy.

That night a special session was held with the associate executive director, the camp director, myself, my program assistant, and the boys. Their parents were called about the gambling, and they were warned that they would be sent home if involved in any other violation of camp policy.

This whole search issue upset both counselors and kids. The administration had dealt with these six boys, but now I had to deal with the feelings of everyone else in the unit. The kids accused the counselors and the supervisors of planning this raid against them, and the counselors were upset because they were not involved in the decision especially because most did not agree with the search procedure.

The next day, as emotions were still running high, I explained as much as I could (I told them that a parent called with proof of drug usage).

Eventually, things become quiet, but the effect remained for everyone. It is sufficient to say that the kids were most uncooperative, very distrustful, and generally hostile for the last two and a half weeks of camp. Their overt anger was highest when the camp director came to the unit; they were displeased with me for allowing a pioneer to be sent home and argued constantly with their counselors about camp rules and policies.

Control

The administration never lost control of the situation; they dealt with these problems hard and fast. Let us take a quick look at each section of our community.

The administration enforced its rules, with respect to the drug policy, it did all it could to keep a drug-free environment.

My assistant and I, as supervisors, tried to funnel the kids' views to the administration and vice versa, a tough middle position that more often than not left one wondering where his allegiance belonged.

The counselors working everyday with the kids took the complaints and tried to explain camp rules but knew their purpose was to make camp an enjoyable experience for the campers, something they couldn't do both because of kids' actions and administration reactions.

The campers wanted a good time but chose to define it in their terms, not the camp's, causing constant conflict. Their view—the camp should adjust to us. The camp's view—they must adjust for the camp's sake and for the group's sake.

Finally, the important outside influence, the parents. On visiting day, we met with the parents in a group to discuss the drug problems that had taken place. The group setting let us explain the incidents and elicit parental backing before they talked with their children. In general, the parents felt the camp had done the right things.

Analysis of the Administration

It appeared to the administration and to the parents that policy was effectively carried out. But was it? It seems to me that overall policy was overshadowed by the camp's fear of drugs.

A number of major mistakes were made:

1. *The group process was used for informational purposes but not for decision-making.* Neither counselors nor lower level supervisory staff were used when crisis decisions had to be made, especially in the instances of the search and sending home of a camper.
2. *The drug problem was never clear.* Rumors, stories, and contacts were the basis for fear. In its attempts to keep the camp drug-free, overreaction seemed to be the path of the administration. The incident that resulted from one letter probably ruined camp for many—both counselors and kids.
3. *Campers were never allowed input into the system.* A camper council might have alleviated many problems.
4. *Using force and authority alienated the campers.* The search and the decision to send a camper home created wider gaps between administration and kids.

As one soon discovers, summer camp is not all fun and games. Serious issues arise that may seriously affect the feelings of kids toward authority, rules, and society. The camp itself is also influenced by each camper and staff population.

But what about the role of the beginning administrator? From the very start of camp, I was caught in an undefinable position. I was expected to be responsive to those above and below me. The most satisfying aspect of my experience was the relationship with my counselors. I found that supervision helps everyone to grow, and also learned that one can be a boss and a friend at the same time.

The authoritarian approach used very often by the camp director usually worked on me. Although not in agreement, I would consent to follow most of his orders. As I see my responsibility now, I would not accept his decrees, and further, I would establish a mechanism for counselors and campers to advise courses of action when camp policy was violated.

In short, experience, analysis, and personality are important factors leading one to perfect his form of administration. For the beginning camp administrator, I suggest honesty with all, both his supervisors and those under him in authority. I suggest limiting the use of authoritarian approach to the last resort, at camp its continued use is alienating. Finally, I suggest that each decision affecting your unit be your own decision—carefully thought out, after consultation, and that you be prepared to stick to it and to accept the consequences.

QUESTIONS

1. What are some of the special aspects of a camp situation that must be understood?
2. Why must a camp, or any agency for that matter, have a firm policy on drug possession and usage?
3. What do you think of the way the drug problem was handled?
4. Do you agree or disagree with the writer's listing of major mistakes made?

CASE 9

Interpreting a New Youth Program

In the late 1960s, the germ of the idea for Project Youth came into being as the brainchild of the state librarian (Children's Services) and the executive director of a fifty-six-year-old private citizen's group, the Child Welfare Association (CWA). The Department of Youth Services (DYS) had funds of $32,000 in the offing for an agency with a predelinquency demonstration program fitting the guidelines of the congressional Safe Streets Act, which was under the federal auspices of the Law Enforcement Assistance Administration (LEAA). According to the grant proposal submitted and subsequently awarded to the CWA, five main libraries in five towns would be asked to participate in the delinquency prevention program and challenged to make use of the library in a new and novel way—as a town meeting place where youth problems and concerns could be discussed among local youth leaders and townspeople.

The grant called for the full-time services of a project assistant, who would organize and coordinate the program in the five towns. The project assistant was under the part-time supervision of CWA's program director and ultimately accountable to the executive director. The five towns were selected on the basis of diversity in composition and size, local need for improved services to young people, talents of librarians, and their willingness to devote time to the project. After considerable thought and demographic study, the towns of Hampton, Smithville, Rogers, Maitland, and Burnside were chosen as the participating communities. The town of Burnside, however, emerged as a special problem for the executive director and other project organizers, and for this reason, it is presented here for review and evaluation.

Project Youth staff organized and met separately with two key planning groups: an advisory group consisting of community leaders and representatives of linked agencies; and a committee of five library professionals and their assistants. The two groups met jointly after the first six months of the project. The advisory group met on a monthly basis (members were recruited by librarians and CWA planners); librarians met as often as needed—and the need surely grew! Some of the objectives—accomplished with varying degrees of success—of the program were to:

1. have libraries become a part of, and resource to, youth service systems in "Aware" communities.
2. use libraries as a forum setting for discussion groups on youth concerns.
3. create an index of films recommended by participating librarians for youth-adult discussion groups.
4. promote a greater interchange and cooperation among professional agencies in "Aware" communities.
5. provide youth service groups with media exposure.
6. identify youth-related problems.
7. provide input to librarians for youth services directories to be available in the libraries.
8. involve local civic organizations—Junior Women's League, Jaycees, Rotary, and so on—as program sponsors and as participants in youth-adult discussion groups.
9. offer community the expertise of nationally known professionals in the field of juvenile justice.
10. generate interest among individuals, groups, and libraries in nonparticipating communities in hopes that others adopt the forum concept.
11. afford participating librarians the opportunity to become better acquainted with service delivery systems in the state and with current trends in the field.

The Burnside Public Library and the community it served were chosen as one of the five targets of the project for this central reason: Mrs. T., the library director, was a confident, very able, and enthusiastic professional who felt that the library and the town would greatly benefit from the program because the library was somewhat antiquated in outlook and the community was woefully inadequate in services and activities for young people. Having had ample previous experience in a large library in a metropolitan area in another state, Mrs. T. was teeming with ideas for Project Youth in Burnside and was willing to give as much of her time and expertise as needed. When she was approached as a prospective participant by the state librarian, she immediately agreed to be part of the program in spite of the much-bemoaned town budgetary problems. In fact, she even felt that the project would provide an excellent opportunity to showcase the library while bringing a focus on local youth-related problems and concerns. Project organizers, caught up in her contagious enthusiasm, soon welcomed Mrs. T. into the program. It was not long, however, before a monster reared its ugly head. Such opposition was surely unanticipated—namely, the library board of trustees. They would not approve!

With the project already into its third month, it was indeed too late to exclude Burnside from the program and then be forced to go through the arduous process of finding a new community to join Youth Project. Mrs. T., convinced that the project should continue at all costs, girded her sword to do battle, proclaiming this issue a burning one from which she would not retreat. Mindful that her position was at stake, she insisted that a stand should be made against the intransigent board. Emboldened by her courage, the program director and I agreed to meet with her to discuss the opposition of the board and devise a possible mode of persuasion to tilt the balance in our favor. We learned much about the board and its policies. One important fact about the board, one that was not considered or known before, was that they were all elected town officials. None of the other Youth Project towns had such a board, for they were comprised of library- and town-appointed people. Nor were any of the board memmers in other towns as conservative and unyielding as this one. Most of Burnside's board members were reelected many times for four-year terms. The director of the board, Mr. K., could trace his family history back to the founding of the town. No doubt he was firmly entrenched in the town's political bedrock.

The program director and I proceeded to dredge up the board's reasons for vetoing the program at the library. Mrs. T. informed us that the board was of the opinion that the role of community planner was out of character for a library director, that there were some youth service leaders of whom the board did not approve, and that some of the proposed topics of discussion—namely, adolescent sexuality, drugs, and alcohol—were not to be broached in any youth forum in their library.

Bearing this in mind, the CWA staff and the library director decided to move slowly and cautiously within the next few months. Whatever else was done, it was first necessary to woo the favor and approval of the board. This could only be done if the project and its organizers were endowed with "respectability" in the eyes of the board. Sensing this, the executive director of CWA, Mrs. P., decided to invite Mr. K., the board director, to dinner to discuss the matter. Because Mr. K. represented the controlling influence on the board, Mrs. P. felt that it would be most effective to meet him on a one-to-one basis without the intimidation of Aware organizers. Knowing that she was ultimately responsible for the actions of the agency and the goals of the project, she explained to Mr. K. over dinner the role of the agency and the goals of the program. During the course of the conversation, many of the notions and fears of the board were discussed and eventually dispelled. At the end of the dinner discussion, Mr. K. invited Mrs. P. to the next board meeting in the library, assuring her that he would try to sway other board members to approve the project. A week later at the board meeting, Mrs. P. was given the opportunity to present the format and purpose of Project Youth to board members. Mr. K. subsequently cast his vote in favor of the program, provided that the board have some say in the determination of content. The other board members yielded with some reservations to the convincing argument of Mrs. P. and, at the urging of Mr. K., approved the program.

The strategy employed by Mrs. P. was in keeping with the role of administrator as diplomat and conciliator. The administrator, then, is not only responsible for "interpreting the agency to the community and developing a proper public image and financial support," [1] but also performs the following:

His primary moves and subsequent directions are determined not in a prearranged sequence but in terms of where the people are and what they need from him and how well he is related to them. The effective administrator is one who knows how to release the energy of people and how to help relate their separate energies so that they may be thought of as a united team. [2]

The next phase of the program undertaken by CWA staff and the Burnside library director was composed of two tasks: to select a community leader as project advisor and to lower the profiles of CWA staff and the library director by turning over program content to townspeople (adults and young people) attending a series of planning meetings. The plan was devised to convey to the library board that project organizers were not imposing a program on the library and the town and that the content would be based on where the needs were and what the people wanted. In this respect, the program would then take on dimensions of being "bigger than all of them"—that is, than the board members. A budding instructor at a nearby college who attended all the planning meetings was asked to be community advisory member and subsequently accepted. He was dynamic, vibrant, and had natural leadership qualities. From this point on, Project Youth in Burnside arose from its slump and moved forward.

This case illustrates that, in addition to staff and board accountability, a head administrator of a social work agency must be prepared to interact with various elements of the community, using political tact and influence when necessary. Of course, an administrator can misinterpret this role in attempting to speak for the community out of one's own interest or use undue coercion and influence in "selling" programs and policies. This, I feel, is when politicizing—or politicking—becomes inappropriate and goes beyond the scope of a private citizens' group such as CWA. But in the case described, the action was apropos insofar as it was an attempt to protect the reputation of the agency, preserve the integrity of the program, and rescue from futility the effects of those involved in the planning. Rather than employing confrontation tactics or withdrawing from the arena altogether, the executive director opted to hold a meeting with the key person standing in the way of the program to try to modify his stance through dialogue and a genuine spirit of compromise and goodwill. And it worked!

NOTES

1. *Social Work Administration* (New York: National Association of Social Workers, March 1968), pp. 6–7.
2. Harleigh B. Trecker, *Social Work Administration: Principles and Practices* (New York: Association Press, 1971), p. 48.

QUESTIONS

1. What were the goals of this Youth Project, and what did the administration have to keep in mind in striving for these goals?
2. What major problem arose with the Burnside Library, and how would you diagnose it?
3. Evaluate the approach decided upon by Mrs. P.
4. What are some of the subtle differences between interpreting a new program and politicizing it?
5. From the standpoint of good community relations work, how would you evaluate this administration?

CASE 10

The Elderly Are Organized to Fight Crime in the River Front Housing Project

The elderly of River Front Housing Project (RFHP) were in a crisis situation. The crime rate against them was increasing, and no one was responding to their growing fear. There are a number of agencies at River

Front, many possible avenues to air their concerns and have their needs met. It was not until two staff workers from the City Aging Unit, working out of RFHP, mobilized the elderly and the various agencies that any action was taken to combat the crime. It is significant that the crucial intervention came from the one autonomous group working out of RFHP.

What follows is a daily account of the mobilization of the elderly of RFHP and the manner in which they protested their life-threatening situation. After the account, an evaluation is given of the organization and administration behind the grass-roots effort.

Setting: The River Front Housing Project is a low-income, high crime housing project situated in the west end of a large city. It is surrounded by a business district and juxtaposed to a middle-class residental area so that it is virtually isolated. The population of RFHP is approximately 40 percent black families, 40 percent Puerto Rican families, and 20 percent elderly (primarily caucasian).

Clientele: The elderly of RFHP. The only place that the elderly have to congregate is the R.F. Senior Center, housed in the elderly section of the project. The center, therefore, becomes the focus of all elderly activity. It was the efforts of the weekly discussion group at the center that precipitated the formation of the action group to protest crime. These people were the organizers and the spokesmen for all the elderly at the River Front.

Problem: Crime is a constant problem and the elderly are the prime targets of attack. They are victims of assault, robbery (both in the neighborhood and in their houses), extreme vandalism, and constant harassment. The more vulnerable of this peer group, such as those persons with ambulatory difficulties, are recipients of multiple attacks.

Role of Social Workers: Because these elderly are a submissive, discouraged, alienated group, the role of the workers has been in motivating them to advocate their own needs and to gain a sense of autonomy and dignity. Because the group is not yet ready to function independently, the workers have remained the group leaders. This has been the members' continual wish and mandate. When the group is subject-oriented, the workers' role is to stimulate, guide, and clarify discussion; when it becomes task-oriented, the role is then to implement and expedite activity.

It is important to know that prior to the elderly's activities to protest crime there was a three-year preparation in which they gained enough ego-strength to eventually assume an aggressive role. The workers developed their confidence by assigning tasks that could easily be achieved, slowly increasing their complexity and demands of the assignment in accordance with their perception of their own ability. By planning a success-oriented program, the group was ready to act when it became crucial.

What follows is a diary of the events that led to the actualization of the group's requests. An appendix is included containing the correspondence between the group and various city officials, press release, and articles that appeared in the local newspaper.

April 11.

At the weekly discussion group of River Front Senior Center, the issue of crime was raised. The group expressed enough anxiety that the workers suggested writing a letter to the mayor informing him of their concerns. The group then agreed to jointly compose a letter. The workers took responsibility for duplicating it, and the center then distributed the letters to the members of the community. The group decided that those capable of writing their own letters should be encouraged to do so, and those who could not would simply sign the form letter. In order to make it clear that this was a grass-roots effort, one of the group members wrote the letter in her own handwriting. This was the decision of the workers.

April 18.

The response on the part of the elderly community was positive. Approximately one hundred form letters were signed, and twenty individual letters were written. Within that week, one of the women who works in the center wrote a petition, obtained ninety signatures, and submitted it to the mayor's office concerning the same issue.

As a follow-up to this initial protest, the workers suggested requesting an audience with the mayor. The group agreed. When the mayor's office was called by a worker, the mayor immediately accepted, stating that he will invite all other appropriate city officials to attend as well.

The workers then asked the group to jointly compose a letter, in their words and handwriting, stating their concerns and suggestions. The workers also asked for volunteers to serve as spokesmen for the group at the meeting. The group enthusiastically responded to both requests.

(Refer to Appendix A for copy of form letter and Appendix B for copy of requests to the mayor.)

April 19.

The co-workers brought the letters and set of demands to the mayor's office and were asked, at this time, to meet with the mayor.

The co-workers briefed the mayor as to the nature of the concerns. The mayor stated his needs for specific information from the workers and his pessimism at being able to solve the problem. He also informed the workers that the meeting was initially called because of the petition. The meeting established a working relationship between the workers and the mayor.

April 20.

An invitation was sent out to all individuals who signed the petition or wrote a letter. The address list was composed by the co-workers. (Refer to Appendix C for copy of the invitation.)

April 22.

One staff member worked on obtaining a bus to transport the elderly to City Hall. The co-workers met with personnel of the center, who seemed upset and threatened by the center's involvement. By carefully informing the individual of the plans, her anxiety was relieved.

April 23.

The co-workers composed and distributed a press release for the newspapers. (Refer to Appendix D.)

The workers met with the speakers to review what they had written. In one case, the speech was not composed, so the worker used this as an opportunity to include all the factual data not covered by the other two spokesmen. (Refer to Appendix E.) The speech was written in the language of that person, using her colloquialisms.

April 24.

There was an article in the city's most prominent newspaper, a morning edition. (Refer to Appendix F.)

The meeting attracted more elderly than expected. There were at least seventy community people present at the meeting. It was covered by both newspapers, the local television station, giving comprehensive reports sympathetic to the plight of the elderly. (Refer to Appendix G for details of the meeting.)

April 25.

As a result of a meeting between the workers and the RFHP residents, it was suggested to the discussion group that a petition be sent to the chief of police asking to meet with him regarding their concerns. The group agreed, the letter was written, and signatures from those present at the center were obtained. The workers called the chief of police's office, and a meeting was arranged between the three workers and the chief's two top assistants for the following day. (Refer to Appendix H.)

April 26.

At the meeting with Lieutenant Anderson and Major Moore, the three workers informed the police of the severity of the problem and the type of action that was needed. The officers informed the workers of the strong commitment on the part of the new chief of police to act positively on issues such as these. A meeting was arranged at the elderly's convenience with Sergeant Arthur, community service advisor, and Detective Kennedy, in youth services.

April 29.

Due to the absence of the center aide, the time for the meeting was decided upon by a member, one of the first independent decisions made by members at the center. A sign-up sheet was placed at the center to encourage attendance at the meeting with the police.

May 2.

The morning newspaper, without knowledge of the new meeting, ran an editorial on the elderly.

The agenda was set by the three workers and was chaired by one, at the request of the police. The meeting was attended by approximately fifty residents, mainly elderly. At this time, it was announced that all of the elderly's requests had been met in the past week. The resolutions were as follows:

1. A nine-man security patrol beginning July 1
2. Two foot-patrolmen from the police department assigned exclusively to this area
3. Plans by the police for youth recreational programs
4. Promises of new home security measures, that is, viewers
5. Canine patrol to get rid of roaming packs of stray dogs
6. Escort service for the elderly
7. Discouragement of youths from playing in the elderly section
8. Cleaning up the grounds in the project

A press release, which summarizes the meeting, was written and distributed. (Refer to Appendix I.)

May 3.

The meeting was covered by the morning paper.

May 6.

An editorial regarding the elderly appeared in the morning paper. (Refer to Appendix J.)

The social worker worked with a center member to draft a letter to the editor, thanking all of the people involved for their help. Initially, the letter was extremely optimistic, but because of resident reports of continued crime, the letter was revised to emphasize the continual need for intervention in this area. The letter was read to members who happened to be present at the center and was approved. (Refer to Appendix K.)

Unfortunately, a security guard had not gone into effect for the entire summer. Supposedly, a mandate from City Council had been given instructing the July 1 security force to guard the newly constructed Civic Center rather than RFHP.

During the summer, the Human Resources Department (HRD) petitioned CETA for funds. A one-year grant was given starting the beginning of November. It provides enough money for forty-two patrolmen, six of whom are assigned to RFHP. Priority was given to community people. The training of the patrolman is provided by the Police Department. HRD also promised to listen to feedback from the community as to the performance of the guards.

This information was disseminated on October 3.

Analysis

It is hard to determine whether this grass-roots effort was a success or failure. The fact that the initial response to the elderly was so swift and strong indicates the value that the city officials place on the elderly's opinion; the fact that the city reneged on its promise at the last moment, indicates the weakness of the officials' convictions and the ineffectiveness of the elderly as a power base.

There are several levels at which this case can be studied. One of the levels is the public attitude toward the elderly; another level is the administrative structure of the RFHP; and the last level is the role of an independent trained worker in organizing a protest.

It is significant that the group involved in this action is the aged. Much of the community response is influenced by that fact. The elderly are generally a passive group that have the capability of wielding power. Because the elderly make up a large percentage of the vote, and the fact that there are certain traditions of respect attributed to this age group, government does not like to be exposed as negligent in meeting the ageds' needs. The government is also aware, however, that the elderly are a compliant and loyal group; they make very few demands on their representatives and will generally vote along party lines no matter what stance the party takes in regard to elderly related issues. Until the officials saw by the show of force at City Hall that the elderly were not going to silently accept their plight, the elderly were not taken seriously. After that meeting, however, there was a closed session between Housing Authority and city government, at which time $80,000 was "miraculously" discovered to fund a security force. By May 2, all of the demands of the elderly had been met, at least on paper.

What had happened? Because these decisions were made behind closed doors, all that can be said is mere conjecture; one can draw some fairly safe conclusions, however, as to what had influence.

First of all, security was a hot issue in the city. An eight-year-old boy had just been shot in the housing project adjoining RFHP. Not only was Housing Authority under severe attack for this issue but there was talk of disbanding the Housing Authority entirely for general incompetence. Second, the government did not anticipate the group being as organized or sophisticated as it was. Because the workers were the liaisons, the officials were dealing with professionals who would not be so easily influenced or intimidated as an elderly resident. Third, the press took the issue seriously and showed a great deal of support. The television coverage, the editorials, and the various articles, were all sympathetic to the cause. They admonished the officials for their inaction, saying that a response to the elderly's demands was a "must." For all these reasons, and perhaps many more, the initial response was positive. The next question is why the officials did a complete turnabout.

Considering that there are eight agencies directly involved with RFHP, five of which are based at the project, it is baffling that no one followed up on the earlier efforts. Because the workers were apprehensive of the permanent nature of official decision, they had purposely involved powerful, active community members to insure the life of the elderly organization, should it be necessary. The members chosen were staff and residents who would directly benefit from the implementation of the security force either by protection or job security. Unfortunately, it did not work. The residents were still too weak to act independently, and the staff was still too unorganized.

Although the eight agencies have the combined capability of providing efficient, quality care for its residents, it is not being done. This is either duplication of services or a total ignoring of certain types of individual needs and community concerns. It seems that the inefficiency regarding the security issues was a victim of this lack of organization. The reason for this disunity is fear; most of the agencies are constantly threatened— by the cutting off of government funds. The agencies are aware that they are in competition for the same depleting source of monies. This threat is an impetus to remain separate and to protect one's own interests. It also endorses taking safe steps to rectify a situation. Rather than protest City

Hall's ruling, HRD applied to CETA for funds, a safe, nonthreatening action to alleviate the problems. It probably never occurred to HRD to organize all of the agencies to fight a common concern crucial to the entire River Front community; the only time they had all met was when the Aging Unit arranged the meetings, and then the attendance was very poor. The Aging Unit was the one cohesive force in the project.

A variety of tasks were involved in this effort, demanding a multiplicity of skills. The workers had learned the various elements involved in influencing public opinion. Having the elderly write letters in their own shaky handwriting is more dramatic and touching than a neatly typewritten letter. Having elderly, some of whom were disabled, serve as spokesmen at the meeting, using their own language to convey the ideas, makes a greater impact than an articulate, educated younger person. But helping the elderly write speeches to make sure that all of the important events are included ensures the impact of their words. Besides making effective use of a target group, the workers were aware of the importance of press coverage in gaining public support. By writing press releases of all events and constantly inviting the press to the open meetings, a fair amount of coverage was given to these events. Although the workers wanted to include the residents more actively in the decision-making, each time an action or press release was presented to the group, the elderly refused to question decisions or influence future strategies. The workers simply had to second guess the elderly's attitudes through informal conversations that were constantly being held.

The workers were also aware of the complicated logistics of staging a protest. They identified the key persons in the city administration to whom the group should direct their complaints; they understood the necessity of accomplishing the unpleasant tasks of arranging transportation or addressing the mayor's invitations to the meeting to guarantee the greatest possible community participation at the events; and they recognized the need for continual follow-up to various city officials for an actual change to occur in the protection of RFHP.

When it came time to function as professionals, the workers were also prepared. They were able to deal with the aggressiveness of the mayor and the covert defensiveness of the police. The workers made their positions clear without alienating these important figures. Finally, the workers were aware of the necessary formalities involved in an action such as this. It was at the worker's invitation that public thanks were given to the various groups so as to fulfill two necessary purposes: 1) complete the elderly's social obligation and 2) point out to the public that while the elderly were promised help their problems were not yet solved.

Perhaps community members could have accomplished all these tasks. There is no doubt that they are potentially capable of acting effectively in advocating their needs. The reality was, however, that no one person showed a willingness to take responsibility, displayed enough tact to deal with the city officials, or indicated an overall awareness of the numerous tasks involved to successfully stage the protest.

What all of this indicates is that with the proper leadership the elderly can be a powerful group. While it would be best for this leadership to come from the community itself, it often is not available. In this case, the most effective person is an independent, trained community organizer whose only vested interest is to meet the needs of the target group. The other lesson to be learned is that when the responsibility is given back to agencies designated as serving the interests of the group, efforts will be made to meet their needs; the questions are when and how. It may take a very long time before a change goes into effect, and the end result may well be less than sufficient. The more directly involved the target group is in demanding their rights, the more difficult it is for the people in power to ignore their needs.

Appendix A

Dear Mayor:

We the elderly of River Front Housing Project wish to inform you of the robberies taking place against us. In one day, two women were held up, and their purses were stolen by two youths. One of these women also was in her own home when they snatched her purse and molested her.

If this is what happens in April what will occur this summer? When the children are out of school, the greater the number of crimes.

We want the security patrol reinstated and more complete police protection to be given on a twenty-four-hour basis. While the patrol was in effect this year, we didn't have half the number of crimes.

This is a very serious matter to us because it endangers ourselves.

We have worked hard all our lives. Is this what retirement should bring? Fear and more fear?

We want action now ! ! !

Appendix B

Issues and Requests for Mayor—Transcript of Letter

Dear Mayor:

We, the senior citizens of River Front Housing Project, request your consideration on the following problems and offer our suggestions for their solution.

1. Reinstatement of the security patrol
2. Reinstatement of the escort service for the elderly so that we can safely leave our homes in the evening

3. Better twenty-four-hour police protection
4. More control over the children

The problems are:

1. Cases of extreme vandalism
2. Cases of bodily harm in and outside the home
3. Dangerous conditions for walking, i.e., bicycles knocking down elderly, broken glass, beebee guns

Our suggestions are to expand the summer and recreation programs for the children so that it keeps them busy and out of trouble.

We would also like your help concerning another problem we have of transportation. We would like to have bus service on Sunday morning to be able to go to church. We also would like to have bus service extended in the evening.

Before we are killed we would appreciate an interview with you in the near future.

The Elderly of River Front
Housing Project

Appendix C

OFFICE OF THE MAYOR

April 20
FROM: MAYOR
TO: RIVER FRONT PROJECT SENIOR CITIZENS, CITY MANAGER, DIRECTOR, HOUSING DEPARTMENT, CHAIRMAN AND DIRECTOR, HOUSING AUTHORITY ET AL.
MEETING TO BE HELD ON WEDNESDAY, APRIL 24, 3:00 P.M., IN THE CONFERENCE ROOM, SECOND FLOOR, CITY HALL, 150 MAIN STREET.

As a result of a petition signed by many senior citizens of River Front Housing Project, I have called a special meeting with representatives from the Housing Authority, City Administration, and Human Resource Tenants' Councils of the Housing Authority projects to discuss security in the River Front Housing Project area along with other pertinent matters of mutual concern.

This meeting will take place on Wednesday, April 24 at 3:00 P.M. in the Conference Room, Second Floor, City Hall, 150 Main Street.

Please contact my office at 233-3785, weekdays, 9:00 A.M. to 5:00 P.M., to let me know if you will be attending this meeting.

Faithfully yours,
(Signed)
MAYOR

Appendix D

ELDERLY OF RIVER FRONT HOUSING PROJECT MEET WITH MAYOR,
CHIEF OF POLICE, AND HOUSING AUTHORTY
TO DISCUSS CRIME

Press Release

Crime had increased in the River Front Housing Project since the cutback and expected dissolution of the security patrol. The major target of attack has been the elderly.

The elderly have responded in a grass-roots effort by signing a petition and writing letters to the mayor requesting action on the issues and an audience with him. The mayor then invited the RFHP residents to a meeting with him, the city manager, the director of the housing department, the chairman and director of the housing authority, and the chief of police on Wednesday, April 24, 3:00 P.M. in the Conference Room, City Hall.

Some of the incidents in the past month that prompted this spontaneous concern are:

1. assaults and robberies in broad daylight either while walking in the neighborhood or in one's home
2. extreme vandalism—there were six incidents on one block
3. stonings of individuals while working around their homes
4. continued attack on the more vulnerable, disabled elderly. These attacks have been more physically abusive than the others and the assailants have chosen the same victims repeatedly.
5. increased tensions felt throughout the community due to renewed gang activity and rumors of increased gang activity this summer because of the termination of the security patrol
6. fear of reprisal for reporting crimes to the police and consequent inability to act on these incidents.

The elderly are asking for:

1. reinstatement of the security patrol and escort service
2. better twenty-four-hour police protection with an emphasis on positive police-community relations
3. expansion of recreational programs for the youths to offset gang influence.

Some other problems that will be mentioned are the lack of bus service on Sundays and in the evenings; the dangers of roaming packs of dogs; the hazardous living conditions such as broken glass and bicycles knocking over elderly citizens; and inadequate collection of rubbish.

Appendix E

Member's Speech Delivered at Meeting with the Mayor

I'd like to give you a general sketch of what's been happening to us at River Front Housing Project in the past month.

In order to protect our people, we will not give the names of the victims who have been attacked.

In the past month, there were two muggings in one day. One of the women was in her own home. They molested her and took her purse. The other woman was walking home when a group of kids grabbed her purse. Both happened in daylight. In just one block, six houses have had rocks and bricks thrown through their windows in the past month. We have been very fortunate that we weren't hit by the flying glass or the rocks. Remember, we are the elderly citizens and our rock-dodging days are over!

It's even dangerous to work outside your home. A week ago, one man was molested while working in his garden. Six kids threw rocks, bricks, eggs at him and then destroyed his fence. They were waiting outside his door; to waylay him again. It seems that with the construction going on in the project, they have plenty of ammunition to use right on hand.

It's the disabled among us who are the most vulnerable. One woman who has bad arthritis has been knocked down, beaten, and robbed several times, and terrorized in her own home. Another eighty-three-year-old woman who walks very slowly with a cane has been attacked for her grocery money. A little while ago, we found her with a black-and-blue face. She told us she had just been badly beaten by some kids. It's particularly bad the first of the month when the checks are due.

Even as recently as Sunday, one elderly man found a teenager trying to break into his home.

We would report these incidents but we're really scared to death because the first thing we know, we'll get a rock through our window, be molested or robbed.

We need help and hope that you folks will have an idea of what's going on at River Front.

Appendix F

Morning Paper, April 24

MAYOR CALLS MEETING ON COMPLAINTS OF THE ELDERLY

The mayor will hold a special meeting today to discuss complaints about lack of security from elderly residents of the River Front Housing Project. The meeting will be at 3 P.M. at City Hall.

The elderly there say, since the elimination of the Housing Authority Security Patrol at the project, crime has increased.

They recently sent a petition to the mayor asking for either reinstatement of the security patrol and escort service or better police protection, with patrols twenty-four hours a day.

The senior citizens also want better recreation programs for the project's youth "to offset gang influence."

Among their other complaints are a lack of bus service on Sundays and evenings, the dangers created by roaming packs of dogs, hazardous living conditions such as broken glass and youngsters on bicycles knocking over elderly citizens, and inadequate rubbish collection.

They have cited as incidents causing them concern: assaults and robberies in broad daylight, vandalism, increased tensions "due to renewed gang activity," and fear of reprisal if they report crimes to the police.

Many crimes go unreported, they said.

They also said the older and more disabled residents are the ones being victimized.

The situation is especially bad, they say, around the first of each month when the welfare and social security checks arrive.

The housing project is in the southwest section of the city.

Appendix G

Morning Paper, Thursday, April 23

ELDERLY RESIDENTS TELL OF ASSAULTS, VANDALISM BY YOUTHS

Elderly residents of River Front Housing Project say they have been terrorized by youngsters who rob and assault them and vandalize their homes and yards.

More than fifty tenants of the Housing Authority project took their complaints and fears to a meeting with city police and Housing Authority officials Wednesday afternoon.

They told the mayor they were harassed, robbed, and beaten often in daylight, both in and out of their homes; youths throw rocks and bricks at them and at their windows; their small gardens are trampled and fences ripped up.

"If this is our golden age, God help us," on elderly woman said. "I don't want to see another ten years."

The RFHP tenants, many of whom leaned on canes as they walked into City Hall, were joined by residents of other housing projects in asking for increased protection by police and security patrols.

The mayor told them there is little chance the city or the Housing Authority will be able to find funds for security patrols in the near future.

He said he and the councilman, chairman of the Public Safety Committee, will introduce a resolution calling for a "comprehensive study" of the problem at the next council meeting, however.

One of the three speakers representing the RFHP tenants said that many elderly people in the project are afraid to report crimes against them for fear of reprisals.

The police captain said this may be one reason why police statistics show that RFHP ranks 40th of 49 districts in the city in incidence of crime.

Other speakers at the meeting said there is no lack of crime, if victims dared report it. One of the most common complaints was about rocks thrown through windows. "We are elderly citizens," one said. "Our rock-dodging days are over."

The superintendent of the nonprofit Martin Luther King project said he has a similar problem. The sponsors of the project spend $600 to $700 a month just replacing shattered windows, he said.

Other incidents reported at the meeting were more serious. One elderly man working in his garden was stoned by about six youths. An eighty-one-year-old woman was beaten black-and-blue about the face by thieves apparently after her Social Security check.

Most of the suggestions for solving the crime problem involved increased coverage by police and security patrols, but other ideas were offered.

Some said expanded recreational programs would help keep youths off the streets. The city and the Housing Authority operate playgrounds and recreational centers, but the centers close at 10 P.M., while the problems go on until early morning.

"I see only one solution and you probably won't like it," another woman said. "Why in the world can't the city have a curfew and keep the kids off the streets after 9 o'clock?"

Her suggestion was met with strong applause.

Appendix H

April 25

Dear Chief of Police:

We, the elderly residents of River Front Housing Project met with the mayor, city officials, and representatives from the Housing Authority on Wednesday, April 24, to discuss crime in the Housing Project.

According to the mayor, there is little chance that the Security Patrol will be continued after June 15. Although we are trying hard to get them reinstated, it seems that we will need to depend on the police for protection, at least temporarily.

The captain pointed out that the police need to have the crimes reported before we can have increased protection. Even though the statistics may not show it, we are living in constant fear.

We wish to express to you personally the crimes that are occurring and the difficulties that we are having in reporting crimes. We are also concerned about the inadequate follow-up that sometimes happens by the police when crimes are reported.

We are inviting you to meet with us in RFHP sometime next week at your convenience. We hope with you hearing us and our concerns, we can overcome our troubles here.

Sincerely,
(twenty signatures of tenants)

Appendix I

PROJECT TO GET SECURITY PATROL

A nine-man security force will begin patroling the River Front Housing Project July 1, a social worker involved in the housing project said Thursday.

The security force, similar to the one set up in Hansen Court and Martin Village last year, will be funded by the Human Resources Department (HRD).

The HRD is a federal agency connected with the Housing Authority (HA) to improve housing management.

The announcement for a security patrol came at a meeting Thursday afternoon to air complaints about crime in the RFHP area.

The Canine Patrol will also begin clearing the area of stray dogs, as part of the project's general attack on the problems.

Police are also looking into ways to increase security in the project.

The HA and police agreed to set up signs asking youth in the project to stay clear of the area generally served for senior citizens.

Many senior citizens expressed concern about frequent clashes between the younger and elderly residents, including assaults and bicycle-pedestrian collisions.

The HA promised tighter security at the project, particularly around the first of the month, when Social Security checks are mailed.

"Everyone left the meeting feeling that their voice had been heard, their concerns respected and perhaps even a little safer," concluded the social worker.

Appendix J

TERROR IN ELDERLY HOUSING

Elderly residents of housing projects in the city are complaining at City Hall—again—about roving youths who rob and assault them and vandalize their homes and yards.

The problems of violence in the housing projects, those run by the Housing Authority and church and other nonprofit organizations, has been around a long time.

After a recent meeting at which the crimes against the elderly were itemized, the mayor said the City Council will consider a resolution calling for a "comprehensive study" of the problem, and that resolution was later approved by the council.

City officials have said recently they see little hope for funding increased security patrols in the near future.

We hope the "comprehensive study" does not mean what it often means in bureaucratic parlance: The study is going to take a long, long time. There is new evidence in hand—in police reports, interviews that have been published and broadcast with testimony from the elderly, and medical and hospital reports of the injuries the elderly have suffered—to show that the problem is severe and needs immediate attention.

One city councilman recently noted that along with security problems, Housing Authority tenants have also complained of roaches, refuse, outside lighting, maintenance, and recreation facilities.

He commented that "that kind of complaints continually crops up," adding that "I find it difficult to understand why public housing continues to be the worst housing in the city. We are failing in public housing in this city."

We wonder about the priorities of city officials who are wondering where they can "find" more money for security for housing projects, implying they do not have the inclination to budget directly for increased security.

There is also a buck-passing game being played—with arguments about state, federal and city funding—accompanied by the sounds of continued violence in the housing projects. Without waiting for the comprehensive study to be completed, the housing projects should get added police protection; those who know the security problem say the police should get out of the cruisers and concentrate on scooter patrols. Elderly residents, according to the testimony, are afraid of criminal retaliation if they report crime to police, and they should be assured that quick reporting is to their own and the community's best interest.

Security at the projects should be one of the highest priorities of city business. The violence to the city's elderly must be stopped and the projects should be made secure enough that anyone can live in the projects or walk about their grounds without fear.

Appendix K

May 9.

SENIOR CITIZENS SAY "THANK YOU"

To the Editor:

We would like to express our appreciation for all the help we were given concerning crime in our project. We want to thank the paper for its coverage and sensitive editorials as well as all the other news media, the police department for doing everything they can to help us, the Human Resources Department for the nine-man security patrol beginning July 1, and the mayor and City Council for listening to our problems.

Everybody in the project noticed the articles in the paper, and we can tell you that there was a lot of happiness around here since Thursday's meeting with the police. Yes, we still have crime, but if everything's done that's been promised, we'll soon be able to safely go out on our streets.

Our sincere thanks for remembering us and our troubles.

The Seniors of River Front Housing Project

QUESTIONS

1. How would you evaluate the work of the staff assigned to the City Aging Unit?
2. In what ways were the elderly tenants of the housing projects involved?
3. What special considerations go into working with the elderly?
4. If you were an administrator of a program for the elderly, what would be some of your primary objectives?
5. Although this program of crime prevention was far from entirely successful, can you point out some positive gains?
6. If you were in charge, how might you have done things differently?

CASE 11

The Roles and Functions of the Director of the Family Life and Sex Education Center

The Family Life and Sex Education Center (FLSEC) has been designed to meet existing needs in a four-town network in a suburban area. This network is composed of three affluent, suburban towns and a larger industrial town. These communities are situated forty-five miles from a major city and encompass a large commuter group. The combined population of the four communities is 150,000.

Based on the premise that the greatest source of strength available to individuals as they grow and develop is the family, and viewing human sexuality as inseparable from the context of the family, the FLSEC has eight primary objectives.

1. to make information related to areas of family life and human sexuality available to all people living within the four-town area. This information will be dispensed honestly, without value judgments, in a comprehensive form.
2. to provide broad, supportive services to enrich all family and human relations.
3. to provide consultants, speakers, and resources to any interested lay, professional, or community group, agency, clinic, church, hospital, school, or health program.
4. to make literature, low-cost pamphlets, films, and educational materials available to any interested group or person. A library will be maintained on the premises.
5. to make appropriate referrals to other agencies when necessary.
6. to explore objectively and clarify community areas of need.
7. to determine how best to educate the target communities through means such as newsletters, community forums, newspaper articles, and guest speakers.
8. to provide courses, seminars, workshops, consultation, and ongoing training to professionals and paraprofessionals in local churches, social agencies, schools, hospitals, community organizations, special interest groups, and so on.

The services provided by the FLSEC will include an office information service, a drop-in center, a telephone line (to answer questions related to sexuality and family issues), an audio visual and literature library, sponsorship of workshops and seminars, a speaker's bureau, a training program for paraprofessionals and professionals.

The organizational structure of the FLSEC will be designed to utilize a large volunteer staff. There will be a paid, full-time director and a paid secretary. All other personnel will be volunteer.

ORGANIZATIONAL STRUCTURE

Board of Directors

Director

Board of Advisors

Volunteer Workers

The board of directors will consist of representatives from the medical professional community, school counselors, mental health professionals, clergymen, community leaders, laymen, and students. The board will be responsible for the design of the organizational structure of the agency, the program of service, securing funds, public relations, and community liaisons.

The advisory board will be composed of medical doctors, psychiatrists, psychologists, social workers, guidance counselors, clergymen. The advisory board will take prime responsibility for designing and implementing the training program for the volunteer staff. This board will supervise all technical writing and publications issued by the center. Supervision of speaking engagements and consultation in all areas requiring specialized knowledge and skills will be further duties for the board of advisors.

The volunteer workers will staff the agency under the supervision of the director. They will be largely responsible for carrying out the services to be provided by the agency.

The functions of the director, as I view them in light of recent understandings about social work administration, will be explicated in the course of this paper.

Launching a new agency involves a whole series of special problems. Because organizational structure, programs and service, and relationships exist only on paper, the director will have the primary task of setting precedents and establishing policy. Although the community may have been prepared for the appearance of the FLSEC, in all probability there will be much confusion regarding the functions of the agency. Many people will be unaware of its existence. Community leaders and agency heads will undoubtedly have questions and concerns regarding the aims and methods of implementation of goals of the FLSEC. Staff of existing agencies may have only a vague awareness of the formation of a new agency. Physicians and mental health professionals may be unsympathetic, uninformed about the service or unaware of its existence. Some clergymen may be hostile to the whole concept of sex education.

The funding source is anxious for the new agency to be favorably received by the community, attract clients, and fulfill its promise. The director of the FLSEC will need to be acutely aware of the concerns of the funding source, the community, and the clients.

One of the first tasks for the new director is the definition of the community that the agency will serve. It will also be necessary to define the services to be provided by the FLSEC. These definitions will have to be clearly communicated to the existing organizations in the community, the coordinating bodies of the community (community is used here to mean the four towns served by the FLSEC), and the public. Although these definitions have been made on paper, they must be redefined in light of the existence of the new service because any proposal is simply that, a proposal and not an actuality. It may be that once the service has been in operation for a short time goals will need to be reassessed in relation to the service as it is being used. The director will want to establish whether all individuals and groups involved in the new agency are working toward a common purpose. Especially with a new service, the director will have to be particularly sensitive to each person's goals and understanding of the agency.

The director will have to have priorities clearly outlined from the beginning. It will be necessary to reach an accord on priorities among the various groups involved in the FLSEC. The board of directors, board of advisors, volunteer workers, and the director will want to agree on the priorities set for the first days, weeks, and months of operation. These priorities may need to be reevaluated from time to time.

The director of the FLSEC will relate differently to each group involved with the agency. Different roles and tasks will be required, and the director must be sensitive to the needs of each group in order to assume the proper role at the crucial time.

Relation to Workers: Primary among the tasks of the new director is that of gathering together and training a cohesive work force to implement the service. The FLSEC will utilize volunteer help to carry out the programs of the agency, assisted and guided by a board of advisors.

Attracting qualified volunteers will be an important task for the director. Because the director will conduct interviews with each prospective volunteer, the image of the new agency will be conveyed by the director. The director will need all the skills of a personnel director added to those of a salesman. The director will need to build a team and develop team spirit, conveying a sense of excitement about being part of a new and innovative project. The director will provide leadership for the volunteers and will encourage their participation in the training program. The director will convey an attitude of confidence in the abilities of the volunteers to perform the sensitive tasks required of them. Once the tasks have been mastered and the work becomes more or less routine, the director will have the tasks of stimulating interest in the service and of communicating the feeling that the workers are contributing a vital service to the community. One of the ways the director can accomplish this task is to develop an ongoing training program to provide continuing education for the volunteers in the areas of family life issues and human sexuality. Inspiring the workers to educate themselves will be another important task. At each stage, the director must be sensitive to the changing needs of the volunteers. The director will need to keep in mind the importance of the volunteers to the service.

The director can model behavior for the workers. The director can also delineate the duties of the volunteers so that each person knows his responsibilities. The director will set standards of competence and provide nonthreatening ways for the staff to evaluate performance. Because the volunteers will be working with highly charged, emotional subject matter, the director will keep aware of volunteer's concerns and insecurities and will provide assurance and support for the volunteers.

The director will facilitate communication. One of the goals of the agency is to achieve an informal structure with interaction between the volunteers and board of advisors. Encouraging creative input and participation in conceptualizing and planning programs, training sessions, and future directions will be useful in building a team concept for the agency. The director will model behavior that facilitates and promotes staff cohesion. All staff will be encouraged to give feedback as to effectiveness of the service.

The director will need to make constant evaluations of the staff and encourage capable volunteers to assume leadership for various projects and to take on more responsible jobs. Morale of the staff will affect the agency's functioning. Therefore, it becomes doubly important to maintain staff cohesion, provide positive feedback, and provide educational opportunities for staff growth.

Relation to Board of Advisors: The second vital component of the volunteer staff is the board of advisors, composed of professionals working in the community. If the director provides opportunities for creative involvement at a vital level, the likelihood of maintaining an energetic, excited, and highly motivated board of advisors is greater. Professionals in this community are courted by various interest groups. The board of advisors must be convinced that they are spending their valuable time on an important and necessary service. The board of advisors will also function as a public relations team. Each member is in daily contact with a segment of the population and can make referrals to the Family Life and Sex Education Center. The board of advisors is also in a unique position to publicize the service on an informal basis.

Relation to the Board of Directors: In working with the board of directors during this initial period of operation, the director has an opportunity to build enthusiasm for the service and to get each board member involved at a maximum level of participation. The board members will perform various functions. They will publicize the service, provide feedback from the community, assess the effectiveness of the service, plan for the future, seek new funding sources, and so on.

The director will function as a liaison between the two boards and the volunteers, keeping all three groups informed about the activities of each group. Especially during the initial phase of operation of the FLSEC, the director wil make every effort to keep the organization running smoothly and to minimize confusion and to develop an orderly mode of operation.

Each of the three groups, the board of directors, board of advisors, and volunteer workers, is vital to the functioning of the FLSEC. The director can coordinate the activities of the agency in such a way that the three groups work together in a cooperative spirit, operating as a team with common goals and purposes. To achieve this aim, the director will need to be sensitive, on a day-to-day, hour-to-hour basis, to the changing needs of the various segments of the organization.

Relation to the community: The director of the FLSEC must be sensitive to the fact that the image of the agency will be established by the director. For many people, the director will represent the agency, and the director's attitudes and behavior will reflect the FLSEC. The community will be sensitive to any values or judgments made by the director, and these will be interpreted as values or judgments of the FLSEC. Knowledge of this fact can be used advantageously by the director to project an image of the FLSEC that the director and the board of directors wish the community to accept. The director will keep tuned into changes in the community, reflecting developing needs, desires, or abatement of a problem. The FLSEC program should be constantly reevaluated to assure that current needs are being met.

Public relations will be an important task for the director. It will be necessary to establish communication and develop relationships with other agencies in the community. Cooperative agreements may be established with some agencies to facilitate referrals. The possibility of joint sponsorship of educational programs should be explored. The director will create a desire to work cooperatively with the FLSEC if the goals of the FLSEC are clearly established so that other agencies do not view the FLSEC as a threat but an addition to the services offered by the community.

The director must devise ways to keep the public informed of the problems that led to the development of the new agency. As the FLSEC makes inroads into solving some of the problems, such as teenage pregnancy and increasing venereal disease, the public will be kept informed about the progress made.

In a public relations capacity, the director will establish relationships with community leaders to enlist their support of the FLSEC. Some community leaders may also be helpful in assisting the director of FLSEC to obtain further funding.

Relation to Clients: The director will be sensitive to the way clients are received by the agency. Client feedback will be solicited as a way of improving the service. In the early months of operation, the director will be particularly interested in feedback from the community and input by the constituency to aid in determining whether conceptualization of the service has been accurate. Use of this data will determine whether needs remain unmet, new needs are emerging, the target population is being reached.

Other Roles for the Director: Decision-making and policy-setting will be primarily the function of the director. The director must identify emerging problems and, more than any other person in the agency, will be responsible for making major decisions.

The director will maintain contact with planning committees and will participate actively in planning, both initiating new plans and following the development of plans in process, so that planning proceeds in an orderly and systematic way. The director will evaluate feasibility and consider alternatives in planning. Another responsibility will be finding ways to involve the community in need determination and securing of resources. The community itself may be considered as an important resource that the director may explore creatively. Researching future directions for the FLSEC will be an exciting job that the director will supervise.

The director will be responsible for justifying funding and the use of funds in a responsible way. Because future funding depends on the initial success of the agency and careful and judicious use of funds, the director must keep track of the utilization of funds. It will require constant evaluation to assure that monies are being spent most advantageously. The director must be prepared to reallocate funds for maximum benefit.

Working out procedural and organizational problems will be extremely time-consuming during initial months of operation, and the director will need to delegate responsibility to volunteers and members of the board of advisors and board of directors. Delegating responsibilities can have beneficial effects on the organization by getting people involved, making people feel that their efforts are important, and by building worker confidence and developing an atmosphere of cooperative endeavor.

The director of the FLSEC will work toward developing a good working relationship with the chairman of the board of directors to ensure that open communication is maintained between the director and the board of directors. The Chairman of the Board of Directors can cooperate with the director to form a leadership team.

The director will act as coordinator of the service. In order to adequately coordinate the activities of the various groups working for the FLSEC, the director will want to build and maintain high levels of trust between these groups. Each group needs to feel that the agency is functioning smoothly, that all jobs are being performed competently.

Evaluation of the services offered by the FLSEC will aid in planning for the future of the FLSEC. But evaluation also needs to be made of methods of delivery and of staff functions. Working out procedures for evaluation will be a joint responsibility of the three groups plus the director.

As the FLSEC begins to have an impact on the community, the director's skills will be required to judge community reaction and to respond to the community opinion. The director will need to judge the pace that will keep the community from rejecting new programs. If the director pushes the service too fast, the community may not accept it. The director will need to be very sensitive to where the community is in attitudes and thinking about sex education and family life issues. The director will need to exercise patience and to view part of the job as that of educating the community to understand and accept the goals of the FLSEC.

The director of the FLSEC will fill a complex assortment of roles and must be qualified to perform many and varied tasks. To be successful, the director will need to be flexible and to maintain a sense of equilibrium under daily barrages and pressure. Certainly, the ability to think quickly and to make decisions rapidly is essential. The director must understand the systems within which the FLSEC functions.

Organizational abilities will be invaluable for the director, who must keep the organization functioning at optimum level. Finally, the director must inspire, motivate, and involve people to work together enthusiastically and cooperatively to achieve the goals of the Family Life and Sex Education Center.

QUESTIONS

1. What is your evaluation of the way the administrator outlines roles and responsibilities in this new agency?
2. How would you define "role" and "responsibility" in administrative terms?
3. Are you satisfied with the squence of priorities listed?
4. What additional items might have been included?

CASE 12

The Administrator as Coordinator in Community Treatment Settings

William Dado
(Used with Permission)

Introduction

The need for the administrator to function in the role of a coordinator arises from working conditions, where task and agency functioning are divided among many people. Left to individual and noncommunicative relationships, there might develop agency disorganization and ineffectiveness. Task-wise, we have developed worker specialization, which results in numerous workers needed to produce and fulfill an agency's goal. Individual contributions are coordinated to the major tasks of the agency, and all energy is focused upon the mission.[1]

The administrator is the person who must understand and give leadership to the continuous process of coordinating effort. His awareness must entail the defined purposes of his agency, the legal and social sanctions that give him his operating power, and the people and mechanical tools that are at his disposal to perform and achieve the desired product.

To coordinate means to develop a functioning atmosphere within the agency, both on a professional and personal level, to designate areas of competence and responsibility, and to foster personal understanding and respect, which make working together a possibility.

This same coordinating process must take place between the agency and the community. Coordination is needed for integration, to build a sense of wholeness.[2] It is futile to put together a strong and effective program when the population to whom you are directing the services, or the community in which you are working, is very nonaccepting. In this area, the administrator as a coordinator must also be a diplomat and public relations person.

Primary focus in this paper will be on building a communicative, workable relationship between community-based rehabilitation programs and the neighborhood in which it is located.

Two assumptions are made: community treatment is vital to former and present clients in order to give them a realistic chance at appraising and testing their social functioning. Also that there are definite attitudes of disagreement and opposition toward the location and founding of such programs.

This situation presents a variety of difficulties to the administrator. The administrator's rationale for the community-based treatment will be explored and how he can coordinate his objectives with those feelings of possible rejection by the community.

Administrative Philosophy of Community Treatment

For too long, the institution (hospitals, prisons, schools) has been insensitive to the community around it. It predominantly offered custodial care, which was the primary treatment for deviants in the community. There was a philosophy whereby the person had to be separated from those conditions that had an influence on his condition. Along with this, protection was an issue; protecting the deviant from those around him and protecting community residents from the deviant. This form of thinking and treatment developed and perpetuated the myths around institutional care.

Now there is a move for the administrator of such facilities to utilize more humane forms of governing. This is resulting in the emergence of a concept of the "therapeutic community." The administrator of this community must carry with him a dual philosophy of using change for patients and families by the staff when in the hospital, and professional and nonprofessional workers in the community. He believes that the social environment must be used as a therapeutic tool.[3]

The institutional culture has neglected the outside world. We have developed without potential for cure, an institutional personality, and a way of adjustment to custodial life situations. It is a way that not only has affected patients but also the thinking of the administrative staff. Social functioning has been limited and recidivism has remained high. It is a locked and closed pattern, the key to which can be the idea of a new "community."

Leaving an institution is a transitional period, sometimes with severe trauma. Patients need assistance. They need a community-based sheltered workshop, or a carefully planned placement service, to provide an integral part of rehabilitation.[4] The community-minded administrator is knowledgeable about the gradual process of total rehabilitation. He sees the patient as capable of taking an active part in his own recovery. This is one of the aims of the therapeutic community; helping the patients by making optimal use of their own skills, those of the staff, relatives, and neighborhood.[5]

It is not a totality but is aiming to provide a workable treatment resource to supplement conventional services. The administrator in the not-too-distant past has seen his conventional services overused, crowded, and slow and ineffective. His successful treatment factor was minimal and returnee rate great. People with minimal difficulty because of a long, detailed, and physically distant treatment process were denied necessary help. On a practical basis, the community then became the immediate supportive or control element in that persons life. It is practical then that community participation continued to be "used," except on a more organized, planned, and effective basis.

Living within one's own family and neighborhood has more advantages than any kind of placement or institution. A person can maintain the vital use of his social skills; the service can reduce needless deferments. In the event of any neded institutionalization, hopes to reduce recidivism rise and support of the families' impulses for reunions is greater. Studies have shown how with this community treatment in families and in groups the former patient can develop a gradual working in, with a more realistic appraisal of himself and the situations around him.[6] Mental illness and health are the responsibility of the total community.

The administrator works to make that natural community become involved and feel a part of the total health care picture. They can, in addition to providing treatment, be one of the most spontaneous and direct sources of program evaluation. The administrator can use their constant feedback to update, alter, or continue the services his agency is providing.

There is no definite dividing line between administration and therapy. The administrator knows what supportive and corrective services people need. He foremost must be concerned with the welfare of clients and quality of the services offered. There is constant overlapping, and the administrator needs to establish priorities and maintain effective levels of community involvement.[7]

Method of Community Treatment

Initial coordination is internally with the staff. The administrator has a staff comprised of many people with different skills and different personalities. Before services can be delivered to the community, it is necessary to define what those services are and who will dispense them. The administrator must organize and combine all components. They must be coordinated into a team, each performing his own duties for the collective good of clients and the agency.

The people and skills needed are numerous. Initially, there must be community relations experts and fund raisers to conceptually and physically prepare the community for the programs. The administrator must be very much involved in community action and therapy programs, utilizing, if possible, all professionals in the mental health area.

Individual and group practitioners make up the core of the staff. Necessary are: rehabilitation counselors, sociologists, occupational therapists, family physicians, psychologists, local workers and offices of the health and social service departments, social workers, activity therapists, specialized nursing care. We need total participation of ministers, teachers, judges, police, and lawyers—all people who are in constant contact with the citizens, and whose position is influential and can be trusted.

In addition, we need to tap the community itself, to use all available volunteer and nonprofessional help, to enlist aids and trainees, getting them involved in the treatment process.[8]

We need to identify our target populations and develop special programs to meet the needs of the community. Between staff and programs there is much cross-over and mutual work, depending on related skills and interests. What unfolds are activities directed toward: the mentally ill, delinquents and criminals, drug addicts, alcoholics, after-care facilities for a variety of types of people, children's services, crisis centers, short-term hospitalization facilities, marital counseling, geriatric care, family services, and educational and recreational programs.

These open the door to a variety of treatment possibilities. There are so many possible combinations that it is vital that the administrator work to be a coordinator.

Awareness of the situation needs to be transmitted to and assimilated into the awareness of his workers. Everyone needs to be sensitive about the ideas and feelings of all concerned. Communication is a key. Channels must be open, decisions made by a team consensus, including the knowledge of the patients. Use staff meetings as a forum for exchanging ideas, working out difficulties, building communication, and improving working relationships. In essence, work together among yourselves, then build contractural relationships with the community, making both workers and patients a functioning unit.

Community-based treatment is an out-reach of the closed institution. To bridge the gap, the administrator needs to involve the institutional staff in some type of collaborative relationship with the people in the community.[9] As the patients need a gradual adjustment to home, so does the institution need gradual adjustment into the community.

The programs are new, and because of a lack of history of community programs, there is necessitated a total education of workers and the surrounding community. We need to inform all existing agencies of our proposals and enlist their help. Actively try to recruit the citizens to participate in various types of paid and volunteer capacities, and with the staff, help them to move from the idea of the closed institution and think and act community-oriented.[10]

Community Opposition

Community treatment seems to be the needed reform in the cumbersome field of institutional care. It offers a variety of services in quickly available facilities. People are in favor of such programs—until the proposed facility is located in their specific neighborhood. Then opposition builds. Interestingly, people are opposed to community facilities on the basis of assumptions, prejudices, and fears.

To community residents, the people using the facilities would be regarded as undesirable residents of the community. There is an inherent myth that troubled people should be kept isolated. In the community, it would be impossible to provide the proper supervision and control.[11]

Many residents were aware of possible changes in their living conditions. Fear is a prevalent feeling. Fear of a possible malignant influence of a clustering of disturbed individuals. Which led to a fear for their families and for the safety of their children.

There are token ideas of resentment in: unsuitability of property; objection to the removal of property from tax rolls, resulting in increased taxes for residents.[12] There is a strong desire on the part of the families to keep the neighborhood residential, and community-centered programs would infringe upon this. Resentment did go as far as to try and enforce or change zoning laws in order to keep community facilities out.

The sources of opposition were mostly from those people whose lives would be most affected. To some, community care represented a threat to a community leader's power, to a reputation, or to a way of life that had been established. Usually the reasons given were not totally the real facts, but it can be determined that most citizens would rather have such facilities in the "other neighborhood."

Coordinating Programs with the Community

A universal point that is established for starting community-based programs is to be direct with the community. Let residents know of your intentions, be honest, be factual, and be relevant to their point of view.

The administrator has the services and knows the objectives, and he needs to communicate and coordinate them with the community. There is a need to be a public relations person, selling not only the person but also the program. The administrator must be aggressive but cautious, fully assessing the neighborhood and realizing the impact upon the community.[13]

Every administrator should present programs that are acceptable and understood by the patient and the community. New techniques will be more easily accepted if presented with slow concise explanation and trial. Any attempt to depart beyond the acceptable cultural background of a community will inevitably lead to a great deal of misunderstanding. To go too fast, too far will act as a brake, resulting in isolation and even rejection. The administrator who leaves out the feelings of the community is creating unnecessary difficulties and antagonisms.[14]

Patience is a key to working in this area, and so is communication, both within and outside the program. Nonacceptance, prejudice, and lack of information with the general public need to be changed. Misunderstanding, rumor, and conflict are how information can progress before acceptance of new programs. But direct, factual, and complete information is a start, even if it is only one-way communication. If the agency is looked on as an intruder, it has a responsibility to make itself and its purposes known. It needs to be open to the voice and feelings of the community.

Use community impact, but only if it is valuable. Do not disregard or play games with what the community has to say. By doing this, you give the program the opportunity to grow out of the real needs of the people, to be their agency.

The administrator as a person is vital to the establishment of these facilities. Such persons must be in the mainstream, functioning as a buffer and liaison, setting the climate for interaction. They must know the professional, semiprofessional, and nonprofessional staff as well as the community members. They must deal in pluralities, carrying a philosophy of public service and civic responsibility. The administrator has to be a social scientist, psychologist, politician, statesman, economist, scholar, and mutual educator, working in each role with minimum accounts of confusion of terminology.[15]

There is an endless stream of roles and functions that deal with all who are vital to the program. The administrator is constantly being judged by the community and the staff, and often the acceptance of programs is dependent on the impression the administrator makes. Such persons need to set a totally good example, personifying hospital ethics and discipline, with being a community advocate to consumers.

The administrator must be sensitive to current affairs, both inside and outside the hospital, leading workers and clients through many testing situations. But working both roles puts personal relationships in jeopardy, and allegiance and interests sometimes reach questionable positions. This may tend to alienate the administrator from colleagues and clients.[16] To function as an administrator, to coordinate staff and services, there must be:

1. cooperation between superiors and subordinates
2. favorable attitudes and trust among members
3. creative solutions to conflicts
4. job performance of good quality between staff and between superiors. Administration contacts should remain constant. For in this type of treatment, employee attitudes toward an administrator may reflect and affect employee attitudes toward clients.[17]

To be constant, the administrator should incorporate all employees and program members into his public relations and educational scheme, using everyone is a variety of capacities, presenting different levels of interpretation to prospective consumers. These people are in closest contact with the neighborhood, and the information they give can be as important as the director's ideals. They can incorporate into their roles that of a weekly informant, where through brochure, letter, or talk this can constantly relate to the public in positive ways, keeping them updated of programs, process, and looking for improvements or needs to be set.

The community too can be brought in to function on a more direct basis through equal representation on the center's board of advisors. Along with institutional leaders, we can incorporate community spokesmen, who can inform their neighbors as well as endorse effects.[18] The community must be part of the planning process. Community treatment cannot be paternalistic; it must be responsive.

If we can develop initial acceptance, then further education best serves to reinforce the place of that agency. To do this, we can use other community agencies. The clergy, the businessmen, industry, law enforcement, and school groups all have influence and confidence with the residents and can serve as immediate support and public relations agents.

Through coordinated efforts with the schools, we can reach everyone at the earliest time and start to alter some of the frightening myths of illness and community care. If the neighborhood can become aware of the physical setting of the center and see it as other than treatment service, then maybe attitudes can alter. Community centers can be used to bring their social planning skills to deal with other community problems, being not only the treatment center but also the total life therapeutic community.

NOTES

1. Harleigh B. Trecker, *Social Work Administration: Principles and Practices* (New York: Association Press, 1971).
2. Ibid., p. 192.
3. Morris B. Squire, *Current Administrative Practices for Psychiatric Services* (Springfield, Ill.: Charles C. Thomas Publishers, 1970), p. 3.
4. Ibid., p. 53.
5. Maxwell Jones, *Beyond the Therapeutic Community* (New Haven: Yale University Press, 1968), p. 2.
6. Helen Rubenstein, "After Care, Who Cares?" *Child Welfare* 46 (April 1967), p. 196.
7. Squire, *Current Adminstrative Practices*, p. 18.
8. Jones, *Beyond the Therapeutic Community*, p. 18.
9. Squire, *Current Administrative Practices*, p. 18.
10. Ibid., p. 33.
11. Francis Baskind, *An Exploratory Study of Community Opposition to Establishing Halfway Houses* (University of Connecticut School of Social Work, 1971), p. 30.
12. Donald Eldred, "Problems of Opening a Rehabilitation House," *Mental Hospitals* 6 (September 1957), p. 20.
13. Baskind, *An Exploratory Study*, p. 9.
14. Squire, *Current Administrative Practices*, p. ii.
15. Jones, *Beyond the Therapeutic Community*, p. 60.
16. Ibid., p. 38.
17. Trecker, *Social Work Administration*, p. 146.
18. Squire, *Current Administrative Practices*, p. 63.

QUESTIONS

1. With the increasing growth of community-based treatment programs, what new kinds of skills are required of the administrator?
2. What are some of the ways to deal with community opposition to having a community-based treatment program located in *their* community?
3. What suggestions does the author make that seem paramount to you?
4. What is meant by coordination, and why is it important that the administrator be a coordinator in community treatment programs?

CASE 13

Revenue Sharing: Report From the Grass Roots

Carnegie Quarterly, Winter 1976. Used with Permission

Federal revenue sharing is a little like the elephant described by the blind men: it's a wholly different beast depending on where you grab hold of it. Through this program, Washington has, since 1972, given close to $6 billion a year with almost no strings attached to 38,000 state and local governments, and the growing debate over what the provisions of the act should be, as it comes up for renewal, reflects fundamental conflicts in perceptions—and values—between the program's promoters and critics.

State and local officials see revenue sharing as a simple and necessary way to help cities and states with their sometimes staggering financial burdens. They worked hard to get it made into law (formally the State and Local Fiscal Assistance Act), and they are still its most fervent champions. Big city mayors echo Moon Landrieu of New Orleans, who says urban areas cannot survive without it even though "with it, there are cities not making it today." Rural officials want revenue sharing just as badly. One called it "the best thing since the milking machine."

The Ford Administration, which staunchly supported the old act, has put forward the new one with minor changes. Revenue sharing, Treasury Secretary William Simon told Congress, "has contributed to a revitalization of our federal system by shifting some resources to those governments closest to the people, where there is often a clearer perception of the needs of citizens," He reflects the philosophical rationale behind revenue sharing, the "new federalism" that took shape during the Nixon Administration. Its aim is to decentralize government, cut red tape, and encourage citizens to play a larger part in decision-making.

Congress, however, looks at revenue sharing with serious misgivings. For one thing, the program violates the time-honored maxim of political accountability: that "the government which has the pleasure of spending the public's money should not be spared the pain of raising it." For another, under the formula for allocating the funds, the neediest localities do not receive the most money. Not least, some in Congress fear that, because local government has a poor record of concern for minorities and the poor, less of the national tax dollar is now going to help the disadvantaged. Twenty-two civil rights and civic organizations, in fact, have stated that the program "perpetuates discrimination" and deemphasizes citizen participation in government.

The overriding concern is that revenue sharing can become a mechanism for letting the federal government do away with social programs, a concern heightened when the Nixon Administration instituted cutbacks, moratoriums, and impoundments of other federal funds targeted to the poor shortly after this bill was enacted. Since the program does not receive the ongoing congressional scrutiny of programs with annual appropriations, there has been rising demand for debate over the program's merits on the basis of facts—on knowledge of its true impact—before the new bill is enacted.

The fate of revenue sharing this time around is of vital importance as a program and as a concept. The new bill, which deals with general revenue sharing, involves a lot of the pressure on local governments to explain what they have been doing, revenue sharing has dampened citizen interest. More important, few governments encourage civic involvement, and many are outright hostile to public "interference." One parish manager in Louisiana told an intern that open hearings were useless, no more than a shouting match. The mayor of New Bern, North Carolina, who tried to prevent an intern from interviewing officials, said that he had never talked to citizens about revenue sharing because "I know what the people in this town want." Finally, blacks in some towns, civil rights leaders said, felt that if they spoke out on revenue sharing, they might lose jobs.

Often, summary hearings on the use of the federal funds were held only after officials had thrashed out their differences privately and could present a united, nearly impenetrable, front on what to do with the money. Often, too, the funds were dumped into a city's regular budget where, as one intern in Raleigh, North Carolina, reported, "they became as obscure and as difficult to comprehend as the [entire] budget in its 1,400 page glory." Across the South, the interns found that few citizens, and often few city or county council members, were involved in deciding priorities. In Texas, one auditor told an intern that in nineteen years he could not remember the county commission making a single change in the budget presented to them. In short, the important decisions on the entire budget, including revenue sharing, are generally made away from the public eye, and the needs of poor and minorities frequently are overlooked because they have no contacts in the local power structure.

At its worst, revenue sharing sometimes has become a device for officials to short-circuit citizen involvement in local government itself. When the voters of Chatham County, Georgia, defeated a bond issue for a new courthouse, the county commissioners financed it with federal funds, telling voters who objected that the money was "only" revenue sharing, not their taxes. Similarly, in Baton Rouge, Louisiana, where voters twice defeated bond issues for a civic center and the state supreme court invalidated another financing scheme for it, one-half of the city's $16 million in revenue sharing over two years is going to build it. Here and elsewhere, referendum requirements have been bypassed and local participation in government actually diminished.

The way revenue sharing is administered by Washington does not help citizens, the monitoring project found. The Office of Revenue Sharing (ORS), which is part of the Treasury Department, requires localities to file reports. These documents should inform the public about how the money is used, but in fact they are practically worthless. Not only do the reports neglect to announce when and where hearings are held, they merely state the classification in the budget to receive the funds. Governments could, and often did, put the federal money in one budget category and remove a like amount of local money. This substitutability of funds, what economists call "fungibility," makes it impossible to trace the real impact of the money.

Local Government and Discrimination

The record on civil rights compliance in revenue sharing is equally poor. Statistics that interns and community groups found on the employment of minorities and women in city governments suggest a widespread use of funds in departments that discriminate, a practice prohibited in the revenue sharing act. Chattanooga, Tennessee, had 314 white men in its fire department, 25 black men, and, despite the law on equal employment opportunity, just one white and one black woman. In Norfolk, Virginia, there was only one white and one black woman in the fire department, which numbers 438 people, and Asheville, North Carolina, with a department of 149, had one black and two females.

Two-thirds of the governments monitored had no affirmative action plan; the plans that existed worked only on paper. New Orleans officials told an intern that because they knew the police department discriminated they simply shifted revenue sharing funds to other agencies.

Discrimination in services funded by revenue sharing was hard to pin down because it was so difficult to discover what became of the federal funds; nevertheless, the monitoring project found evidence that bias did exist. A much neded health center in Lowndes County, Alabama, was turned down when it black staff asked for revenue sharing funds. When an intern inquired, he was told that the county did not want to fund anything controlled by blacks. Such overt cases of discrimination are not the central issue, however; the real but elusive question, says an intern, "is where money does *not* go. Building courthouses instead of helping to aid or expand social services is not overtly discriminatory, but it shows an insensitivity to the poor—often minority people."

The Office of Revenue Sharing's response to discrimination, which Senator Muskie categorized as "very cautious, very restrained, and very inhibited," does little to ameliorate the problem. Last December, in Spartanburg, South Carolina, for example, an ORS auditor checking the books found everything in order, but he said there was evidence of discrimination in almost all city departments. An intern, and subsequently the project staff, helped Spartanburg groups to prepare documentation of flagrant discrimination, to make attempts to get ORS to investigate the situation, and, most recently, to find legal representation. As in other cases where the project has been instrumental in helping citizens enter a complaint with ORS, nothing has happened. In the entire year gone by, Spartanburg has done little to end discrimination. As the mayor puts it: "We haven't heard from Washington." Overall, of 136 cases before the ORS civil rights staff, only 16 have been settled.

The Office of Revenue Sharing points out that it has a staff of just five. It says that while it has toughened its regulations and asked for more staff, it can act against discrimination only when the evidence is overwhelming. In one instance, when a civil rights officer visited Rankin County, Mississippi, to investigate a complaint of unequal services to the black community, a white deputy sheriff accompanied him on his visits to black families. Not unexpectedly, the blacks declined to complain. Overall, ORS manifests the attitude that civil rights issues *should* be assigned a low priority, because, says one of its staff, "revenue sharing is not a civil rights program."

The National Overview

The lack of citizen participation and the seemingly ubiquitous discrimination that the Southern Governmental Monitoring Project uncovered in its investigations in eleven southern states is not unique. The National Revenue Sharing Project, established by four organizations (the Center for National Policy Review, the League of Women Voters Education Fund, the National Urban Coalition, and the Center for Community Change) and supported by six foundations, saw a similar pattern emerge in its intensive eighteen-month study.

Gathering and analyzing data from a survey developed by the Harvard-MIT Joint Center for Urban Studies, the national project, with headquarters at the Center for National Policy Review in Washington, D.C., concluded that, as in the southern study, there was little public involvement in revenue sharing. Many citizens had difficulty finding out where administrators were putting the money, a conclusion seconded by the General Accounting Office (GAO), which stated that, "accounting designations of the uses of revenue sharing are illusory." Moreover, not a single government that one group monitored had a hearing on the funds, and in the six states that another studied, 35 percent of the legislators did not know where the money was going.

Again, the national project found that discrimination was a widespread problem, complicated by the fungibility of funds. In his budget message, the mayor of Los Angeles said that because there was a discrimination problem in the police and fire departments, revenue sharing funds would go to other agencies, but police and fire departments would still get as much money as when they received the federal tax dollars. Again, the study found that the Office of Revenue Sharing failed to provide, in the words of the U.S. Civil Rights Commission, "even a minimally effective civil rights enforcement program." The only time it withheld funds because of discrimination was when a suit initiated by the center caused a federal court to order ORS to stop payments to Chicago. And again, the project discovered widespread ignorance about the civil rights provisions in the program. No one in the civil rights agencies in the states that it studied knew about the antibias regulations.

Assessing the Fiscal Issues

Looking beyond the purely political outcomes of the program, the Center for National Policy Review also assessed the economic aspects of the bill: its distribution formula and its fiscal effects. The center's conclusions do not bolster support for the program as a means of delivering services in an equitable and effective manner.

The revenue sharing formula gives money to government units on the basis of population, need, and tax effort, with one-third of the funds going to the state and the rest to local governments. A stipulation restricts a local grant to not less than 20 percent or more than 145 percent of the per capita state grant, a device to ensure wide distribution of funds. However, the center, the Brookings Institution, and GAO all agree that the 20 percent floor often only props up virtually nonfunctioning small governments. The 145 percent ceiling, on the other hand, prevents poor cities, with vast numbers of poor people, high costs of providing services, and eroding tax bases, from getting money for which they would qualify if there were no ceiling. As an economist on the staff that wrote the bill admits: "The formula created a program that's a mile wide and an inch deep. The aid is simply too thin to help cities in a significant way." Moreover, governments with minority populations get proportionately less aid than others. The Census Bureau, which provides the figures by which the per capita payments are determined, admits that with its current procedures minorities tend to be undercounted.

The new revenue sharing bill presented by the administration makes a token gesture of bringing more equity into allocations by moving the ceiling from 145 percent to 175 percent. But the center and other researchers suggest that a 300 percent ceiling—or no maximum and no minimum payment at all—would be fairer. Even so, William Taylor, director of the center, says that such a change "would go only a small part of the way toward redressing the formula's inequities." Analysis by the center suggests that per capita income is not so good an index of need as the percentage of the population with incomes below the poverty line.

From a fiscal viewpoint, too, the center found that revenue sharing was not living up to the expectation that it would encourage tax reform. By giving money to states and cities with fiscal problems borne of an antiquated and regressvie tax structure, says Taylor, "the federal government, in fact, took the pressure off officials to face up to initiating progressive forms of taxation." Not a single state introduced an income tax where one did not exist, although revenue sharing was supposed to be an incentive to do so.

Richard Nathan, who directs a Brookings Institution study of revenue sharing, takes a more sanguine view of the program's fiscal effects. He notes that the program allowed half of the 60 governments he studied to lower or stabilize property taxes. Newark, for example, chose not to fund social services but to hold down taxes, and in doing so was able to stem property owners' flight from the city. He says that this benefits Newark's poor and minorities. Taylor believes no city should have to choose between preventing urban flight or funding social services. He points out that Newark's basic source of difficulty, the refusal of the state to enact an income tax, has not changed. He asks: "Should federal money help perpetuate this inequitable situation? Should the government give money to states that are not making an effort to meet their own needs?"

Ultimately, both the Southern Governmental Monitoring Project and the National Revenue Sharing Project raise more questions than they answer. Is revenue sharing an adequate approach to solving social problems? Is it the best way to reduce financial pressures on state and local governments? Does it cure the ills of a federal system that seems overweighted by Washington? To state the obvious, putting federal money in revenue sharing means not putting money in other types of programs. That decision reflects a set of choices about national priorities and how to reach them. No monitoring program can set priorities, but the projects have shown very clearly that in certain areas—encouraging citizen participation, rooting out discrimination in local government employment and services, distributing funds to the localities with the most need, and helping local reform—revenue sharing has not been very effective.

By highlighting the trouble spots in the revenue sharing program, the monitoring projects may help to correct the problems. The center's analysis of the bill's inequitable formula has laid the groundwork for developing a better program. The southern project has made a convincing case for building citizen involvement into any future bill. In special revenue sharing programs in which participation is mandated by law, so the project discovered, there is a marked increase in citizen input in decision-making. And both projects' documentation on bias in agencies receiving revenue sharing may lead Congress to make more specific directions on enforcing the bill's civil rights provisions.

Both projects have had a catalytic effect on local government. For one thing, interviewing civic leaders and talking with the media focused attention on the program. At the same time, civic groups discovered the importance of the budget in government, and that recognition has acted as a launching pad for more informed involvement in local policy-making. What is more, the questionnaires and materials that the monitoring groups developed have given community groups a solid start on continuing oversight.

In the final analysis, the monitoring staffs realize that evidence of how programs operate or how reforms might be introduced goes only so far. Revenue sharing involves fundamental political questions that cannot be answered neatly. What makes the current renewal debate—and the final bill—so important is that, as one observer put it, "the law of momentum operates in politics as well as physics. What happens to revenue sharing now is going to have an impact on the nation for a long, long time."

QUESTIONS

1. What are some of the essential points in the rationale for Revenue Sharing?
2. What are some of the major problems with Revenue Sharing as it has operated?
3. To what extent has the public been involved in the decision-making process?
4. What changes would you like to see in Revenue Sharing?

CASE 14

Bitter Racial Dispute Divides Grosvenor House

By Barbara Campbell, *New York Times,* March 8, 1973
Used with Permission.

The dismissal of Grosvenor Neighborhood House's first black program director last summer has triggered a bitter and continuing dispute for control of the Upper West Side center.

On one side is the board of directors, with forty-one socially prominent women on it. On the other is a predominantly black and Puerto Rican group known as the Committee on Community Control of Grosvenor.

At the center is William Burnes, who last week filed a complaint with the City Commission on Human Rights against the women, whom he charged with "blatant racism." He is asking $500,000 in damages.

The women, all of whom are volunteers, deny that the dismissal of the thirty-six-year-old Mr. Burnes was racially motivated. They contend that he was asked to leave because of "incompetency."

The women have brought an action in Supreme Court against Mr. Burnes and an associate, Ted Veal, who are leaders in the community committee, to remove them from interfering with the board's operation of Grosvenor.

Control Seized

Members of the committee took control of the settlement house at 176 West 105th Street in a nonviolent action last August and stayed in power until January, when the board obtained a court order evicting the group.

During the takeover, Mr. Burnes said, seventy-five committee volunteers staffed the house when most of the forty-five-member Grosvenor staff left their posts. The community group implemented the day-care, counseling and after-school programs with such activities as drug counseling, black and Puerto Rican studies, and tennis tournaments.

Dr. Eugene Callender, president of the New York Urban Coalition, has also filed an affidavit at the request of the board, he said, describing a disruption in the Sunday services at his Church of the Master in Harlem by members of the committee led by Mr. Burnes and Mr. Veal.

The committee accused Dr. Callender of having supported the board in the dispute over community control, a charge that Dr. Callender denies.

As a result of the prolonged fight between the board and the committee, the financial future of privately supported Grosvenor is uncertain, according to the board president, Mrs. Charles I. Pierce, who said that no money was able to be raised through benefits, society balls, and annual appeals during the takeover.

$400,000 Budget

The board, said Mrs. Pierce, whose husband is a partner in the law firm of Debevoise, Plimpton, Lyons & Gates, raised 70 percent of Grosvenor's $400,000 annual budget.

"We are terribly worried about Grosvenor," Mrs. Pierce said while visiting the four-story settlement building recently. "Our main concern, now that we have the house back is to keep it going."

Grosvenor was founded in 1915 in the East 40s but moved to West 105th Street twelve years ago. The board raised $1 million to build the house, which offers programs for children and the elderly. The house is used mostly by blacks and Puerto Ricans.

Getting New View

Women on the board said that they had considered their job primarily that of fund-raisers. As a result of the dispute, according to one board member, they have begun to painfully reexamine their roles as "social workers."

"I don't think we realized how terribly important it was to have community representation," Mrs. Pierce said. "I suppose all of this sounds terribly patronizing but it wasn't meant that way."

The Committee for Community Control was formed shortly after Mr. Burnes was dismissed. According to Mr. Veal, there are seventy people on the committee and 90 percent are black and Puerto Rican.

"The membership is open-ended" he said. "We go out in the community and get people when we need them."

The group has demanded that Mr. Burnes be reinstated and that a substantial number of "community" representatives be put on the board of the settlement house. The committee contends that the people who use Grosvenor have no voice in what programs are provided for them and no say in who is hired to supervise their children.

A month after the committee took over Grosvenor, four mediators were brought in to help negotiate the dispute.

The mediators were Elihu Hill, member of the board of United Neighborhood Houses, David W. Barry, executive director of the New York City Mission Society; Anthony Drexel Duke, president of Boys Harbor, and Lonnie Williams, executive director of Boys Harbor.

Talks Broken Off

By January, the board had agreed to change its bylaws to add eighteen community people to the board. (Last spring three persons from the area were added; they were white and of similar background to other board members. During the controversy last summer, the board added one black and two Puerto Rican women, leaving 12 places open.)

But negotiations broke down in January, when the board refused to fill the remaining twelve places with people chosen by the committee.

The women also agreed to rehire Mr. Burnes in an unspecified position, but he rejected the offer because, he said, it was a move by the board to "keep me in my place."

Mr. Burnes, who was paid $10,500 a year as program director, added that the board had told him he could return to Grosvenor for a probationary period, with his tenure subject to the discretion of the executive director.

The board's former executive director, Russell Inserra, who is white, resigned in January because he said his position there was "untenable." The community group had charged that Grosvenor was run like a "plantation," with Mr. Inserra in charge of the mostly black and Puerto Rican staff.

Last week the board hired a new executive director, André Kent Peters, who is black.

Board Member Picketed

Recently, the board members have been confronted with the aggressive tactics of community protest. Pickets have marched in the lobbies of the West Side apartment houses of some women.

Mrs. Edward T. Chase, who was president of the board when Mr. Burnes was dismissed, has been a particular target of the pickets.

"I was so embarrassed," Mrs. Chase said the other day in the sunlit library of her Park Avenue apartment.

"A lot of people here know my commitment to social work, but there are some who just don't understand." Mrs. Chase is a former president of the Junior League.

The board members have had their meetings invaded by the committee and have been shouted down in face-to-face confrontations.

"Some of the women reacted with fear to the flak and rhetoric of the group," said Mrs. John I. B. McCulloch, a younger and newer member of the board who is working with a fellow board member, Mrs. Roy M. Goodman, five days a week in the community to garner support. "Many of our members live such insulated lives."

Some board members recall having stood by helplessly in August when the committee took over Grosvenor after unsuccessfully negotiating for Mr. Burnes's reinstatement.

"Everything snowballed," Mrs. Pierce said. "We couldn't believe it when they took over the house. We tried to think of what to do—we didn't want violence."

QUESTIONS

1. What were some of the basic reasons for this dispute and conflict?
2. What does it signify when an agency is "taken over" by the community?
3. Evaluate the steps taken by the board of directors.
4. How important is it to have wide community representation on boards of directors?
5. Could this conflict and confrontation have been prevented?

CASE 15

Revenue Sharing—National Association of Social Workers News

Introduction

The proposed NASW policy statement on general revenue sharing, prepared by Pablo Eisenberg of the Center for Community Change, delineates the key issues and suggests an NASW position in an area in which the association has needed clearer direction.

The statement focuses on the following major themes: 1) lack of significant citizen participation; 2) weaknesses in public reporting and accountability; 3) deficiences in civil rights enforcement and lack of adequate monitoring by the Office of Revenue Sharing (ORS); 4) Inequities in local allocation of general revenue sharing funds to the detriment of the poor, the elderly, and minority groups; 5) inadequacies in the distribution formula; 6) overabundance of eligible jurisdictions.

Background and Source of Social Work Concern

The introduction of general revenue sharing late in 1972 was accompanied by the sponsors' promise that it would be a significant mechanism for involving citizens and the general public more closely in local priority-setting and in the affairs of local government. General revenue sharing, in short, was to bring greater power to the people by decentralizing the authority to spend an annual $6 billion in federal funds for a three-year period.

The program was also touted as an effective way of assisting fiscally strapped state and local governments to pay for urgently needed public services, including those for the poor and the elderly. The hard-pressed cities and other jurisdictions with concentrations of disadvantaged people were therefore to receive some measure of relief and help. General revenue sharing was to be new money, supplementing the categorical and block grants already authorized.

The few limitations that were included in both the legislation and regulations were designed as minimal assurance of public accountability. The requirements for reporting, public information, and civil rights enforcement, it was stated, would be adequate for the Congress, the federal government, and the public at large to exercise their oversight responsibilities.

Despite promises and early expectations, the program has failed to reach, even seriously address, these objectives.

Generally, citizens have not been involved in the general revenue sharing process, nor have they had access to information that might have generated their increased participation in both the program and local budgetary processes.

The distribution formula and the program's universality (over 38,000 recipient units of government) have reduced the need factor to a minimum.

The big cities and other jurisdictions with the greatest problems have not been allocated nearly enough money to meet their minimal requirements. Every indication points to the fact that the poor and the elderly are not receiving a fair share of the general revenue sharing pie.

The reporting and accountability provisions have proved to be either inadequate or unenforceable by a Treasury Department, which continues to maintain a "hands off" attitude. The responsibility for oversight has thus been placed entirely on individual citizens and community groups.

General revenue sharing, unfortunately, has not meant new money. During the past two years, many of the categorical programs targeted primarily at the poor, near-poor, and minorities have been either eliminated, substantially reduced, or modified. These losses have not been fully replaced by revenue sharing funds, either general or special. Only in limited cases has general revenue sharing been substituted for cutbacks in social programs for the poor and the elderly.

The recent shift from categorical to block and revenue sharing grants, on the whole, has had an adverse effect on the nations' most disadvantaged constituencies. It has tended to provide them less money and assistance than before. It has removed some federal restrictions and guarantees that previously helped keep local action in line with national priorities. And it has not been accompanied by any incentives or requirements for state and local government reform.

Statement of Policy Issues

If continued in its present form, general revenue sharing will perpetuate: the minimal and ineffectual involvement of citizens in their state and local governments; discriminatory practices of state and local governments and their departments; existing inequities in the distribution of these federal funds; and the delay of necessary government reforms, both administrative and fiscal.

Nowhere is this need more evident than in the case of citizen participation. Neither the act nor the regulations require any citizen involvement other than requiring that state and local governments must go through their normal budgetary procedures in allocating their general revenue sharing funds. The assumption that such a requirement would provide some public involvement has not been warranted. Many jurisdictions, including over half of the counties, are not legally obligated to hold public hearings on their general budgets. Moreover, general budget hearings in most jurisdictions are too poorly advertised and attended, are too pro forma in nature, and come too late in the budgetary process to provide any meaningful citizen involvement and influence. Special hearings on general revenue sharing have been the exception rather than the rule.

The findings of monitoring groups, both local and national, indicate that there has been little citizen involvement in the general revenue sharing process throughout the country. Where there has been community participation, it has been, with rare exceptions, the result of citizen initiatives. Elected officials have not viewed the program as an opportunity through which to involve community groups and the public, nor have they demonstrated any desire to open their local budgetary processes. They continue to regard citizen involvement as a concept essentially limited to the electoral process. They are not likely to change their attitudes unless they are forced to do so.

The few community groups that have been most successful in influencing the general revenue sharing process are those that have had considerable resources, organizational capabilities, and outside stimuli and assistance.

Unless there is official encouragement, the overwhelming majority of communities will not be able to organize similar efforts.

The lack of public information about the program has been another deterrent to citizen involvement and public accountability. Publication in the media of planned and actual use reports and the availability of information for interested citizens have proved to be totally inadequate. More often than not the reports are published in reduced size among the newspapers' legal notices.

Nor do the reports provide much useful data either on the expenditure or impact of funds. The categories are too general to be even indicative of actual projects or programs. Information that was included on the initial reports, such as the distinction between old and new programs, now is no longer required. Because of their fungibility, funds may be earmarked for purposes—reduction of taxes or nonpriority expenditures—that actually hide their real use.

Although there are strong legislative provisions against discrimination in the act, its potential for ending existing civil rights abuses is not being tapped. General revenue sharing, in a sense, is helping to reinforce discriminatory practices in many local communities. At fault are inadequate local compliance mechanisms and more significantly, the unwillingness of the Office of Revenue Sharing to enforce the civil rights provisions with energy and determination. For example, ORS has refused to use its authority to defer funds from jurisdictions found to be discriminatory by a court, state human rights agency, or an administrative law judge.

The planned and actual use reports, as well as a number of independent studies, indicate that a very small portion of general revenue sharing money—between 3 to 5 percent—has been channeled into social programs for the poor and the elderly. Although certain capital projects and other programs can be said to have benefited the poor and the elderly as well, the low priority placed by state and local governments on projects and programs for disadvantaged constituencies appears well established. Among the smaller citites, suburban jurisdictions, and rural areas, the neglect of the poor and the elderly has probably been even greater.

The formula on which allocations have been based has not adequately stressed the need factor. Census undercounts of minorities, as well as the statutory limitation on per capita payments to local governments, have added to this problem. The distribution of money to over 38,000 jurisdictions has spread limited resources much too thinly, and many governments that did not need additional money have received a federal bonus. Others are receiving too little money to provide any meaningful programs of relief.

In a real sense, the movement for local government reform has been delayed by general revenue sharing About 25,000 of the supposedly 38,000 plus general-purpose governments receiving funds are jurisdictions or towns that exercise only a single function. Many others are responsible for only two or three functions normally associated with a true general-purpose government. These governments that should have been either absorbed by, or consolidated with, other governments have been encouraged to survive through their inclusion in the revenue sharing system. Supporters who saw the program as a means of achieving intergovernmental cooperation have also been disappointed. While a few local governments have coordinated their approaches to the allocation of funds, the overwhelming majority have paid no attention to the use of funds by their neighboring jurisdictions. The current practice, therefore, appears to be enhancing intergovernmental competition, organizational fragmentation, and duplication.

Nor has general revenue sharing provided any incentives for progressive tax reform. Although the funds are raised through the progressive federal income tax, the allocation formula takes no special account of similarly progressive state and local taxes.

There are no incentives for states to adopt or expand an income tax. Jurdisdictions have been permitted to reduce their tax rates, although one of the initial objectives of general revenue sharing was the provision of desperately needed public services. Where local taxes have been reduced, no special consideration has been given to those who can least afford regressive taxes.

Declaration of Policy

The National Association of Social Workers has become increasingly concerned with the serious limitations and inequities of general revenue sharing.

Members and chapters must continue to evaluate the program, particularly its implications for the poor, near poor, and minorities. Alternatives to general revenue sharing—including tax reforms, the federalization of programs such as welfare and health, and large block grants to the neediest jurisdictions—should be carefully evaluated and compared. Congress should conduct similar assessments from an open and objective perspective during the coming year.

If the Congress decides to renew general revenue sharing in 1976, the legislation should be amended to eliminate the major program weaknesses that have been identified. We recommend the following amendments to achieve this purpose:

1. Citizen Participation

The legislation should mandate citizen involvement by requiring all recipient governments to hold special hearings on general revenue sharing. All recipient governments with over 5,000 in population and/or receiving more than $25,000 should also be required to form citizen advisory committees to assist them in planning, operation, and evaluation of programs and projects financed through these funds.

All recipient governments should be required to hold general budget hearings and to begin opening local governments to greater citizen involvement.

2. Public Reports and Accountability

The planned and actual use reports should be modified to include additional information such as the distinction between old and new programs, a list of specific projects and programs funded and their locations, and the jurisdiction plans or activities to involve citizens. The reports should include the impact statement regarding the programs' beneficiaries and the community at large. The planned and actual use reports should also require the jurisdictions to cite the state or local official responsible for civil rights problems and compliance, as well as any pending complaints about discrimination in the use of revenue sharing funds or active civil rights litigation against the local government.

The actual use reports should note any changes between the planned and actual use reports.

3. Public Information and Requirements

The planned and actual use reports should be published in a general circulation newspaper for two consecutive days in type not smaller than that used for ordinary front-page stories. This would apply to all jurisdictions over 5,000 in population. Smaller jurisdictions would be required to publish the reports only one day.

Responsibility for making such reports available to the media, including minority and foreign language, would be that of the recipient government.

A reasonable number of such reports should be available to the general public in jurisdictions of over 5,000 in population.

4. Civil Rights Enforcement

The legislation must reaffirm and strengthen the responsibility and obligation of the Office of Revenue Sharing for carrying out the Congressional mandate to eliminate civil rights violations in the use of General Revenue Sharing Funds.

Special emphasis should be placed on effective mechanisms for implementing an active enforcement policy, including the suspension of funds from jurisdictions found to be discriminatory, and the imposition of stiff financial penalties for those governments guilty of continued violations.

The legislation should provide a precise and reasonable timetable for all stages involved in the administrative process of investigating and adjudicating complaints about violations.

In contrast to past practice, periodic complaince checks need to be undertaken by the Office of Revenue Sharing. The ORS should be authorized additional personnel to carry out this and other functions related to civil rights enforcement.

No agreements delegating auditing or compliance responsibilities to state governments should be enacted unless the Office of Revenue Sharing has adequate evidence that the government in question is capable and willing to exercise these responsibilities effectively.

In addition, prompt federal action should be required in those cases where civil rights problems have been discovered (i.e., examination of EEO–4 forms) through the joint efforts of the federal agencies in question.

5. Priority Expenditures

If a significant portion of general revenue sharing is to be directed to programs and projects for the poor and elderly, it will have to be mandated by the legislation. For this reason, at least 25 percent of all funds received by any recipient government should be earmarked for social services designed primarily to benefit the poor and the elderly.

The priority categories should be retained. One additional category should be introduced to permit revenue sharing funds to be directed to efforts to build greater citizen involvement in the government planning and evaluation process. The prohibition against the use of revenue sharing money as matching funds for federal grants should be dropped because it has tended in some localities to discourage social programs.

6. Distribution of Funds

The allocation formula must be revised to give added weight to the needs or poverty factor, possibly by doubling this factor as in the case of the Housing and Community Development Act of 1974. The statutory limits on per capita payments to local governments should be raised substantially, while the requirements for minimal per capita payments could be eliminated. If the allocation formula is to work equitably, the legislation will have to require the use of the most up-to-date census information about minority populations.

7. Eligible Jurisdictions.

The number of eligible local governments should be limited to jurisdictions that are true general-purpose governments, administering a minimal number of recognized public service functions and serving a population of at least 2,500.

State governments with budget surpluses should receive only that portion of their scheduled entitlement amounting to the difference between the entitlement and their surpluses. The unused funds from their entitlement should be redistributed among the local governments in that state on a "needs" basis.

Implementation Statement

There will be strong opposition to any substantial revisions of the general revenue sharing legislation, including many of NASW's recommendations for a more responsible program. If many or some of the suggested amendments are to have a chance of passing, NASW members throughout the country will have to organize to make their concerns and views heard. Meeting with congressmen in their home districts, as well as direct mailings to Washington, will be in order. Coordinated planning and action with other organizations, locally and nationally, will add considerable force to the movement for reform.

QUESTIONS

1. To what extent has the original Revenue Sharing Program accomplished its objectives?
2. What recommendations would you make for improving and strengthening Revenue Sharing?
3. What are some of the major policy issues in the program?
4. Evaluate the NASW Declaration of Policy Regarding Revenue Sharing.

Bibliography of
Selected Readings

The literature of administration has grown significantly in recent years. This growth represents the rising interest in the field and the frankness with which practitioners have been willing to share their experiences and views. At the same time, many of the earlier writings about administration have enduring value for the student and teacher. This bibliography of selected readings is an attempt to combine the early and basic material with the newer writings. For persons who have missed some of the earlier publications, this listing will serve as an important research tool. For others who are familiar with the earlier works, the more recent references will be of special value.

ABRAMSON, MARK. *The Professional in the Organization.* Chicago: Rand McNally, 1967.

ADDAMS, JANE. "Community Advisory Boards and Maximum Feasible Participation," *American Journal of Public Health,* February 1971.

Administration of Organization and Methods Services. Department of Economic and Social Affairs, United Nations, New York, 1969.

ALBERS, HENRY. *Organized Executive Action.* New York: John Wiley and Sons, 1961.

————. *Principles of Management.* 3rd ed. New York: John Wiley and Sons, 1969.

ALDRICH, HOWARD. "Organizational Boundaries and Inter-Organizational Conflict," *Human Relations,* August 1971.

ALESHIRE, ROBERT A. "Organizing for Neighborhood Management: Drawing on the Federal Experience," *Public Management,* January 1971.

ALFORD, ROBERT A. *Bureaucracy and Participation.* Chicago: Rand-McNally, 1969.

ALLEN, LOUIS A. *The Management Profession.* New York: McGraw-Hill Book Company, 1964.

ALSTON, JON, and DEAN, IMOGENE K. "Socioeconomic Factors Associated with

Attitudes Toward Welfare Recipients and the Cause of Poverty," *Social Service Review,* March 1972.

ALTSCHULER, ALAN. *Community Control.* New York: Pegasus, 1970.

ANDERSON, THEODORE, and MARKOV, SEYMOUR. "Organizational Size and Functional Complexity: A Study of Administration in Hospitals," *American Sociological Review,* February 1961.

APPLEY, LAWRENCE A. *Management in Action.* New York: American Management Association, 1956.

Approaches to Racial Understanding and Social Justice. National Federation of Settlements and Neighborhood Houses, Study Outline III, New York (undated).

ARGYRIS, CHRIS. *Diagnosing Human Relations in Organization—A Case Study of a Hospital.* Studies in Organizational Behavior No. 2—Labor Management Center. New Haven: Yale University, 1956.

————. *Executive Leadership.* New York: Harper and Row, 1953.

————. *Integrating the Individual and the Organization.* New York: John Wiley and Sons, 1964.

————. *Interpersonal Competence and Organizational Effectivness.* Homewood, Ill.: The Dorsey Press, 1962.

————. *On Organizations and the Future.* Beverly Hills: Sage Publications, 1973.

————. *Personality and Organization.* New York: Harper and Row, 1957.

————. "The Organization—What Makes It Healthy?" *Harvard Business Review,* November–December 1958.

————. *Social Science Approaches to Business Behavior.* Homewood, Ill.: The Dorsey Press, 1962.

————. *Understadning Organizational Behavior.* Homewood, Ill.: The Dorsey Press, 1960.

ARONSON, ALBERT H. "Emerging Problems of Personnel Administration," *Personnel Administration,* May–June 1962.

Attica—The Official Report of the New York State Special Commission on ATTICA. New York: Praeger Publisher, 1972.

AUERBACH, ARNOLD J. "Aspirations of Power People and Agency Goals," *Social Work,* January 1961.

BALDWIN, J. E. "Applying Management Principles to Public Welfare Administration," *Social Service Review,* March 1957.

BANNON, JOSEPH J. *Outreach, Extending Community Service in Urban Areas.* Springfield, Ill.: Charles C. Thomas, Publishers, 1973.

BARBER, JAMES. *Power in Committees: An Experiment in the Governmental Process.* Chicago: Rand-McNally, 1966.

BARKER, ROBERT L., and BRIGGS, THOMAS L. *Differential Use of Social Work Manpower.* New York: National Association of Social Workers, 1968.

BARNARD, CHESTER L. *The Functions of the Executive.* Thirtieth Anniversary Edition. Cambridge: Harvard University Press, 1968.

————. *Organization and Management.* Cambridge: Harvard University Press, 1948.

BASS, BERNARD M. *Leadership Psychology and Organizational Behavior.* New York: Harper and Row, 1960.

BAUER, DOUGLAS. "Sisyphus in Chicago," *Harper's Magazine,* June 1976.

BAUER, SAMUEL P. "The Impact of Automation on Public Welfare Systems," *Public Welfare,* Winter 1973.

BECHILL, WILLIAM, and BERMAN, J. "Some Key Issues in the Administration of Welfare Reform Legislation," *Public Administration Review*, September–October 1972.

BECK, BERTRAM. "Community Control: A Distraction Not an Answer," *Social Work*, October 1969.

BECK, WALTER E. "Agency Structure Related to the Use of Staff," *Social Casework*, June 1969.

BECKER, ROBERT T., M.D. "The Organization and Management of Community Mental Health Services," *Community Mental Health Journal*, 1972.

BECKER, SELWYN W. "Personality and Effective Communication in the Organization," *Personnel Administration*, July–August 1964.

BEIGELMAN, ALLAN, and LEVENSON, ALAN I. *The Community Mental Health Center—Strategies and Programs*. New York: Basic Books, 1972.

BELLOWS, ROGER, et al, *Executive Skills—Their Dynamics and Development*. Englewood Cliffs, N.J.: Prentice-Hall, 1962.

BENNIS, WARREN G. "Leadership Theory and Administrative Behavior," *Administrative Science Quarterly*, December 1959.

————. *Organization Development—Its Nature, Origins, and Prospects*. Reading, Mass.: Addison-Wesley Publishing, 1969.

————. "Post Bureaucratic Leadership," in Donald N. Michael, *The Future Society*, Transaction Books. Aldine Publishing Co., 1970.

————. "Revisionist Theory and Leadership," *Harvard Business Review*. January–February 1961.

————. *The Planning of Change*. New York: Henry Holt, 1961.

————. "The University Leader," *Saturday Review*, January 1973.

BENTON, LEWIS R. *Supervision and Management*. New York: McGraw-Hill, 1972.

BENZ, LORETTA N. "Citizen Participation Reconsidered," *Social Work*, March 1975.

BERGEN, GARRET L., and HANEY, WILLIAM V. *Organizational Relations and Management Action*. New York: McGraw-Hill, 1966.

BERKELEY, GEORGE E. *The Administrative Revolution*. Englewood Cliffs, N.J.: Prentice-Hall, 1971.

BERLINER, A. K. "Some Pitfalls in Administrative Behavior," *Social Casework*, November 1971.

BERNARD, SYDNEY E., and ISHIYAMA, TOARU. "Authority Conflicts in the Structure of Psychiatric Teams," *Social Work*, July 1960.

BERNTHAL, WILMAR F. "Leadership Among Professional People," *Hospital Administration*, Winter 1965.

BIDWELL, CHARLES E. "Some Effects of Administrative Behavior: A Study of Role Theory," *Administrative Science Quarterly*, September 1957.

BILLINGSLEY, ANDREW. "Bureaucratic and Professional Orientation Patterns in Social Casework," *Social Service Review*, December 1964.

BLAKE, ROBERT F. "Three Strategies for Exercising Authority," *Personnel Administration*, July–August 1964.

BLAU, PETER M. *Bureaucracy in Modern Society*. New York: Random House, 1956.

————."Orientation Toward Clients in a Public Welfare Agency," *Administrative Science Quarterly*, December 1960.

————. *The Dynamics of Bureaucracy*. Chicago: University of Chicago Press, 1955.

————. "The Structure of Small Bureaucracies," *American Sociological Review*, April 1966.

————, and SCHOENHERR, RICHARD. *The Structure of Organizations*. New York: Basic Books, 1970.

————, and SCOTT, RICHARD W. *Formal Organizations: A Comparative Approach*. San Francisco: Chandler Publishing Co., 1962.

BLEDSOE, R. C. et al. "Productivity Management in the California Social Services Program," *Public Administration Review*, November–December 1972.

BLUM, HENDRICK L., and LEONARD, ALVIN P. *Public Administration—A Public Health Viewpoint*. New York: Prentice-Hall, Inc., 1951.

BLUMBERG, DEBORAH D., et al. "Clients' Evaluation of Medical Social Services," *Social Work*, January 1975.

Boards of Directors: A Study of Current Practices in Board Management Operations and Board Operations in Voluntary Hospital, Health, and Welfare Organizations sponsored by the Greater New York Fund, 1974. Oceana Publications, Dobbs Ferry, N.Y.

BONJEAN, CHARLES M., CLARK, TERRY N., and LINEBERRY, ROBERT L. *Community Politics—A Behavioral Approach*. New York: The Free Press, 1971.

BOULDING, KENNETH E. "The Boundaries of Social Policy," *Social Work*, January 1967.

BOYER, WILLIAM W. *Bureaucracy on Trial: Policy Making by Government Agencies*. New York: Bobbs-Merrill, 1964.

BRAGER, GEORGE A. "Advocacy and Political Behavior," *Social Work*, April 1968.

————. "Institutional Change: Perimeters of the Possible," *Social Work*, January 1967.

————, and MICHAEL, JOHN. "The Sex Distribution in Social Work—Causes and Consequences," *Social Casework*, December 1969.

CAMPBELL, ROALD F., and GREGG, RUSSELL T. *Administrative Behavior in Education*. New York: Harper and Row, 1957.

CAPLOW, THEODORE. *Principles of Organization*. New York: Harcourt Brace and World, 1964.

CARROLL, STEPHEN J., and TOSI, HENRY L. "Goal Characteristics and Personality Factors in a Management-by-Objectives Program," *Administrative Science Quarterly*, 1970.

CASS, ROSEMARY HIGGINS. "New Demands on the Private Sector." New York: The National Assembly for Social Policy and Development, Inc., October 1973.

CAUDILL, WILLIAM A. *The Psychiatric Hospital as a Small Society*. Cambridge: Harvard University Press, 1958.

CHAFETZ, JANET S. "Women in Social Work," *Social Work*, September 1972.

CHAIKLIN, HARRIS, and FRANK, CAROL L. "Separation, Service Delivery and Family Functioning," *Public Welfare*, Winter 1973.

Changing Services for Changing Clients. New York: National Association of Social Workers. New York: Columbia University Press, 1969.

CHAPPLE, ELIOT D., and SAYLES, LEONARD R. *The Measure of Management*. New York: The Macmillan Company, 1961.

CHEEK, JAMES M. "Cost Effectiveness Comes to the Personnel Function," *Harvard Business Review*, May 1973.

CHELIMSKY, E. "Welfare Administration and Possibilities for Automation," *Public Welfare*, July 1973.

CLEGG, REED K. *The Administrator in Public Welfare*. Springfield, Ill.: Charles C. Thomas Publisher, 1966.

COHEN, ALAN M. "Change and Program Evaluation in Social Organization," *Journal of Sociology and Social Welfare,* Winter 1974 Supplement.

COHEN, MICHAEL D., and MARCH, JAMES G. *Leadership and Ambiguity—The American College President.* Carnegie Foundation for the Advancement of Teaching, New York, 1974.

COHEN, NATHAN E., ed. *The Citizen Volunteer.* New York: Harper and Row, 1960.

COHEN, WILBUR J. "What Every Social Worker Should Know About Political Action," *Social Work,* July 1966.

COLEMAN, JAMES S. *Power and the Structure of Society.* New York: W. W. Norton and Co., 1974.

COLEMAN, MORTON, et al. "Is Conflict Utilization Underestimated in the Management of Social Welfare." Revised. West Hartford: University of Connecticut School of Social Work, September 1973.

COLLIER, ABRAM. *Management, Men and Values.* New York: Harper and Row, 1962.

COLLINS, BARRY E., and GUETZKOW, HAROLD. *A Social Psychology of Group Processes for Decision Making.* New York: John Wiley, 1964.

CORSON, JOHN J. "Innovation Challenges Conformity." *Harvard Business Review,* May–June 1962.

CORWIN, RONALD G. "Strategies for Organizational Innovation: An Empirical Comparison," *American Sociological Review,* August 1972.

COSER, ROSE L. "Authority and Decision Making in a Hospital: A Comparative Analysis," *American Sociological Review,* February 1958.

COSTELLO, TIMOTHY, and ZALKIND, SHELDON. *Psychology in Administration.* Englewood Cliffs, N.J.: Prentice-Hall, 1963.

CROZIER, MICHEL. *The Bureaucratic Phenomenon.* Chicago: University of Chicago Press, 1964.

CULBERT, SAMUEL A. *The Organization Trap and How to Get Out of It.* New York: Basic Books, 1974.

CULBERTSON, JACK A. *Administrative Relationships—A Casebook.* Englewood Cliffs, N.J.: Prentice-Hall, 1960.

CULL, JOHN G., and HARDY, RICHARD E. *The Big Welfare Mess: Public Assistance and Rehabilitation Approaches.* Springfield, Ill.: Charles C. Thomas Publishers, 1973.

DALE, ERNEST. *Readings in Management—Landmarks and New Frontiers.* 2nd ed. New York: McGraw-Hill, 1970.

DALE, LEON A., and AKULA, WILLIAM G. "Managers for a Changing Society," *Personnel Administration,* 1970.

DALTON, GENE W., BARNES, LOUIS B., and ZALEZNIK, ABRAHAM. *The Distribution of Authority in Formal Organizations.* Boston: Harvard University, Division of Research, Graduate School of Business, 1968.

DALTON, MELVILLE. "Explicit and Implicit Administration," *Hospital Administration,* Winter 1962.

DAVIS, JAMES W. *Politics, Programs, and Budgets: A Reader in Government Budgeting.* Englewood Cliffs, N.J.: Prentice-Hall, 1969.

DAVIS, KEITH. "The Organization That's Not on the Chart." *Supervisory Management,* July 1961.

———, and SCOTT, WILLIAM G. *Readings in Human Relations.* 2nd ed. New York: McGraw-Hill, 1964.

DEMONE, HAROLD W., JR., and HARSHBERGER, DWIGHT. *The Planning and*

Administration of the Human Services. New York: Behavioral Publications, 1973.

DIMOCK, MARSHALL E. *Administrative Vitality—The Conflict with Bureaucracy.* New York: Harper and Row, 1958.

————. *A Philosophy of Administration—Towards Creative Growth.* New York: Harper and Row, 1958.

DOLGOFF, THOMAS. "Power, Conflict, and Structure in Mental Health Organizations: A General Systems Analysis," *Administration in Mental Health,* Winter 1972.

DOWLING, WILLIAM F., JR., and SAYLES, LEONARD. *How Managers Motivate—The Imperatives of Supervision.* New York: McGraw-Hill, 1971.

DOWNING, JOSEPH J. "Building the Program," in H. Richard Lam and Joseph Downing, ed. *Handbook of Community Mental Health Practice.* San Francisco: Jossey-Bass, 1969.

DREW, E. B. "HEW Grapples with PPBS," *The Public Interest,* Summer 1967.

DRUCKER, PETER F. *Management Tasks, Responsibilities, Practices.* New York: Harper and Row, 1974.

————. *Managing for Results.* New York: Harper and Row, 1964.

————. "The Effective Decision," *Harvard Business Review,* January–February 1967.

————. *The Practice of Management.* New York: Harper and Row, 1954.

DUBEY, SUMATI N. "Community Action Programs and Citizen Participation: Issues and Confusions," *Social Work,* January 1970.

————. "Powerlessness and the Adaptive Response of Disadvantaged Blacks: A Pilot Study," *Human Organization,* 1971.

DUCE, LEONARD. "A Philosophical Dimension of Administration," *Hospital Administration,* Summer 1966.

DUHL, LEONARD J., and ROBERT L. LEOPOLD. *Mental Health and Urban Social Policy.* San Francisco: Jossey-Bass, 1965.

DUNN, J. D., et al. *Management Essentials: Resource.* New York: McGraw-Hill Book Co., 1973.

EATON, JOSEPH. "Role Expectations: The Social Worker Looks in the Mirror," *Public Administration Review.* September 1963.

EHLERS, WALTER H., et al. *Administration for the Human Services—An Introductory Programmed Text.* New York: Harper and Row, 1976.

ENELOW, ALLEN J., M.D., and WESTON, W. DONALD, M.D. "Cooperation or Chaos: The Mental Health Administrator's Dilemma," *American Journal of Orthopsychiatry,* July 1972.

EPSTEIN, LAURA. "Differential Use of Staff: A Method to Expand Social Services," *Social Work,* October 1962.

ETZIONI, AMITAI. *Complex Organizations.* New York: Holt, Rinehart, and Winston, Inc., 1962.

————. *Modern Organizations.* Englewood Cliffs, N.J.: Prentice-Hall, 1964.

————. *A Sociological Reader on Complex Organizations.* New York: Holt, Rinehart, and Winston, Inc., 1969.

p. 15, Chester Barnard, "Organizations as Systems of Cooperation."

p. 47, Robert K. Merton, "Bureaucratic Structure and Personality."

p. 59, Amitai Etzioni, "A Basis for Comparative Analysis of Complex Organizations."

p. 158, Herbert A. Simon, "On the Concept of Organizational Goals."

p. 187, James D. Thompson and William J. McEwen, "Organizational Goals and Environment."

p. 387, Peter M. Blau, "The Dynamics of Bureaucracy."

EWING, JOHN D. "Patterns of Delegation," *Harvard Business Review*, July–August 1961.

FANSHEL, DAVID, ed. *Research in Social Welfare Administration*. New York: National Association of Social Workers, 1962.

FEIN, EDITH. "A Data System for an Agency," *Social Work*, January 1975.

FELDMAN, SAUL. "Problems and Prospects—Administration in Mental Health," *Administration in Mental Health*, Winter 1972.

————. *The Administration of Mental Health Services*. Springfield, Ill.: Charles C. Thomas Publishers, 1973.

FINCH, WILBUR A., JR. "Social Workers Versus Bureaucracy," *Social Work*, September 1976.

FISK, GEORGE, ed. *The Frontier of Management Psychology*. New York: Harper and Row, 1964.

FITZGERALD, THOMAS H. "What Motivation Theory Doesn't Work," *Harvard Business Review*, July–August 1971.

FIZDALE, RUTH. *Social Agency Structure and Accountability*. Fairlawn, N.J.: R. E. Burdick, Inc., Publisher, 1974.

FOLEY, ARCHIE P., and BRODIE, H. KEITH. "The Administrative Process as an Instrument of Change," *Hospital and Community Psychiatry*, January 1969.

FOLSOM, MARION B. *Executive Decision-Making—In Business and Government*, New York: McGraw-Hill Book Company, 1962.

FRANKEL, GODFREY. "The Nature and Significance of Administrative Communication," *Public Welfare*, July 1967.

FRANKLIN, JEROME L. *Organization Development—An Annotated Bibliography*. Center for Research on Utilization of Scientific Knowledge, Institute for Social Research, University of Michigan, Ann Arbor, Mich., 1973.

FREEDMAN, ALFRED M. "The Role of the Administrator," in Alan Biegal and Alan Levinson, *The Community Mental Health Center*, New York: Basic Books, 1972.

FREEMAN, RUTH B., and HOLMES, EDWARD M., JR. *Administration of Public Health Services*. Philadelphia, W. B. Saunders, 1960.

FREMONT-SMITH, MARION R. *Philanthropy and the Business Corporation*. New York: Russell Sage Foundation, 1972.

FRENCH, DAVID G., ed *Planning Responsibilities of State Departments of Public Welfare*. Chicago: American Public Welfare Association, 1967.

FRIEDRICH, CARL J., ed. *Authority*. Cambridge: Harvard University Press, 1958.

FRITSCHLER, LEE. "Bureaucracy and Democracy: The Unanswered Question," *Public Administration Review*, March 1966.

GANS, HERBERT J. "The New Egalitarianism," *Saturday Review*, May 6, 1972.

GANS, SHELDON P. *Integration of Human Services*. New York: Praeger, 1975.

GARDNER, JOHN W. *Self-Renewal—The Individual and the Innovative Society*. New York: Harper and Row, 1964.

GAWTHROP, LOUIS G. *Bureaucratic Behavior in the Executive Branch*. New York: Free Press, 1969.

GILBERT, NEIL. *Clients or Constituents*. San Francisco: Jossey-Bass, Inc., 1970.

GLASER, WILLIAM, and SILLS, DAVID L. *The Government of Associations: Selections from the Behavioral Sciences*. New Jersey: Bedminister Press, Inc., 1967.

GLASSER, WILLIAM A. *Social Setting and Medical Organization*. New York: Atherton, 1970.

GLENNERSTER, HOWARD. *Social Service Budgets and Social Policy.* New York: Harper and Row, 1975.

GLOVER, E. E. "Social Welfare Administration: A Social Work Method," *Child Welfare,* August 1965.

GLOVER, JOHN D., and HOWER, RALPH M. *The Administrator—Cases on Human Relations in Business.* Homewood, Ill.: Richard D. Irwin, 1963.

GOLDMAN, SAMUEL. *The School Principal.* New York: The Center for Applied Research in Education, Inc., 1966.

GOLDMAN, THOMAS A. *Cost Effectiveness Analysis—New Approaches in Decision Making.* New York: Praeger Publishers, 1967.

GOLEMBIEWSKI, ROBERT T., and GIBSON, FRANK. *Managerial Behavior and Organizational Demands.* Chicago: Rand-McNally, 1967.

GOODNER, JACK. "A Check List for Top Administrators." *College Management,* May 1974.

GORE, WILLIAM J. *Administrative Decision-Making.* New York: John Wiley and Sons, 1964.

GORHAM, WILLIAM. "Allocating Federal Resources Among Competing Social Needs," *Health, Education, and Welfare Indicators,* August 1966. Includes Comprehensive Bibliography on PPBS.

GOROFF, NORMAN. "Conflict Theories and Social Work Education." West Hartford, Conn.: University of Connecticut, School of Social Work (mimeographed).

GOTTESFELD, HARRY, et. al. *Strategies in Innovative Human Service Programs, 1973.* Behavioral Publications, 2852 Broadway, Morningside Heights, New York, N.Y. 10025. A Separate of Volume I, *Development in Human Services* edited by Herbert T. Schulber, Frank Baker, and Sheldon R. Roen.

GOTTLIEB, NAOMI. *The Welfare Bind.* New York: Columbia University Press, 1974.

GOULDNER, HELEN P. "Dimensions of Organizational Commitment," *Administrative Science Quarterly,* March 1960.

Governance of Higher Education—Six Priority Problems. A Report and Recommendation by the Carnegie Commission on Higher Education, April 1973.

GREEN, A. D. "The Professional Social Worker in the Bureaucracy," *Social Service Review,* March 1966.

GREENE, WADE. "A Farewell to Alms," *The New York Times Magazine,* May 23, 1976.

GREINER, Larry E. "Patterns of Organization Change," *Harvard Business Review,* May–June 1967.

GROSS, BERTRAM H. *The Management of Organizations: The Administrative Struggle.* 2 vols. The Free Press of Glencoe, 1964.

GRUBER, ARNOLD. "The High Cost of Delivering Services," *Social Work,* July 1973.

GUEST, ROBERT H. *Organizational Change—The Effect of Successful Leadership.* Homewood, Ill.: The Dorsey Press, Richard D. Irwin, Inc., 1962.

GUETZKOW, HAROLD; KOTLER, PHILIP; and SCHULTZ, RANDALL L. *Simulation in Social and Administrative Science—Overviews and Case Examples.* Englewood Cliffs, N.J.: Prentice-Hall, Inc., 1972.

GUMMER, BURTON, "Social Planning and Social Administration: Implications for Curriculum Development," *Journal of Social Work Education,* Winter 1976.

HAGE, JERALD. "An Axiomatic Theory of Organization," *Administrative Science Quarterly,* 1965.

————, and AIKEN, MICHAEL. "Relationship of Centralization to Other Structural Properties," *Administrative Science Quarterly,* June 1967.

HAIRE, MASON, ed. *Modern Organization Theory—A Symposium of the Foundation for Research on Human Behavior.* New York: John Wiley and Sons, 1959.

HALL, RICHARD H. *The Formal Organization.* New York: Basic Books, 1972.

HALLMAN, HOWARD W. "Administrative Decentralization and Citizen Control." Pamphlet Number 7. Washington, D.C.: Center for Governmental Studies," 1971.

HALPERN, JOSEPH, and BIINEER, PAUL R. "A Model for Output Value Analysis of Mental Health Programs," *Administration in Mental Health,* Winter 1972.

HALPIN, ANDREW W., ed. *Administrative Theory in Education.* Chicago: Midwest Administration Center, University of Chicago, 1958.

HAMILTON, JAMES A. *Decision-Making in Hospital Administration and Medical Care—A Casebook.* Minneapolis: University of Minnesota Press, 1960.

HAMPTON, DAVID R.; SUMMER, CHARLES E.; and WEBBER, ROSS A. *Organizational Behavior and the Practice of Management.* Glenview, Ill.: Scott, Foresman and Co., 1968.

HANCHETTE, HELEN et al. *Some Dynamics of Social Agency Administration.* New York: Family Service Association, 1960.

HANDLER, JOEL F., and HOLLINGSWORTH, ELLEN JANE. *The Deserving Poor—A Study of Welfare Administration.* University of Wisconsin, Institute for Research on Poverty, Monograph Series 1971. Chicago: Markham Publishing Co.

HANDLIN, N. "The Organization of a Client's Advisory Committee," *Public Welfare,* October 1967.

HANLAN, ARCHIE. "Casework Beyond Bureaucracy," *Social Casework,* April 1971.

HARDCASTLE, DAVID A. "General Revenue Sharing and Social Work," *Social Work,* September 1973.

HARDWICK, CLYDE T., and LANDUYT, BERNARD F. *Administrative Strategy.* New York: Simmons-Boardman Publishing Co., 1961.

HARDY, OWEN. "Voluntary Cooperation and Coordination—Requisites for Effective Hospital Administration," *Hospital Administration,* Fall 1966.

HARDY, RICHARD. *Organization and Administration of Service Programs for Older Americans.* Springfield, Ill.: C. C. Thomas Publishers, 1975.

HARPER, DEAN, and BABIGIAN, H. B. "The Three Evaluations of Social Work Programs," *Journal of Sociology and Social Welfare,* Winter 1974 Supplement.

HARRISON, ETHEL G., and HOFFMAN, ISAAC L. *The Management of Time, Case Assignment, and Communication in the Team Approach.* St. Paul: Amherst H. Wilder Foundation, January 1960.

HARTLEY, HARRY J. *Educational Planning—Programming—Budgeting—A Systems Approach.* Englewood Cliffs, N.J.: Prentice-Hall, 1968.

HASENFELD, YEHESKEL, and ENGLISH, RICHARD A. *Human Service Organizations—A Book of Readings.* Ann Arbor: University of Michigan Press, 1974.

HAWKES, ROBERT W. "The Role of the Psychiatric Administrator," *Administrative Science Quarterly,* June 1961.

HAWLEY, JOHN M., JR. "An Agency's Preparation for Internal Advocacy," *Social Casework,* April 1972.

HELD, VIRGINIA. "PPBS Comes to Washington," *Public Interest,* September 1966.

HENDERSON, HAZEL. "Toward Managing Social Conflict," *Harvard Business Review,* May–June 1971.

HENDRY, CHARLES E., and ROSS, MURRAY. *New Understandings of Leadership.* New York: Association Press, 1957.

HENNESSEY, JOHN. "The Administrator and Policy Processes," *Hospital Administration,* Winter 1965.

HERSEY, PAUL, and BLANCHARD, K. *Management of Organizational Behavior.* Englewood Cliffs, N.J.: Prentice-Hall, 1972.

HICKEY, W. J. "Power, Conflict and the Administrator," *Hospital Administration,* Winter 1968.

HICKS, HERBERT J. *The Management of Organizations: A Systems and Human Relations Approach.* 2nd ed. New York: McGraw-Hill, 1972.

―――. *Management, Organization, and Human Resources—Selected Readings.* New York: McGraw-Hill, 1972.

HOSHINO, GEORGE, and MCDONALD, THOMAS P. "Agencies in the Computer Age," *Social Work,* January 1975.

Hospital Governing Boards. Departmental Evaluation Series. Management Program Review. Chicago: American Hospital Association, 1968.

HOULE, CYRIL O. *The Effective Board.* New York: Association Press, 1960.

HOUSTON, LAURA P. "Black People, New Careers and Humane Human Resources," *Social Casework,* May 1970.

HUNGATE, JOSEPH. *A Guide for Training Social Welfare Administrators.* Washington, D.C.: U.S. Department of Health, Education, and Welfare, Welfare Administration, Bureau of Family Services, 1964.

HUNGATE, JOSEPH I., JR. "The Concept of Programmed Responsibility." *Child Welfare,* November 1966.

HUSH, HOWARD. "Collective Bargaining in Voluntary Agencies," *Social Casework,* April 1969.

JENSON, THEODORE J., and CLARK, DAVID L. *Educational Administration.* New York: Center for Applied Research in Education, Inc., 1964.

JOHNS, RAY. *Confronting Organizational Change.* New York: Association Press, 1963.

―――. *Executive Responsibility.* New York: Association Press, 1954.

JOHNSON, ARLIEN. "Social Policy Goals of Voluntary Agencies," *NASW News,* National Association of Social Workers, February 1967.

JOHNSON, R. L. "Courage and Administrative Strategy," *Hospital Administration,* Fall 1968.

JOHNSON, RICHARD A., et al. *The Theory and Management of Systems.* New York: McGraw-Hill Book Company, 1963.

JONES, GARTH N. *Planned Organizational Change.* New York: Frederick A. Praeger, 1969.

KAHLE, J. H. "Structuring and Administering a Modern Voluntary Agency," *Social Work,* September 1969.

KAHN, ALFRED J. *Theory and Practice of Social Planning.* New York: Russell Sage Foundation, 1969. Chapter 9—Program Budgeting and Cost Effectiveness; Chapter 10—Programming Problems in Social Service Delivery.

KAHN, ROBERT L., et al. "Americans Love Their Bureaucrats," *Psychology Today,* June 1975.

―――, and KATZ, DANIEL. "Social Work and Organizational Change," *Social Welfare Forum 1965.* Published for the National Conference on Social Welfare by Columbia University Press, New York.

————. *The Social Psychology of Organization.* New York: John Wiley and Sons, Inc. 1966.
Chapter 2—Organizations and the Systems Concept
Chapter 4—Development of Organizational Structure
Chapter 11—Leadership

KAST, FREMONT E., and ROSENWEIG, JAMES E. "Hospital Administration and Systems Concepts," *Hospital Administration,* Fall 1966.

KATZ, ELIHU, and DANET, BRENDA, eds. *Bureaucracy and the Public: A Reader in Official Client Relations.* New York: Basic Books, 1973.

KATZ, ROBERT L. "Skills of an Effective Administrator," *Harvard Business Review,"* January–February, 1955.

KATZELL, MILDRED E., and BYNAM, WILLIAM C., eds. *Women in the Work Force.* Confrontation with Change Series. New York: Behavioral Publications, Inc., 1972.

KAUFMAN, HERBERT. "The Administrative Function," in David L. Sills, ed., *International Encyclopedia of Social Sciences.* New York: The Macmillan Company and Free Press, 1968. Vol. 1, p. 61.

————, and COUZENS, MICHAEL. "Administrative Feedback-Monitoring Subordinates Behavior." Washington, D.C.: The Brookings Institution, 1973.

KELLY, JOE. "Make Conflict Work for You," *Harvard Business Review,* July–August 1970.

KEPNER, CHARLES E., and TREGOE, BENJAMIN B. *The Rational Manager: A Systematic Approach to Problem Solving and Decision Making.* New York: McGraw-Hill, 1965.

KIDNEIGH, JOHN C. "Simplification in Administration—A Point of View," *Social Service Review,* June 1954.

————. "Social Work Administration—An Area of Social Work Practice?" *Social Work Journal,* April 1950.

————, and JAMBOR, HELEN M. "Role Perception in Social Casework Supervision—A Concern of Social Work Administration." School of Social Work, University of Minnesota based on unpublished Ph.D. thesis of Helen M. Jambor, *Discrepancies in Role Perceptions for the Supervisory Position—A Concern of Social Work Administration,* University of Minnesota, June 1954.

KNUDSEN, HARRY R. *Human Elements in Administration.* New York: Holt, Rinehart, and Winston, 1963.

KOONTZ, HAROLD. *Toward a Unified Theory of Management.* New York: McGraw-Hill, 1964.

————, and O'DONNELL, CYRIL. *Principles of Management—An Analysis of Management Functions.* 3rd ed. New York: McGraw-Hill, 1964.

KOPPLE, F. A. "An Administrator's Evaluation," *Social Casework,* April 1972.

KOTIN, JOEL, and SHARAP, MYRON R. "Management Succession and Administrative Style," *Psychiatry,* August 1967.

KRAFT, IVOR. "Governance and the Professional School," *Journal of Social Work Education,* Spring 1975.

KRAMER, RALPH M. *Participation of the Poor—Comparative Community Case Studies in the War on Poverty.* Englewood Cliffs, N.J.: Prentice-Hall, Inc., 1969.

KRAUS, WILMA R. "Toward a Theory of Political Participation of Public Bureaucrats," *Administrative Science Quarterly,* June 1971.

KRIESBURG, MARTIN, and GUETZKOW, HAROLD. "The Use of Conferences in the Administrative Process," *Public Administration Review,* Spring 1950.

KYLE, JOHN D. "Informal Relationships in the Hospital," *Hospital Administration*, Fall 1961.

LAWRENCE, PAUL R. *The Changing of Organizational Behavior Patterns*. Boston: Harvard University, Graduate School of Business, 1958.

LEAVITT, HAROLD. *Managerial Psychology*. Chicago: University of Chicago Press, 1958.

———. *The Social Science of Organizations*. Englewood Cliffs, N.J.: Prentice-Hall, 1963.

LEBRETON, PRESTON P. *Comparative Administrative Theory*. Seattle: University of Washington Press, 1968.

LEE, JAMES A. "Behavioral Theory vs. Reality," *Harvard Business Review*, March–April 1971.

LEFTON, MARK, and ROSENGREN, WILLIAM R. "Organizations and Clients: Lateral and Longitudinal Dimensions," *American Sociological Review*, December 1966.

LEVINE, A. S. "Cost-Benefit Analysis and Social Welfare Program Evaluation," *Social Service Review*, July 1968.

LEVINE, HAROLD, and LEVINE, CAROL. *Effective Public Relations for Community Groups*. New York: Association Press, 1969.

LEVINSON, DANIEL J., and KLERMAN, GERALD L. "The Clinician Executive," *Administration in Mental Health*, Winter 1972.

LEVINSON, HARRY, et al. *Men, Management and Mental Health*. Cambridge: Harvard University Press, 1963.

———. *Organizational Diagnosis*. Cambridge, Mass.: Harvard University Press, 1972.

LIKERT, RENSIS. *New Patterns of Management*. New York: McGraw-Hill, 1961.

———. *The Human Organization—Its Management and Value*. New York: McGraw-Hill, 1967.

LILIENTHAL, DAVID E. *Management: A Humanistic Art*. Carnegie Institute of Technology. Distributed by Columbia University Press, New York, 1967.

LIPPINCOTT, EARLE, and AANNESTAD, ELLING. "Management of Voluntary Welfare Agencies," *Harvard Business Review*, November–December 1964.

LITTLE, VIRGINIA, ed. *Program Budgeting—An Introduction*. Monograph 1, Spring 1975. University of Connecticut School of Social Work, West Hartford, Conn.

LITWACK, EUGENE. "Models of Bureaucracy which Permit Conflict," *The American Journal of Sociology*, September 1961.

LOHMANN, ROGER A. "Break-Even Analysis: Tool for Budget Planning," *Social Work*, July 1976.

LOWENSTEIN, E. R. "Citizens Participation and the Administrative Agency in Urban Development: Some Problems and Proposals." *Social Service Review*, September 1971.

———, et al. "The Management of Organizational Change: Some Findings and Suggestions," *Public Welfare*, Winter 1973.

LUNDSTEDT, SVEN. "Administration Leadership and Use of Social Power," *Public Administration Review*, June 1963.

LYDEN, F., and LEE, L. "Evaluating Program Change," *Social Work*, March 1973.

LYDEN, FREMONT J., and MILLER, ERNEST G., eds. *Planning, Programming, Budgeting: A Systems Approach to Management*. Chicago: Markham, 1968.

MacRae, Robert T. "Changing Patterns of Financial Support," *Child Welfare*, December 1973.

Maier, Norman R. F. *Creative Management*. New York: John Wiley and Sons, 1962.

Maine Social Services Delivery System. Maine Bureau of Social Welfare, Augusta, Maine, May 1973.

Managing Major Changes in Organizations. Ann Arbor, Mich.: Foundation for Research in Human Behavior, 1961.

Manser, Gordon. "Implication of Purchase of Service for Voluntary Agencies," *Social Casework*, June 1972.

March, James G., and Simon, Herbert A. *Organizations*. New York: John Wiley and Sons, 1958, pp. 36–46, "Dysfunctions in Organizations."

Martona, S. V. *College Boards of Trustees*. New York: Center for Applied Research in Education, Inc., 1963.

Massie, Joseph L. *Essentials of Management*. Englewood Cliffs, N.J.: Prentice-Hall, 1964.

McGregor, Douglas. *The Human Side of Enterprise*. New York: McGraw-Hill, 1960.

———. *Leadership and Motivation*. Cambridge: Massachusetts Institute of Technology Press, 1966.

McLean, Alan, ed. *To Work Is Human—Mental Health and the Business Community*. New York: Macmillan, 1967.

McLeod, R. K. "Program Budgeting Worker in Non-Profit Institutions," *Harvard Business Review*, September–October 1971.

Meade, Marvin. "Participative Administration—Emerging Reality or Wishful Thinking," in Dwight Waldo, ed., *Public Administration in a Time of Turbulence*. Scranton, Pa.: Chandler, 1971.

Meravitz, Leonard, and Sosnick, Stephen H. *The Budget's New Clothes: Critique of Planning, Programming. Budgeting and Cost Benefit Analysis*. Chicago: Markham Publishing Co., 1972.

Merton, Robert K., ed. *Reader in Bureaucracy*. Glencoe, Ill.: Free Press, 1953.

Metcalf, Henry C., and Urwick, L. *Dynamic Administration—The Collected Papers of Mary Parker Follett*. New York: Harpers, 1942.

Miles, Matthew B. *Change Processes in Public Schools*. Center for Advanced Study of Educational Administration, Oregon University, Eugene, Oregon, 1965.

Miller, Delbert, and Shull, Fremont. "Administrative Role Conflict Resolutions," *Administrative Science Quarterly*, September 1962.

Miller, George A., and Wager, L. Wesley. "Adult Socialization, Organizational Structure and Role Orientation," *Administrative Science Quarterly*, 1971.

Miller, Ronald, and Podell, Lawrence. *Role Conflict in Public Social Services*. 1972 State of New York, Office for Community Affairs, Division of Research and Innovation.

Miller, S. M., and Rein, Martin. "Participation, Poverty, and Administration," *Public Administration Review*, January–February 1969.

Millett, John D. *Decision Making and Administration in Higher Education*. The Kent State University Press, 1968.

———. *Organization for the Public Service*. Princeton: D. Van Nostrand, Inc., 1966.

MOELLER, GERALD H., and CHARTERS, W. W. "Relation of Bureaucratization to Sense of Power Among Teachers," *Administrative Science Quarterly*, 1966.

MOGULOF, M. B. "Involving Low-Income Neighborhoods in Anti-Delinquency Programs," *Social Work*, October 1965.

———. "Special Revenue Sharing and the Social Services," *Social Work*, September 1972.

MOMENT, DAVID, and ZALEZNIK, ABRAHAM. *Role Development and Interpersonal Competence*. Boston: Harvard University, Graduate School of Business, Division of Research, 1963.

MONTGOMERY, HELEN B. "Practice of Administration: Role of the Executive," *Child Welfare*, February 1962.

MOORE, HAROLD E. *The Administration of Public School Personnel*. New York: Center for Applied Research in Education, Inc., 1966.

MORELL, R. W. *Managerial Decision-Making*. Milwaukee: The Bruce Publishing Co., 1960.

MORRIS, WILLIAM T. *Decentralization in Management*. Columbus: Ohio State University Press, 1968.

MORROW, DANIEL G. "The Role of the County Welfare Director: W.R.O. vs. The Taxpayer," *Public Welfare*, July 1970.

MOSS, CELIA R. *Administration of a Hospital Social Service Department*. Washington, D.C.: American Association of Medical Social Workers, 1955.

MOUZELIS, NICO P. *Organizing and Bureaucracy*. Chicago: Aldine Publishing Co., 1968.

MOYNIHAN, DANIEL P. *The Politics of a Guaranteed Income*. New York: Random House, 1973.

MULDER, MARK. "Power Equalization thru Participation," *Administrative Science Quarterly*, March 1971.

NEBO, JOHN E., ed. *Administration of School Social Work*. New York: National Association of Social Workers, 1960.

Neighborhood Action on Local Problems. New York: National Federation of Settlements and Neighborhood Centers, Study Outline III (undated).

NEWELL, ALLEN, and SIMON, HERBERT. *Human Problem Solving*. Englewood Cliffs, N.J.: Prentice-Hall, 1972.

NEWLAND, CHESTER A. "Current Concepts and Characteristics of Administration," *Child Welfare*, June 1963.

NEWMAN, EDWARD, and TUREM, JERRY "The Crisis of Accountability," *Social Work*, January 1974.

NEWMAN, WILLIAM H., and SUMMER, CHARLES E., JR. *The Process of Management*. Englewood Cliffs, N.J.: Prentice-Hall, 1961.

NIGRO, FELIX A. *Modern Public Administration*. New York: Harper and Row, 1965.

ORCHARD, BERNICE. "The Use of Authority in Supervision," *Public Welfare*, January 1965.

OSBORN, PHYLLIS, "Meeting the Needs of People: An Administrative Responsibility," *Social Work*, July 1958.

PATTI, R. J., and RESNICK, H. "Changing the Agency from Within," *Social Work*, July 1972.

PAULL, J. E. "Recipients Aroused: The New Welfare Rights Movement," *Social Work*, April 1967.

PAWLAK, EDWARD J. "Organizational Tinkering," *Social Work*, September 1976.

PEABODY, ROBERT L. "Authority Relations in Three Organizations," *Public Administration Review*, June 1963.

———. *Organizational Authority*. New York: Atherton Press, 1964.

———. "Perceptions of Organizational Authority." *Administrative Science Quarterly*, March 1962.

PENCHANSKY, ROY. *Health Services Administration Policy Cases and the Case Method*. Cambridge: Harvard University Press, 1968.

PERLMUTTER, FELICE. "A Theoretical Model of Social Agency Development." *Social Casework*, October 1969.

PFIFFNER, JOHN, and SHERWOOD, FRANK P. *Administrative Organization*. Englewood Cliffs, N.J.: Prentice-Hall, 1960.

PHILLIPS, BEATRICE. "A Director Examines the Director's Role," *Social Work*, October 1964.

PIGORS, PAUL, et al. *Management of Human Resources—Readings in Personnel Administration*. New York: McGraw-Hill, 1964.

———. and MYERS, CHARLES A. *Personnel Administration*. New York: McGraw-Hill, 1961.

PIVEN, FRANCES. "Participation of Residents in Neighborhood Community Action Programs," *Social Work,* January 1966.

———. "The Great Society as Political Strategy," *Columbia Forum,* Summer 1970. New York: Columbia University.

POE, WILLIAM R. *The Hidden Agenda: The Administration of Mental Health and the Mental Health of Administration*. Ph.D. dissertation, April 1975, School of Education, University of Massachusetts, Amherst, Mass.

Policy Questions Related to Programs Moving in New Directions. New York: National Federation of Settlements and Neighborhood Centers, Study Outline V (undated).

Policy Statement on Racism and Poverty. Washington, D.C.: National Association of Social Workers, 1971.

POMEROY, RICHARD. *Studies in Public Welfare: Reactions of Welfare Clients to Social Services*. Center for the Study of Urban Problems, Graduate Division, Bernard M. Baruch College, City University of New York, 1969.

POST, DUDLEY. "Requiem for Model Cities," *The New Republic,* April 14, 1973.

"PPBS: Its Scope and Limits," Special Section, *The Public Interest,* Summer 1967.

PRESTHUS, ROBERT. *Behavioral Approaches to Public Administration*. University of Alabama Press, 1965.

———. *The Organizational Society*. New York: Alfred A. Knopf, 1962.

PRICE, JAMES L. "The Impact of Governing Boards on Organizational Effectiveness," *Administrative Science Quarterly,* December 1963.

Program Budgeting—A Case Study from the Greenwich Public Schools. Communiity Development Aid 9, Department of Community Affairs, State of Connecticut, October 1973.

PUGH, D. S., et al. "A Scheme for Organizational Analysis," *Administrative Science Quarterly*, December 1963.

RADLOFF, BARBARA. "Revenue Sharing: Report from the Grass Roots," *Carnegie Quarterly*. Carnegie Corporation of New York, Winter 1976.

RAMOS, ALBERTO. "Models of Man and Administrative Theory," *Public Administration Review,* May–June 1972.

RAMSER, CHARLES. "Job Satisfaction in an Institution for the Mentally Retarded," *Mental Hygiene,* Winter 1972.

REED, ELLA W., ed. *Social Welfare Administration*. New York: Columbia University Press, National Conference on Social Welfare, 1961.

REINERT, PAUL C., S. J. "The Problem with Search Committees," *College Managements*, February 1974.

Responsibility for Community Change—New Faces and New Hats for Boards of Directors. New York: National Federation of Settlements and Neighborhood Houses, Study Outline IV (undated).

RICHTER, ANDERS. "The Existentialist Executive," *Public Administration Review*, July–August, 1970.

RICKLEFS, ROGER. "Learning to Cope—How a Social Worker Helps People Adjust to an 'Unjust' System," *The Wall Street Journal*, December 21, 1972.

RILEY, PATRICK V. "Family Advocacy: Case to Cause and Back to Case," *Child Welfare*, July 1971.

ROCKMORE, MYRON JOHN, and CONKLIN, JOHN J. "A Blending of Two Roles —The Administrator-Psychiatric Social Worker," *State Government*, Summer 1971. Published by the Council of State Governments.

RONKEN, HARRIET O., and LAWRENCE, PAUL. *Administering Changes—A Case Study of Human Relations in a Factory*. Boston: Harvard University, Graduate School of Business Administration, Division of Research, 1952.

ROSENBERG, MARVIN, and BRODY, RALPH. "New Directions in Public Social Services: Threat or Challenge?" National Institute for Training in Integrated Service Delivery. School of Applied Social Sciences, Case Western Reserve University, Cleveland, May 1973.

———, and RICHMAN, LEON. *Service Management in Action*. National Institute for Training in Integrated Service Delivery, School of Applied Social Sciences, Case Western Reserve University, Cleveland, January 1973.

ROTHMAN, JACK. *Planning and Organizing for Social Change—Action Principles from Social Science Research*. New York: Columbia University Press, 1974.

ROY, ROBERT H. *The Administrative Process*. Baltimore: Johns Hopkins Press, 1965.

RYAN, JOHN J. "Social Work Executive: Generalist or Specialist," *Social Work*, April, 1964.

RYAN, WILLIAM. *Blaming the Victim*. New York: Pantheon Books, 1971.

SARASON, SEYMOUR. *The Culture of the School and the Problems of Change*. Boston: Allyn and Bacon, Inc., 1971.

SARRI, ROSEMARY C. "Administration in Social Welfare," in *Encyclopedia of Social Work*, Vol. I, 1971, p. 39ff. New York: National Association of Social Workers, 1971.

SAYLES, LEONARD R., and STRAUSS, GEORGE. *Human Behavior in Organizations*. Englewood Cliffs, N.J.: Prentice-Hall, 1966.

SCHALLER, LYLE E. "Is the Citizens Advisory Committee a Threat to Representative Government?" *Public Administration Review*, September 1964.

SCHATZ, HARRY A., ed. *A Casebook in Social Work Administration*. New York: Council on Social Work Administration, 1970.

———. *Social Work Administration—A Resource Book*. New York: Council on Social Work Administration, 1970.

SCHEIN, EDGAR. *Organizational Psychology*. Englewood Cliffs, N.J.: Prentice-Hall, Inc., 1965. Chapter 6, "The Organization as a Complex System."

———. *Process Consultation: Its Role in Organization Development*. Reading, Mass.: Addison-Wesley Publishing Co., 1969.

————, and BENNIS, WARREN G. *Personal and Organizational Change Through Group Methods.* New York: John Wiley and Sons, Inc., 1965.

SCHMIDT, William D. *The Executive and the Board in Social Welfare.* Cleveland: Howard Allen, Inc., 1959.

SCHNITZER, MARTIN, and CHEN, YUNG-PING. *Public Finance and Public Policy Issues.* Scranton: Intext Educational Publishers, 1972.

SCHWARTZ, JEROME, and CHERNIN, MILTON. "Participation of Recipients in Public Welfare Planning and Administration," *Social Service Review,* March 1967.

SCOTCH, BERNARD C. "Sex Status in Social Work," *Social Work,* July 1971.

SCOTT, WILLIAM G. "Organization Government: The Prospects for a Truly Participative System," *Public Administration Review,* January-February 1969.

SEGAL, BRIAN. "Planning and Power in Hospital Social Service," *Social Casework,* July 1970.

SELZNICK, PHILIP. *Leadership in Administration—A Sociological Interpretation.* Evanston, Ill.: Row Peterson, 1957.

SHAFFER, A. "Welfare Rights Organizations: Friend or Foe?" *Social Work Practice 1967.* Selected Papers from the National Conference on Social Welfare, Columbia University Press.

SHANNON, WILLIAM V. "A Radical, Direct, Simple, Utopian Alternative to Day-Care Centers." *The New York Times Magazine,* April 30, 1972.

SHARKANSKY, IRA. *Public Administration Policy-Making in Government Agencies.* Chicago: Markham Publishing Co., 1970.

SHEEHAN, NEIL. *The Arnheiter Affair.* New York: Random House, 1972.

SIGEL, ROBERTA S. "Citizens Committees—Advice vs. Consent," *Transaction,* May 1967.

SIMON, HERBERT A. *Administrative Behavior—A Study of Decision-Making in Administrative Organizations.* 2nd ed. New York: Macmillan, 1957.

————. "Administrative Decision-Making," *Public Administration Review,* March 1965.

————. *The New Science of Management Decision.* New York: Harper and Row, 1960.

SINGER, HENRY A. "The Changing Role of the Administrators in the 1970's," *Hospital Administration,* Summer 1966.

SJOBERG, GIDEON, et al. "Bureaucracy and the Lower Classes," *Sociology and Social Research,* April 1966. Also in Dean L. Yarwood, ed., *The National Administrative System.* New York: John Wiley and Sons, Inc. 1971.

SMITH, HOWARD R. "The Management Function: A Socio-Dynamic Overview," *Hospital Administration,* Spring 1966.

Social Work Administration. Pamphlet. New York: National Association of Social Workers, March 1968.

SOFER, CYRIL. *Organization in Theory and Practice.* New York: Basic Books, 1972.

SORENSON, ROY. *The Art of Board Membership.* New York: Association Press, 1950.

SPECHT, HARRY. "Casework Practice and Social Policy Formulation," *Social Work,* January 1968.

SPENCER, SUE W. *The Administration Method in Social Work.* Curriculum Study on Social Work Education. Vol. III. New York: Council on Social Work Education, 1959.

SQUIRES, MORRIS B., ed. *Current Administrative Practices for Psychiatric Services*. Springfield, Ill.: Charles C. Thomas Publishers, 1970.

STEIN, HERMAN D. "Administration." *Encyclopedia of Social Work 1965*. New York: National Association of Social Workers, 1965.

———. "Administrative Implications of Bureaucratic Theory," *Social Work*, July 1961.

———. "Board, Executive, and Staff." *Social Welfare Forum 1962*. Published in 1962 for the National Conference on Social Welfare by Columbia University Press, New York.

———. "The Study of Organizational Effectiveness," in David Fanshel, ed., *Research in Social Welfare Administration—Its Contributions and Problems*. New York: National Association of Social Workers, 1962.

STEIN, IRMA. *Systems Theory and Social Work*. New York: Scarecrow Press, 1974.

STEINER, JEROME. "What Price Success?" *Harvard Business Review*, March–April 1972.

STOGDILL, RALPH M. *Handbook of Leadership*. New York: Free Press, 1974.

STRANGE, J. H. "The Impact of Citizen Participation on Public Administration," *Public Administration Review*, September 1972.

STUDT, ELIOT. "Worker-Client Authority Relationships in Social Work," *Social Work*, January 1959.

SUMMER, CHARLES E., and O'CONNELL, JEREMIAH J. *The Managerial Mind—Science and Theory in Policy Decisions*. Rev. ed. Homewood, Ill.: Richard D. Irwin, Inc., 1968.

TAEBEL, D. A. "Strategies to Make Bureaucratic Responsive," *Social Work*, November 1972.

TANNENBAUM, ROBERT, and SCHMIDT, WARREN H. "How to Choose a Leadership Pattern," *Harvard Business Review*, March–April 1958.

———; WESCHLER, IRVING R.; and MASSARIK, FRED. *Leadership and Organization—A Behavioral Approach*. New York: McGraw-Hill, 1961.

TEAD, ORDWAY. *Administration: Its Purpose and Performance*. New York: Harper and Row, 1959.

———. "Reflections on the Art of Administration," *Hospital Administration*, Winter 1959.

———. *The Art of Administration*. New York: McGraw-Hill, 1951.

The Escalation of Change—The Urban Scene in America. New York: National Federation of Settlements and Neighborhood Houses, Study Outline I (undated).

"The New and the Old in Social Work Administration," *Child Welfare*, October 1974.

THOMPSON, JAMES D. "Common and Uncommon Elements in Administration," *Social Welfare Forum, 1962*. National Conference on Social Welfare, Columbia University Press, New York, 1962.

———. *Organizations in Action: Social Sciences Bases of Administrative Theory*. New York: McGraw-Hill, 1967.

———, et al. *Comparative Studies in Administration*. Pittsburgh: University of Pittsburgh Press, 1959.

THOMPSON, VICTOR A. "Hierarchy, Specialization and Organizational Conflict," *Administrative Science Quarterly*, March 1961.

TITMUSS, RICHARD M. *Commitment to Welfare*. New York: Pantheon Books—A Division of Random House, 1968.

———. *Social Policy*. New York: Pantheon Books, 1974.

TRAXLER, RALPH N. "The Qualities of an Administrator," *Hospital Administration,* Fall 1961.

TRECKER, HARLEIGH B. *Citizen Boards at Work—New Challenges to Effective Action.* New York: Association Press, 1970.

———, ed. *Goals for Social Welfare 1973–1993: An Overview of the Next Two Decades.* New York: Association Press, 1973.

———. *Group Process in Administration.* New York: Association Press, 1950.

———. *New Understandings of Administration.* New York: Association Press, 1961.

TRIPODI, TONY; FELLIN, PHILLIP; and EPSTEIN, IRWIN. *Social Program Evaluation—Guidelines for Health, Education and Welfare Administration.* Ithaca, Ill.: F. W. Peacock Publishers, 1971.

TROTTER, VIRGINIA Y. "Women in Leadership and Decision Making," *Vital Speeches,* February 15, 1975.

UNDERWOOD, HAROLD W. "Emotional Health of Executives," *Personnel Administration,* 1970, pp. 54-55.

URWICK, L. F. *Leadership in the 20th Century.* New York: Pitman, 1957.

———. *The Pattern of Management.* Minneapolis: University of Minnesota Press, 1956.

UTZ, CORNELIUS. "The Responsibility of Administration for Maximizing the Contribution of the Casework Staff," *Social Casework,* March 1964.

VASEY, WAYNE. *Government and Social Welfare.* New York: Holt, Rinehart, and Winston, 1958.

———. "Partnership Between Administrator and Staff in Developing Social Welfare Programs," *Social Casework,* April 1952.

VORWALLER, D. J. "The Voluntary Agency as a Vendor of Social Services," *Child Welfare,* July 1972.

WALTON, JOHN. *Administration and Policy-Making in Education.* Baltimore: Johns Hopkins Press, 1959.

WANGENSTEIN, MILES G. "Worker and Administrator: Bridging the Gaps," *Public Welfare,* April 1970.

"Wanted: Qualified Administrators," *College Management,* May 1972.

WARHAM, JOYCE. *An Introduction to Administration for Social Workers.* New York: The Humanities Press, 1967.

WATZLAWICK, PAUL, et al. *Change-Principles of Problem Formulation and Problem Resolution.* New York: W. W. Norton and Co., 1974.

WAX, JOHN. "Power Theory and Institutional Change," *Social Service Review,* September 1971.

WEBER, MAX. *Essays in Sociology.* Translated by H. H. Gerth and C. W. Mills. New York: Oxford University Press, 1946.

WEIL, THOMAS P. "Some Guidelines for Evaluating the Performance of an Administrator," *Hospital Administration,* Spring 1967.

WEINBERGER, PAUL E. "Job Satisfaction and Staff Retention in Social Work," *National Association of Social Workers News,* March 1970.

WEISS, CAROL H. "Alternative Models of Program Evaluation," *Social Work,* November 1974.

———. *Evaluation Research—Methods of Assessing Program Effectiveness.* Englewood Cliffs, N.J.: Prentice-Hall, 1972.

WEISSMAN, HAROLD H. *Overcoming Mismanagement in the Human Service Professions: A Casework of Staff Initiatives.* San Francisco: Jossey-Bass Publications, 1973.

WHITE, VIRGINIA. *Grants: How to Find Out About Them and What to Do Next*. New York: Plenum Press, 1975.

WHYTE, WILLIAM F. *Organizational Behavior—Theory and Application*. Homewood, Ill.: Richard D. Irwin, Inc. and the Dorsey Press, 1969.

WIEHE, VERNON. "Management by Objectives in a Family Service Agency," *Social Casework*, March 1973.

WILCOX, HERBERT G. "Hierarchy, Human Nature and the Participative Panacea," *Public Administration Review*, January–February 1969.

WILDAVSKY, AARON. *The Politics of the Budgetary Process*. Boston: Little, Brown and Co., 1964.

WILSON, JAMES Q. "The Bureaucracy Problem," *The Public Interest*, Winter 1967.

WORTHY, JAMES C. "Ethical and Moral Responsibilities of the Executive," *Hospital Administration*, Summer 1962.

WORTMAN, MAX S., and LUTHANS, FRED. *Emerging Concepts in Management*. New York: The Macmillan Co., 1969.

YARWOOD, DEAN L., ed. *The National Administrative System*. New York: John Wiley and Son, Inc. 1971.

YOUNG, VIRGINIA C. *The Library Trustee—A Practical Guidebook*. New York: R. R. Bowker, 1969.

ZALD, MEYER. "Organizations as Politics: An Analysis of Community Organization Agencies," *Social Work*, October 1966.

ZALEZNIK, ABRAHAM. *Human Dilemmas of Leadership*. New York: Harper and Row, 1966.

———. "Management of Disappointment," *Harvard Business Review*, November–December 1967.

ZAND, D. E. "Trust and Managerial Problem Solving," *Administrative Science Quarterly*, June 1972.

ZANDER, ALVIN. *Motives and Goals in Groups*. New York: Academic Press, 1971.

ZELTER, ROBERT C. "The Newcomer's Acceptance in Open and Closed Groups," *Personnel Administration*, September–October, 1962.

Index